# THE THINKING MAN'S SOLDIER

## THE LIFE AND CAREER OF GENERAL SIR HENRY BRACKENBURY 1837–1914

Helion Studies in Military History Number 10

### Christopher Brice

Helion & Company Ltd

In Memory of Clifford Arthur McTighe and Olive May Brice

Helion & Company Limited
26 Willow Road
Solihull
West Midlands
B91 1UE
England
Tel. 0121 705 3393
Fax 0121 711 4075
Email: info@helion.co.uk
Website: www.helion.co.uk

Published by Helion & Company 2012

Designed and typeset by Bookcraft Ltd, Stroud, Gloucestershire
Cover designed by Bookcraft Ltd, Stroud, Gloucestershire
Printed by TJ International, Padstow, Cornwall

Text © Christopher Brice 2012
Images © as individually credited
Maps © Helion & Company Limited

ISBN 978-1-907677-69-4

British Library Cataloguing-in-Publication Data.
A catalogue record for this book is available from the British Library.

All rights reserved. No part of this publication may be reproduced, stored in a retrieval system,or transmitted, in any form, or by any means, electronic, mechanical, photocopying, recording or otherwise, without the express written consent of Helion & Company Limited.

Dustjacket illustrations: Front cover – Henry Brackenbury. This photograph was taken after his promotion to General in 1902 and before retirement in 1904, and is quite possibly the last picture of him taken in military uniform (Private collection). Rear cover – Henry Brackenbury. Undated but likely to have been taken around 1882. (Private collection)

For details of other military history titles published by Helion & Company Limited contact the above address, or visit our website: http://www.helion.co.uk.

We always welcome receiving book proposals from prospective authors.

# Contents

| | |
|---|---|
| List of illustrations | vi |
| List of maps | vi |
| Foreword by Professor Hew Strachan | vii |
| Preface | ix |
| Acknowledgements | xiv |
| Introduction | xv |
| Maps | xxvi |
| 1. The Brackenburys of Lincolnshire | 1 |
| 2. Early Years | 11 |
| 3. The Late Victorian British Army | 17 |
|     The Standing of the British Army | 18 |
|     Control of the Army | 19 |
|     Army Reform | 21 |
|     Colonial Warfare | 27 |
|     Conclusion | 31 |
| 4. The Indian Mutiny | 32 |
| 5. The Literary Work of Henry Brackenbury | 38 |
|     A Journalistic Career | 41 |
|     Military Campaigns | 44 |
|     Military Tactics | 45 |
|     Summary of Literary Career | 51 |
| 6. Army Reform | 53 |
|     Background to Reform | 54 |
|     'Military Reform' | 54 |
|     Soldiers' Welfare | 60 |
|     Chief of Staff | 63 |
|     Parliament and the Army | 63 |
| 7. Brackenbury's Women | 68 |
| 8. The Franco-Prussian War | 75 |
| 9. The National Aid Society | 82 |
| 10. Aftermath of the Franco-Prussian War | 97 |
| 11. The Ashanti War | 107 |
|     The Founding of the 'Ashanti Ring' | 108 |
| 12. Return from Ashantiland and Experiences in Natal and Cyprus | 115 |
|     Natal | 117 |
|     Egypt and Crete | 118 |

|     | Writing and Regimental Duty | 119 |
|     | Cyprus | 122 |
| 13. | The Zulu War, the Sekhukhune Expedition and Beyond | 125 |
|     | The Zulu War | 125 |
|     | Sekhukhune Expedition | 126 |
|     | India | 130 |
|     | Military Attaché in Paris | 131 |
| 14. | Ireland: Disappointment and Near Disaster | 133 |
|     | Ireland and Disappointment | 133 |
| 15. | Redemption in the Sudan | 147 |
|     | Back from Ireland | 147 |
|     | The Gordon Relief Expedition | 149 |
| 16. | The Intelligence Branch | 161 |
|     | Background to the Intelligence Branch | 163 |
|     | Brackenbury's Arrival at the Intelligence Branch | 164 |
| 17. | The Mobilisation Plans | 168 |
| 18. | Intelligence Work | 174 |
|     | Producing Intelligence | 174 |
| 19. | The Hartington Commission | 184 |
| 20. | Legacy of Intelligence Work | 194 |
|     | Brackenbury's Legacy | 195 |
| 21. | The Challenge of India | 198 |
|     | Introduction | 198 |
|     | British Power in India | 198 |
|     | The Military in India | 199 |
|     | 'The Great Game' | 200 |
| 22. | Military Member | 203 |
|     | Military Member of the Council of the Viceroy of India | 203 |
|     | Brackenbury and Roberts | 207 |
| 23. | Brackenbury and the 'Russian Menace' | 212 |
| 24. | The Reorganisation of the Indian Army and Farewell to India | 221 |
|     | Reorganisation of the Indian Army | 221 |
|     | Legacy | 226 |
| 25. | President of the Ordnance Board: The Calm Before the Storm | 230 |
| 26. | Director General of the Ordnance | 235 |
|     | The South African War | 235 |
|     | The Ordnance Department | 237 |
|     | The Transfer of the Ordnance Factories | 237 |
| 27. | The State of the Ordnance Department | 242 |
|     | Brackenbury's Report on the Ordnance Department | 242 |

| | | |
|---|---|---|
| 28. | The Mowatt Committee | 248 |
| 29. | Army Contracts and the Trade | 253 |
| | Over Reliance on 'the Trade' | 253 |
| | Army Contracts | 254 |
| | 'The Trade' | 255 |
| 30. | Problems of Production | 261 |
| | Quality and Inspection | 261 |
| | Ammunition | 263 |
| 31. | The Ehrhardt Gun | 267 |
| | Artillery in the South African War | 267 |
| | The Erhardt Gun | 271 |
| 32. | The Conclusion of the South African War | 274 |
| | Small Arms Ammunition | 274 |
| | Artillery Ammunition | 276 |
| | Establishing Reserves | 277 |
| | Brackenbury and Secretaries of State | 279 |
| 33. | Ill-Health and Retirement | 281 |
| | Overwork and Ill-Health | 282 |
| | Honours | 284 |
| | Assessment | 286 |
| | Retirement | 288 |
| 34. | Conclusion and Assessment | 292 |

Appendices

| | | |
|---|---|---|
| I | Timeline of the Career of General Sir Henry Brackenbury | 304 |
| II | List of books and articles by Sir Henry Brackenbury | 306 |
| | Books | 306 |
| | Journal Articles and Published Lectures | 307 |
| | Newspaper Articles | 308 |
| | Miscellaneous | 309 |

Bibliography 310

| | |
|---|---|
| Archives | 310 |
| British Public Documents | 311 |
| Newspapers and Periodicals | 313 |
| Edited Diaries | 313 |
| Contemporary Books, Autobiographies and Journal Articles | 313 |
| Later Published Sources – Books | 316 |
| Later Published Sources – Articles | 326 |
| Unpublished Dissertations | 329 |

Index 330

# List of Illustrations

| | |
|---|---|
| Lieutenant-Colonel Sir Edward Brackenbury | 4 |
| Lieutenant William Brackenbury | 6 |
| Major-General Charles Booth Brackenbury | 42 |
| Photograph of a handsome young Henry Brackenbury | 43 |
| Lord Wolseley | 109 |
| Robert Bulwer-Lytton, 1st Earl of Lytton | 129 |
| This photograph of Henry Brackenbury was taken in March 1885, when he was commanding the River Column during the Gordon Relief Expedition | 130 |
| Henry Brackenbury. Undated but likely to have been taken around 1882 | 134 |
| Edward Stanhope | 149 |
| Major-General William Earle | 152 |
| Henry Brackenbury. A photograph taken during his time in India | 206 |
| Lord Lansdowne | 214 |
| Lord Roberts | 223 |
| Henry Brackenbury. Another photograph showing Henry in India | 224 |
| Field Marshal Sir George White | 226 |
| Henry Brackenbury, taken after his promotion to General in 1902 | 277 |
| Henry Brackenbury seen in his uniform and robes as member of the Privy Council, circa 1904 | 285 |
| Henry Brackenbury in retirement, circa 1909 | 289 |

# List of Maps

| | |
|---|---|
| Franco-German border | xxvi |
| India | xxvii |

# Foreword

The reputation of Garnet Wolseley, the Victorian army's 'only general', was assured by the success of the Ashanti war in 1873–74. Careful staff work and excellent preparation ensured that a campaign in west Africa, notorious as a graveyard for European troops, was conducted in short order with minimal loss of life. Within months a two-volume account was available in London's bookshops. Wolseley understood the importance of the press, and the book's publishers, William Blackwood, knew how fast popular interest in such events could fade. Its 795 pages were written in six weeks. The author, assisted by two shorthand writers, worked twelve to fourteen hours a day, and, when he had finished, collapsed with exhaustion.

His name was Henry Brackenbury, and this is the first full account of his life. Wolseley launched Brackenbury on his career and he was therefore always and rightly identified with what came to be called 'the Wolseley ring'. Brackenbury accompanied Wolseley to Zululand in 1879 and held his most senior operational command in what proved to be his and Wolseley's last campaign, the Gordon relief expedition of 1884–85. Brackenbury wrote another book about that. So too did J.F. Maurice, another member of the 'ring'. Maurice was dubbed 'the second pen of Sir Garnet', but Brackenbury has as good a claim to the title. He had been professor of military history at the Royal Military Academy Woolwich, and, while he never wrote the big book on strategic theory that many believed he had in him, he was part of a current of intellectual engagement which stands at odds with popular – if often ill-conceived – images of the army in which he served.

Brackenbury's career can be partly understood in terms of paradox. An Etonian who initially planned a career in the law, he joined one of the army's two 'scientific arms', the Royal Artillery. In the era of the purchase of commissions, which accelerated promotion for the wealthy, artillery officers – who served in a corps which did not have purchase and were promoted by seniority – could struggle to reach senior rank. Brackenbury became a full general. Wolseley's patronage was an important part of this success, and yet Brackenbury's career does not confirm the idea of an army divided in two – between those backed by Wolseley and those backed by Britain's only 'other general', Lord Roberts. In 1891 Brackenbury became the military member of the Viceroy's council in India when Roberts was still the sub-continent's commander-in-chief, and Roberts supported the proposal to erect a memorial to Brackenbury after his death. Wolseley, a deeply politicised officer, battled with Lord Lansdowne, the secretary of state for war, during the South African War, while Brackenbury, who was so determined to remain apolitical that he did not even vote while serving, remained on good terms with Landsdowne – and with other politicians.

As a result Brackenbury was appointed to jobs which we would now see as lying on the cusp of the civil-military divide. In particular he served on the Hartington Commission which in 1890 recommended the creation of a general staff and the abolition of the post of commander-in-chief of the British army. Its recommendations were not implemented until after the South African War, but they reflected the real significance of Brackenbury's career. In 1866, as a young officer, he wrote a series of articles on military reform which – among other things – called for the army to have a chief of staff rather than a commander-in-chief. His service with Wolseley, and the latter's cultivation of certain key officers whom he called upon for each of his campaigns, highlighted the army's lack of – and need for – a proper general staff. In 1885 Brackenbury was appointed to head the Intelligence Branch of the War Office, a body tasked not just with the collection of information but also with preparations for mobilisation. He appointed to the department those who were (unlike himself) Staff College graduates, and he nurtured young talents – like Charles Callwell, John Grierson, Wully Robertson and Henry Wilson. Here, in the evolution from Wolseley 'ring' to the Intelligence Branch, was the genesis of the army's general staff, even if that body would not be fully formed until 1906. In 1886 Brackenbury's department drew up a mobilisation plan in 1886, and the work on which he then engaged, both in India and on his return in 1896 with the Ordnance Board, was similarly devoted to creating an army that could be expanded in the event of war, and then both properly equipped before it was deployed and fully supplied once it was in the field.

In some ways, therefore, Brackenbury was, even more than his mentor, 'the model of a modern major-general'. Scientific and immensely hard-working, he recognised, as did the best officers of the Prussian general staff whom he had encountered in the Franco-Prussian War of 1870–71, that waging modern war was about administration and good management as much as courage and inspiration. Such work tends to remain unsung; in Brackenbury's case it has – until now. Christopher Brice has made good the deficit with the exhaustive biography which Brackenbury deserves and whose research he would surely have appreciated.

Professor Hew Strachan

# Preface

Sir Henry Brackenbury rose from fairly humble beginnings to become an extremely important figure within the late Victorian British army and state. His family had little wealth and as the youngest son of a youngest son it was always clear he would have to work for a living. However his social status would require entry into a profession rather than merely a job. In many ways he was a surprising soldier and Professor Joseph Lehmann recorded that "In uniform he appeared to be a businessman in disguise".[1] Yet in many ways he embodied the period of change within military campaigning where technology and mass mobilisation meant that equally important to a good fighting general in the field was a man in the War Office with a fine military, administrative, strategic and logistical brain. His career spanned almost half a century by the end of which he had reached the top of his profession.

No work of this nature has ever been undertaken before and Henry Brackenbury remains a largely forgotten Victorian soldier. To an extent he has suffered from the fact that this era has been largely forgotten by many historians who understandably find more interest in the eras either side of it, the Napoleonic Wars or the two world wars of the twentieth century. Yet the significance of this period should be no more neglected than the significance of Sir Henry Brackenbury. In undertaking this study I have pulled together all the documents in the public domain, but have also been fortunate in having access to a private collection not available to historians before. In 2009 I completed a PhD Thesis on the military career of Sir Henry Brackenbury. I was then approached by Duncan Rogers of Helion with a view to publishing my work on Brackenbury. From the outset I was determined that this should be a biography of his life rather than simply his military career. This has not been the easiest of tasks. However I have attempted to include as much of Henry Brackenbury the 'man' as the 'soldier'. On the other hand I have tried to keep all the information relevant to the basic theme of his life and career rather than simply be 'everything I know about Henry Brackenbury'. The intention is to show the significance and scope of his career in a way never attempted before. Through examining the life of Henry Brackenbury we see a different view of events and the late Victorian British Army than is normally seen.

---

1   Lehmann, Joseph H., *All Sir Garnet: A life of Field Marshal Lord Wolseley* (London: Jonathan Lane, 1964), p.168.

A major problem is the scattered nature of his private papers. Since completing my PhD thesis on the military career of Sir Henry Brackenbury I have made the acquaintance of members of the Brackenbury family who have a collection of private papers once belonging to Sir Henry. Their assistance, and particularly that of Mr Mark Brackenbury, the great-great-nephew of Sir Henry, has filled in some of the gaps regarding his personal life. Whilst this private collection is very useful there is very little correspondence prior to 1870, and perhaps unsurprisingly the majority of letters are from the later period of his life. At some stage Henry either lost or destroyed his earlier correspondence, and this is perhaps not surprising given that there are several hundred letters remaining within the collection. It may well be that at some stage Sir Henry sorted his papers and removed older correspondence to save space. However what remains is a private collection to which the author is grateful to have been granted unprecedented access. Here we have evidence of Henry Brackenbury's relationships and friendships. Some of this is surprising. Despite the fact that they appeared to be very close work colleagues there are no letters in the collection from James Grierson, later Lieutenant-General Sir, which suggests that their relationship was largely professional. We see clearly the personal friendship that Brackenbury had with Lord and Lady Lytton and Lord and Lady Lansdowne, a relationship that surpassed their professional association. We also see that amongst members of the Wolseley's 'ring' of officers he was closest to Henry Evelyn Wood and particularly Baker Russell who always started his letters with "My Dear Brack", the latter being one of the few occasions when his nickname was used in correspondence. The other interesting thing about this collection is that we see some very personal moments, particularly in the correspondence with his first wife. Whilst this collection of papers has not filled in all the gaps it has provided answers to many and given support to many of the authors conclusions.

What remains of his papers in the public domain are a mixture of letters and official documents scattered amongst the archives of those with whom he had contact during his life. One period of his life that is covered extensively in the public papers is between 1891 and 1896 when he was military member of the Council of the Viceroy of India. The British Library holds official documents and letters from this period, whilst the Royal Artillery Museum at Woolwich has his letter books. Added to this, and for obvious reasons, much of his correspondence with Lord Roberts concerns his time in India and survives in the Roberts papers at the National Army Museum. However, again we have the problem that much of this is regarding official matters. The Brackenbury family private collection of Brackenbury's papers does shed some light on the personal nature as there are a series of letters from Colonel, later General Sir, Bindon Blood, an officer serving in India who Brackenbury seems to be very close to. Much of their correspondence is official and regarding practical military matters, but interestingly continues long after Brackenbury has left India.

However there are also elements of what might be called Army and India 'gossip', referring to personal and private matters. One such example is Blood writing a letter of introduction, in September 1900, for a young army officer called Winston Churchill. Churchill was interested in military equipment for his latest book and Blood pointed him in the direction of Brackenbury, who agreed to meet Churchill to discuss the matter.[2]

The majority of the material surviving in the public domain is mostly concerned with official matters. However there are exceptions to this, such as his correspondence with T.H.S Escott and Lord Wolseley. Especially in his letters to Wolseley we get an insight into his views on his work and his career. We can see some of the insecurity that he had, most significantly when it came to how others viewed him as a soldier. He felt that he was treated with suspicion, and this added to his insecurity and as a result he did not feel his skills were appreciated. He also tells Wolseley that he prefers promotion to honours, as a reward for serving in various campaigns. We see elements of his hypochondria, but also the way in which his practice of working would exhaust him to the point of breakdown. This happened periodically, most notably on his return from the Franco-Prussian War, the Ashanti campaign, and the Gordon Relief expedition and during the South African War. Indeed the latter was the most significant. The severe strain that was placed upon him and the Ordnance Department led to a complete breakdown of his health, to the extent that he offered his resignation, but was persuaded to take a holiday instead. Brackenbury's working pattern was based on long days and very late nights.[3] The problem was that by the time of the South African War he was in his early sixties, the years of such hard work were taking their toll, and he became very anxious about his ability to carry on. Consequently he was finding that what little sleep he had was fitful and brief.

One has to be careful when examining the letters of Wolseley. They have their value, but often have to be examined for deeper motives. Most of these letters were to Lady Wolseley. She appears to have been an incurable gossip and her husband seems to have indulged her by keeping her fully informed. As a consequence it is sometimes difficult to differentiate between gossip and fact. Also, Wolseley was very much a man of moods. Even a brief look at Wolseley's campaign journals illustrates that his opinion of his staff changed from day to day. His praise could quickly turn to vitriolic condemnation. His Sudan journal best illustrates this. On one page he describes Brackenbury as being hated throughout the army in the Sudan and

---

2 Bindon Blood to Brackenbury, 26th September 1900, Winston Churchill to Brackenbury, 17th October 1900, private collection. There are numerous letters from Blood to Brackenbury and a bundled collection of ten letters written by Blood when he was serving during the Chitral Expedition in 1895.

3 In *Some Memories of My Spare Time*, pp.51-52, Brackenbury talks of having discussed his working practice with the author Anthony Trollope, who was a close friend. Trollope believed in working from five o'clock in the morning, and not working after breakfast. He told Brackenbury that, "I give the freshest hours of the day to my work; you give the fag end of the day to yours".

generally condemns his leadership, but in the next entry an attack on the character of Buller leads Wolseley to say that on his next campaign he will have Brackenbury as his Chief of Staff, praising his leadership quality, and saying that Brackenbury is one of only two men worth employing again. On one occasion Wolseley criticises Brackenbury for complaining about being forced to serve under officers junior to him during the Gordon relief expedition. Wolseley continued: "If in my career I had refused to serve under a junior, I wonder where I should have been?", conveniently forgetting that he had never been in that position.[4] The Wolseley papers and journals are useful and interesting but their limitations should always be remembered. Again in this instance it is unfortunate that Brackenbury's personal recollection of events has not fully survived. It would have been very interesting to have compared them with Wolseley's. To a similar extent the correspondence with T.H.S. Escott has a similar bias. Escott and Brackenbury were close friends and this obviously influenced his judgement. This is illustrated in Escott's article 'Henry Brackenbury and his school'. It is an interesting tribute to Brackenbury but does not even attempt to look at his faults or failings.[5]

An interesting archive are the letters Brackenbury wrote to Lord Spencer whilst serving in Ireland.[6] Here we get a good picture of his mind and administrative skills at work. We see the formulation of his plans to deal with the Fenian threat, and how he recommends the creation of a sophisticated intelligence network. We also see in these letters the incredulity he felt when his plans were not adopted. Here we also see his lack of ability to play the political game and to realise that he was in a highly politicised position and environment. This is one of the best archives that shows how he worked, rather than simply the product of his work. Another archive that gives some valuable insights into Brackenbury's thinking can be found in his letters to Edward Stanhope, when the latter was Secretary of State for War between January 1887 and August 1892. Stanhope and Brackenbury knew each other before their time together at the War Office. The full extent of this relationship is unclear, but we do know that Stanhope had been sufficiently impressed by Brackenbury to ask him to become the chief political and election agent for the Conservative party. Their friendship meant that Brackenbury was extremely open in his letters to Stanhope. In them we get a picture of Brackenbury's insecurity and concern about his future. He seems to have had a real fear that once his time as Head of the Intelligence Branch was over he would simply not be given another appointment. This is extremely interesting given that to the outside observer it would have appeared that Brackenbury's star was in the ascendance.

---

4  The handwritten original journal survives in the National Archives, Kew, WO 147/8.
5  T.H.S. Escott Papers, British Library Add58775 and Escott, T.H.S., 'Henry Brackenbury and his school' *Contemporary Review* 105 (January/June 1914).
6  Brackenbury correspondence with 5th Earl Spencer, Spencer papers, British Library Add 77088.

In general this is a straightforward biography in chronological order. However there are some exceptions to this. Due to the fact that the Victorian military era is not very well known I have included a chapter on the late Victorian British Army, which whilst it cannot tell the whole story does give some background on the issues of the time. The other exception is that the majority of his literary career has been condensed into two chapters. The idea behind this is so that the significance and scope of his literary career can be illustrated, rather than introducing it piecemeal in other chapters. An attempt has been made to keep the chapters relatively short and of similar length, however this has not always been possible.

Dr Christopher Brice

# Acknowledgements

I am grateful to Helion & Co for all the assistance provided in turning a PhD thesis into a book, particularly Duncan Rogers, who has assisted me personally in its preparation and has been extremely understanding throughout.

Dr Anthony Clayton, formerly of the War Studies Department of The Royal Military Academy, Sandhurst, deserves foremost thanks for his help, support and advice throughout my studies. Originally serving as First Supervisor for my PhD, he has continued to support me throughout the period of study and beyond despite no longer having an official interest. His advice and contacts have been invaluable, and I am extremely grateful to him.

This book has been built largely on my PhD thesis and it is therefore right that I should acknowledge the academics who acted as my supervisors, namely Professor Tony Mason, Professor Mike Cronin and Professor Richard Holt.

I am grateful to many academics who have so kindly given me their advice and assistance throughout my studies and preparation of this book, namely Professor Hew Strachan, Dr Stephen Badsey, Dr T.A Heathcote, Dr Christian Leitzbach, Brigadier B.A.H Parritt and Mr Matthew Buck. I would also like to express my gratitude to Professor Strachan for agreeing to write the foreword to this book, despite his very busy schedule. My thanks are also due to members of the Brackenbury family who have assisted me in my research, particularly Mark Brackenbury and Robin Brackenbury.

Thanks must also go to the various archives that I have visited and had contact with. Firstly the staff of The National Archives at Kew, The British Library, The National Library of Scotland and the National Army Museum at Chelsea. Also Mr Andrew Orgill and the staff of The Central Library at the Royal Military Academy, Sandhurst provided much help in the early days of my study. Thanks must also go to Mr Paul Evans at the Royal Artillery Museum, Woolwich for his help and assistance regarding the letter books of Sir Henry Brackenbury from his time in India. Also Zoë Lubowiecka at the Central Library, Hove for her assistance when going through the Wolseley Papers, and the staff of the Centre for Kentish Studies in Maidstone. Thanks must also go to Major Alan Edwards and the staff at the Military Intelligence Museum at Chicksands. Also Eliza Newton at the Devon Record Office in Exeter for help with the Buller Papers.

Finally I would like to thank my parents for their help and support during my studies, in particular my father, who at times has acted as 'chauffeur' and has also read through the large majority of the work for me.

# Introduction

In May 1916, a little over two years after Sir Henry Brackenbury's death, the Earl of Derby made a speech in the House of Lords:

> When I had the honour of being the Financial Secretary at the War Office under my noble friend Lord Middleton there was at the time in the Service a General officer whom personally I have always looked upon as one of the most brilliant officers that have ever been in His Majesty's Army. The noble Marques will know him well—I refer to Sir Henry Brackenbury.[1]

This is perhaps surprising. Few people outside a small number of military historians will ever have heard the name. Yet he was being held up in the House of Lords as one of the most brilliant officers to have ever served in the army. The Earl of Derby was not a particularly close friend of Brackenbury's, nor can it be argued that this was a 'glowing' tribute in the aftermath of Henry Brackenbury's death as a little over two years had passed. Whilst few others would have gone as far as the Earl of Derby there were plenty of people at the time that recognised not only Brackenbury's ability but the very significant and real impact he had upon the army.

The 'brilliance' that the Earl of Derby and others claimed for Brackenbury was not of the conventional kind. He was not a great battlefield commander, and despite the fact that he had considerable service in colonial campaigns, this alone would not be enough to justify such a claim. Perhaps his 'brilliance' was better explained by a comment of Sir Garnet, later Lord, Wolseley who remarked that Brackenbury was "...not one of the cleverest but the cleverest man in the British Army".[2] In an era when 'breeding rather than brains' remained important this clearly makes Brackenbury stand out from the crowd. He was of limited private means so here was a man who entered the Army as a profession. A man of great intellectual ability he had the talent to think and write about his profession. However there was more than simply an intellectual ability. He demonstrated great administrative skill and management ability. In his early years this made his reputation and earned him

---

1   *Hansard*, House of Lords Debate, 23rd May 1916, Vol 22, cc101-26. The comments were made by the 17th Earl of Derby, Edward George Villiers Stanley, who served as Financial Secretary to the War Office between 1901-1903 and would later serve as Secretary of State for War between 1916-1918 and 1922-1924.

2   Maurice, Sir Frederick and Arthur, Sir George, *The Life of Lord Wolseley* (London: William Heinemann, 1924), pp.223-4.

his next appointment and in later years he became something of a 'trouble-shooter' being sent in to struggling departments to reorganise them and turn them around. He was a staff officer in the best sense of the word, an organiser and administrator who combined with this a tactical and strategic knowledge that few of his contemporaries shared.

At the same time this professional approach and 'radical' perception had drawbacks. Major-General Lord Edward Gleichen told the following story about a meeting with the Commander-in-Chief, the Duke of Cambridge, when Gleichen was a young officer.

> He (the Duke of Cambridge) very kindly asked me what I was doing, but when I had broken to him that I was working in the Intelligence Department he looked grave: and, leaning over and putting his hand on my knee, he said, "So you are under Brackenbury? A dangerous man, my dear Gleichen, a very dangerous man![3]

As Gleichen went on to say, this was a curious thing for the Commander-in-Chief to say to a young subaltern about his chief. More than that, why did the Duke feel it his duty to warn a young officer serving under this 'dangerous' man? It is interesting to compare this with Wolseley's comment that Brackenbury was "not one of the cleverest, but the cleverest man in the British Army". It could be argued that this was part of the reason why the Commander-in-Chief considered him dangerous.[4] Yet there must have been far more to it than that. Gleichen himself could be called a man of 'brains', yet he seemed acceptable to the Commander-in Chief. However Gleichen had the advantage of breeding alongside 'brains' being the son of Prince Victor Hohenlohe-Langenburg. Perhaps social status did come in to it, but the main difference was that Brackenbury was not only a thinker but also a reformer, and a radical one at that. Some of the reforms that Brackenbury supported would have destroyed the 'order' that the Duke of Cambridge championed. There was also a more personal point in that one of Brackenbury's key reforms was to abolish the office of Commander-in-Chief and replace him with a Chief of Staff. Brackenbury saw this as a key move in 'professionalising' the army. Many of his other reforms to this end would also have been unacceptable to the Commander-in-Chief. Indeed in some respects he could be called the most radical of Britain's military reformers in the late Victorian era.[5] The problem was that to a large extent many of his reforms

---

3   Gleichen, Major Lord Edward Gleichen, *A Guardsman's Memories* (London: William Blackwood, 1932), p.142. The Duke of Cambridge also told Edward Stanhope, Secretary of State for War at the time, that Brackenbury was a dangerous man to have in the War Office. See Duke of Cambridge to Edward Stanhope 30th July 1887, Stanhope Papers, Centre for Kentish Studies, Maidstone.
4   The Duke of Cambridge is alleged to have said that he preferred "Breeding rather than brains" when it came to army officers. This concept is supported by Wolseley's comments that "H.R.H would prefer nonentities belonging to his own club, men socially agreeable to him and his own set".
5   Certainly his idea, mentioned in his articles for *Fraser's Magazine* on Army Reform, that every fifth

remained in the realm of theory as he was never in a position to put them all into practice. As a consequence the merit and effectiveness of these proposed reforms, which will be discussed in more detail later, is largely supposition.

The intention of this book is to provide a biography of an extremely significant but largely forgotten Victorian soldier who was in many ways unique amongst the British officer corps. No work of this nature has ever been done before.[6] Whereas the majority of his contemporaries made their reputations on the battlefields of the empire, Brackenbury made his in military administration and his literary career. The work that he did in the organisation of the various campaigns in the field and at the War Office has never truly been recognised, and rarely recorded. A brief synopsis of his career makes this hard to understand. He served in many of the key colonial wars of that period: the Indian Mutiny, the Ashanti Campaign, the Zulu War and the Gordon Relief expedition. He had two key War Office appointments, as Head of the Intelligence Branch and Director General of the Ordnance, and was generally accepted to have left both in a far better state than when first appointed. Indeed in both instances he entered departments in a state of some disarray. He also had two very significant semi-military appointments as Under Secretary for Police and Crime in Ireland and as the Military Member of the Council of the Viceroy of India. Added to this he also witnessed the Franco-Prussian War at close quarters when working for the National Aid Society providing medicine and stores to the sick and wounded of both sides. As a consequence he had probably the best view of the Franco-Prussian War of any Englishman. He saw both armies in operation, and because of the capacity in which he was serving was treated in a friendly and cordial manner and given full access to the military hierarchies of both combatant nations.[7] In addition to this he had also developed a considerable reputation as a writer, largely, but interestingly not exclusively, on military matters. His literary work was vital to his career advancement. It was a two-part article written for *The Standard* that brought him to the attention of the founders of the National Aid Society. It was also his writing on army reform that introduced him to the leading military reformers of the day, both civilian and military, and in particular Garnet Wolseley. Given his lack of personal means his literary work also gave him some financial security. However, more importantly, it provided an importance and recognition beyond his military rank. His writing on military reform gave him a

---

officers commission should be given to someone from the ranks, would have been too radical for many of his contemporaries.
6   It would be unfair not to recognise the few attempts to chronicle Brackenbury's life that have been made. Foremost is Ian Harvie's 'A Very Dangerous Man', which appeared in Issue 96 of *Soldiers of the Queen*. Two thorough reports of his life have been made for the *Dictionary of National Biography*, the most recent by Ian Beckett.
7   Because of his service in this capacity he became, as far as I am aware, the only man to be decorated with both the German Iron Cross and the French Legion of Honour

public profile that brought him to the attention of leading politicians. His series of articles on military reform were written before, and in many cases anticipated, the Cardwell Reforms. It was here that he advocated the creation of a General Staff nearly forty years before it was ultimately introduced.

Yet despite these achievements he remains largely unknown. There are several reasons for this. First, he was largely a behind-the-scenes figure, and his most significant achievements were in the War Office rather than the battlefield. Second, the importance of the work he undertook has been overlooked, mostly because of the lack of importance attached to administration and staff work by generations of soldiers and civilians alike. His work, although vital, was unappreciated. Such administrative work within the military was, and to an extent remains, unfashionable. It is interesting to note that many of the Secretaries of State under whom he served were far more appreciative of his skills than his military contemporaries. However, gradually the importance of the behind the scenes work, which enables an army to take the field, started to be understood. To a large extent this happened after he had retired in 1904, but there were a few, both soldiers and civilians, who appreciated the vital and demanding work he had done from the War Office during the South African War, a conflict that perhaps started an appreciation of such work.

There has been a key problem with the historiography regarding Brackenbury. Due to his close links with Wolseley the large majority of references to Brackenbury come straight from the former. However this sometimes misses the point that Brackenbury was far more than just one of the 'Wolseley ring'. His career brought him into a close working relationship with Wolseley's great rival Lord Roberts and many leading politicians of the day. Indeed he was closer, and worked closer, with Roberts, Stanhope and Lansdowne in particular, than he ever did with Wolseley. To Wolseley he always remained a subordinate, whereas the others treated him as closer to an equal. One of the key aims of this biography is to illustrate his career away from Wolseley. Although Brackenbury was dependent upon Wolseley's patronage in the early days his later career owed little to his influence. His three key administrative appointments towards the end of his career owed much more to political intervention than Wolseley's influence. Certainly whenever historians have written about Wolseley and his exploits the name of Brackenbury has not been far away, but to get a fuller picture of Brackenbury it is necessary to move beyond this association. As a consequence this study has tried to cover all the other available sources. Looking at the papers of people such as Roberts, Campbell-Bannerman, Arnold-Forster, Lansdowne, Escott, Stanhope, Buller and others, alongside the private family collection, has allowed for a much wider view than the tradition

INTRODUCTION

Wolseley centric view of Brackenbury.[8] The aim is to move beyond the narrow view of Brackenbury that exists and put his whole career in its wider context.

Henry Brackenbury was once described as "a scientific soldier at the dawn of scientific soldiering".[9] This is a very pertinent comment that raises several points. In some respects he could be said to be 'ahead of his time'. Had he been born twenty years later he would have been more in tune with prevailing military attitudes and would most likely have been the Chief of Staff that he had so long campaigned for. However, questioning of this style ignores the fact that his advancement was due to the circumstances of the time, and because there was a wider movement for army reform, with which he could associate. He also benefited, at least initially, from the patronage of Lord Wolseley. Also because in some ways he was the first of a new breed or at least style of officer he became, and indeed made himself, a focal point for like-minded young officers when he was Head of the Intelligence Branch. It could be said that the Intelligence Branch during this era was the closest thing the British Army had to a General Staff. This was not simply because of the duties that it undertook. Under Brackenbury in particular it attracted, and indeed sought out, the capable young officers of the Army who in European nations would have formed the General Staff.

Indeed it was here that many of the senior figures of the War Office during the First World War gained that initial training. Amongst the junior officers he selected or recommended for the department were two future Field Marshals, a future Chief of the Imperial General Staff, and five Major-Generals. Not only does this show the quality of men he selected but it perhaps lends weight to the argument that the quality of such officers was starting to be understood. Brackenbury was also in a way a champion of the graduates of the Staff College, despite never having attended it himself. Although there were obvious exceptions, such as Edward Gleichen, who had proved his worth when serving under Brackenbury in the Sudan, within a year of Brackenbury's appointment at the Intelligence Branch there were thirteen officers either attached or permanent who were Staff College graduates.[10] All those who served under him during this period had great respect for him. The relationship worked both ways. If Brackenbury were ever to be Chief of Staff these were the men who would serve under him. On the other hand they saw him as a patron who would assist their military advancement, and also one of the few senior

---

8   One of the closest people to Brackenbury professionally was the future Lieutenant General Sir James Grierson, but unfortunately his papers have not survived. The Grierson diaries would have been extremely useful, as he was probably closer to him than any other officer and in some ways his protégé. Unfortunately all that survives if D.S Macdiarmid's biography of him, as on the author's death the papers were destroyed.
9   Macdiarmid, D.S., *The Life of Lieutenant-General Sir James Moncrieff Grierson* (London: Constable & Company Ltd, 1923), p.63.
10  That is to say they were PSCs, which simply stood for Passed Staff College.

officers with whom their particular administrative talents were recognised for their importance. In their many autobiographies all of them commented upon his devotion, hard work, and professional manner. With their support Brackenbury achieved a great deal, not least because he, supported by Wolseley as Adjutant-General and Stanhope as Secretary of State for War, managed to create the political and military will to gather such a group of like-minded intellectual officers together and make it into the hub of the War Office. However, the practice of appointing people to the War Office on the back of military achievements in the field would remain a problem for many years to come.[11]

He turned all the offices he worked in, whether in the War Office or throughout the empire, into professional well run going concerns. The words 'professional' and 'business-like' were still something of an insult in the army of this period. The future Lord Kitchener was once called a 'professional soldier', and this was clearly intended as an insult; if you were professional you were probably not a gentleman. Even Wolseley once commented in this regard of Brackenbury that "I have looked upon him as not quite a gentleman".[12] This is part of a much wider discussion about the professionalisation of late Victorian society, which in turn forms part of a wider debate about the army and the merits of 'brains' versus 'breeding', to use the words of the Duke of Cambridge. Although joining the army before the abolition of purchase, Brackenbury never had to purchase a commission as officers of the Royal Artillery, and Royal Engineers, were not covered by the system.[13] Still he had to maintain the 'lifestyle' of an officer and with no real private income his situation was difficult. This was someone who came from a minor landowning family so the problem for the middle classes is self-evident. His problem of finance was partly solved by his writing, which was almost a full-time occupation on occasions. He also made a financially motivated first marriage. There was no issue from ether marriage, and consequently there are no direct descendants of Henry Brackenbury. This in itself has caused a problem as it is commonly the descendants who keep the memory alive, and this is another factor in understanding why so little has been written about Henry Brackenbury.

Although he could be considered a consummate professional Brackenbury's ideas about soldiering have been called into question. Ian Hamilton, who was a friend of Brackenbury's, criticised him for "hating" soldiers. "On paper he appreciated them well; that is to say he wrote what military instructors barbarously call 'appreciations'

---

11 The practice continued well into the 20th Century. Indeed the continuance of such a policy led to Field Marshal Montgomery's famous comment that due to the practice of appointing men who had distinguished themselves in World War One, "the Army entered the Second World War in 1939 admirably organised and equipped to fight the 1914 war".
12 Wolseley Sudan Campaign Journal, 31st December 1884, National Archives, Kew WO147/8.
13 The theory was that officers in these branches, the so-called scientific services, had to have an element of professionalism and training.

about them, but Brackenbury, the real Brackenbury, hated them in practice".[14] Not only is this an unusual criticism but also it is hard to understand what point Hamilton was trying to make. His motivation here, as in the rest of the same chapter, was to criticise Wolseley for his selection of officers and his conduct of the Gordon Relief expedition. If Hamilton was trying to say that Brackenbury did not care for them that is hard to support in the light of his writing on military reform, much of which, if carried out, would dramatically improve the life of the average soldier. It must be added that Brackenbury's primary motivation was to improve efficiency and aid recruitment. However, Brackenbury did not have much experience in dealing with ordinary soldiers. His career was largely based around dealing with officers and in the brief times in his early career that he had commanded soldiers they were artillerymen rather than infantry. The artillery was a very different organisation to the rest of the army as a degree of specialism was required, and if as a result Brackenbury was unsure of how to deal with ordinary soldiers then that is to a large extent understandable. Another key phrase is Hamilton's reference to military instructors and it is no coincidence that this was Brackenbury's background. If, however, Hamilton is suggesting he did not care about the welfare of his men then the point is harder to support. Brackenbury's very nature would have meant that he did not show much concern, but that did not mean that he did not care. However he would have cared for them as soldiers, and their efficiency as such, rather than as individuals. Whilst he always had ambitions to be a field commander and had shown he was more than capable, this was not where his greatest talents lay. Indeed perhaps his most useful position was not to be at the seat of war but at the War Office where, as an administrator, he could organise and plan campaigns. In this sense it is tempting to refer to him as the 'English Von Moltke'.[15]

The fact that this was not appreciated says a lot about the army of that time. Ideals about soldiering centred on romantic notions of the battlefield. In almost every campaign the British forces would be outnumbered, although they would almost always have technical and material superiority over their adversaries. This was the place to be for career advancement. There was, and to an extent still is, a lack of 'glamour' about staff work even though it is vital to allow an army to take the field. The folly of this attitude was partly realised during the South African

---

14  Hamilton, Ian, *Listening for the Drums* (London: Faber & Faber, 1944), pp.179–180.
15  Helmuth von Moltke (1800–1891) was Chief of the Prussian, later German, General Staff for over thirty years and widely considered to be one of the greatest staff officers of all time. He was at the very heart of the foundation and development of the Prussian/German Military machine that dominated Europe from the mid nineteenth to the early twentieth century. In *Our Greatest Living Soldiers* Charles Lowe described Brackenbury as being "a Soldier of the type of Moltke – cool, studious, accomplished, far-seeing, a finished soldier-scientist, the kind of man well entitled to the honour of being called 'the brain of an army'" (Lowe, Charles, *Our Greatest Living Soldiers*. London: Chatto & Windus, 1900), p.171.

War when the staff arrangements were wholly inadequate for the demands of the conflict. Most of the staff was selected purely because of their availability and few had met before let alone served together. This arrangement led the author of *The Times History of the South African War* to comment:

> Englishmen, who would not dream of sending a crew to Henley Regatta whose members had never rowed together before, were quite content that a general's staff should be hastily improvised at the last moment from officers scraped together from every corner.[16]

An interesting view on his career was given by Brackenbury in February 1883 when he wrote to Wolseley:

> Never yet have I been offered even the humblest employment on the staff in England – never once have I been asked to serve on a committee or commission, or in any way whatever to help in the work of organisation and administration of the army.[17]

It seems rather ironic that a man who wanted such work and had proved he could do it was overlooked in favour of men who would much rather have seen service in the field. His liking for management was largely due to his professional background to work, but also because of his educational background. The years he had spent teaching at the Royal Military Academy, Woolwich as Professor of Military History had set his mind to studying his profession more seriously than most, and it was at this time that his literary output was at its most prestigious. Wolseley praised him for administrative work on many occasions. Perhaps more significant was the praise he received from several Secretaries of State for War. Indeed the individual who seemed the most aggrieved by Brackenbury's omission from the honours list for the South African War was the Secretary of State for War, H.O Arnold-Forster. His position is understandable. Brackenbury was one of the few men to come out of the South African War with any credit, yet it was never officially recognised.

Henry Brackenbury seems to have been a slightly unusually character in some ways. That he often appeared aloof, superior, condescending and arrogant is probably true but these were hardly unique characteristics for a Victorian army officer. Indeed this might have been part of the 'disguise' he used to make himself seem acceptable to his fellow officers. Yet his supposed arrogance might often have been self-confidence, particularly when he saw himself as an expert of the matter under discussion. However he was certainly able to realise his own limitations. There had

---

16   Amery, Leo, *The Times History of the War in South Africa* Volume II (London: Smith Elder & Co, 1902), pp.37-8.
17   Brackenbury to Wolseley, 4th February 1883, Wolseley Papers, Central Library, Hove.

been some suggestions that Brackenbury might be the man to succeed Roberts as Commander-in-Chief in India. In a very frank and honest letter to Lord Lansdowne Brackenbury rejected the idea in self-deprecating terms, but we shall look at that in more detail later.

Although a highly intelligent and professional man Brackenbury adopted what has been called a 'silly ass' manner. He developed a 'haw haw' laugh, much to Wolseley's annoyance. Perhaps most incomprehensible was his affectation of a lisp, a common practice at the time in the fashionable regiments, which meant his own name became 'Whackenbaywe'.[18] Although this was very popular during the mid-nineteenth century it started to fall out of fashion. We have no evidence but it is likely that Brackenbury abandoned the affectation at some point. It would be interesting to known when he did as during the late 1880s he had many private meetings with Lord Randolph Churchill, well known for his lisp which might have been slightly affected. It would have been bizarre to say the least to have heard two intelligent men lisping their way through a conversation on such weighty matters as the future of the army and imperial defence. It is clear that his use of a lisp and a 'haw haw' laugh can be seen as part of his attempt to be accepted and was almost a disguise for the unacceptable nature of his professionalism. Given that he joined the Crimean era army the use of such mannerisms is perhaps more understandable.[19] Clinging to the fashions of the day would have given him a certain security and acceptability that his professionalism would not have secured alone. It might also have made people believe that he was of slightly higher social status than he indeed was.

For whatever reason Brackenbury appears to have been difficult to like personally, but even those who disliked him would admit admiration for his work. He had an ability to rub people up the wrong way. Sir George White, for instance, claimed that Brackenbury was an "intriguer" who tried "...to turn everything to his own credit".[20] In a sense it was inevitable that Brackenbury would gain some credit for all things done in the Indian Army, as he was ultimately the senior man, and in theory White's 'boss'. It would be interesting to know if White realised that Brackenbury had championed his claim to be Commander-in-Chief in India, despite his juniority, and had written to both Stanhope, as Secretary of State for War, and Lord Lansdowne as Viceroy, in his favour. Indeed in both letters he said White was the only option. So whatever view White had of Brackenbury it did not affect

---

18  Brackenbury, Charles E., *The Brackenburys of Lincolnshire* (Lincoln: The Society for Lincolnshire History and Archaeology, 1983), p.69.
19  It is said that Lord Cardigan launched the infamous Charge of the Light Brigade with the words "The Bwigade will advance". See Turner, E.S., *Gallant gentleman: A portrait of the British Officer 1600-1956* (London: Michael Joseph Ltd, 1956) pp.244-245 for further examples of the affected lisp and 'haw haw' laugh.
20  Sir George White to John White, 7th April 1898, White papers, British Library P3/132.

Brackenbury's view of White. Whilst there are other examples of this ability to rub people up the wrong way, including his actions towards the government during his time in Ireland, there is however no record of anyone criticising or denigrating his work or professionalism.[21]

The idea that he was hard to get to know and generally disliked is contradicted by his time in the Intelligence Branch where the officers serving under him were full of praise and genuinely liked him. It can be argued that this was because he had surrounded himself with likeminded officers and for perhaps the first time in his military career could genuinely be himself. It is clear that Brackenbury felt a pressure on himself to prove that he was more than a teacher or thinker. In the same way he felt himself pressured to prove that he was 'an officer and a gentleman' rather than a 'professional'. He had an uneasy relationship with politicians, although he got on well with a good many. The problem was Brackenbury's lack of tact and unwillingness to play the political game. Again his view was simple, if not arrogant. He was the expert, and if he said something needed to be done then it was their duty to make sure that he was able to carry it out. This was certainly the case with Ireland and his time as Director General of the Ordnance. He was slightly more tactful when Head of the Intelligence Branch. This was perhaps due to the fact that the conflict he had in Ireland with his political masters was still fresh in his memory. The other reason might be that in this latter case he had the full support of Wolseley and Stanhope who would play the political game for him. This change in Brackenbury was noticed by Lord Wantage, who when writing to congratulate him on his promotion to Major-General noted that "It has been an additional pleasure to me to witness how much prosperity has softened and improved your character".[22]

Brackenbury entered the army at an important time. The army had been called upon to undertake two major operations, the war in the Crimea and the mutiny in India, within a short space of time. In particular the Crimean War showed up the inadequacies and inefficiencies of the military machine in all its aspects. Indeed, the situation was such that a major overhaul of the military system was undertaken whilst the war was still being fought. Whilst these reforms simplified the situation

---

21  Another criticism of Brackenbury can be found in General Sir Horace Smith-Dorrien's autobiography. Brackenbury had made a speech in which he had apparently questioned the value of the Staff College certificate. Unfortunately the speech does not appear to have survived anywhere, and Smith-Dorrien gives few details. What is unfair however is Smith-Dorrien's attempt to make Brackenbury appear to be one of the conservatives of the army resistant to change, which illustrates a complete ignorance on his part of Brackenbury's career. It is also contrary to Smith-Dorrien's own statement about the Staff College that, "I do not think we were taught as much as we might have been, but there was plenty of sport and not too much work". Brian Bond says of Smith-Dorrien's time at the Staff College that, "Legend says that after he had been there three months he was found wandering about the corridors asking the way to the library!" Bond, Brian, *The Victorian Army and the Staff College* (London: Eyre Methuen Ltd, 1972), p.141.

22  Lord Wantage to Brackenbury, 30th September 1885, private collection.

they were only part of what was needed. Thus there was a continuing interest in reforming the army. At the time Brackenbury started writing, in the mid-1860s, parliamentary interest in army reform was growing though never could it be said that it was considered to be a high priority. It can be seen as Brackenbury's career advanced he was often in the right place at the right time. An interesting question would be whether the events of the time turned Brackenbury into a reformer or whether he helped to set the agenda of reform. Although other generals of the period such as Wolseley, Kitchener and Roberts were undoubtedly professionals they were of a different type.[23] Brackenbury could be called an intellectual soldier. His literary career demonstrates the amount of time and thought he put into so many areas of his profession as well as his concern about the fighting efficiency of the army.

Brackenbury was unique in combining a significant literary career with active service and key administrative appointments at the highest level of the British Army. No other soldier compared in this respect and through looking at his career we gain a different perspective on the British Army than that provided by other scholars. There is also the matter of the sheer length of his career, spanning some forty-eight years, encompassed the large majority of the Victorian era, which means that he is a key witness to the period.[24] However, what is more important than the length of his career is what he was able to achieve during it. From a subaltern in the Royal Artillery he moved on to a significant active service career before ending his military service with three major administrative appointments. Through using a much wider set of archives than has ever been used before, we are able to place Henry Brackenbury in his correct context, and illustrate his importance within the army and the state during this period. The aim is to move away from the narrow view of his association with Wolseley to illustrate the career of a significant officer of the late Victorian army.

---

23   It is worthy of note that all four generals were sons of army officers.
24   For simplicity the date of April 1856, when he was first commissioned as a Lieutenant, is used for the start of his Army career. It could be argued that 1855, when he first entered Woolwich, or 1853, when he was made an Ensign in the Quebec Militia, could be used.

# MAPS

Franco-German border

India

CHAPTER 1

# THE BRACKENBURYS OF LINCOLNSHIRE

Henry Brackenbury was part of the Lincolnshire Brackenburys, a minor landowning family who were an important part of the life of that county. As a result of their limited private income many of the family had gone into one profession or another to make a living. Some in the legal profession many in the church and an increasing number in either the army or the navy. Although a detailed account of the history of the Brackenburys of Lincolnshire is not necessary it is important to understand something of Henry's heritage and how it affected his life and career.[1]

Perhaps the most famous, or perhaps that should be infamous, Brackenbury in British history is Sir Robert Brackenbury, Constable of the Tower of London during the reign of Richard III. Like so many of the late King's followers his reputation suffered from Tudor propaganda. Sir Robert was part of the Hampshire Brackenburys who could trace their origins back to the Norman invasion. It is extremely likely that the Brackenburys of Lincolnshire were an off-shoot of this family, indirectly, through the County Durham branch of the family. It is believed that there is a link between the Lincolnshire Brackenburys and those of County Durham, but there is no definitive proof. As Charles E. Brackenbury, a family historian for the Lincolnshire Brackenburys, wrote, "There must have been a connection between these two families, if only one could find evidence of it".[2] There is an alternative theory which says the Brackenburys of Lincolnshire were not of Norman decent at all and that the name is a derivation of Brackenborough, a village just north of Louth

---

[1] There are two very useful sources regarding the Lincolnshire Brackenbury family. Firstly there is Charles. E. Brackenbury's *The Brackenbury's of Lincolnshire* (Lincoln: Lincolnshire Society for History and Archaeology, 1983). This is a published version of the Brackenbury Memorial Lecture given for that year. The second is Henry Brackenbury's 'A Letter from Salamanca' *Blackwood's Magazine* Volume 165 (March 1899).

[2] Brackenbury, *The Brackenburys of Lincolnshire*, p.1.

in Lincolnshire. The earliest recorded accounts of Brackenburys being resident in Lincolnshire are in 1155. The family is recorded as being financial supporters for the Gilbertine Order, a monastic group which had been founded in Lincolnshire in 1130 by Saint Gilbert. The family seemed to take a keen interest in religious and business life in the county, so much so that by the start of the 18th century the Brackenburys of Lincolnshire were made up mostly of churchmen and solicitors.

When looking through the history of the Brackenbury family of Lincolnshire, it can be seen that certain Christian names go through the generations. One of these is the slightly unusual name of Carr. This is in memory of the Carrs of Sleaford, who were a rich and powerful family, with links to the Brackenburys. One of the people named in memory of the Carrs was Henry Brackenbury's great-great-grandfather Carr Brackenbury, born in 1688. It was through his legal career and his appointment as Receiver General of Lincolnshire that the family first rose to prominence in that county. His eldest son, Henry's great-grandfather, was also named Carr, and inherited the family wealth, which when added to a 'good' marriage meant that he died a very wealthy man. He had ten children but under the terms of his will only the first six benefited. As a consequence Henry's grandfather, Richard, born in 1758, inherited nothing. Richard's need for a 'career' meant that he became the first member of the family to enter the army. With money borrowed from his uncle he purchased a commission in the 70th Regiment of Foot. He had a brief career in the army and married an 'admiral's' daughter in 1776.[3] He became the Colonel of the Lincolnshire Militia and became a powerful figure in county life. The source of Richard Brackenbury's wealth is unclear. In 1818 he inherited the family property in Aswardby, Lincolnshire, but it was estimated that the rental income from the tenants of the estate was only £373 a year (about £12,000 in modern money). Yet despite this he was a wealthy man and left an enviable collection of art work including pictures by Thomas Gainsborough, Aelbert Cuyp, Phillips Wouwerman, and Jan Breughel.[4]

As Colonel of the local militia he became a man of great importance. Interestingly his main use of the militia was to intimidate those who sought to develop Methodism in Lincolnshire, and he would regularly station militia units outside Methodist Chapels during morning worship. The irony of this was that his brother Robert was an important figure in the growth of Methodism, one of its key financial backers, and was responsible for the building of Raithby Chapel one of the oldest Methodist Chapels in the world. On his death Robert left all his money to the church at the cost of his own family. Despite Richard's anti-Methodist past he himself converted

---

[3] Although George Gunn is often referred to as an Admiral there is no record of him on the Royal Navy List.
[4] Charles. E. Brackenbury *op.cit.*, pp.12-13.

to Methodism at some point in his life and ultimately became a local preacher.[5] The prominence of Methodism within the Brackenbury family raises some interesting questions about Henry. There is little reference to his own beliefs but he does appear to have been a regular churchgoer. It should be remembered that this was an era when to a great extent someone of his social standing and family connections would have been expected to attend and support the local church. It would have been as much about keeping up appearances as any personal expression of faith. On two occasions Henry Brackenbury made reference in his writing to having been in a church service and on both occasions it was a Church of England service. This is perhaps not too surprising. As we shall see Henry enjoyed nothing better than ingratiating himself with the establishment.

Richard Brackenbury married Janetta Gunn when he was only eighteen. As the daughter of 'Admiral' George Gunn it was a socially acceptable marriage for the family but one that did little for their financial security. When Janetta died in 1827 he soon remarried. Three years later at the age of seventy-one he married Alice Horn of Bollingbroke, Lincolnshire.[6] The marriage caused something of a family scandal on two accounts. Firstly she was considerably his junior. Although her exact age is unclear it is unlikely that she was over thirty, and quite possibly much younger. Whilst her age might have met with disapproval it is more likely that the real cause of scandal was the fact that she was of 'low' birth. She was in fact the daughter of a tenant farmer on the Brackenbury estate. To a family of middle rank like the Brackenburys who were constantly trying to climb the social ladder this would not have met with approval. It also caused real problems regarding the inheritance of the children, as many of them were most likely considerably older than she was. Despite the age difference they were married for fourteen years before Richard died in 1844 at the age of eighty-six. Alice lived until 1868 and on her death the main beneficiary was her sister's family.

Richard and Janetta had six sons and five daughters. Two of the sons died in childhood and another, Robert, died at the age of twenty whilst serving in the Royal Navy. The three remaining sons all had military careers. The eldest surviving son John Macpherson Brackenbury served in the 25th Light Dragoons although his career was short. He later served as superintendent for shipwreck survivors along the Lancashire coast, and was appointed His Majesty's Consul in Cadiz, a position he retained for twenty years. This line of the family continued the military tradition. John Macpherson Brackenbury's son, William Congreave Brackenbury, joined the Royal Navy, but later followed his father into the Consular Service, serving as Consul in Madrid, Bilbao, Vigo and Coruna. His family continued the Spanish connection,

---

5 Ibid., pp.9-13.
6 According to Charles. E. Brackenbury's account of the family Henry Brackenbury rather tactfully referred to Alice Horn as a "woman of immense proportions".

which exists to this day. His eldest son John William Brackenbury, also joined the Royal Navy and had a distinguished career retiring with the rank of Admiral, and his second son, Maule Brackenbury, joined the army and finished as a Colonel.

The next oldest surviving son of Richard Brackenbury was Edward. He joined the 61st Regiment and saw service with them in the Peninsular War. Later on he commanded a battalion in the reconstituted Portuguese army commanded by a British officer General William Beresford. The Portuguese army offer the opportunity of command to those like Edward Brackenbury who lacked either the money or connections to obtain command in the British Army. Edward Brackenbury was the most successful soldier the family had produced up until that point. He saw considerable service fighting in Sicily, at Calabria, and then during the Peninsular Campaign being present at the battles of Talavera, Bussaco, Fuentes de Oñoro, Badajoz, Salamanca, Villa Muriel, Osuna, Vitoria and San Sebastian. His service saw him awarded a British knighthood along with the Spanish and Portuguese versions. At the battle of Salamanca his Portuguese battalion was involved in fierce hand to hand fighting with a French column attempting to outflank the Allied army. At the same battle he is recorded as capturing an enemy gun guarded by four men without any assistance. He remained in the army after the Napoleonic Wars and left in 1845 with the rank of Lieutenant-Colonel. In retirement he sat as a magistrate and was Deputy Lieutenant for Lincolnshire. The many contacts he had made would prove useful to Henry in his early days, as we shall see later.[7]

**Lieutenant-Colonel Sir Edward Brackenbury, Henry's uncle, who was a more successful soldier than his younger brother William, and saw far more active service. He commanded a Portuguese Regiment during the latter stages of the Peninsular War and played a useful part in Henry's early career. (Private collection)**

---

7   *Oxford Dictionary of National Biography* (Oxford: Oxford University Press, 2004), p.149.

The fifth son of Richard Brackenbury died before reaching maturity. We now come to the youngest son, William, the father of Henry. William was also a soldier and whilst his bravery was on a par with his brother he received few of the rewards that his brother did. Nor was he as lucky. William was serving as a Lieutenant in the 1st battalion of the 61st Regiment during their deployment to the Spanish peninsular. At the battle of Talavera on 28th July 1809 he was severely wounded by being shot between the shoulders. He returned to England and when fit again joined the 2nd battalion in Ireland. In 1811 he returned to Spain, volunteering for further action. Once in Spain he realised that he had rushed himself and suffered from continual pain as his wounds had not healed sufficiently. Despite the pain he continued to serve and was present at the battle of Salamanca on 22nd July 1812. During the battle as the 61st came under attack from a French column William rescued the fallen colours of the battalion and defended them stoutly, despite being shot in the left foot and the left cheek, the latter blow breaking his jaw. He continued to fight on until relieved.[8] Edward wrote a letter to their parents telling them of the battle and of his brother's injuries. Many years later Henry Brackenbury used this letter as the basis of a journal article simply entitled 'A letter from Salamanca'. William remained in Spain to recover from his injuries and did not return to England until 1814. His latest wounds left him lame and in great pain. He was apparently liable to self-pity and exaggeration, although there is no doubt that his injuries were severe. This was an accusation later levelled at his son Henry. Both seemed to make the most of their 'misery'. There is another similarity in that neither took care of themselves. William had rushed back to Spain before he was fully recovered from wounds received at Talavera, and later paid the price for it. Henry would work himself to exhaustion almost to the point of collapse and then need total rest to recover. To those who did not know the way he worked the times when he would take himself away for several weeks to recover would appear to be self-pity, as during that time he would act and behave as an invalid.

This time William's wounds, added to those from Talavera, were sufficient to make sure he saw no further active service. He spent most of what was left of his military career stationed in Ireland. It was there that he first met Maria Atkinson, and although they fell in love, marriage was out of the question due to financial limitations. Instead Maria married a James Wallace, but in due course she was widowed and in 1820 William now retired on half-pay and with a pension for the wounds received during the war was in a position to marry her. William and Maria had four sons and four daughters. The eldest William Atkinson Brackenbury died unmarried

---

8   The events of that day are covered by Henry Brackenbury in 'A Letter from Salamanca' and in *The Brackenburys of Lincolnshire*, the latter includes the letter as Appendix IV. The letter and an account of the battle can be found in David Scott Daniell's *Cap of Honour: The Story of The Gloucestershire Regiment (The 28th/61st Foot) 1694-1975* (London: White Lion Publishers, 1975), pp.111-114.

Lieutenant William Brackenbury, Henry's father, who had a difficult time as a soldier and suffered from severe wounds received during the Peninsular War. He rescued the 61st colours at the battle of Salamanca. He died when Henry was only six years old. (Private collection)

at the age of nineteen. Catherine Mary Brackenbury was next and she married and had one daughter but died at the age of twenty-three. She was followed by Richard Gunn Brackenbury, who joined the army and served in his father's old regiment the 61st. He saw service during the Indian Mutiny. In 1859, still serving in India, he died of cholera at Poona unmarried at the age of thirty-four. Next came two daughters, Hannah Maria and Jemima Gordon, both of whom were unmarried and died at the age of nine and nineteen respectively. The final daughter, born in 1833, Henrietta Brackenbury died only three years later.

This meant that the eldest surviving son was now Charles Booth Brackenbury, born in 1831[9]. He also joined the army, being commissioned into the Royal Artillery in December 1850. He served with chestnut troop of the Royal Horse Artillery in the Crimea War from June 1855. He served in Malta and in March 1860 was appointed Assistant Instructor in Artillery at the Royal Military Academy, Woolwich. It is natural enough to think that his brother's entry in the Royal Artillery was a contributing factor in Henry's decision to join a few years later. It is also very likely that Charles's active service in the Crimea had a lot to do with Henry's desperation to see

---

9   Charles left few private papers. The only papers that survive are his letters to Spenser Wilkinson at both the National Army Museum and the British Library, and his letters to Lord Rendel at the Archive Centre, Newcastle upon Tyne.

active service in the Indian Mutiny. In fact many elements of Henry's life seem to be based around emulation of, if not jealousy of, his brother. For instance Charles developed a literary career before his brother, albeit never on the same scale as Henry who as we shall see effectively wrote for a living for periods of his career. Charles however devoted his literary talents exclusively to military matters, and indeed much of his work appeared in the military press. Charles also developed a reputation as a military correspondent and to this end Henry admitted his envy, as he wrote:

> My brother, Captain (afterwards Major-General) Charles Brackenbury, had acted as military correspondent of *The Times* in the war of 1866. At the battle of Koeniggratz he had ridden with Benedek into the thick of the fire at Chlum. He had gone on to Italy, and described the naval battle of Lissa and the handing over of Venetia. He had become a personage of some importance, and I was fired with emulation.[10]

Indeed it has been said of Charles Brackenbury that, "Few men had seen so much of modern warfare on a large scale as General Charles Brackenbury and no one did more to spread sound ideas in England about the tactical changes demanded by the change in weapons".[11] Ironically two of Henry's key appointments were also previously held by Charles, namely the Intelligence Branch and on the staff of the Royal Military Academy, Woolwich.[12] The brothers also shared the same reforming streak, although it is arguable that Henry was more 'radical' in some of his proposals. Charles was also more willing to deal with tactics than his brother. Even Henry's article 'Tactics of the Three Arms' is remarkably void of military detail, and is largely about administration and training. Despite his reforming tendencies Charles was never associated with the 'Wolseley ring', which as much as anything shows the danger in believing that reform only came from within that group. Unfortunately we know little of his views on such matters.[13] What we do know is that he was one of the 'continentalist' school of thinkers who looked at the British Army in terms of it fighting continental warfare. This was hardly surprising as Charles had only ever witnessed European warfare, not only through his time fighting in the Crimea but also through the work he had done as a correspondent during the European wars of the 1860s and 1870s. It is known that like Henry he also earned the enmity of the Commander-in-Chief the Duke of Cambridge, and for the same reason, namely

---

10  Brackenbury, Henry, *Some Memories of My Spare Time* (London: William Blackwood & Sons, 1909), pp.57-58.
11  *Oxford Dictionary of National Biography* (Oxford: Oxford University Press, 2004).
12  Although Charles was never technically head of the Branch he played a key role in its development and reorganisation in the 1870s. It will also be noted that Charles was both Assistant Instructor in Artillery and later Director of Artillery Studies at Woolwich.
13  He, like his brother Henry, left few private papers.

their reforming tendencies. One key reform they shared, that would have been opposed by the Duke of Cambridge, was the creation of a Chief of Staff. In 1889 Charles wrote to Spenser Wilkinson, a journalist and well known as a champion of Army reform, urging the importance of a Chief of Staff. He compared the situation with that of Germany and complained that whilst they had a dedicated staff planning for the possibilities of war and the army taking the field, what few staff officers existed in the British Army were "swallowed up in a sea of documents and red tape".[14] He continued by criticising the current system and the Commander-in-Chief, both as a position and as an individual. He believed many of the problems of command, organisation and planning would be solved, "once we had a General Staff Department, for it would be too strong to be sat upon, and the very appointment of a Chief of Staff would cause the Duke's resignation. We don't want a peace Commander-in-Chief but we want one all ready for war. It is too absurd to have a Commander-in-Chief permanently on our necks and never intended to take the field at all".[15]

Whilst there were similarities between the two in terms of their opinions there were also key differences. Charles's admiration of the Prussian, later German army, whom he had seen in action many times, led him to champion the cause of reform in the British Army by suggesting an almost exact duplication of the training, tactics, and administration of the Prussians.[16] Whilst the brothers shared their admiration for the Prussian artillery, Henry, whilst recognising the triumph of the reforms that the Prussians had achieved, also recognised the limitation of that system when applied to the British Army. The Prussian Army was designed for merely one purpose: to fight a European war from within its own borders. The British Army considered European warfare to be one of its lesser priorities. More pressing was the demand of imperial defence and the conduct of expeditionary warfare around the globe. The other key problem Henry saw was that the Prussian system was dependent upon conscription, which was the key to many of the other reforms. This was largely why the Cardwellian reform of localisation failed in the sense of increasing recruitment. Henry took the view that whilst there were great lessons to be learnt from the Prussian Army the system that existed would have to be altered to meet the peculiar demands of the British Army.

Charles was promoted Major in July 1872 and Lieutenant Colonel in January 1876. From September 1873 until April 1876 he served in the Intelligence Branch of the War Office. Further appointments followed as Superintendent of Garrison

---

14  C.B. Brackenbury to Wilkinson, 2nd June 1889, Spenser Wilkinson Papers.
15  C.B. Brackenbury to Wilkinson, 2nd June 1889, Spenser Wilkinson Papers.
16  Bailes, Howard: 'Patterns of Thought in the Late Victorian Army', *Journal of Strategic Studies*, March 1981 Volume 4 Part 1, p.38. This page has a particular reference to criticism of Charles Brackenbury's advocacy of Prussian (German) methods, but the whole article covers much of the debate regarding advocacy of Prussian tactics.

Instruction at Aldershot from April 1876 to June 1880, as Superintendent of the gunpowder factory at Waltham Abbey from July 1880 until June 1885, and from May 1886 he commanded the artillery in the eastern district until June 1887. He was appointed Director of Artillery Studies at Woolwich in 1887. In February 1890 Charles collapsed in the street. The illness was put down to overwork, a trait he shared with his brother, but his strength left him and he never fully recovered despite returning to work. On 20th June 1890, whilst returning by train to his home in Chelsea from Woolwich, he suffered a fatal heart attack, at the age of fifty-eight. By the time of Charles's premature death, the brothers had become important figures within the army. Had Charles lived it would have been interesting to see where his appointments would have taken him. Had he returned to high office within the Royal Artillery he might have been invaluable to his brother during his time as Director-General of Ordnance. The fact that there were two Brackenburys, with similar careers, has caused some confusion amongst historians.[17] This is compounded by the fact that for many years their ranks were very similar. It is interesting to note that despite his 'head start' Henry not only caught his brother up in terms of rank, but also surpassed him. This again says much about the importance of active service overseas as an aid to promotion. Indeed the position had changed so much that in 1885 Henry had recommended Charles as the next Director of Artillery to be "… the only man who would dare stand up to the Duke of Cambridge" and in April 1890 it was Henry who wrote to Sir Ralph Thompson, Permanent Secretary to the War Office, asking for Charles's temporary rank of Major General to be confirmed, as there was now a vacancy in the Royal Artillery at that rank, also recommending him as Director of Artillery.[18]

Unlike Henry, Charles and his wife Hilda had children, six sons and three daughters, who had an interesting set of careers.[19] Two of his sons joined the Indian

---

17  There are two notable mistakes in this regard. Lt-Colonel (later Brigadier) B.A.H Parritt in his book *The Intelligencers* confuses the brothers, and thus when he says that Henry had served in the Intelligence Branch before being appointed its head he is mistaken; this is understandable as at this time both had a tendency simply to refer to themselves as 'Major Brackenbury'. A less defendable mistake is made by Jay Luvaas in his book *Education of an Army* (pp.259-260) where his quotation is actually from Charles Brackenbury rather than Henry, which leads the reader to believe that Henry was lobbying politicians of the day to be made Chief of Staff. Whilst this might have happened, the evidence from which he quotes is the opinion of his brother and cannot be considered Henry's opinion.
18  Brackenbury to Lord Wolseley, 14th October 1885, Wolseley Papers, Central Library, Hove, and Brackenbury to Sir Ralph Thompson, 28th April 1890, Stanhope Papers, Centre for Kentish Studies, Maidstone. Charles was at the time acting Major General, being a Major General in the Army but only a Colonel in the Royal Artillery.
19  Two sons became engineers and worked both in this country and the empire. Another became a very successful and wealthy rancher in Denver, Colorado. Two of his daughters were suffragettes, and according to Charles. E. Brackenbury, "the portrait of Mrs Pankhurst in the National Portrait Gallery is by one of them, who was an artist of some competence".

Army but both died in India, Charles Herbert due to typhoid fever contracted in the Bolan Pass in 1885 aged twenty-three and Lionel Wilhelm in defence of the Residency at Manipur in 1891 also aged twenty-three. Hilda disliked house work and it is interesting to note that the celebrated journalist and writer Flora Shaw, later Lady Lugard, a distant relation of the Brackenburys by marriage, lived with them as housekeeper and governess during the 1870–80s. Indeed it is said that it was Charles Brackenbury's contacts that helped to start her journalistic career.[20] The death of Charles and two of his sons placed a further financial burden on Henry, who was supporting Charles widow and family, although the exact extent of this is unclear.

It can be seen that Henry Brackenbury came from a family with longstanding public service who were just wealthy enough to be comfortable but had to work for a living. From being a family of landowners they became a family of professionals. They made use of family connections and 'advantageous' marriages to advance. Much of the family wealth came through marriage to wealthy families. Indeed there is a saying that the Brackenburys were as rich as their wives' money. They had become an important family in the county of Lincolnshire and through the military careers of Edward, Charles and Henry they became important within the country for a time. Indeed, even in the 2004 revision of the *Dictionary of National Biography*, three of the Lincolnshire Brackenburys, the aforementioned soldiers, retained their entries.

---

20  *Oxford Dictionary of National Biography* (Oxford: Oxford University Press, 2004), p.149.

CHAPTER 2

# Early Years

Henry Brackenbury was born on 1st September 1837 in the small Lincolnshire village of Bolingbroke, now referred to as old Bolingbroke. As we have already seen the Brackenburys of Lincolnshire were an important family in the life of that county but they were in reality only a mixture of minor landowners and professionals. What wealth there was in the family was also somewhat removed from Henry. His father, William, was comfortable due to his pension and additions to that which he received on account of his wounds. However rather than landowners they were in fact tenants. Accounts differ but either in 1838 or 1841 the family left Bolingbroke Hall and moved to Usselby Hall, also in Lincolnshire. Here they were the tenants of Charles Tennyson d'Eyncourt, M.P. who owned considerable land in the county. When Henry was only four his father suffered a stroke and was left partly paralysed, which added to his war wounds and general ill-health meant that his life expectance was not good. Partly due to finance, and also to help with William's care, the family moved to Ahascragh in County Galway a year after his stroke where they lived with his wife's sister and her husband. William Brackenbury died in June 1844.

Unfortunately little is known of Henry's childhood. He never referred to it in any detail in any of his literary work. Again we come across the problem of the fact that he had no children, no direct descendants to pass on stories and anecdotes of his childhood memories. Nothing is known of his life after moving to Ireland in 1843 until he enters Tonbridge School in 1846, where he remained until 1849. One wonders what, if any schooling, he had up to that point. Rural education was not renowned in that period of history, nor in that part of Ireland. It is also likely that due to the limited nature of the finances of the family, particularly since the death of his father, that they were unable to afford a private tutor. This might go some way to explaining why he did not excel at school. However this might have had more to do with a lack of interest rather than intelligence. From Tonbridge he moved to Eton College where he was from September 1850 to Easter 1852. At Eton he was in the House of Rev Charles Wolley, later Wolley-Dod, and as was common at the time he lodged with one of the school 'dames', Mrs De Rosen.[1] At the time he attended Eton the curriculum was still largely 'classical' in format, although it was during his time at Eton that Mathematics became compulsory for most pupils. Although there is no record of which subjects he took it is logical to surmise that he took Latin, German, French, and Mathematics given the high marks he would receive for these subjects in his entrance exam for the Royal Military Academy Woolwich, but more will be said of that later. Another interesting point to note regarding his time at Eton is that he was not a 'scholar' and therefore someone was paying for his schooling. Exactly where this money came from is unclear, and no record exists as to whether it was a family member or family friend who made his education at Eton possible.

Although he attended two of the finest schools in England at that time there was no suggestion at this stage that there was any particular flair for administration or writing. The original *Dictionary of National Biography* entry for him records that "Henry Brackenbury's schooling was interrupted by youthful vagaries".[2] Again we suffer from the fact that there are no direct descendants to give us any hint of what that might actually mean. Whilst there is the possibility that it involved some 'scandal' it might simply be the case that formal 'schooling' did not appeal to him. If so it is quite ironic that Brackenbury himself would become little more than a teacher when on the staff of the Royal Military Academy Woolwich. Indeed it seems that he did not really settle down to work seriously until he entered the Army. Even at an early stage this shows a somewhat different approach. Although it might be something of a stereotype it was often the case that most young officers stopped working once they had joined the army rather than start. Indeed it could often be something of a struggle to pass officer examinations and military 'crammers' were common for many years. 'Crammers' were teachers who knew exactly what it took to pass the exam and would provide an intense study programme for would-be officers. Winston Churchill, who himself went to a 'crammer', attested to their usefulness by saying "It was said that none but a congenital idiot could have avoided passing thence into the Army".[3] So, the fact that Brackenbury did not have to turn to a 'crammer' suggests that he had learnt something from his schooling, even if he had not excelled. It might simply be the case that formal education did not appeal to him. Given what we know of his later life it is likely that cricket and women were higher up his list of priorities.

Brackenbury seems to have lacked direction until he entered the army. Being the youngest son of a youngest son, from a family who lacked considerable wealth, there would always be a need to work. His social standing would necessitate him

---

1   For this information I am grateful to Mrs Hatfield, the college archivist at Eton.
2   *Dictionary of National Biography* (London: Smith, Elder & Co, 1921).
3   Turner, E.S., *Gallant Gentlemen: A portrait of the British Officer 1600-1956* (London: Michael Joseph Ltd, 1956), p.244.

entering one of the professions. In short he needed a career rather than simply a job. The three main professions for the sons of gentlemen were the military, the Church, and the legal profession. His later life would show that he was clearly unsuited to the Church, particularly the Methodist Church to which the majority of his family now belonged. The Army, or perhaps the Royal Navy, would have seemed obvious given his family history and tradition, perhaps particularly in light of his father. One wonders how well Henry knew his father. He died when Henry was only six years old. Even for those few years William's health had been such that even by the standards of the time he probably had little contact with his son. It is likely that Henry knew his father best for his accomplishments in battle, particularly the heroic action at Salamanca. When in later life Henry would deliberately place himself in harm's way when on active service, it is easy to view it, to an extent, as a desire to emulate his father.

Despite this he did not initially embark upon a military career. Instead he started to study for the law. It is likely that this path was chosen for him. The exact reasons for this are unknown. However we do know that the family used its influence to obtain what was a great opportunity for any young man. Through contact with Mr Archibald Campbell, Her Majesty's Notary in Quebec, he was offered probation in that office. In short he was to study law with quite a senior colonial lawyer. Mr Campbell was a friend of the family and would later become father-in-law to Henry's brother Charles. Campbell was a significant figure in Canadian life. His father was an American loyalist who had moved to Canada shortly after the American Revolution. Archibald studied law in Quebec and set up practice as a notary in Quebec in 1812. His practice was briefly interrupted by the War of 1812 where he saw active service in the repulse of the United States invasion of Canada. After the war his close relationship and support for the Governor General, the 9th Earl of Dalhousie, led to him being granted the largely honorific title of His Majesty's Notary. However this did mean that all Crown business in Quebec had to pass through his office. He was a great patron of the arts and seems to have been the man who raised subscriptions for various building projects as diverse as Music Halls, Hotels and Churches. His previous military service also meant that he was appointed Colonel of the Seventh Battalion of the Quebec Militia.

The significance of this period of Henry Brackenbury's life should not be underestimated. In 1852 when he left for Quebec he was only fifteen years old. The opportunity to travel and see part of the Empire must have been a great experience for him. However the greatest significance of his time in Canada was the approach it gave him to his future work. That period immersed in the professional and business like atmosphere of a Notary's office had a profound and lasting impact upon him. Unlike many of his contemporaries he had an experience not only of the wider world but in particular the business world. This was still a period when, "For most

British officers the acquisition of a commission represented a stage in the life of a 'gentlemen', not a long-term commitment, and its main importance was a confirmer of social status".[4] Brackenbury from the outset had a professional approach to his career, which undoubtedly had much to do with his experience in Quebec. Very few had this business like experience. Indeed very few had any experience at all. John Ardagh, a name we shall here more of later, was another of the few intellectually gifted officers of this period. He also had outside experience having been prepared for a career in the Church he had passed out with an honours degree from Trinity College Dublin. It is also likely that it was at this point that Brackenbury started to become aware of his aptitude, and liking, for administrative work.

His time in Quebec was also important for one other reason. It gave him his first taste of military life. Again he had Campbell to thank for this opportunity, who as Colonel of the Battalion had secured the appointment. Henry Brackenbury was commissioned as an Ensign in the Seventh Battalion of the Quebec Militia in 1853. It appears that he could have stayed longer in Quebec than he did. However by 1854 Brackenbury had decided that he would embark on a military career. By this stage the Crimean War had started and there was a real shortage of artillery officers. So much so that it was announced that the entry examination for the Royal Military Academy Woolwich was to be opened to general competition. However there was more to his decision to join the Royal Artillery than simply the opening up of the examination. The so-called 'scientific' branches of the army, namely the Royal Artillery and the Royal Engineers, were known to require a certain level of professionalism from their officers, even if only on a technical level. The Royal Artillery was also exempt from the purchase system, although this was a double-edged sword. Whilst it meant that the ability to buy your next commission was avoided, it meant that promotion was merely on the grounds of seniority and could therefore be painfully slow. Another reason for joining the Royal Artillery was the fact that his brother Charles was already an officer in that regiment, seeing active service in the Crimea. We know of at least one occasion when Henry visited his brother in the Royal Artillery so he obviously knew something of the life, and it must have appealed to him.[5] There was also something of a friendly rival with his brother and a chance to emulate him, along with living up to the reputation of his father and uncle, might also have inspired his decision.

---

4 Searle, G.R., *A New England? Peace and War 1886-1918* (Oxford: Oxford University Press, 2003), p.255.
5 Brackenbury, Henry, *Some Memories of My Spare Time* (London: William Blackwood & Sons, 1909), p.63. An amusing story from this visit tells of how one morning the young Henry took his horse for a ride and ended up riding through Greenwich Park, unaware that only the Royal Family and the Park Ranger were allowed this privilege. There was talk of arresting him until the young Brackenbury pointed out to the park keepers that they might equally be in trouble for allowing him into the park in the first place.

It is said that it was only now that Henry really started to settle down to serious study.[6] This makes a lot of sense as it appears he had now found what he was looking for and a sense of direction. The requirement had always been to find a career: now he had. He passed out fifth in his examination group, with particularly high marks in Mathematics, Latin, German and French, which obviously shows that his schooling had not been a complete waste of time. In 1855 he entered the Royal Military Academy Woolwich, and found that due to his previous commission in the Quebec Militia he was appointed Senior Under Officer of his intake of 'gentlemen cadets'. Henry later recalled that he never mentioned to the authorities that his entire experience with the militia consisted of one muster parade![7]

As has already been mentioned, the Crimean War had created a great demand for artillery officers. As a consequence only a year later, in April 1856, he was commissioned as a Lieutenant in the Royal Artillery. His commissioning had been rushed through, and it has been said that he had not completed all the necessary courses.[8] The Army had been preparing for the campaign season in the Crimea for 1856. Thus the on-going need for artillery officers was the reason for the apparent haste. However the Treaty of Paris brought an end to the war in March 1856. By that stage Brackenbury's commissioning would have already been organised and thus was allowed to stand. In June he commenced his service spending a short period at Woolwich before in early August his company of garrison artillery was ordered to Plymouth to take up duty. Plymouth, or more accurately Devonport, seems to have been a dreary but pleasant station for the young subaltern. There was little work but social activities were plentiful. An account of his time there suggests that his life seemed to revolve around, boating, archery, picnicking, cricket, dances, hunting and Devonshire girls.[9]

Two events are recorded by Brackenbury of his time on the garrison artillery, one of which led to an amusing observation whilst the other may have had a lasting impact on him. In August 1856 the Royal Yacht encountered bad weather in the Channel and consequently put into Plymouth so that the Royal party could continue their journey by train. Before departing they reviewed the garrison and Henry Brackenbury for the first, but not the last time, had the honour of leading his troop on the march past Queen Victoria and Prince Albert. Many of the garrison had not long returned from the Crimea where it had become fashionable to wear a beard, partly due to the lack of shaving facilities and equipment. After the march past an order was issued to Brackenbury to be passed on to the whole garrison. It ordered

---

6   *Dictionary of National Biography* (London: Smith, Elder & Co, 1921).
7   Brackenbury, *Some Memories of My Spare Time*, p.2.
8   His not having completed all his courses is mentioned in the *Dictionary of National Biography* entry, but I have found no other evidence for this.
9   Brackenbury, *Some Memories of My Spare Time*, p.6.

that the Queen, "for the sake of uniformity has commanded all the army shall wear a moustache", and that consequently beards were banned. Many years later Henry recorded that, "It was easy for them to shave off their beards, but not so easy for the young subaltern of eighteen to wear a moustache!"[10] The second incident clearly had a profound effect on his later career. During his time in Plymouth he heard William Makepeace Thackeray deliver a lecture on "The Four Georges". The fact that writing in 1909 Brackenbury recalled that "I can remember, as though it were yesterday" is testament to the lasting impact this meeting had on him. This is a period in which his own intellectual leaning was still developing, after all it must be remembered that despite being an army officer he was only eighteen. Hearing and meeting one of the great figures of English literature obviously helped him to realise his own talents and ambitions in that direction. Also, his administrative skills were starting to be put to good use. From August 1856 he had been acting as Adjutant for the Royal Artillery in the whole of the western district.[11]

Whilst Plymouth was an attractive posting for any young officer Henry Brackenbury wanted more. He was eager for active service, a situation which was doubtless exacerbated by the fact that he had obviously been preparing for service in the Crimea which failed to materialise due to the ending of the war. He did not have to wait long as an opportunity for service in the force being sent to supress the Indian Mutiny was obtained for him. However for the moment we will leave the narrative of his life to take a brief look at the organisation which the young Brackenbury had joined: the British Army of the Victorian era.

---

10 Brackenbury, *Some Memories of My Spare Time*, pp.7-8. There is also the suggestion that a beard helped to prevent frostbite, but whether that has any medical veracity I do not know.
11 Brackenbury, *Some Memories of My Spare Time*, pp.8-9.

CHAPTER 3

# THE LATE VICTORIAN BRITISH ARMY

The era in which Henry Brackenbury served was an important one for the development of the British Army. When he joined the Army in 1856 it had just emerged from the Crimean War which had been a severe shock to the system. It had illustrated almost forty years of neglect since the ending of the Napoleonic wars. Indeed the era in which Brackenbury served can be viewed as a period between two great conflicts; the Napoleonic wars and the First World War. It saw the Army move away from the Napoleonic era army to the foundations of what would be the British Expeditionary Force (B.E.F.) in 1914. It was also a period of dramatic technological advances in weaponry and equipment. So the importance of this period is clear as we see a movement from the disorganisation and poor quality of the army in the Crimean War to the B.E.F., widely considered to be the best trained and organised army ever to come out of this country. Much of this book looks at Henry Brackenbury's role in this period of change and reform. Whilst there is no room in such a book for a detailed account of the British Army during this period it will be useful to the reader to have some of the key areas of the period highlighted. Although a very important era the late Victorian period is largely overlooked, mainly because, as has already been mentioned, it comes between two major wars of global proportions. The aim is to give a brief explanation and understanding of the organisation of which Henry Brackenbury was for so long an important member.[1]

---

1   There are many good books that look at this era from various angles. For the academic point of view Edward Spiers *The Late Victorian Army* (Manchester: Manchester University Press, 1992) is unsurpassed. For the campaigns of the period see Philip J. Haythornthwaite *The Colonial Wars Source Book* (London: Caxton Publishing Group, 2000) or Byron Farwell *Queen Victoria's Little Wars* (London: Allen Lane, 1973). The political and military debates of the latter half of the period are expertly covered by W.S. Hamer *The British Army Civil-Military Relations 1885-1905* (Oxford: Clarendon Press, 1970). Brian Bond has written numerous journal articles looking at this period and

## The Standing of the British Army

The British Army was in a unique position when compared to its European rivals because unlike them they had no land borders at home needing permanent protection. This, along with the presumed supremacy of the Royal Navy, allowed a great deal of complacency in the British approach to its army and was the reason why it could afford to have only a small army recruited by means of voluntary enlistment. The average size of the army during this period was around 150,000 men, if one excludes the British garrison in India which after the 1857 rebellion was maintained at a fixed level of 70,000 men. This compares poorly with the German Army or French Army of this period which averaged around 550,000 men or the Russians who averaged nearly 900,000, although the latter was obviously spread out over vast distances. Yet the real pictures was far worse as all these nations had some form of compulsory service and thus could quickly double their manpower with trained soldiers. This was one of the reasons why the Prussian/German system of short service, three years with the frontline army and then continued service with the various levels of reserve until the age of forty-five, caused so much interest within Britain. This compared badly to the British system at the start of this period in which a soldier spent twenty-one years with the colours, thus meaning that even the youngest soldiers were at least nearing their forties by the time they joined any sort of reserve. As a consequence there was little practical backup for the standing army, and such volunteer forces as there were had limited and specific terms of service which greatly affected their use.[2]

There were many factors affecting the standing of the British Army. Firstly the presumed supremacy of the Royal Navy, the first line of defence and in itself an expensive organisation to support, meant that it was always tempting to ignore the importance of the army. This is borne out by the fact that it is only when questions are being raised about the strength of the Royal Navy that many of the improvements in the army occurred, particularly during the invasion scares that occurred periodically throughout the late nineteenth century. There were also reasons of economy, but there was also a much wider point regarding the standing of the army and the idea of a large standing army was not simply unpopular with regards to expense. There were much wider concerns particularly harking back to the time of the Commonwealth when Cromwell's large standing army had supported his dictatorship. This concept was also supported by recent history, especially in France, and

---

    his book *The Victorian Army and the Staff College, 1854-1914* (London: Eyre Methuen, 1972) gives an interesting insight into the officer corps and its training. For the Army and society see Edward Spiers *The Army and Society 1815-1914* (London: Longman, 1980) and A.R. Skelley *The Victorian Army at Home* (London: Croom Helm, 1977).

2    All figures for average size of the armies of Europe are taken from David Woodward *Armies of the World 1854-1914* (London: Sidgwick and Jackson Ltd, 1978).

as a result the perception existed within Britain that a large army was synonymous with dictatorship. There were also wider social issues regarding loss of liberty. A soldier's life was not particularly pleasant. They were subject to brutal and humiliating punishment, often for quite minor offences even by Victorian standards, and living conditions were poor, as was pay and life expectancy. There was also a very real chance of death, or perhaps worse being crippled and confined, more often than not, to life as a beggar. A stigma arose around being a soldier, and many stories exist of families saying that members were dead rather than admit to the humiliation of having a soldier in the family.[3] All this resulted in the army only being able to recruit from the lowest section of society, and joining the army for many was an act of desperation. The obvious consequence was that recruitment became harder. It has been said that:

> Recruiting a Regular Army by voluntary enlistment in an industrial and profoundly anti-militarist country like Britain has so far proved an insoluble problem. In Victoria's reign even the harsh incentives of insecurity, a high level of unemployment, and a low standard of living failed to supply a steady flow of candidates for the Queen's shilling.[4]

Whilst the public enjoyed the sight of the army in grand parades and took pride in its exploits in the ever-expanding empire, what it did not want was to see soldiers in their towns or cities or have to pay any more in taxes to support them. As a consequence the only time that reform of the army was taken seriously was during times of threat. When invasion scares, which came and went throughout the Victorian period, arose so did the clamour for action to reform the army, but governments began to realise that if they were perceived to be doing something, normally by establishing a commission or committee, the clamour would soon subside. Even the briefest look at the invasion scares of the late Victorian era highlights this.

## Control of the Army

The Crimean War of 1854–56 did more than anything else to highlight the need for reform of the army.[5] Nearly forty years of neglect and economy were clearly illustrated as the army almost collapsed under the strain of the conflict. Perhaps an equally

---

3 Harries-Jenkins, Gwyn, *The Army in Victorian Society* (London: Routledge & Kegan Paul, 1977). Also see Rudyard Kipling's poems 'Tommy' or 'The Absent minded Beggar' which gives a very accurate, if dramatic, account of how the common soldier was treated, and perceived, by society at large.
4 Bond, Brian, 'Recruiting the Victorian Army 1870-92', *Victorian Studies* 5 1961.
5 It is common amongst British historians to use the dates stated. However technically the conflict started in 1853 if one includes the Russian campaigns against Britain's future ally, the Ottoman Empire.

significant problem was the presence of the Duke of Wellington as Commander-in-Chief for much of the intervening period. Deeply conservative in many ways, he refused to alter the military system that he had so bitterly complained about during his period as a commander in the field. The Duke did his best to keep the army out of view both physically and economically, fearing demands for economy.

What caused the greatest problems was a divided system of command and control at home. There were nine different, and even in some cases conflicting, offices responsible for the army.[6] It was in fact during the war that this system was changed, such were its obvious flaws, and in 1855 the army was reorganised, to be controlled by the Secretary of State for War and the Commander-in-Chief. Control of the army was in many ways a constant battle. Parliamentary control was assured by financial control but the army remained very much a royal body. Queen Victoria in particular viewed the army very much as hers, and in this she was assisted by the fact that from 1856 to 1895 her cousin, Prince George the Duke of Cambridge, was Commander-in-Chief. A succession of Secretaries of State for War found their attempts at reform halted by this royal combination. They had even tried to halt Cardwell in his reforms by attempting to have him appointed Speaker of the House of Commons, a prestigious appointment but not one that interested Cardwell.[7] It was in ways like this and through such influence that royal control remained important within the army.

Whilst parliamentary control was said to be stronger because of the changes made immediately after the Crimean War, an alternative argument can be made. Indeed Brackenbury himself argued that the change had actually weakened parliamentary control as the whole burden for the army, within parliament, rested on one man: the Secretary of State for War. He acknowledged that the Commander-in-Chief sat in the House of Lords but in the case of the Duke of Cambridge there was little parliament could do to exercise power over, "a Prince of the blood Royal".[8] In fact trying to control the Duke of Cambridge was a constant problem. If he could not stop a minister himself he felt no compunction about appealing directly to the Queen. Whilst ultimately control of the army rested with parliament, many schemes for the improvement of the army, most notably the replacement of the Commander-in-Chief with a Chief of Staff, were abandoned because whilst politicians saw the

---

6   Bond, Brian, 'The Late Victorian Army', *History Today* 11:9 (Sept 1961) p.617. This included the Secretary of War, Secretary at War, Master General of the Ordnance, the Home Office, the Colonial Office, the Treasury, etc.

7   Bond, Brian, 'The Late Victorian Army', p.618. Although Queen Victorian and the Duke of Cambridge both opposed his reforms they also appreciated the dangerous ground they were on constitutionally, had they not enforced the will of the House of Commons. If they had not Cardwell threatened to allow the House of Commons the opportunity to debate the future of the Duke of Cambridge with the very real threat that he might be removed.

8   Brackenbury, Henry, 'Military Reform' Part V *Fraser's Magazine*, Vol 76 (1867), pp.206-208.

merits of the schemes they knew that royal opposition would make the process more trouble than it was worth. The Duke was a deeply conservative individual sometimes rather unfairly called a 'bow and arrow' general. Whatever else, no one could doubt that he deeply cared for the army and the individual soldier. Indeed despite his conservatism the creation of the Staff College would not have been possible without his championing of it. He genuinely believed that he knew what was best for the army and men who thought they knew better, like Wolseley and Brackenbury, earned his disapproval. He opposed Cardwell's reforms and used the Prussian success, given they were officered by 'gentleman', and Britain's military problems during the 1870s and 1880s as evidence that Cardwell was wrong.[9]

Not only was this a period in which groups of soldiers, whether reformers or conservatives, supporters of Wolseley or Roberts, would battle to influence and control the army, there remained the battle between monarch and parliament over whom the army 'belonged' to. It was to take the First World War to ultimately decide this issue, although the legacy of this dispute can still be seen today in the oath of allegiance that every soldier takes. It refers to the monarch and officers of the army but makes no reference to Her Majesty's Government, either implicitly or explicitly.

## Army Reform

This was a period of continual Army Reform and every Secretary of State for War made a contribution to the process. The two outstanding Secretaries of State for War in this regard were Edward Cardwell, between December 1868 and February 1874, and Edward Stanhope, between January 1887 and August 1892. Both had the dubious advantage of a long stay at the War Office. Whilst this allowed them to achieve a great deal it was at the detriment of their health, and this was an era in which a long stay at the War Office often meant an early death because of the sheer volume of work.[10]

---

9   See Colonel Willoughby Verner *The Military Life of H.R.H. George, Duke of Cambridge* (London: John Murray, 1905, 2 volumes). This remains the best account of the Duke, largely because of the unrestricted access to his correspondence that Verner was allowed. Verner was undoubtedly an admirer of the Duke but his work is not without criticism of him. He does however try, and to an extent succeeds, in painting a more balanced portrait of the Duke, than the 'blimp' like reactionary image that is generally held

10  Some may be surprised that there is no mention of the Childers Reforms. Whilst important they were largely administrative. In many ways the reorganisation and creation of new regiments and battalions was simply carrying on the work of Cardwell. Others may view it as an attempt to rectify the problems of the Cardwell system. The only other major reform attempted was to standardise uniform and dress, which as we shall see was still something of a problem that Brackenbury had to deal with in the aftermath of the South African War.

There has been a tendency to overstate the magnitude of the Cardwell Reforms. They did much to sweep away the more antiquated elements of the army and were in many ways a belated response to the deficiencies and organisational problems that the Crimean War had highlighted. However their intention must be understood. They were not designed to improve the army as a fighting force but to improve its efficiency and hopefully reduce costs. Indeed Gladstone's administration of 1868–1874 is widely regarded as one of the great reforming governments and to an extent the Cardwell's reforms were simply part of that. Cardwell himself had no military background and had not been active in military debate before his appointment. In a way this helped him as he had a detached view without prejudice for tradition or 'esprit de corps'.

Many of his reforms were simply administrative such as withdrawing troops from self-governing colonies, realigning the relationship between the Commander-in-chief and Secretary of State, and abolishing the bounty for new recruits, thus slightly improving the recruiting system. He also abolished flogging in peacetime and placed restrictions on its use in time of war, and the system of 'branding' soldiers for desertion or other offences was abolished altogether. This was part of a long process of improving the lot of the common soldier.

Cardwell was influenced, as were many in Britain, by the success of the Prussian Army. Prussia was smaller both in terms of territory and population and less industrialised than Britain, yet it had produced a military system that had allowed its army to become the strongest in Europe and had defeated Denmark, Austria, and later on France, with relative ease. Their military system became the envy of Europe. It relied on conscription, localisation and above all good administration and organisation of the forces available. Prussia, and later Germany, was split into military districts each providing an army corps made up of a combination of regulars and the different levels of reserves. Prussia had short service based on two years in the infantry, or three in the cavalry and artillery, and then four or five years with the reserves. The peculiarities of the British position, with regards the garrisoning of a global empire, meant that much of the Prussian system was impractical. Conscription was politically and social unacceptable and even short service based upon even three years would make it difficult and costly to garrison the empire as a large part of service would be taken up with travel to and from the empire. A compromise of six years with the colours, although in reality most chose to sign on for the full twelve years, and then six years with the reserves was introduced. An element of localisation was adopted in the form of linked battalions, with the theory being that each regiment would have two battalions, one stationed at home and the other abroad. The one at home would keep the other up to strength with a draft of men until it replaced the battalion overseas. However this often failed in practice.[11] Using the Prussian example the militia were linked with the regular battalions therefore forming a theoretical brigade. The only real advantage to emerge from the changes was the development of a reserve. In 1882 it was used for the first time as 10,800 reservists were recalled to the colours for service in Egypt. However even raising this small number proved difficult. The fact that for a colonial campaign, using an army of 20,000 British troops, it was necessary to have half the force made up of reservists only served to highlight the weakness of the British Army.

The most controversial of Cardwell's reforms was the abolition of the purchase system whereby officers bought their initial commission and every promotion thereafter up to the rank of Colonel. It was argued that the purchase system of itself would not have prevented any of Cardwell's other reforms, however this missed the point. As one historian has noted "Purchase was the standard under which military reactionaries congregated".[12] It was therefore necessary to confront this issue that did a great deal to reduce efficiency and professionalism. Such a system not only discouraged professionalism but meant that a regiment became virtually the property of its colonel. As Cardwell wrote to Gladstone, "Our principle is that the officers shall be made for the Army. Their principle is that the Army is made for the officers". The attempt to abolish this system initially drew little attention, but once it started to be debated in Parliament a storm of criticism was directed towards Cardwell. The accusations were varied. Some said he was tampering with a system that suited the Prussians very well as their officers were 'gentleman of breeding', although this was a slightly misrepresentation. Other said that this was the system that had 'beaten Napoleon', others that it would create greater militarism, and a good number that it would prove prohibitively expensive to reimburse all the officers for their commissions, an estimated £8,000,000 (about £365,000,000 in modern money). Despite opposition the Bill passed through the House of Commons, largely due to the enforcement of strict party discipline and the unofficial support of Benjamin Disraeli, the leader of the opposition. The Bill to abolish the purchase system was defeated in the House of Lords and the Government introduced the Bill through a Royal Warrant in November 1871, as the purchase system only existed by Royal command, the Brokerage Act of 1809 having already made the practice illegal save for the approval of the Crown.

The abolition of purchase did not lead to a radical alteration in the background of officers or create a more professional spirit. However it removed an important factor which stopped this and over time things did change, but it would take the First World War to fundamentally change the social background of officers. However the

---

11 Sometimes the system did not work according to the theory. A notable example of this is the 24th Regiment of Foot during the Zulu War, when both battalions were there at the same time.
12 Bond, Brian, 'The Late Victorian Army', p.619.

abolition of purchase created the possibility of change. This is supported by W.S. Hamer's view of the post abolition system where,

> Men of lesser means could gain rapid promotion through intellectual distinction, but the aristocracy and landed gentry still sent their sons 'for to be a soldier'. Men such as Henry Brackenbury and Sir Frederick Maurice were promoted on grounds of their own personal achievements. Others such as Sir Henry Wilson, Lord Chelmsford, Douglas Haig, were sons of the well-to-do.[13]

Cardwell had done much to aid the development and modernisation of the British Army. There were obvious problems with the system of linked battalion and the reserve that became obvious in future years, but this was largely due to the fact that Cardwell had not been able to successfully tackle the problem of recruitment. The legacy of Cardwell is best summed up by Brian Bond who wrote, "Cardwell should be regarded as a pioneer who blazed the trail for later reformers – not, as Sir Robert Biddulph suggested in his biography, "the man who revolutionised the British Army".[14]

Edward Stanhope's period of Secretary of State for War has often been overlooked, but many of the changes and reforms that he implemented were of equal importance to those of Cardwell.[15] He entered the War Office at a difficult time, with many of the failures of Cardwell's reforms having recently been highlighted. Both the Stephen Commission on Warlike Stores and the Morley Committee's inquiry into the manufacturing departments of the army were in progress. Both had been appointed as a consequence of problems encountered in the Sudan in 1884–85. The Stephen Commission was very critical of the whole administration of the army, and the Morley Committee found that the manufacturing departments were wholly inefficient and inadequate to meet military needs. The Government was also under pressure from the recently resigned Lord Randolph Churchill, whose resignation had led to the reshuffle that brought Stanhope to the War Office. Churchill attacked what he saw as gross extravagance in military spending. After less than six months in the job Stanhope faced aggressive questioning from Churchill and other members of

---

13  Hamer, W.S., *The British Army Civil-Military Relations 1885-1905* (Oxford: Clarendon Press, 1970), p.17. Hamer's assertion that Brackenbury was promoted by merit does ignore the fact that he was largely dependent upon the patronage of Wolseley, and it is right to question whether Brackenbury would have risen to the level he did without such patronage.
14  Bond, Brian, 'The Late Victorian Army', p.621.
15  Professor Ian Beckett has done much to highlight the importance of Stanhope's period as Secretary Of State. See 'Edward Stanhope at the War Office, 1887-1892', *Journal of Strategic Studies* 5 (1982) and 'The Stanhope Memorandum of 1888: A Reinterpretation' *Bulletin of the Institute of Historical Research*, 57 (1984). Chapters 14, 15 and 16 of Ian Beckett's book *The Victorians at War* (London: Hambeldon & London, 2003) also deal with the Stanhope era.

the Select Committee on Army and Navy Estimates. All this shows that Stanhope came to the War Office at a very difficult time.

One of Stanhope's earliest moves came out of the reports of the two committees.[16] Stanhope increased military administrative control, but held back from creating the council of senior military figures that the Stephen Commission had recommended. This reorganisation of 1888 helped to clarify the division of responsibility between civilians and soldiers that had begun during the Crimean War. Stanhope declared that the soldiers now had the power to use the military resources as they saw fit to meet the requirements and needs of the moment; in his words, "All the threads are in their own hands".[17] Yet this missed the fact that financial control was still very much in civilian hands and had in fact been strengthened.

There were other important reforms such as the creation of the Army Service Corps, which helped to improve the support service for the army in the field. It was Stanhope's pressure, against Treasury opposition, which finally saw the magazine rifle introduced. A committee had first looked at this in 1883 but it took Stanhope's personal intervention to see its introduction in 1888. He also obtained money for the building of a series of new barrack rooms which were desperately needed due to the unsanitary conditions that existed in many camps, although the argument he used was that it would save on repairs and the fact that the small size of barracks meant that many soldiers had to be housed elsewhere at extra cost. It was also during his tenure that breech-loading artillery was re-introduced, despite the fact that British industry had first developed this method twenty years before. In response to Brackenbury's warnings about the lack of defensive positions around London sixteen mobilisation centres were built, the so-called 'Stanhope Storehouses', which would supply and maintain the defensive positions around London if invasion ever happened. Stanhope established, in 1891, the Naval and Military Committee, which was set up to coordinate the defence of ports and coaling stations throughout the empire. This was the precursor of the later Committee of Imperial Defence.

Stanhope's legacy was embodied in the so-called Stanhope Memorandum.[18] Its significance has perhaps been misunderstood. The Stanhope Memorandum defined

---

16 The official name was *The Royal Commission appointed to enquire into the system under which patterns of Warlike Stores are adopted and the stores obtained and passed for Her Majesty's service* (1887) H.M.S.O, London. It was commonly called the Stephen Commission, after its Chairman Sir James Fitzjames Stephen. The Report of the Stephen Commission is interesting when compared to that of the Hartington Commission, of which more will be said in a later chapter. Both looked at the same problems but whereas the Stephen Commission concluded that the problems stemmed from the concentration of too much power in the hands of one civilian, namely the Secretary Of State for War, the Hartington Commission concluded that the problems were created by too much power in the hands of one soldier, namely the Commander-in-Chief.

17 *Memorandum of the Secretary of State relating to the Army Estimates 1888-1889* (1888) Cd 5303. LXVI, 4.

18 Although historically always known as the Stanhope Memorandum it was in effect merely a copy of Wolseley's recommendations of January 1888, which had probably been prepared with the as-

the purposes of the army. Up to this point no list of expected duties had been set down. The memorandum, originally written on 8th December 1888, set out five purposes in order of priority. First was to support the civil power within the United Kingdom, which largely meant the maintenance of law and order. Second, the army had to find and supply the necessary men for the draft for India that was set at a level agreed with the Government of India. Third, it was charged with garrisoning fortresses and coaling stations at home and abroad. Fourth, after providing for the aforementioned duties, it was expected to mobilise two Army Corps of regular troops rapidly for home defence and a third made up partly of regulars augmented by the militia. The fifth purpose was little more than an afterthought, which envisaged the possibility of sending abroad two army corps, a cavalry division and line of communication troops. Fulfilling the fourth and fifth aims created problems in terms of a lack of sufficient support troops, and an explanation of the problems identified by Brackenbury in this area will be undertaken in more detail later. The weakness of the memorandum was that it largely ignored imperial defence, which had become the main purpose, in reality, of the army. It is also uncertain how widely this memorandum was known, even within military circles. It did not become public knowledge until 1901.[19]

Criticism has been made of the order of priorities. Gooch has asserted that the order of priorities – most notably the inclusion of support for the civil power as first priority – was "More suited to the conditions of 1818 than those of 1888". This may be correct but does ignore the particular problems of the time. The late 1880s and early 1890s saw a particularly high level of civil unrest, and this period also saw the infamous 'mutiny' of the 2nd Battalion of the Grenadier Guards in July 1890, which only added to the fears of the time.[20] With further civil unrest anticipated the order

---

sistance of Brackenbury as it was the latter's desire to create a mobilisation scheme that gave fresh impetus to the long-term request for such a list of priorities. The only alteration was that the army would be at a two corps standard rather than the three suggested by Wolseley.

19  Although originally written in 1888 in response to Lord Wolseley, it was later reissued on 1st June 1891. Yet it was never published until 1901, as part of the response to allegations coming out of the South African War that there had been no military planning or set of established purposes for which the Army was maintained.

20  Gooch, John, *The Plans of War* (London: Routledge & Kegan Paul, 1974), p.12. There had been disturbances in Lancashire, the 'Crofters War' in the Western Isles and the 'Tithe War' in north Wales. There had also been the Home Rule riot in Trafalgar Square in November 1887. It is important to remember that support of the civil power also included Ireland and that during the 1880s there had been an increase in Fenian attacks both in Ireland and on the mainland. Added to this the early 1890s saw a rise in industrial unrest, and troops were used to cover during the London dock strike of late 1889 and the police strike of July 1890, whilst preparations were made for the army to take over the running of the Gas, Light and Coke Company in September 1890 when a strike threatened to cut off all power to the City of London. For further details of the extent of the employment of the Army in support of the civil power see Spiers, *The Late Victorian Army*, Chapter 8 'Military Duties in the United Kingdom'. See also Webb, J.V., 'Trouble in the 2nd Grenadier Guards in 1890', *Soldiers of the Queen, Journal of the Victorian Military Society* Issue 95 (December 1998). The military-political

of priorities was hardly surprising. It is easy to criticise the memorandum for failing to confront the issue of imperial defence or wider strategic issues. It is questionable whether Stanhope had the power to do anything about such matters. What the memorandum did was create a framework within which military planning could take place. It was within this framework that the hugely successful mobilisations plans, which worked with such ease and efficiency during the South African War and the First World War, were drawn up.

The continual reform during the late Victorian era did much to improve the state of the British Army. At times there was political impetus and public concern over defence. Often this led to improvements. However it needed the shock of the South African War to finally concentrate the country as a whole on just how important the army was. The B.E.F. is often referred to as the best trained and best equipped army ever to leave these shores, even if its numerical size was insufficient for a modern war. Much of the work done to get the army to that point happened during the late Victorian and early Edwardian period.

## Colonial Warfare

Between 1815 and 1914 Britain only once fought a European power, during the Crimean War of 1854–56. Although at times it faced enemies with modern weapons and European training, most notably Egypt in 1882 and the Boers in 1881 and from 1899–1902, and although the latter conflict saw the despatch of the largest army ever to leave Britain up to that point, it did to all intents and purposes remain a colonial campaign. During this period, however, it was always presumed that the largest force that Britain would deploy in the event of a war would be around 40,000 men. In an era when European armies were starting to be measured in millions of men it showed the weakness of the British position. The answer, as always, was that Britain brought to any alliance control of the seas through the power of the Royal Navy. There is a sense in which the British Army is always a step behind during this period, measuring its army in tens of thousands when the rest of Europe is measuring it in hundreds of thousands, and then measuring it in hundreds of thousands when the rest of Europe is counting in millions.[21]

At the same time the British Empire was still expanding and the army was never short of work. Opponents and conditions varied greatly. They came up against the highly disciplined and well trained Zulus and Maoris, the 'fanatical' charges of the warriors of the Sudan but also the more conventional armies of Egypt and the

---
establishment seems to have taken this extremely seriously because it was a Guards battalion.
21  It is worth noting that during the latter half of the nineteenth century the German Army could call on over 6 million trained men, the French 4½, Austria-Hungary 3 and Russia 4 million. In such a context should Britain's difficulties to place even 40,000 men in the field be placed.

Boers.[22] Such a variety of opponents naturally led to a belief that the British Army faced a unique set of circumstances and could not therefore always conform to the traditions and tactics of European armies. More often than not the key to success in such colonial campaigns was not tactical doctrine but an ability to cope with the climate and conditions of the area, as witnessed by the success of the Abyssinian Campaign of 1868 and the Ashanti war of 1873–74 both of which succeeded in difficult conditions because of thorough preparation and organisation. This period was not without its dramatic and embarrassing defeats, but on the whole the British army became quite adapt at what today would be called expeditionary warfare. The defeats were, and perhaps still are, given more attention than they deserve. There is a sense in which the 'professional' and technologically advanced British Army should not have suffered defeats at the hands of colonial enemies no matter how well trained they were. Yet military history is full of such incidences, where victory is gained against the odds. More often than not the defeats could justifiably be put down to poor command decisions, such as Lord Chelmsford before Isandlwana and George Colley before Majuba Hill. In both cases there was a degree of arrogance and an underestimation of the enemy, the latter being a particular flaw throughout this period. On the other hand sometimes the victories had exaggerated praise heaped upon them, such as Rorke's Drift but more pertinently the Red River Expedition in 1870. Here a British force moved 1,118 miles through the Canadian wilderness between 14th May and 24th August 1870. Not a shot was fired but the campaign was praised for a logistical feat thought impossible my many. It again highlights the position of the British Army; whilst they were engaged in a bloodless expedition in the empire the Franco-Prussian War was raging in Europe seeing huge armies of hundreds of thousands of men go up against each other.

Despite the obvious failures it can be argued that the British Army became quite proficient at fighting colonial wars, and had a far better record than any other European power. As one historian has noted, "Although disasters periodically occurred, triumphs were much more frequent".[23] The Royal Navy and the size of Britain's mercantile marine were important factors in this success. Forces were organised and deployed without too much trouble. It is true that the practice of drawing men from other regiments was still common for forces going overseas, as they needed to bring their battalion up to strength, but this had more to do with the peculiarities of the regimental system, particularly after the Cardwell Reforms, than anything else. It is often suggested that such forces were 'cobbled' together for particular expeditions and it is true that many times, especially after

---

22   The Boers were in fact the closest that Britain came to facing a European power during this period, and not simply because of their ancestry. They were armed with modern artillery, rifles and machine guns, and were supported by a small but prosperous economy.
23   Spiers, *The Late Victorian Army*, p.272.

an early setback, troops were sent from other parts of the empire. In some ways this showed a strength of the British position. In a similar way to the United States today, wherever in the world an incident occurred there were always British, Colonial or Royal Navy assets available to lend support. The obvious example of this is India from where troops, mostly British but occasionally Indian, were sent to support operations in Africa and the Mediterranean.

The army was under constant pressure to provide men for expeditions. This often meant that fixed formations and structures, such as was seen on the continent, were unworkable given the size of the army. As a result many such campaigns required the creation of *ad hoc* groups with men and staff often serving in unfamiliar formations. As a consequence British military thinking tended to be very much based around the regiment rather than brigades, divisions or corps. This is a contributing reason as to why the importance attached to the regiment and the sense of regimental esprit de corps was greater than in many other armies.

During this period the British Army gained a great deal of combat experience, although there was considerable debate on the value of such experience. 'Imperialists' saw the benefits of colonial wars but the so-called 'continentalists' derided the value of such exploits and looked to learn from European warfare, in most cases Prussia. Colonel Lonsdale Hale, a vigorous continentalist, wrote that,

> An Officer who has seen service must sweep from his mind all recollections of that service, for between Afghan, Egyptian, or Zulu warfare and that of Europe, there is no similarity whatever. To the latter the former is merely the play of children.[24]

Hale did make a legitimate point in terms of the difference of such styles of warfare, but he and others of the continentalist school were too obsessed with the Franco-Prussian War. Hale recommended to all officers that the official German account, "should be studied page by page, paragraph by paragraph, line by line", at the exclusion of all else.[25] Indeed this seems to have been a problem in the approach of the continentalists. They never actually made a study of the conflicts but rather preferred to take the official accounts of the war at face value. The continentalists stuck rigidly to the lessons of the war as the official history had described it, whereas the imperialist school was more concerned with serious analysis and using events as evidence. As Bailes wrote, "The one (continentalists) was concerned to exemplify, the other (imperialists) to demonstrate".[26]

---

24  Hale, Colonel Lonsdale, 'The Spirit of Tactical Operations of Today', *Proceedings of the Royal Artillery Institution* 16 (1889), pp.449-464.
25  Hale, Colonel Lonsdale, 'The Study of Military History by the Regimental Officers of the Army', *Journal of the Royal United Service Institute* 20, (1876), p.522.
26  Bailes, Howard, 'Patterns of Thought in the Late Victorian Army', pp.40-41.

The imperialists, not least of all Brackenbury, felt that there were unquestionable benefits to be had from small wars. Wolseley also pointed out that if nothing else it got British troops used to being under fire and in combat and, as he underlined in 1890, the Germans had not fired a shot in anger since 1871.[27] Perhaps the definitive work of this period was Colonel Charles Callwell's *Small Wars: Their Principles and Practice*. This became in effect the textbook for the British Army in this period. Callwell wrote that, "The Conduct of small wars is in fact in certain respects an art by itself, diverging widely from what is adapted to the conditions of regular warfare, but not so widely that there are not in all its branches points which permit comparisons to be established".[28] After all colonial wars were now the main occupation of the army.

As the Stanhope Memorandum had made clear involvement in a European war was unlikely, so there was little point in preparing an army to fight on the continent of Europe if it was to spend most of its time fighting throughout the Empire. The military writer T.M. Maguire also warned of too much concentration on European warfare,

> While looking at the stars we may tumble in a ditch, and while lost in wonder at how to move effectively from Strasbourg, Mayence, and Metz towards Paris with many divisions of cavalry and armies consisting each of from three to eight corps, we may forget how to handle a few battalions in the passes of the Suleiman Range or in the deserts of Upper Egypt.[29]

A famous example of this attitude was Sir Edward Hamley's *Operations of War*, first published in 1872, which was a standard text at the Staff College for many years and, indeed, until 1894 was the sole text for the entrance exam to the Staff College.[30] This completely ignored colonial campaigning, and as Bailes states, "It is remarkable that the most famous military treatise of late nineteenth-century Britain should have said almost nothing about the immediate problems facing its army", namely the constant fighting to maintain the Empire.[31]

---

27  Spiers, *The Late Victorian Army*, p.21.
28  Callwell, Charles E., *Small Wars: Their Principles and Practice* (London: H.M.S.O, 1896), p.21. This work was probably the closest thing there was in the Late Victorian era to a theoretical military textbook. Originally published in 1896 it was revised and republished several times, most recently in 1996 by University of Nebraska Press.
29  Maguire, T.M., 'Our Art of War as "Made in Germany"' *United Service Magazine* (13 April-Sept 1896), p.126.
30  Jay Luvaas devotes a whole chapter to Edward Hamley in *The Education of an Army* (London: Cassell, 1965), pp.130-168. This is a well-balanced account that focuses on both his strengths and weaknesses and gives the best account of his quite public falling out with Wolseley.
31  Bailes, Howard, 'Patterns of Thought in the Late Victorian Army', p.34.

## Conclusion

The question remains whether a better organisational structure could have been found for the British Army that would have successfully enabled both preparations for fighting a European war and continued imperial expeditions. The problem was that it would have concerned an increase in the army estimates, and there was constant pressure from the Treasury on every Secretary of State for War to reduce the estimates; or would have required the implementation of conscription, which was out of the question during this era. No matter what successive governments said about the likelihood of having to fight a European war, it was appreciated by many soldiers and politicians that this might be necessary. The South African War led to large-scale reform in the British Army and ultimately the establishment of the British Expeditionary Force (B.E.F.), which was largely set up to fight in Europe.

During this period there was a growth in the number of soldiers who saw it as a profession rather than merely a duty. There were an increasing number of officers who took their profession seriously, studied, and prepared for it. This is clearly seen through the expansion of such organisations as the Royal United Service Institute and the Royal Artillery Institution. Unfortunately men of such calibre rarely achieved high office during this era. Often they found their niche in an administrative post and never moved on because they were considered too valuable. Moreover the system of awarding high military office to those who had distinguished themselves in the field, regardless of the suitability for such office, continued to deny the more intellectual soldier high office. Indeed this is what makes Brackenbury's career so unique.

Although there were periods of great activity, such as Cardwell and Stanhope's tenures in office, the whole period was one of continuous military reform. The significance and importance of this is often lost as the second half of the nineteenth century started with a disastrous war, the Crimean, and finished with one, the South African War. This often detracts from the significance of the improvements that took place. Indeed it ought to be remembered that the Royal Commissions that investigated the South African War concluded that if the Hartington Commissions proposals had been accepted then the disaster of South Africa might not have taken place.[32] So the momentum for effective reform was there, even if there was often pressure from the forces of entrenched conservatism to prevent it from being carried through.

---

32 Both the Elgin and Esher Commissions suggested this. The Esher Committee went so far as to assert this directly. *Report of the War Office Reconstitution Committee* (Esher Committee). Part I (1904) H.M.S.O, London, p.161.

# Chapter 4

# The Indian Mutiny

Even a hundred and fifty years after the conflict the 'Mutiny' of 1857 remains an incredibly controversial and sensitive issue. Indeed controversy is rife even regarding the nomenclature of the conflict. In the United Kingdom it is still commonly referred to as the 'Indian Mutiny'. This is as inaccurate as the modern tendency in Indian to refer to the conflict as the 'First Indian War of Independence'. Both terms ignore the fact that the mutiny, or rebellion if one prefers, was to a large extent a localised phenomenon. India was at the time of the conflict governed by the British East India Company which operated under a Royal charter. India did not exist as a single country and much of the land was still ruled by local princes. One or two of them saw the opportunity to make political capital and perhaps regain some of their land and prestige which had been lost to the British, but it was only a handful. Indeed even amongst the mutineers their political thought was to look backwards to restoring the Mogul Empire rather than attempting to create a modern Indian State. As Byron Farwell put it, "They sought a King not an elected President".[1]

Another problem with using the term 'Indian' in the title of the conflict is that it suggests that it spread throughout the subcontinent and was a general uprising. Had this been the case the consequences for the British would have been fatal. If several million Indians had rebelled, including several hundred thousand soldiers who had been trained in arms by the British, it is incredulous to think that the estimated 60,000 British soldiers spread throughout India, or even any relieve force sent from home, could have stopped such a popular uprising. The problem was that only in a few areas were the mutineers supported by the local populace in any significant way, most notably in the Oudh. In many parts of the country, social, ethnic, religious and class differences were significant enough to ensure that if any section supported the mutineers the British were guaranteed an ally. The old saying that "my enemy's enemy is my friend" reigned supreme.[2] Whilst the term Sepoy

---
1  Farwell, Byron, *Armies of the Raj, 1858-1947* (New York: W.W. Norton and Co, 1989), p.44.
2  There is insufficient space within this work to go into a detailed account of the 'mutiny'. It is

rebellion or Bengal Mutiny might be more accurate without an accepted and agreed alternative the title Indian Mutiny will continue to be used.

The Company's military forces in its territory were split into three, namely the army of Bengal, Bombay and Madras. Often referred to as the presidency armies, the geographical division would remain in effect after control of the territory transferred from Company to Crown. The 'mutiny' was limited almost in its entirety to the men of the Bengal Army. There was little trouble in the Bombay Army and the only trouble in the Madras Army saw a battalion refused to serve outside their normal territory, an incident which was handled with tact by the British. However such tact was in short supply during the conflict. The surprise and shock of the mutiny and the indiscriminate murder of British civilians, including large numbers of women and children, released a torrent of British fury that would see the conflict become very bloody and controversial. Here is not the time or place to debate the rights and wrongs of the actions of either side. The mutineers committed many atrocities that led to a wave of British retribution that would be of equally questionable morality. Very few prisoners were taken by the British, and those that were faced show trials before execution, mainly by hanging or shooting. However, even in the heat of British revenge the manner of some of the executions left an unpleasant legacy. On rare occasions British officers tied sentenced mutineers to the front of loaded cannon before having them 'blown from the guns'. Although barbaric it was a legitimate form of execution for mutiny at that time. Much of the response simply illustrates the shock and surprise with which the mutiny caught the British, but that in no way justifies or excuses it.

The mutiny of 1857 was by no means the first, or the last, mutiny to take place during the period of British rule in India. In 1806 Indian soldiers at Vellore rose up and killed their British officers and the wounded in the hospital and in 1824 a Bengal Regiment had objected to having to serve in Burma and on parade refused to ground arms. The British officer in command dealt with this ruthlessly and ordered up cannon and had his own regiment blown away! Yet the surprise and severity of the 1857 mutiny would affect Britain's relationship to and with India for the

---

difficult to know where to begin when suggesting further reading with regards to the 'mutiny'. One of the best of the more recent works is Saul David's *The Indian Mutiny 1857* (London: Penguin, 2003). This is clearly of good academic value, whilst remaining thoroughly 'readable'. Julian Spilsbury's book *The Indian Mutiny* (London: Weidenfeld & Nicolson, 2007) is a good general work but very much takes the British side. Very few of the Indian interpretations of the mutiny have been published in English. For the British military response either *The British Military in India* (Manchester: Manchester University Press, 1995) or *The Indian Army: The Garrison of British Imperial India, 1822–1922* (Vancouver: David and Charles, 1974) both by T.A. Heathcote, give very good detail. Byron Farwell's *Queen Victoria's Little Wars* (London: Allen Lane, 1973) or *Armies of the Raj, 1858–1947* (New York: W.W. Norton and Co, 1989), give basic yet informative accounts of the conflict. Two important works from the Indian perspective are Surendra Nath Sen's *Eighteen Fifty-Seven* (Delhi: Ministry of Information & Broadcasting, 1957) and Henry Scholberg's *The Indian Literature of the Great Rebellion* (New Delhi: Promilla, 1993).

remainder of British rule. As we shall see in a later chapter much of British policy in India would be coloured by the events of the mutiny and a fear of a repeat.

In the previous chapter we looked at Brackenbury's motivation for seeing 'action'. Although he missed the opportunity to serve in the Crimean War he did not have to wait long for his first experience. With forces being readied for service in Indian to deal with the Sepoy mutiny, the young Lieutenant Brackenbury at once volunteered for service. Eventually he was accepted but not without incident. It will be remembered that by this stage Brackenbury was serving as Adjutant for the Royal Artillery in the western district. He had impressed in this role and when Brackenbury asked his Colonel to forward his name, and recommend him for service in India, his Colonel said that he would forward his name but *not* recommend him, going on to say that his services could not be spared. To put this incident into context given the nature and national anger that the mutiny had caused, virtually every officer in the army would have been trying to gain service in India. The chance of action, the opportunity to avenge and for revenge, along with the possibility of 'glory' and advancement for those who survived meant that there was no shortage of volunteers. The Colonel's viewpoint is understandable, and whilst not prepared to stand in Brackenbury's way, he obviously felt that there would be plenty of young officers who could serve in India but few who could fill the role of Adjutant so well. As we shall see, in later years Brackenbury's reputation for administrative work became legendary and it is clear that in those years as Adjutant this was coming to the fore. His Colonel even went so far as to say he 'could not be spared'. However Brackenbury turned the Colonel's words to his advantage. He enlisted the support of his uncle, Lieutenant-Colonel Sir Edward Brackenbury, who appealed directly to the Adjutant-General of Artillery Sir Hew Ross, who as luck would have it was a former Peninsular War comrade of Sir Edward. In later years Henry recalled the conversation between the two men as it had been told to him by his uncle.

> He (Sir Edward Brackenbury) called on Sir Hew, who sent for the papers. "How old is the lad?" said Sir Hew. "Only nineteen", said my Uncle. "What, only nineteen, and his colonel says he can't be spared! He must be a good lad, he ought to have a chance on service". And so the very remark which was intended to keep me back was the cause of my being chosen.[3]

Having been informed that he would be leaving for India he prepared in a very traditionally British way, spending the last two days playing cricket for the Royal Artillery against the famous I Zingari XI.[4]

---

3   Brackenbury, Henry, *Some Memories of My Spare Time* (London: William Blackwood & Sons, 1909), p.9.
4   Brackenbury top scored in the first innings with 27 and when keeping wicket stumped two and caught three. Brackenbury took pride in the fact that he had been dismissed by Spencer Ponsonby Fane, the MCC and Surrey cricketer.

At the end of August 1857 he sailed for India, to be precise Madras. As has already been mentioned that was an area little affected by the mutiny and was being used as a base to gather together British forces for the relief of besieged garrisons. Indeed in Madras large numbers of 'loyal' Indians were hastily being recruited to serve the British cause. The supply system and logistics in general had been found wanting in the recent campaign in the Crimea, and the campaign in India was little better. Brackenbury recorded many years later "I have often wondered how any of us survived".[5] Even his arrival in India was eventful. There was no pier in Madras at that time and he was landed directly on the beach, a perilous exercise at the best of times. For what, one can only presume, were reasons of smartness and presentation he was landed on the beach in full tunic and busby. Seeing several hundred men in full uniform, busbies included, wading ashore from their boats must have been a rather interesting sight to say the least. Things did not get much better once they were landed and having gone ashore at 7am it was not until 7pm that they were finally given orders to march ten miles to St Thomas' Mount.

After a week or two of acclimatisation they were ordered back to the beach to re-embark for transport to Masulipatam (modern day Macilipatnam). This also became something of a farce. They were ordered out at midnight in a tremendous storm and marched to the beach at Madras. Nobody was there to meet them, and Brackenbury later remarked that this was surely what staff officers were for. When finally someone did arrive it was simply to inform them that they had no right to be on the beach at that hour! It transpired that a message had been dispatched the night before telling the Brigadier in command at St Thomas Mount to delay their march as the high surf made embarkation impossible. The message never reached the Brigadier as he had retired early that evening and his servants did not dare disturb him until the morning, by which time the message had been forgotten. Soaked to the skin the officers and men were escorted to the Governor's residence in Guindy, a suburb of Madras. There they spent an uncomfortable three days as their baggage had already been taken on board ship prior to their march to the beach.[6]

This was not the end of the administrative blunders. When finally they were landed at Masulipatam and started their way in land they did so without helmets, and the men of the batteries of artillery only had forage caps, which gave virtually no protection from the sun. Although helmets had not been organised someone had issued them with white covers for their forage caps, obviously presuming this would make all the difference! The inevitable happened and Brackenbury recorded that his battery lost twenty per cent of its officers and men in one month due to "solar apoplexy": in other words severe sunstroke. At the time the only known 'cure' for

---

5   Brackenbury, *Some Memories of My Spare Time*, p.10.
6   Brackenbury, *Some Memories of My Spare Time*. His experiences during the 'mutiny' can be found on pp.10-16.

this was to tie the patient down on a stone floor and pour buckets of water on the patients head and chest. All this unnecessary suffering had been caused by a lack of even basic equipment.[7]

On their march in land from Masulipatam they arrived at Hyderabad. The Nizam, the princely ruler of the territory, had remained loyal to the British and had done his best to keep his people from joining the mutineers. Although they were welcomed with friendship by the Nizam, his government and his court, there was less enthusiasm from the local population. Brackenbury felt that had it not been made very clear that they were under the protection of the Nizam they may have been attacked. As it was the populace confined itself to "scowling looks and curses, while from some of the roofs of the low houses men spat at us as we passed".[8] This perhaps says as much about the unpopularity of the Nizam as it does that of the British, but it helps illustrate that these were dangerous times for British rule in India and the longer the rebellion went on the more danger of it possibly growing into a continent wide revolt.

Brackenbury served with G Battery of the 14th Brigade, Royal Artillery and this unit was attached to the Nerbudda Field Force under the then Major-General George Whitlock. Whitlock was an Indian veteran having first joined the Madras army in 1818 as an Ensign. He had seen service in the Mahratta War in India. He had risen steadily through the ranks and in June 1857 was promoted to Major-General at the age of fifty-nine. During the mutiny he was given command of the Nerbudda Field Force, sometimes referred to as the Madras Column. Its task was to advance inland from Madras through the territory of the Nizam, clearing the mutineers on the way, to Nagpore and Jubbulpore where friendly India leaders were holding out against mutineers. The initial force at his disposal was quite considerable, consisting of two troops of horse artillery, three companies of field artillery, with two light field batteries attached; the 12th Lancers, and the 6th and 7th Madras Light Cavalry; the 43rd Light Infantry, the 3rd Madras Europeans, and the 1st, 19th, and 50th Madras Native Infantry; with two companies of sappers.

The column took part in what is commonly referred to as the Central India Campaign, mostly in the modern day states of Madhya Pradesh and Rajasthan. A detailed look at the campaign is not necessary to our narrative. The column was mostly concerned with relieving British and allied towns and garrisons that were under threat from the mutineers. The most famous incident associated with the column was the capture of what became known as the Banda and Kirwee prize money, which later necessitated a legal case to determine each man's share. The battle of Banda on 19th April 1858 had seen the column face an enemy of upwards

---

7   Out of a total of 11,021 British casualties during the war 8,987 died from sickness, a large number believed to be sunstroke.
8   Brackenbury, *Some Memories of My Spare Time*, pp.12-13.

of 7,000 mutineers, and unsurprisingly the artillery played an important part in driving back and defeating a numerically superior force.[9] Brackenbury is not particularly good at giving dates when referring to this period. Much of that may be due to the fact that he waited fifty years before recording these events. It is likely that Brackenbury joined Whitlock's column in early February 1858 and continued until nearly the end of the year, when he was invalided home. The exact nature of his injuries is unclear, and no record exists. It may simply be that he finally succumbed to 'sun stroke' like so many others.

The experience of India stayed with Brackenbury for many years and he learnt many important lessons. It was advantageous that his first taste of combat came at such an early age, only just twenty, so that he could learn from the experience, but also it gave him a bit more credibility. He was no longer just a young subaltern of the Royal Artillery: he was now a 'soldier' and returned with an Indian service medal with the clasp 'Central India'. That would also have added to his prestige as it was known to be a particularly difficult and grueling part on the suppression of the mutiny. The experience also taught him many valuable lessons about organisation and military administration. The fiasco of his landing directly on to a beach, in full uniform, and that no preparations having been made for their arrival. His midnight march to the beach because of a lack of communication, and perhaps most importantly the need for the correct equipment. This would be something that would be in his mind many years later when charged with supplying the army in South Africa. However that is to jump ahead in our story. It is sufficient to say that his experience in India coloured his future career, in many ways showing him the need for good administration and staff work.

---

9    For further information on the Banda and Kirwee prize money see Robson, Brian 'The Banda and Kirwi Prize Money', *Soldiers of the Queen, Journal of the Victorian Military Society*, Issue 97 (June 1999).

# Chapter 5

# The Literary Work of Henry Brackenbury

On his return from India in 1858 Brackenbury was sent to Woolwich where he served as a subaltern on the depot brigade. In early 1860 he was offered the position of adjutant of the brigade but the circumstances surrounding it are a curious story. Brackenbury was told that the offer was conditional. His predecessor in the role had been a very keen cricketer and as a consequence had neglected his duties, and had been asked to resign. Brackenbury was offered the post on the condition that he would give up cricket for his tenure as adjutant. As has already been mentioned Brackenbury was a keen cricketer himself and had developed quite a reputation as a wicketkeeper batsman, representing the Royal Artillery on several occasions. Somewhat surprisingly he agreed to the conditions and for two and a half years played no cricket. In his own words he elected "for work in preference to play".[1] Sport was an important part of an officer's life in this era, in which being a 'gentleman' was more appropriate than being the dreaded 'professional', the latter applying to the army officer corps as much as to cricket. His willingness to give up sport to concentrate on his work shows us several things. It is an early indication that he was of a different 'type' to the majority of the officer corps. It is also a mark of his professional approach to his work and his intention to make a career out of the army. This is perhaps not that surprising when one thinks of his brief professional experience in Quebec. It also points to what might be called 'a young man in a hurry'. His eagerness to see active service and the fact that at such a young age he was being considered for appointment as adjutant of the depot brigade at Woolwich, illustrate a young man keen to make his mark in his chosen profession. Indeed it should be remembered that he was still only twenty-two, an age when he could have been forgiven for thinking more about sport than work.

---

1   Brackenbury, Henry, *Some Memories of My Spare Time* (London: William Blackwood & Sons, 1909), p.17.

The decision to put work before play was one which perhaps belied his years. Brackenbury recorded that this period was one of very hard work, and we see an indication that he was a 'workaholic'. His skill in administration was starting to come to the fore. After two and a half years of all work and no play he left his appointment as adjutant and became Lieutenant of a company of gentleman cadets at the Royal Military Academy Woolwich. This was the start of what could be referred to as a series of teaching appointments. In his new appointment he found that he had lots of spare time, and sport once again played an important part in his life as he started to play cricket again along with racket sports and billiards. However his spare time was not entirely devoted to leisure activities. He started to make a study of, as he put it, "the art of military administration, of strategy and of tactics". He found that there was a distinct lack of books on this topic written in English.[2]

In 1864 he took on the additional responsibility of being Assistant-Instructor in Artillery at the Royal Military Academy, Woolwich. Later that year this became his sole responsibility and he now found he had a great deal of spare time. Indeed he had two whole days a week devoid of any teaching, added to which were the Easter, summer and Christmas vacations. Once again he was determined to put this to good use, later writing that "I was anxious to employ this time more profitably than in mere amusement".[3] He had the good fortune that one of the more enlightened minds of the army was his direct superior. Colonel, later General Sir, John Henry Lefroy, Director of the Advanced Class for Artillery Officers at Woolwich, encouraged him in his studies and suggested that he make a study of the origins and early history of artillery in Europe and particularly England. In the Royal Artillery a certain level of technical training was necessary and thus study was not quite so 'alien' to the artillery, or engineer, officer as it would be to the rest of the army. In the majority of the army his activities would have been the source of amusement and scorn. Many cases abound of officers who became pariahs in their own regiment because their motives were suspect. Such extra study was often viewed as a crude attempt at self-advancement. It also fitted in with the dislike of staff officers who it was often felt used their position in time of war to take the 'glory' away from regimental officers.[4]

Brackenbury took to his task seriously. Whilst he undertook his initial research in the military libraries of Woolwich and London he decided that he would have to move beyond this to produce a substantial account. Through Colonel Lefroy he contacted Mr John Hewitt author of the contemporary book *Ancient Armour and Weapons in Europe*, who introduced him to useful documents and background reading. From here Brackenbury went to the British Museum and over several months he poured over the archives going through medieval chronicles and even identifying some errors in

---

2  Brackenbury, *Some Memories of My Spare Time*, p.18.
3  Brackenbury, *Some Memories of My Spare Time*, pp.23-24.
4  Turner, E.S., *Gallant Gentlemen: A portrait of the British Officer 1600-1956*, pp.203-205.

the collections.[5] He seems to have enjoyed the process and in later years spoke fondly of the many writers and academics he met during this era. He also consulted the Public Records Office and the Bodleian Library, but with little yield for his study. He was assisted by the contacts of another officer at Woolwich. Colonel C.H. Owen was Professor of Artillery at Woolwich and had published widely on the matter of artillery. Owen's brother was Mr Sydney Owen who was a reader in Indian Law and History at Oxford University. Both men assisted him, particularly by pointing him in the right direction towards various resources. Another contact was made through Mr Bond of the British Library who wrote to his opposite number at the Bodleian saying that Brackenbury was interested in any drawings of fourteenth century cannon they might have. He was told to contact Dr Payne-Smith, who was later Regius Professor of Divinity. On their meeting an amusing incident happened. Having been told that Brackenbury wanted to see any drawings they had of fourteenth century cannon, Dr Payne-Smith asked him what it was he wanted to ascertain. It soon became clear they were talking at cross purposes and as Brackenbury later recorded "The ecclesiastical mind had leapt to the human canon of the Church!", and he asked him if it was some matter of dress that he wished to query.[6]

In 1865 he produced his first article on 'Ancient Cannon in Europe' published in the *Proceedings of the Royal Artillery*, followed by a second paper the following year. This charted the subject matter to around the year 1400. It was his intention to produce a third article which would have included detailed sketches and drawing, which were copies of artists of the fifteenth century. However before this could be done his material was lost in a fire. With the loss of material which had taken him so long to produce he decided to end the series. As he later confessed "I had neither time nor heart to commence over again". There is also a suggestion that with the benefit of hindsight he was slightly relieved, as he felt his study was somewhat taking over his life. "It was perhaps as well for me that it was so, for nothing is more fascinating than antiquarian research, and it is all-absorbing".[7] It is quite ironic given his previous experience with an officer who was allowing sport to take up too much of his time that Brackenbury felt that he was in danger of allowing his 'hobby' to detract from his military duties. Whilst perhaps a more worthy distraction, it is still interesting to note that he felt it was taking him away from his military duties, especially considering that this was just the start of his literary output. It also points to the fact that although he had outside interests he was determined to make the Army his career.

---

5    Brackenbury, *Some Memories of My Spare Time*, pp.25-27.
6    Brackenbury, *Some Memories of My Spare Time*, pp.23-31. This gives a full account of Brackenbury's study and the many contacts he made.
7    Brackenbury, *Some Memories of My Spare Time*, p.31.

## A Journalistic Career

Although the articles on ancient cannon had been a useful intellectual exercise it had been unpaid work. However it had established his credentials. Colonel Lefroy, who had urged him to write in the first place, now offered him his first paid literary work. This consisted of writing the military articles for a new edition of Brande's *Dictionary of Literature, Science, and Art*. This was published by Messrs Longmans, Green and Co, and through this he was introduced to the publisher William Longman. They found they had a common interest as William Longman was writing *The History of the Life and Times of Edward III*, a period which Brackenbury's articles on 'Ancient Cannon' had looked at in detail. It is interesting how one contact led to another. Longman introduced him to Mr Walford editor of *The Gentleman's Magazine*, who commissioned him to write an article entitled 'Warfare in the Middle Ages' published in December 1866. After the success of this article he was again approached by Longman asking if he would edit a book by General Michael W. Smith entitled *Drill and Manoeuvres of Cavalry combined with Horse Artillery*. This book appealed to his reforming nature. It was a modern, technical, account of artillery tactics and deployment. It was hardly likely to be a bestseller as it contained "elaborate mathematical calculations" and "trigonometrical formulae two printed lines in length".[8] However his performance in editing the book for publication impressed William Longman, who recommended him to Mr J.A. Froude the editor of *Fraser's Magazine*. His first article for *Fraser's* was a review of an American author's book about the action around Charleston during the American Civil War. This was to lead to further work for the magazine, most notably a series on Army reform. His association with *Fraser's* was the start of a long literary career.

No other Victorian soldier produced the same amount, and variety, of literature as Henry Brackenbury. He produced five books but they were only a small part of his writing[9]. He wrote numerous articles for the weekly and monthly journals of the day – not all on military matters – as well as a considerable amount for the daily press.[10] Brackenbury's literary career which had started out of boredom, continued partly out of necessity but also because he found great benefit from it. Whilst Brackenbury's

---

8   Brackenbury, *Some Memories of My Spare Time*, pp.36-37. The reviewer in *The Athenaeum* concluded that "If General Smith had dispensed with the first 150 pages of his work and the last 100, he would have found plenty of readers for the intermediate 70 pages".

9   There is some debate over the number of publications that could actually be referred to as books. *The Dictionary of National Biography* includes amongst this number his lecture and journal article entitled 'The tactics of the three arms'. I would not include this as a book. Often ignored is his book on the Franco-Prussian War, written in French, which was never published and of which only a handful of copies survive.

10  The sheer scale and scope of Brackenbury's literary output means that a full account is impossible within the boundaries of this biography. It has been decided to concentrate on those articles that in particular refer to the themes of this book, such as army reform, military tactics, campaign memories, and anything else that is considered significant.

literary contributions allowed him to explore the issues surrounding military reform and to express his ideas on all manner of military and non-military subjects they also had a wider benefit. Given his family background he had virtually no private means. This was a severe drawback at a time when an officer's pay was insufficient to meet the cost of the lifestyle they were expected, and in some cases required, to keep. Brackenbury had now found a way of supplementing his pay, which at the same time helped to build his reputation as a thinker and reformer within and outside the army. Brackenbury's private circumstances explain not only the continuance of his literary career but also the publications for which he wrote. A comparison can be made with his brother Charles. Although the third son, the untimely deaths of his elder brothers meant that he would inherit the family estate, such as it was and as we have already seen he had married into a very wealthy family. Charles shared many of his brother's reformist and intellectual ideals. Yet due to his financial circumstances he wrote most of his articles for the 'trade', his articles appearing in the *United Services Journal*, the *Royal Artillery Journal*, and the *Army Magazine*, amongst others.[11] Henry on the other

Major-General Charles Booth Brackenbury, Henry's only surviving brother. A friendly rivalry existed between the two. Henry's career moves were often motivated by a desire to emulate his brother. (*The Graphic*)

---

11   The exact nature of Charles's finances is unclear. Despite the fact that he had nine children, although not all survived infancy, he never appeared to have the financial problems of his brother. Charles Brackenbury did write occasionally for newspapers, but never on the scale of his brother. Charles acted as military correspondent for *The Times* during the war of 1866, which saw Prussia and Italy allied against Austria, but this was an exception to the rule.

hand wrote rarely for such publications, instead writing for the popular press, in other words, those who would pay.[12]

Along with writing for many leading Victorian periodicals Henry Brackenbury also formed a strong association with some daily newspapers. In 1867 *The Standard* employed him to write a series of occasional articles on military matters, his first being on the subject of 'Corporal Punishment in the Army'.[13] This association also included articles for *The Morning Herald* and *The Evening Standard*, which were owned by the same proprietor. His connection with *The Standard* continued until he went to the continent to work for the National Aid Society in 1870, and their

Although unidentified, this appears to be a photograph of a handsome young Henry Brackenbury. The medal ribbon appears to be that of the Indian Mutiny. (Private collection)

---

12  The Blackwood Papers at the National Library of Scotland contain some details of the amount of money he was paid, and not just for his work for Blackwoods. From these papers we know that Brackenbury was paid £300 for his book on *The Ashanti Campaign*, that for *The Illustrated London News* he was writing an average of 25 columns at four guineas a column, and that his work for *The Daily Telegraph* saw him paid £5 a column. Brackenbury to Blackwood, 27th November 1874, Blackwood Papers, National Library of Scotland, MSS MS 4315 and Brackenbury to Blackwood, 2nd June 1877, Blackwood Papers, National Library of Scotland, MSS MS 4356.
13  This was published in *The Standard* on Monday 18th March 1867. Brackenbury wrote that corporal punishment should only be used on active service, a view which the later Cardwell Reforms would make practice.

association ended badly.[14] In late 1876 he began a connection with *The Daily Telegraph*, which was to see him contribute occasional articles, most of which, due to their highly politicised nature, were written under the penname of 'Anglophile'. This later led to a brief association with the newspaper *The World* in the late 1870s. Some of his work was extremely well paid and Brackenbury was capable of making a considerable amount of money out of his literary career. It also gave him a chance to highlight his credentials as an army reformer, and to gain what today would be called 'name recognition'.

## Military campaigns

Perhaps his best-known work was in the field of military campaigns dealing with the Ashanti War and the Gordon Relief Expedition. Both books on these two colonial campaigns are still available to this day and have been republished many times. He did, however, also write about a much smaller and less significant campaign conducted in South Africa, namely the Sekhukhune expedition. In none of these does he use the exercise as an attempt at self-publicity or aggrandisement, and he rarely mentions his own part in such events. Indeed in his final book on his military campaigns, *The River Column* first published in 1885, he refrained from comment or praise for any of the individuals concerned. As he wrote,

> It would have been a pleasure to me to take this opportunity of praising those individuals to whom, in my opinion, such success as the Column attained is chiefly due; but my position demands so strict a neutrality that I have thought it right to avoid all words of praise, lest in any case their accidental omission might appear to impute the semblance of blame.

Again this supports the view that Brackenbury did not write for personal glory. Indeed Brackenbury stated that his own motivations were, in a sense, to provide a lasting record of an extraordinary military expedition.

> I have written this simple narrative in the belief that the advance and return of four regiments of infantry through a hundred miles of cataracts and rapids in an enemy's country deserve, as a military operation, some

---

14  From the commencement of the Franco-Prussian War, Brackenbury had been writing a 'Diary of the War' that appeared in each day's paper. The editor had wanted him to sign a formal contract, which Brackenbury had refused to do on the grounds that his military duties could take him away at any moment. When Brackenbury announced that he was leaving to work in Europe for the National Aid Society some rather acrimonious correspondence took place between the editor and Brackenbury. The upshot of it was that Brackenbury considered they would not welcome him in the future and thus the association ended.

permanent record, and because death has removed the only other officers possessing sufficient knowledge of all details to write that record with accuracy.[15]

Although he never wrote a major military thesis, such a work as this was a useful contribution to those who studied the 'art of war'. It was a well-organised campaign, although there were clearly supply problems, in hostile territory, due to the enemy and also the difficulty of the terrain and climatic conditions. Whilst it has already been explained that he wrote largely for financial benefit, he was also writing to illustrate to the wider public the problems which soldiers faced. As a writer he was also capable of exerting a wider influence. Brackenbury believed that reform of the army would have to come from outside. Clearly the forum for this was the House of Commons. The type of publication Brackenbury wrote for was widely read by the members of that house. It is inconceivable that Brackenbury did not realise the scope of his influence, therefore it is clear that rather than just writing for financial gain or career advancement he was also writing to influence army reform. Brackenbury never touched on the controversy that the campaign provoked. His was purely a military and logistical account of a quite remarkable military manoeuvre. As an account of a military operation it was interesting and its republication in the 1990s for the US Military illustrates the lasting value of such a work.

## Military Tactics

A criticism levelled at Brackenbury is that despite his prolific writing and his promotion of intellectual soldiering he never wrote a major theoretical work.[16] Cynically it could be suggested that this was because there was no financial gain in such a book but the truth is probably that, whilst there was perhaps a need for such a work, there was no demand. Within the Army itself an amateur ethos still existed, and little value was placed on studies of military history or contemporary tactics. Brackenbury himself had experience of this. Lieutenant-Colonel G.F.R. Henderson, Professor of Military History at the Staff College, had written a notable work entitled *Stonewall Jackson and the American Civil War*. Jackson's tactics during the war had given him a somewhat legendary status and the book did well commercially. However, despite its tactical interest Henderson told Brackenbury that, "Beside yourself, only one other General, or even Colonel, on the active list has said a word about

---
15  Both quotations from Brackenbury, Henry, *The River Column* (London: Blackwoods, 1885), pp.v-vi.
16  This criticism was most recently made by Ian Beckett in *The Victorians at War*, p.189, although it has also been alluded to by Howard Bailes in *Patterns of Thought* and Brian Bond in *The Victorian Army and the Staff College 1854-1914*.

the book to me".[17] It was a clear illustration of the lack of interest in such matters that existed at the time. Further evidence of this can be found in Colonel Lonsdale Hale's lecture and subsequent article for the Royal United Service Institute, in 1891, on "The Professional Study of Military History", delivered largely as a criticism of the unprofessional nature of the officer corps and their dislike of study. Hale concluded that the average army officer, "found 'study' and 'history' bad enough by themselves, but when in juxtaposition, forming a combination absolutely detestable".[18]

This goes a long way to explaining why there was no distinctively British theoretical work on tactics. The closest was Charles Callwell's *Small Wars*, first published in 1896, but this looked purely at the colonial style of small wars. German literature and the Swiss-born writer Henri Jomini largely influenced other notable works, such as Edward Hamley's *Operations of War*, first published in 1866. Brackenbury recounted stories that illustrated the point that the majority of tactical and theoretical military history was being written for a small audience within the army. He did, however, write two articles, both for *Saint Paul's Monthly Magazine*, in 1867 and 1869, which dealt largely with the tactical side of his profession. The first of these concerned itself with a review of 'The Military Armaments of the Five Great Powers'.[19] In looking at the weaponry of the nation's Brackenbury felt it natural to comment on the tactical application of such resources. His starting point was the Paris Exhibition of 1867 which had seen an uncommonly high display of military equipment. Although all types of military hardware were covered at the exhibition there was a particular emphasis on artillery. This had gone through something of a revolution with the introduction of rifled guns, which had dramatically improved their distance and accuracy. He also wrote about the developments and benefits of the new breech-loading rifles. In a rare note of praise for British governments he commended the speed with which they had recognised the benefits of such a weapon and had appreciated the lesson of the Danish-Prussian War long before the majority of European powers.[20] The fact that the decision had been to adapt and modify the Enfield rifle rather than adopt a completely new weapon also met with his approval. Brackenbury took the view that, as this was an emerging technology, it was far better to modify an existing weapon, thus giving the benefit of breech loading, and to await the further development of such technology.

Even in an article that was supposed to be largely about military technology and tactics Brackenbury came back to his continuing concern over recruitment in the British Army. His view was that as tactics and technology were changing so must

---

17    Brackenbury, *Some Memories of My Spare Time*, p.86.
18    Hale, Colonel Lonsdale, 'The Professional Study of Military History', *Royal United Service Institute Journal*, Volume 1 (1897), p.690.
19    The Five Great Powers were defined as Prussia, France, Austria, Russia and Great Britain.
20    Brackenbury, Henry, 'The Military Armaments of the Five Great Powers', *Saint Paul's: A Monthly Magazine*, (13) Volume 1 (November 1867), pp.190-191.

the old idea that the soldier was, in his words, "a mere machine". It was therefore necessary for Britain to change the practice of recruiting from the lowest members in society. As he wrote,

> Other nations take the flower of manhood of the country for their armies, and the highest and lowest of their sons fight side by side in the ranks. Too independent to accept compulsory service even for our country, we yet are unwilling to pay the cost of our exemption, and instead of making the army the best of all professions, so as to attract men of intelligence and ability into its ranks, we seek only for how small a sum it is possible to get men of any stamp, and we lower our bidding till we can just fill our army with the dregs of our cities, and only raise the offer when even they cannot be drawn, even by the lies of a recruiting sergeant, into the ranks.[21]

This was quite hard-hitting language and the subject of recruiting was one that he was particularly passionate about, and to which he regularly returned. This is not surprising for someone who was concerned about efficiency in all that he did. At the heart of Brackenbury's passion on this subject was the fact that all his other suggested reforms would not work efficiently unless a settled and effective system of recruiting existed.

It is sometimes difficult to understand where Brackenbury stood on the issue of compulsory service. He never publicly advocated its introduction, not even when a popular movement in its favour was started with the support of Lord Roberts in the aftermath of the South African War. Perhaps this was because he believed that such a measure could never be accepted in peacetime. This view would certainly be supported by many of his articles on army reform. Yet he continually mentioned the idea in his writing with language which seems to suggest a longing for such a measure. Another interesting point from the passage quoted above is that relating to highest and the lowest serving together in the ranks. This only truly happened in the French army, and even then there were loopholes that could be exploited by those with power or money, yet Brackenbury emphasises the point in such a way as to make it sound as though this was the common practice in Europe. One possible reason for this can be found in his previous articles on army reform when he wrote that compulsory service was not only impossible in Britain for historical and political reasons, but also because of liberal reforms that had made such a measure almost impossible.[22] It could be argued that Brackenbury's concept of the highest and the lowest serving together side by side in the ranks was an attempt to appeal to liberal ideas of equality. Having said this it does seem unlikely that Brackenbury was in favour of compulsory service as there is no direct mention of

---

21 Brackenbury, 'The Military Armaments of the Five Great Powers', p.194.
22 Brackenbury, Henry, 'Military Reform: Part I', pp.685-686.

his support for it, and he was certainly not reticent about expressing his views on other, perhaps even more controversial, matters. Brackenbury may well have sought to make compulsory service seem more generally acceptable. If this was his view it is supported by the evidence of the South African War, where a large number of volunteers from all levels of society willingly served together in the ranks. It was perhaps hoped that those in power who were diametrically opposed to this idea would seek to improve the state of the army of voluntary service so as to avoid any pressure for compulsory service.

Brackenbury also wrote on 'The Influence of Modern Improvements Upon Strategy', again for *Saint Paul's Monthly Magazine.* This was during an era when there were several similar articles published.[23] The reason for this was that emerging technology, especially rifled artillery, had recently been demonstrated in action, most notably in the conflict between Prussia and Austria. There were also incidents in the Danish-Prussian War that had highlighted the ability of the breech-loading rifle. However Brackenbury stated clearly that his aim was to look at strategy, which he defined as the movement of troops in war, rather than tactics, the art of handling troops in the presence of the enemy. The first elements he looked at were the electric telegraph and the influence of railroads. He recognised that this had particular significance for Russia, and if applied correctly would enormously increase Russia's role as a great power. The railroads in particular were important in that they had increased the ability to concentrate troops at any one point and the ability to keep them supplied. He gave various examples from the recent wars in Europe and the American Civil War, where tens and indeed hundreds of thousands of troops were moved, along with guns and equipment, quickly and efficiently for battle. All this meant that mobilisation which in the past had taken weeks or months now took a matter of days. He did, however, appreciate that this now meant that considerable numbers of troops had to be used to protect the railroads. Brackenbury could not resist the temptation to compare this with the chaos caused in Britain when volunteers were moved to Brighton for manoeuvres, which required the closing of the railway for four days simply to prepare for one day's movement, consisting of troops only without the extra problems and delays of guns, horses and stores.[24] This was perhaps a somewhat unfair criticism, as unlike their state owned continental counterparts, British railways were largely private companies. It could also be argued that this was only a concern for European warfare. Rarely were railways available during the British army's colonial campaigns, and the likelihood of the army being significantly involved in a European war was considered slim.

---

23  Most notably Sir Patrick MacDougall's *Modern Warfare as Influenced by Modern Artillery* published in 1864.
24  Brackenbury, Henry, 'The Influence of Modern Improvements upon Strategy', *St Paul's: A Monthly Magazine*, (141) Volume 3 (March 1869), p.704.

He also highlighted the importance of the telegraph, using the example of the recent conflict between Prussia and Austria, where the Prussian King and the General Staff had been in constant contact with the Headquarters of the three army corps. Again, this was subject to attack by the enemy but he pointed out that in this case it was quick and easy to repair, unlike railroads. Another technological advance he noted was the use of steam to power shipping which now negated the need to wait for a favourable wind before landing or collecting troops, and had the obvious effect of speeding such transportation. Brackenbury used such advances in technology to once again press for improvement in the education of officers. An officer who understood and could apply such technologies would be able to move his troops around rapidly so as to increase the chance of catching his enemy off guard. This was the strategy that was now important and Brackenbury supported his views with the words of General Sir Charles Napier: "An ignorant general is a murderer. All brave men confide in the knowledge that he pretends to possess, and when the death-trial comes, their generous blood flows in vain". Brackenbury did sound a note of optimism, stating that he felt such things were beginning to be understood: "The day is not far distant when a man who combines ability with study may make certain of a career in the British army".[25]

His only other foray into the field of tactical thought in any considerable way was his lecture to the Royal United Service Institute, which was later published. 'The Tactics of the Three Arms as Modified to meet the requirements of the Present Day', looked at the recent improvements in technology and weaponry and how they had affected tactics. Brackenbury started by simply defining the object of a battle which in his view was, "... to break down the enemy's moral force, and to sustain the moral force of our own troops". He continued by saying that "It is better to kill fifty men in an enemy battalion, if that makes the rest run away, than to kill a hundred men if the rest stand firm". Although sounding somewhat simplistic its accuracy cannot be questioned. The simplest way to achieve this was "... to obtain the greatest possible development of accurate fire".[26] This was made easier by the new developments such as rifled artillery and both breech loading artillery and rifles. Such increased firepower made it difficult to maintain the 'moral power' of your own troops and the solution to this was discipline, war like training and confidence, the latter coming largely from the commander and the smoothness with which operations took place. He felt it was also necessary to have tactics in regards to formations determined before an operation as a sudden change in tactics could weaken morale. He then debated the tactics of attack and defence with examples of the Napoleonic Wars

---

25  Brackenbury, 'The Influence of Modern Improvements upon Strategy', p.713.
26  Brackenbury Henry, 'The Tactics of the Three Arms as Modified to meet the Requirements of the Present Day' *Royal United Service Institution Journal*, 17 (1874). It needs to be pointed out that the actual lecture took place 31st May 1873.

and the more pertinent campaigns of recent years particularly the Austro-Prussian War and the Franco-Prussian War. At this point the lecture became concentrated on the military history of these campaigns. The lecture was important to Brackenbury on several levels. Not only did it give him a fine opportunity to demonstrate his knowledge and intelligence in front of an audience of his peers, but he gives us clear evidence that he understood the modern tactical environment. Reading this lecture, and his aforementioned work on strategic improvements, it can never be argued that he was simply a 'colonial' soldier. This is why it is incorrect to place Henry Brackenbury entirely in the 'Imperialist' school of military thought. He clearly demonstrates a grasp of the requirements of a modern campaign. One might even go further and say that given this tactical and strategic understanding and his skill as an administrator that he showed that in the future he would be ideally suited for command in a major conflict.

This was as far down the road of theory and strategy that Brackenbury ever went. It might be suggested that Brackenbury's main reason for not writing a major theoretical work was because he saw no financial gain in such an enterprise. Perhaps it is more pertinent to say that he was too busy writing for the popular press, which it must be remembered was vital to his financial security. Another point that needs to be made is that such a work would not necessarily have suited his style of writing. Brackenbury was at his best when writing a descriptive narrative. Even some of his official reports take on such a style, especially when he felt it necessary to give an account of how the present situation had arisen by filling in the background.[27] The financial imperative of Brackenbury's writing needs to be understood. It gave him the money he needed to maintain a military career. Maintaining the lifestyle expected of an officer was an expensive business. If this money had not been forthcoming he may well have taken one of the many job opportunities outside of the army that he was offered.[28] His literary career also gave him a means of advancement as it was the ideas he promoted in his articles which brought him to the attention of political and military reformers with whom he became associated. The fact that he had built up a considerable reputation can be seen not only by the reviews of his work but in the fact that he started to be approached to write on military subjects at considerable rates of pay. Whilst the payment of 100 guineas for one article, paid by *The Illustrated London News*, was exceptional it does show the level to which his reputation as a writer had risen. Whilst the figure of £300, about £13,000 in modern money, for his book on the Ashanti War might seem insignificant given the amount of times it has been republished, it was a significant amount for a first book, even if he did have previous literary experience. Editors were attracted by his

---

27 A good example of this is the report Brackenbury wrote on the defence of India.
28 It is worth remembering that he had initial legal training as a notary before entering the army. *Some Memories of My Spare Time* recounts several offers he received to work in the City or in politics.

ability to engage with the non-military reader. Virtually all his articles appeared in the popular press rather than 'trade' journals such as *United Service Journal*. He had a clear narrative style which, whilst largely free of military jargon, was still technical enough to engage the military reader.

## Summary of literary career

His reputation as a writer moved him into new circles of associates, both socially and professionally. Socially he found himself mixing with some of the leading lights of the artistic scene of Victorian London, including Henry Irving, Arthur Sullivan and W.H. Russell. He was on good personal terms with John Blackwood, the editor of several periodicals, and continued this relationship with his nephew who succeeded him as editor. He also enjoyed good relations with other literary editors and proprietors including J.A. Froude, William Longman, and Edward Lawson (proprietor and editor of *The Daily Telegraph* and later Lord Burnham). The fact that he was writing for 'general' publication also gave him an advantage in that his articles were being read and considered by the leading politicians of the day, who whilst they might not read the *United Service Journal*, were likely to read *Fraser's Magazine*, *The Fortnightly Review*, or *Blackwood's Magazine*.[29] This undoubtedly benefited him, if only simply because of name recognition. It is doubtful that politicians were aware of many captains or majors who they did not know personally, yet Brackenbury's name may well have been familiar to many of them largely because of his writing.[30]

A fitting summary of the importance of his literary career can be found in the final pages of his book *Some Memories of My Spare Time*.

> I attribute to a great extent whatever measure of success I had in my profession to it. It is not merely that to my pen I owed the means, which enabled me to keep my head above water, to buy books, to travel, and to study theatres of campaigns and battlefields, and the administration of foreign armies. Writing for the press compelled constant observation and constant work, preventing the brain from rusting. It brought me into contact with superior minds. It was my studies for this outside work that enabled me to take up the Professorship of Military History. It was my work for the press that brought about that connection with the Red Cross Society, which gave me my first insights into administration. It was this Red Cross work and

---

29 In addition to which are the articles he wrote for the daily press, although it must be understood that many of these were written under a pseudonym so had little effect on his reputation.
30 The exact benefit of this is difficult to determine. The complication is that Brackenbury already knew personally many future Secretaries of State for War, such as Stanhope, Campbell-Bannerman and Lord Hartington. Certainly Cardwell was aware of his literary work, but had also come to know him because of his work for the National Aid Society during the Franco-Prussian War.

my work as a lecturer, outside my professional duties, which brought me under the notice of Sir Garnet Wolseley, and so gave me my first employment as a staff officer in the field.[31]

At the time of his writing the British army officer was still largely an amateur. Although slightly exaggerated, the idea that being a gentleman of breeding and background was more important than making a thorough study of your chosen profession was still the majority view. This was starting to change at the time Brackenbury was writing. The Crimean War 'shook' some of the complacency out of the officer corps and the realisation that technology was making 'intelligence' and study as important as moral and physical courage was growing. Men like Edward Hamley, C.B. Mayne, Francis Clery, W.H. James, J.F. Maurice, George Colley, and even Wolseley, were developing literary careers and were studying their profession. To borrow one of the phrases of D.S. Macdiarmid, this was 'the dawn of scientific soldiering'.[32]

---

31  Brackenbury, *Some Memories of My Spare Time*, pp.354-355.
32  Macdiarmid, D.S., *The Life of Lieut. General Sir James Moncrieff Grierson* (London: Constable & Co Ltd, 1923), p.63.

CHAPTER 6

# Army Reform

After his review of operations against Charleston Brackenbury was asked to write a series of articles for *Fraser's Magazine* and he proposed the subject of Army Reform. He produced five articles published between December 1866 and August 1867. They were radical, outspoken, and highly critical of governments and soldiers alike and, as Brackenbury admitted in one of the articles, likely to gain him the enmity of Horse Guards and the War Office. Military discipline limited the extent to which soldiers could criticise the military workings of the state, and he pushed the limits of what was acceptable. He was taking a considerable risk, perhaps even jeopardising his own career, by being critical of the very people who had control over his career advancement. Officers who write for public consumption have never been well thought of by the army, particularly when they are writing for financial gain. However this is not just confined to the military. Any junior member of an organisation who is publically critical will never be well liked. His lack of experience to date could be pointed to as an issue. His active service was limited to a year in India during the suppression of the mutiny. His administrative experience was as an Adjutant in the Royal Artillery and as an Assistant Instructor in Artillery at Woolwich. So in effect he was an inexperienced twenty-nine year old subaltern offering grand opinions on the state of the army both politically and militarily. It could be seen as great arrogance to presume to write such articles, but one must remember that the era was one when army reform was something of a hot topic. In the previous chapter we examined the wider literary career of Henry Brackenbury. In this chapter we will look specifically at the literary work of Henry Brackenbury that dealt with army reform.

## Background to reform

The Crimean War had highlighted the failures not only in the army but the system of management and control that existed. The situation had been so dire that during the war itself action had to be taken to reform the military system. At the time there had been several government departments and ministers responsible for the army. The Home Office was responsible for the army at home, along with the militia and yeomanry. The army abroad was the responsibility of the Colonial Office. There existed both a Secretary at War and a Secretary of War, and then there was also the Board of Ordnance which had separate responsibility for Artillery. As Brackenbury said,

> In one swoop, during war with one of the great powers, the whole of these immense interests were removed from the control of the officers in which they had hitherto been vested, and were consolidated or rather heaped together in a mass under a Secretary of State for War, who was made head of the new war department and the sole responsible officer for the entire administration of the army![1]

Many were still critical of the reforms that had taken place during and after the war. The timing of his articles is also interesting from the point of view that they came just after the conclusion of the Seven Weeks War, or Austro-Prussian War, in Europe where the balance of power had been drastically altered due to Prussia's crushing victory over Austria and her allies. Prussia had radically reformed her army and the relative ease with which she had defeated Austria had caused shockwaves throughout Europe. This in turn gave impetus to those who wished to reform the British Army and was the start of a decade or more of admiration for Prussian military reforms.

## 'Military Reform'

The date at which the articles on army reform were published by *Fraser's* is also significant because they predate Edward Cardwell's entry to the War Office and the commencement of the series of army reforms that collectively became known as the Cardwell Reforms. Not only do they predate Cardwell but also Brackenbury's association with Wolseley. The significance of the articles are that they mark Brackenbury as a radical and passionate army reformer in his own right and were published at a time when debate was still going on and interest was high in the matter of army reform. Given the circumstances abroad at that moment and the fact that

---

1   Brackenbury, Henry, 'Military Reform: Part V', *Fraser's Magazine*, Volume 76 (August 1867), pp.206-207.

Brackenbury was being paid essential for his military knowledge in his literary work it would have been surprising had he not written on the matter of army reform.

The actual writing of the articles brought him into conflict with his editor Mr Froude, not because of the highly controversial nature of them, but due to their length. Brackenbury became a little annoyed with this, particularly as he had originally been told that "If, therefore, you like to go on and enlarge your present article to double its size you can do so".[2] Although Brackenbury later recorded that he was grateful for his constructive criticism, he seems to have had several disagreements along the way. Perhaps some of this stemmed from the fact that he found it difficult to get close to Mr Froude who, according to Brackenbury, was a very private man. When Froude went to Ireland in March 1867 the Rev. Charles Kingsley took over as editor on a temporary basis, himself a published author of some note best remembered for his books *Alton Locke, Westward Ho!* and *The Water-Babies*. Brackenbury found Kingsley easier to get on with, particularly on a personal level, and they developed a strong friendship which lasted until Kingsley's death in 1875. Kingsley was much more supportive and encouraging of Brackenbury than Froude had been. That is not to say that Froude had been discouraging but had been more content to concentrate on the negative rather than the positive. Whilst this is undoubtedly part of an editor's 'art' it did not suit Brackenbury, who at this stage in his literary career needed encouragement more than criticism, even if it was constructive. For example Brackenbury later wrote that Kingsley always ended his letters with the friendly term 'Yours ever', "which from an editor does so much more to get the best out of a contributor than the cold 'Yours faithfully' of Froude".[3] This might sound a very minor point but one must remember the circumstances of the time. He was still very much finding his way as a writer. It also hints to a slight uncertainty and insecurity over his work at this stage. Whilst always giving the impression of great self-confidence one occasionally sees Brackenbury's need to be assured, normally in private, that he is doing the right thing. This becomes apparent in some of his later correspondence. Perhaps what he needed at this stage in his career from a publisher was reassurance and encouragement rather than criticism, no matter how well intentioned it was. Having said that, many years later he looked back at Froude's advice and was grateful.

Whilst Kingsley was encouraging about the quality of his work he sounded a note of caution regarding the effectiveness of his articles.

> You will do very little good, I warn you, because beside the military party which will wish to keep things as they are, the whole of the dissenting Radical party will be opposed to any real reform of the army. They are

---

[2] Brackenbury, Henry, *Some Memories of My Spare Time* (London: William Blackwood & Sons, 1909), p.41.
[3] Brackenbury, *Some Memories of My Spare Time*, p.43.

glad enough to revile its faults, but would be sorry to see them amended, lest it should become strong and popular. Moreover, you will not mend Sandhurst till you mend the education given at schools. Sandhurst lads' time is taken up there in learning what they ought to have learnt at school. What Sandhurst wants is discipline and public spirit. The former can be got. The latter not till a great war, which will make the officer again necessary and valuable in the eyes of the people.[4]

However at the time he was writing interest in Army reform was at the highest it had been for many years. In his articles he mentions many debates in the House of Commons that had recently taken place on such matters and indeed uses them as a starting point for his articles. That was why such articles were written for a popular magazine in the public domain. Brackenbury stated in his first article that the impetus for reform would have to come from outside the army due to limits of military discipline and the suspicion with which army officers were treated. He continued that the debates that were had in the professional journals, such as the *United Service Journal*, were largely academic as they were read purely by those who already had a keen interest in military reform: In short 'preaching to the converted'. By writing in a popular magazine he reached a wider audience. Whilst few politicians would read the *United Service Journal*, a great deal more were likely to read *Fraser's Magazine*.

The first article set the scene regarding military reform describing the problems with bringing the matter to the public attention. On this matter Brackenbury wrote that "In fact it is only under the pressure of some excitement that the condition of the army, and the welfare of the troops composing it, can command any attention from the public". Brackenbury spoke his mind during this series of articles, often being highly critical of governments and soldiers alike. He was using these articles, in a magazine within the public rather than the military domain, to urge that military reform would have to come from outside the army. The main problem that Brackenbury saw was the over-centralisation of the military machine; far too much responsibility, and therefore work, devolved on one man. Brackenbury used the early deaths of Secretaries of State for War, Lord Herbert and Sir George Cornewall Lewis, as examples of the extreme pressure of the office.[5] This was a prophetic statement as both Cardwell and Stanhope would also die relatively young largely as a result of the exhausting work of a long stay at the War Office. Brackenbury's objections were not a defence of the old system, where he believed there had been too many people involved. He did however think that it had gone too far the other

---

4   Brackenbury, *Some Memories of My Spare Time*, p.44. The letter is quoted in the aforementioned book but has not survived amongst his private papers.
5   Brackenbury, Henry, 'Military Reform: Part V', p.209.

way in endowing one man with such demanding responsibilities. This would be borne out by what happened during the tenure of both Cardwell and Stanhope where the organisation of the War Office was returned to a more balanced distribution, even if this did cement the supremacy of the Secretary of State over the Commander-in-Chief. One of Brackenbury's main points was the growth of administrative departments, pointing out that a large proportion of the army estimates "... goes to maintain an army of clerks in London, who only obstruct and delay business instead of furthering it".[6] Whilst this has been an age-old cry of the soldier about civilian administration, it does have some legitimacy in the period in question given the huge reduction in the number of departments, but not the number of administrators, responsible for the army. Brackenbury's skill lay in administration, although up to this point it had only be seen in his own regiment rather than the grander appointments that were to come, so he more than most soldiers recognised its importance. His complaints about bureaucracy should be seen in that light.

The success of the Prussian Army during the 1860s and 1870s meant that their unique military system became the envy of much of Europe. This was particularly true in Britain where many sought to copy it almost in its entirety.[7] Brackenbury was less enthusiastic about the Prussian system than many of his contemporaries. Whilst he saw there were lessons to be learnt from the Prussians, it was clear to him that it was for the large part incompatible with the demands placed on the British Army. One of the key benefits of Prussian success in his eyes was the debate it had stimulated. As he wrote, "Just at present the public mind is more awake to military affairs than it has been for years past. The nation has been startled out of its slumber by the extraordinary successes of the Prussian Army, and has learnt that those successes have been due to provision and forethought". Brackenbury urged that rather than adopt the Prussian system in its entirety "we must search and carefully examine how far the Prussian system would harmonise with the institutions of this country".[8]

Whilst he thought there were problems he did accept that "there is doubtless something very captivating in the results of the Prussian organisation".[9] He recognised that it had been efficient and extremely cost effective, "a mere fraction of our expenditure on the Crimean campaign". The problem in his mind was that the system was reliant on compulsory service. This was totally unacceptable politically,

---

6  Brackenbury, 'Military Reform: Part V', p.212.
7  Amongst these were Colonel Lonsdale Hale, F.N. Maude, and Charles Brackenbury, Henry's brother. There was slowly a reaction to this movement which united Ian Hamilton and Garnet Wolseley for probably the only time, in condemning the 'slavish imitations from the Prussians' as Hamilton put it in *The Fighting of the Future* (London: Kegan Paul, 1885), p.16.
8  Brackenbury, 'Military Reform: Part I', *Fraser's Magazine*, Volume 74 (December 1866), p.684.
9  Brackenbury, 'Military Reform: Part I', p.684.

and Brackenbury argued, liberal reform was also making it socially unacceptable.[10] However to Brackenbury there was a much wider problem than conscription, which concerned the demands that each nation placed upon its army. Both armies had the objective of defence of the realm, but this meant very different things. As Brackenbury explained,

> With us the realm means not only England, not only Great Britain and Ireland, but immense tracts of territory in Asia, in Africa, in America, in Australasia, territories whose two hundred millions of inhabitants are no less than seven times as numerous as those of the United Kingdom itself, and to some of which the mere journey occupies months, during which the voyager is out of all possible communication with home.

Service in India for instance, which was where nearly 60,000 of the British army was stationed, would be impractical for the conscript soldier as "the training of a recruit at home to fit him for foreign service, together with his voyages out and home, would swallow up a large portion of his entire term of service".[11]

Even in 1866 Brackenbury was asking for a formal definition of the duties of the army, explaining to his readers that no formal preparation could be made until one existed. He would again plead this case when Head of the Intelligence Branch, and for the same reason, namely so that plans for the defence of Great Britain and Ireland could be prepared. Whilst Brackenbury was dubious about the possibility, and indeed likelihood, of invasion he was practical enough to realise that it could happen. He questioned the policy of relying solely on the Royal Navy to prevent it, using the recent Battle of Lissa to prove that naval superiority was never assured.[12] Brackenbury realised that with the many commitments in the empire it was impossible for an army of 150,000 or more to be kept in Britain on the off-chance of invasion. His answer was to reform the reserve forces. He envisaged a well trained body of reserves, militia and volunteers who if invasion ever happened would form the basis of an army to resist it. It is interesting to note that in 1866 he is in many ways envisaging the creation of the Territorial Army, which was not created until 1907. The idea that former or part-time soldiers would be asked to defend against the cream of an invading army does sound a little strange, but Brackenbury envisaged a reserve force that would be trained along the principles of the Prussian system. They would be grouped into local formations that would train together for part

---

10   It is worth remembering that Prussia was in fact a smaller and less industrialised country than the United Kingdom. The population was about two-thirds that of the United Kingdom and military expenditure was half that of the United Kingdom. Brackenbury, 'Military Reform: Part I', p.686.
11   Brackenbury, 'Military Reform: Part I', p.687.
12   At the Battle of Lissa in 1866 the more modern and numerically superior Italian fleet had been virtually wiped out by a supposedly inferior Austrian fleet. The battle had added significance in that it was the first major engagement between ironclad warships.

of the year. Reservists, volunteers and militia would form brigades and divisions that would not merely exist on paper but would be capable of taking the field fully supported by artillery, engineers and other support services. In his view they must to all intents and purposes be professional, if not full time, soldiers; as he wrote "we do not entrust the cure of our diseases to an amateur physician, nor the legal defence of our property to an amateur student of law, and we cannot entrust our honour entirely to the keeping of amateur soldiers".[13]

This then, in Brackenbury's view, was the lesson that could and indeed should be learnt from the Prussian system, namely that a reserve was not only desirable but also essential. A key problem with keeping reservists up to standard was that they found difficulty in gaining civilian employment. This was understandable as employers were hardly likely to want to employ someone who could be away training part of the year or could be recalled to the colours instantly. In a later issue on military reform Brackenbury did respond to this problem, and suggested that as many as possible should be found employment where the Government was the employer. His idea was sensible and was formed no doubt as a solution to the fact that compulsory service was impossible, but it had many problems. Perhaps this was a good case of Brackenbury the theorist, not being entirely realistic. The Government would never have supported an idea, which by its very nature would have been extremely expensive, albeit not as expensive as regular troops. His ideas were also perhaps a little before their time as at this stage there was no reserve to speak of. Only after the Cardwell Reforms did one begin to emerge. It also envisaged the creation of storehouses, as places where supplies could be kept and the Army would congregate to meet any possible invasion, some twenty years before the creation of the 'Stanhope storehouses'. Given his close working relationship with Stanhope one cannot help but think that Brackenbury must have played an important role in influencing their creation. All this is evidence of a soldier and officer who was thinking seriously about his profession and the ways in which it could be improved. If sometimes the 'theory' seemed a little naïve and unrealistic his lack of experience and relative youth – he was only twenty-nine when these articles were published – can explain that. At this stage he had no real experience outside his own regiment, and at this point all he had seen of war was his short period in India during the mutiny. Despite this it is remarkable how many of the ideas he put forward during this period were to be put into practice many years later.

---

13   Brackenbury, 'Military Reform: Part I', p.689.

## Soldiers' welfare

This is one subject on which he was surprisingly active in his articles on military reform. Brackenbury was later criticised by Wolseley and Ian Hamilton for not caring about the conditions and welfare of the common solider.[14] Yet the poor conditions that the soldier endured were a constant theme throughout Brackenbury's five articles on military reform, with one being dedicated entirely to the discussion of this subject. However Brackenbury's main concern was improving the quality of the recruit and therefore the efficiency of the army. Whether this was his only motivation is impossible to know, but it rings true of a man who was constantly looking towards making the army a more efficient organisation. Whatever his motives he did suggest ideas which would have considerably improved the lot of the common soldier. Some were later to be adopted, most notably the idea of shorter service and the abolition of flogging, together with the improvement of barrack rooms and facilities, which although they were never raised to the standard that Brackenbury had wanted, were dramatically improved during Stanhope's period as Secretary of State for War.

Brackenbury's starting point was the very real problem of recruiting, which had long existed.[15] At the time not only was there no discernible reserve but it was often impossible to meet the established level of the regular army. To Brackenbury the main problem in recruiting the necessary numbers were the conditions of service. It was also a constant theme of his articles that this was also discouraging a better class of recruit from coming forward. The problems were a combination of harsh conditions of service and the social stigma attached to the army, but also in Brackenbury's view there was no prospect of advancement. One of Brackenbury's more radical inducements to service was the suggestion that what would now be referred to as a quota system should be introduced where every fourth or fifth officer's commission should be reserved for a non-commissioned officer.[16] It was perhaps radical ideas such as this that led to the Duke of Cambridge to refer to him as "a very dangerous man".

---

14  In fairness it must be added that both men had their own motivations. Wolseley was at the time falling out with all the members of the 'ring' and had become rather bitter about their attitudes towards him. His relationship with Brackenbury was at this time rather strange. Reading his campaign journal and the letters he wrote to his wife during this period one can see instances where he bitterly attacks Brackenbury on one page and on the next is full of praise for him. By this stage Wolseley was suffering from ill health. Ian Hamilton, although a personal friend of Brackenbury, was quite often extremely critical of him as a way of attacking Wolseley who he despised, and blamed for his lack of advancement.

15  As Brackenbury wrote his first article a Royal Commission chaired by Lord Dalhousie was looking at the subject of recruiting. The recommendation led to the Reserve Act in 1867, which created a paper reserve that didn't exist in practice until the implementation of short service, as part of the Cardwell Reforms. Brackenbury was highly critical of the Royal Commission for ignoring such matters as food and living quarters as disincentives for recruitment.

16  On 5th March 1855 *The Times'* editorial had suggested commissions for NCOs, but had refrained

There were more conventional inducements to service also suggested by Brackenbury, such as improved pay, rations and living conditions. On the subject of pay he recommended an increase in the basic pay but he was more concerned with ending many of the needless 'stoppages', so that the soldier had more money in his pocket.[17] He also used evidence to support the idea that this would reduce drunkenness, as the prevailing wisdom was that soldiers drank largely because they didn't have enough food. Another monetary inducement was the improvement of the army pension, which at that time stood at 8d a day after twenty-one years' service.[18] The treatment of retired soldiers had recently been national news after the appearance in *The Times* of an article entitled 'Waterloo and the Workhouse'. Brackenbury wrote of a similar tale of a soldier who had served heroically throughout the Peninsular Campaign, had fought at the Battle of New Orleans, where he saved the life of a wounded officer, and subsequently the Battle of Waterloo.[19] He had then gone on to serve in the West Indies and in the Portuguese Expedition of 1827–28. After leaving the Army he worked for the Dockyard Police. He and his wife were now in their seventies and reduced to living on 10d a day. Brackenbury finished off by saying, "Eight sieges and battles, including Waterloo; two forlorn hopes, a wounded limb; a commanding officer's life saved; twenty-one years services in Spain, Belgium, America, the West Indies, and Portugal; and tenpence a day for a reward!" Whilst Brackenbury's comments were of an emotional nature his true colours, namely the efficiency of the army and the quest for a better class of recruit, were on display later in the article when he wrote that, "This matter of pension is of vital importance; and if we want soldiers, we must treat it in no niggardly spirit, remembering that every pensioner who goes back into civil life leavens his own neighbourhood with good or bad opinions of the army".[20] Brackenbury's recommendation was that the pension should start at no less than a shilling a day, returning it to the pre 1847 amount, which could rise to as much as 1s 6d per day for soldiers with good conduct or service before the enemy. This illustrates the intelligence with which Brackenbury

---

from setting a fixed number. One wonders if Brackenbury was even aware of this editorial. To an extent this was already done in the French Army, where a large number of officers came from the ranks. Many of the conservatives within the British army, most notably the Duke of Cambridge, thought this was a key reason for the failure of the French army against the Prussians, who of course were officered by 'gentlemen'.

17 'Stoppages' was the term used to refer to money deducted at source for messing and washing expenses. This meant that whilst an infantryman's pay was 7s 7d a week, after stoppages he only had 2s 11d.
18 Before the Army Service Act of 1847 the pension had been 1s a day after twenty-one years' service.
19 The fact that the soldier in question served at both New Orleans and Waterloo is remarkable in itself. The former took place on 8th January 1815 and the latter on 18th June 1815. Given the travelling time between America and Europe, it is understandable that few men were present at both battles.
20 Both quotations are from Brackenbury, 'Military Reform: Part II', *Fraser's Magazine*, Volume 75 (March 1867), p.289.

wrote. Rather than making the case purely in the emotional vein, as so many did, he also made the case practically, by showing that the ill-treatment of soldiers, and a miserly pension were in effect bad public relations for the army. It created a negative view and hampered recruitment and, particularly for Brackenbury, it prevented the recruitment of a better class of soldier.

Brackenbury devoted a whole article to military discipline. Again this was a popular subject at the time, due to the case of Private Robert Slim who had died during a flogging. Debates in the House of Commons, during June 1867, had seen a motion passed by one vote to abolish flogging, which the government had ignored. The resolution had caused panic in the government and, in the words of Brackenbury, "In three successive nights, the Secretary of State for War enunciated three distinct and totally different policies".[21] The result was that flogging had been abolished in time of peace except for mutiny and insubordination with violence. In itself Brackenbury felt that little good would come of this in terms of recruitment, but he argued that officers would now be more inclined to remove soldiers from the ranks for persistent bad behaviour, and as a consequence a better class of recruit would be essential. Flogging was just one matter he touched on. He went into detail about the unfairness of the present regimental court system, the unsuitability of many officers for the task of presiding over such courts, and the general illegality of them when compared with the civil courts.[22]

Brackenbury did not only want a better class of recruit, but he also believed that he knew where such men could be obtained.

> We have a race of hardy villagers and stalwart country lads fond of sport, of all games that require pluck and skill, a quick eye, a strong hand, and a fleet foot, to whom the spice of danger enhances the pleasure of such games as football and cricket, and who are ready to join in anything promising a chance of adventure. It would seem that a soldier's life is exactly the career suited to such as these; but the fact stares us in the face that these men will not come in any numbers to the army.[23]

Brackenbury believed that if his recommendations in terms of pay, pension and conditions were enacted then such men would join the army. Whilst this would have removed many of the drawbacks to service it still ignored the social stigma attached to the army, which was only partly to do with money. There was still a wider dislike of militarism in any form that could not so easily be solved. There is no doubt that Brackenbury's recommendations would have improved the lot of the

---

21 Brackenbury, 'Military Reform: Part IV', *Fraser's Magazine*, Volume 75 (June 1867), p.743.
22 The details of his arguments are too extensive for this chapter. See Brackenbury, 'Military Reform: Part IV', pp.743-749.
23 Brackenbury, 'Military Reform: Part I', p.692.

soldier and would have helped recruitment but the type of recruit he sought would not be induced purely by such changes.

## Chief of Staff

His first article on 'Military Reform' had touched on War Office organisation but it was in the fifth that he set out many of his key ideas and reforms. It was here that he first championed the idea of a Chief of Staff, an important point to remember given that he was much criticised in 1890 when it was suggested that he put forward this idea purely for personal gain. To him such an appointment was obvious. It would reduce the substantial workload of the Commander-in-Chief and Secretary of State for War, and would give the army much needed planning and strategy. If nothing else should have been copied from the Prussian successes it was surely this.[24] He recommended many alterations to the War Office administration, some of which he would enact as Director General of Ordnance between 1899–1904. A large problem in his opinion was the matter of supervision and control. It was impossible for one man, the Secretary of State, to do this for both the civilian and military side. The Commander-in-Chief was rapidly losing control over subordinate militarily controlled departments, a problem that attempts to rein in the Duke of Cambridge would exacerbate. There was a gap where a Chief of Staff should be. This lack of coordination and supervision was part of the reason for so many Royal Commission and committees being established, a situation that would continue throughout the century. Writing in 1867 Brackenbury stated that in the last eleven years there had been:

> Seventeen Royal Commissions, eighteen Select Committees of the House of Commons, nineteen committees of officers within the War Office, besides thirty-five committees of military officers, making a total of no less than eighty-nine committees and commissions, which have been held to consider one question or another, and in the majority of cases their reports have not been attended to at all, or at most only partially acted upon.[25]

## Parliament and the Army

Brackenbury returned to the subject of army reform when he wrote two articles for *Saint Paul's Magazine* in 1868. The first was on 'Parliament and Army Reform' and

---

24  It is worth remembering the words of the Royal Commission on the War in South Africa who stated that if the recommendations of the Hartington Commission of 1890 had been enacted the disasters of South Africa could have been largely avoided. Key in this was the creation of a Chief of Staff.
25  Brackenbury, 'Military Reform: Part V', p.211.

concentrated solely on the issue of the purchasing of commissions, a practice which was still in place. This was written in the last months of the Conservative government, and thus before Cardwell and the Liberal Party came to office. Brackenbury was confident that the new government would abolish the purchase system. He noted that abolition now attracted more support in parliament than previously and that the press was now largely in favour. Brackenbury was very clear:

> The whole issue lies in this. Is the army to be a profession or not? Are the officers to enter it with a view to making it the pursuit of their lives, and devoting their entire energies to military service; or are they to enter for a brief space as a pastime, and therefore, as a matter of course, not to look seriously upon their duties?[26]

This view is similar to that taken by Cardwell a few years later when he wrote that, "Our principle is that the officers shall be made for the Army. Their principle is that the Army is made for officers".[27] Both comments fitted into a wider feeling of a growth in professional society that occurred during the late Victorian era. For Brackenbury to suggest that 'soldiering' was a profession was to put it on a par with the medical and legal profession. It was therefore something that one should study and take seriously rather than to be seen as a duty of social status, or as Brackenbury put it, "a pastime". Brackenbury also expressed a rather modern view about the nature of 'officership'. Many who defended purchase did so in terms of social character, as he put it 'pluck and courage'. Brackenbury espoused the view that courage before the enemy was only part of an officer's duty; "the duties of war are rare and far between, and the duties of peace are constant, and ever at hand".[28] It is very similar to the current creed of the British Army that states there is more to being an officer than simply behaving like an officer. Brackenbury's point was that there was far more to being a good officer than many believed. It was more than merely having natural leadership and courage, whether this came from social background or not. The army was a profession and it was Brackenbury's view that like any other profession it had to be studied and trained for and taken seriously. Active service played only a small part of an officer's life.

The second article was entitled 'Our Army as it is, and as it should be'. This was clearly written as a response to the Prussian success against the Austrians in 1866 which had stimulated much debate in the British press. In it he provided an overview of the 'evils' of the present military system. Once again he expressed

---

26 Brackenbury, Henry, 'Parliament and Army Reform', *Saint Paul's: A Monthly Magazine* 78 Volume 2, (July 1868), p.457. Although the article was on the purchase system he did take the opportunity to reiterate his views on short service and commissions for NCOs.
27 Bond, Brian 'The Late Victorian Army', *History Today*, 11:9 September 1961, p.619.
28 Brackenbury, 'Parliament and Army Reform', p.457.

the view that the greatest problem facing the army was recruiting and once again Brackenbury took up the subject of promotion through the ranks.[29] This time he argued that such a move was the natural progression from the opening up of the military colleges to anyone, rather than merely to those who were highborn. If there was no longer anything other than money preventing anyone becoming an officer surely, he argued, those who already had experience of the army were ideal candidates. In this article he referred to the fact that those few NCOs who were commissioned as officers were often treated, "as a kind of outcast from the society of his brother officers ... if a third of the officers had thus risen, such social ostracism could no longer exist. And, indeed, it is probable that a very superior class of men would be promoted".[30] The promotion of officers through the ranks was a continual theme in Brackenbury's writing on the state of the army. The two main benefits he saw were that it would improve the class of recruit if there was a reasonable possibility of a commission and that it would further improve the efficiency of the army because such men would naturally have a more professional attitude. There is a question as to whether either of the desired effects would have occurred, but Brackenbury made a compelling case that was supported by the example of the French Army where such a system was in place. At this time the French Army was still held up as an example by many in the British military establishment, in a way that the Prussians were starting to be at this time and would further be after their success in 1870. At the same time Brackenbury also suggested the possibility that in the future 'Hindoos', as he called them, might even be commissioned as officers in the British Army or the possibility that this would be part of an Imperial Army including all the races of the Empire. Again this is an extremely radical suggestion, perhaps even more so than NCOs becoming officers and raises questions of race and ethnicity in the Victorian age, which are far beyond the scope of this book.

One possible drawback to promotion through the ranks was clearly money. An officer's pay was insufficient to meet the array of expenses that occurred whilst still providing a living wage. Thus some form of private income was always necessary. The reason for this was that officers' pay had not been altered for quite some time. Again this reflected the 'amateur ideal' that officers should not be making money out of serving the crown. Competitive rates of pay with other professions were unacceptable, partly because of cost but also because of the fear that this would create a professional military spirit which was considered by Victorian society to be both unacceptable and dangerous. The problem was that, whilst pay had not been altered since 1806, Brackenbury estimated that an officer's costs had increased by 50% over

---

29  This article appeared after the Royal Commission on recruiting had been published, but before it became clear that the recommendations were to be largely ignored.
30  Brackenbury, Henry, 'Our Army as it is, and as it should be', *Saint Paul's: A Monthly Magazine* 40 Volume 1 February 1868, p.610.

the same period.[31] Obviously any improvement in pay was dependent upon the abolition of the purchase system otherwise professional officers would be barred by financial limitations.

It was in this piece that he included some equally outspoken comments upon military expenditure. For those who wanted a reduction there was a simple alternative, namely the introduction of conscription. This would give the country a cheap standing army and a considerable trained reserve and would allow further adoption of elements of the Prussian system. Brackenbury realised that this was extremely unlikely; therefore the alternative was a more expensive, smaller, volunteer army. In this case the only way in which expenditure could be reduced was "by placing all our military institutions, recruiting and promotion especially, on a sound and honest footing". Whilst his words alluded to the corruption that undoubtedly existed, especially when it came to recruitment, it was more importantly a call for efficiency. He felt that the number of officers could safely be reduced and that the double administration of the War Office and Horse Guards could be ended. To an extent the latter was achieved during the Cardwell Reforms, but the reduction in expenditure was negligible. The much wider point was that without conscription an army adequate for home and imperial defence would always be an expensive operation. As Brackenbury wrote, "If Englishmen will not pay in person for the defence of England's possessions, they must pay in purse".[32]

Brackenbury was, in this way at least, one of the imperialist school of writers, who felt that the uniqueness of the British position and their differing commitments called for an altogether different military system. He therefore did not fall into the trap of many military writers of wanting to copy excessively the practices of one of the great military powers of Europe. There were parts that Brackenbury admired in the Prussian system, namely their reservist system and localisation, and similarly parts he admired in the French system, most notably promotion through the ranks. His key aim was always to promote reforms that would, in his view, increase the efficiency of the army. That such recommendations were often radical was not necessarily his intent. Like Wolseley, being seen as a reformer and a 'radical' he was often associated with the Liberal party and liberal views. However neither had any affinity with the Liberal Party, indeed Brackenbury grew to hate them for the stall in his career they had caused. He was basically a conservative both politically and socially.[33] So when he recommended liberal and radical policies it was merely in what he saw to be the best interests of the efficiency and effectiveness of the army.

---

31   Brackenbury, 'Our Army as it is, and as it should be', p.611. The pay scales for officers had been set in 1806 and would remarkably not alter until 1st January 1914.
32   Brackenbury, 'Our Army as it is, and as it should be', p.613.
33   Brackenbury's political conservatism is supported by the fact that he was once approached to become the chief election agent for the Conservative Party.

Yet he was classed as a radical reformer, most notably by the Duke of Cambridge, and was therefore "a very dangerous man".

The many reforms Brackenbury proposed would have had a profound impact upon the British Army. It would have been intriguing to see the result of many of them. Many might not have achieved the desired effect. Many seemed strange and usual, whilst some seemed just like common sense. However even the more unusual ideas, such as a quota system regarding commissions for NCOs or the creation of an Imperial Army with all colours and races working together, were so well presented and carefully reasoned that it would take either a brave man or a foolish one to dismiss them as 'nonsense'. This is surely testament to the quality of Brackenbury's ability. His skill at writing, at reasoning and intellectual argument, meant that his work took the debate to another level, one where emotion and pride in the army were combined with practical ideas regarding efficiency and economy. Given this it is no wonder that he was in such demand as a writer.

# Chapter 7

# Brackenbury's Women

The slightly unusual title for this chapter in many ways speaks for itself. Although this book is primarily concerned with the life and career of a soldier it would be wrong to ignore his personal life. This chapter will look at the relationship he had with women. He was married twice but there appear to have been numerous affairs, only one of which we have direct evidence of. In many ways his actions were not uncommon for the era. A number of high profile careers during this period were destroyed by sexual scandal such as Hector Macdonald, Valentine Baker and Charles à Court Repington to name but three. There were however others who managed to keep their affairs out of the press or the divorce courts and continued to have successful carers, such as Sir John French and Sir John Cowans and even, one might say, Sir Henry Brackenbury. One has to be very careful when looking back at such matters and interpreting too much from comments of the time. A good example of this can be seen in the case of Sir Henry Evelyn Wood, where many historians have claimed homosexual tendencies on the basis of a misquoted letter.[1] In the case of Sir Henry Brackenbury we have the problem that a great deal of the information about his sexual indiscretions comes from the pen of Lord and Lady Wolseley. The latter was an incurable gossip, as even a cursory glance at their correspondence illustrates, and Lord Wolseley indulged her by keeping her informed of all that occurred.

Although not wishing to delve into psychology one has to wonder about the relationship Brackenbury had with his mother. Already a widow before she married William Brackenbury, she spent most of her second marriage nursing her invalid husband. She had eight children and lived to see six of them predecease her. Whilst this was not uncommon for the era, it does not lessen the impact and one wonders what consequence it had for her relationship with her two remaining children Charles and Henry. Henry wrote little about his mother, briefly mentioning her death in 1870 as the reason he was delayed during his Franco-Prussian War

---

[1] For more on the sexual scandals of the late Victorian British Army see Beckett, Ian, *The Victorians at War* (London: Hambeldon, 2003) Chapter 8.

experiences. What we can draw from this is difficult to say, but it surely had some impact on his general relationship with women.

Henry Brackenbury married relatively young, in an era when army officers did not tend to married until they were thirty. In 1861 at the age of twenty-three he married Emilia Morley, née Haswell, and widow of Reginald Morley. Eight years Brackenbury's senior the marriage is believed to have been motivated largely by money. In short he married her to pay off his mounting debts. Exactly how long they continued to live together is unclear. The first evidence to point to their separation is a letter from Lord to Lady Wolseley in August 1875, but the likelihood is they were apart long before this.[2] Exactly what happened and why they separated can only ever be speculation. They had no children and one wonders how much that had to do with their marital problems. Wolseley suggested that Brackenbury immediately knew he had made a mistake, but we know no more than that. Regardless of the reasons for the failure of the marriage it is clear from her letters to Henry that she must have been a very difficult woman to live with. Of the few letters that have survived most deteriorate into little short of a rant. There is an interesting comparison to be made about the letters between the two. Henry's letters were very matter-of-fact and practical; one might even say business-like, whereas Emilia's were extremely emotional. In fact it was probably the tone of Henry's letters that added to her infuriation, and consequently she responded with emotion. Although it might have more to do with a matter of style, there is no love or emotion in Henry's letters, no warmth and no sense that he considered the marriage had any future. The latter might explain his practical and business-like approach in his letter, where he was simply trying to make the best of a bad situation.

Whatever her complaints regarding his behaviour she had no grounds to complain about his generosity in later years when his finances were in a better state. In 1897, after five years in India where the low costs and generous salary had improved his financial position, he wrote to Emilia, or Milly as he always called her, to discuss finances. Henry wrote to her that "I cannot afford to allow you more than £600 a year".[3] Exactly what his income was since his return from India we do not know, but to place the figure in context he had been paid £1,900 a year whilst in India. The figure of £600 was generous and equates to about £34,000 in modern money. Out of this she was expected to maintain the 'family house'. Their relationship at this stage is rather strange. Whilst they had long since ceased to live together it does appear that he still spent some weekends with her at this stage. At this time their relationship was on the verge of collapse. The modern reader might ask the question why they did not simply divorce. Even if one takes away the social stigma attached to

---

2    Lord to Lady Wolseley, 22nd August 1875, Wolseley Papers, Central Library, Hove. A comment by Hilda Brackenbury alludes to 1872 as being the time they stopped living together.
3    Henry Brackenbury to Emilia Brackenbury, 18th August 1897, private collection.

divorce during this era there was another more practical reason, namely a divorcee could not hold the Queen's commission. Had he divorced it would have been the end of his military career.

Emilia wrote to him in emotional terms saying "I realise that the sight of me is loathsome to you and so I yield to the other option that commends itself most to you and go out of your sight. It is the most dignified for me". This is a dramatic statement and had nothing to do with Henry's letter to which she was responding. This had merely talked of her moving to a new house in the country, something which she had originally proposed! She clearly had a lot of resentment, either justly or unjustly, for Henry by this stage, as the following extract makes clear:

> I have had much to forgive and freely forgiven, but what I cannot forgive is – what for want of a better expression – I call your social persecution of me ever since you have risen socially yourself, to see me ignored to begrudge me any share in your life and being content to see me treated with disrespect never taking me who as your wife you ought to call on, and only too glad if people did not call upon me, letting the world form the conclusion I was perhaps a drunken woman, or that you had made a bad alliance or that I was "only a woman you had kept" ... I know you never wish to see me again but in any house I live of my own you would always be welcomed by me. I know how tender you can be and a kind word has often soothed our fears of resentment.[4]

It is truly a remarkable letter which is extremely emotional and demonstrates a great deal of hurt feelings. Whether much of this was simply her imagination we cannot say. The idea that he was somewhat ashamed of her since he had risen socially, as Emilia put it, has something of a ring of truth about it and fits in with the social climbing and somewhat snobbish image of Henry Brackenbury. When she says she had much to forgive she obviously referred to his extra-marital affairs, and undoubtedly she was correct. However her next statement about social persecution is a little harder to understand. There is evidence to suggest that Henry shunned large social gatherings, but one wonders why he did not take her with him to the many dinners and weekends he spent with his close friends, such as Lord Lansdowne and Lord Lytton. Perhaps the age difference was starting to tell, with Henry in his early sixties and Emilia nearing seventy. One can over-analyse the wording but the fact that she says that he was happy to see her be ignored suggest the possibility that people were ignoring her anyway.

It is also interesting that she puts the phrase "only a woman you had kept" in quotation marks suggesting that it is something she has heard someone say in

---

4    Emilia Brackenbury to Henry Brackenbury, 10th August 1897, private collection.

reference to her. Henry's reply was remarkably calm and measured. Whilst she wrote with emotion he again stated the facts, as he saw them, calmly and plainly. The fact that he did not reply with emotion perhaps says as much about the way he felt about Emilia as it does his natural character. It can be assumed that he simply did not care anymore. What survives of her correspondence is in similar vein, and Henry appears simply to have had enough. That said, it must be pointed out that he had not been a good husband. The only person to write to Henry about his wife was his sister-in-law Hilda, the wife of the late Charles Brackenbury. One gathers from the letter that Emilia had shown her all the correspondence between them. Hilda Brackenbury wrote to Henry:

> I think it was inevitable with both your temperaments you could no longer live together, but you must not think all the suffering has been on your side ... Milly has been neglected for 25 years, even your friends I know have felt for her, while loving you. She had no children to take her mind from dwelling on her wrongs, and there is no denying that you were ashamed of her. Yet many men are tied to women far less presentable than Milly is and was.

This letter perhaps raises more questions than it answers. One wonders what 'suffering' Henry had been through as alluded to in the letter and why he was supposedly ashamed of her. The letter from Hilda Brackenbury went further and openly referred to his affairs.

> As to infidelity you know she has condoned that, and did not talk about it, but people found out (at Woolwich). You are not an exception, many men do the same but outwardly they show a sort of respect to the woman whom they once loved ... she has often said to me "I could bear anything of that sort if he would give me a kind word, and show me proper respect before others – I know that he is valuable to the world and I am not".[5]

The attributed words of Emilia Brackenbury again demonstrate her rather melodramatic nature. It is interesting to note that it appears that not only did Emilia know of his extra marital affairs but that she understood and accepted them. In return she wanted to be treated as a wife in public with respect and social status. Clearly this was not what Henry wanted and one wonders whether or not he was already living 'as man and wife' with the woman who would become the second Mrs Brackenbury. They married only a matter of months after Emilia's death in 1905.

We do not know how many relationships with other women that Henry had during his marriage to Emilia. We are led to believe by certain comments that there

---

5    Hilda Brackenbury to Henry Brackenbury, 21st August 1897, private collection.

were a considerable number. In only one case do we have direct evidence, and in another case we have what could at best be called circumstantial evidence. The one we know the most about occurred in Natal in 1875. This is referred to several times in the correspondence between Lord and Lady Wolseley. Exact dates are unclear but in June 1875 Wolseley wrote to his wife that "Brackenbury's affair goes on stronger than ever and I really believe that he and the lady concerned are deeply in love with one another".[6] The only problem was that the woman concerned was already married. Even worse than that she was married into the all-powerful Shepstone family, who virtually ran Natal. Helen Shepstone was the wife of Theophilus Shepstone Jnr, a noted lawyer and a Captain in the Royal Natal Carbineers Volunteers who would distinguish himself on active service during the Ninth Cape Frontier campaign and the Zulu War.[7] Wolseley's comments on the matter largely concern how the fallout of the affair could affect him. He was concerned that Theophilus had a reputation for being very jealous and was also renowned as a marksman. Wolseley clearly feared that if Theophilus found out about the affair then Brackenbury's life could be in danger. Indeed Brackenbury, usually so professional, was taking a very emotional approach without considering the repercussions that revelations about his affair could have upon Wolseley's mission to Natal. This supports the view that Brackenbury was genuinely in love and not thinking straight, as the effect of the shooting dead of a British officer by a colonial politician for an extra marital affair would have been news that would have spread throughout the empire. The scandal that might have followed such an event would have seriously damaged Wolseley's career also. Exactly why the relationship ended is unclear and it may well have continued until Brackenbury left Natal. Wolseley makes some interesting comments both on Brackenbury's marriage and Helen Shepstone. Of the latter he said that she was "... really a pretty woman with plenty of fun and wit". This he compared with Emilia Brackenbury whom he described by writing that "... really his wife is so dull that I am not surprised he is glad to be away from her".[8]

The other relationship he might have had is largely based upon guesswork and supposition. There is a little circumstantial evidence to suggest that he had an affair with Madame Canrobert, the wife of Marshal Francois Canrobert. The veteran French soldier had a much younger wife. When they married in 1863 he was fifty-four and she was twenty-five. Indeed she was less than a year younger than Brackenbury. Her full name was Leila Flora Canrobert, née MacDonald, and she was said to be a direct decedent of the Jacobite heroine Flora MacDonald. Henry

---

6   Lord Wolseley to Lady Wolseley, 22nd June 1875, Wolseley Papers.
7   Details of Helen Shepstone are very limited, and her exact age is unclear. It is believed she was born in 1873, making her about twenty-two during their relationship, whilst Henry was aged thirty-seven.
8   Lord Wolseley to Lady Wolseley, 22nd June 1875, Wolseley Papers.

Brackenbury and she would have many things in common other than both being British by birth. Both were children of army officers and both came from respectable but hardly wealthy families. They first met during the Franco-Prussian War and spent a lot of time together. That may well have been the start of a friendship but it is unlikely there was anything more than that at that time. However in future years they saw a lot of each other and there are two comments by the Wolseleys that suggest that there might have been something more than friendship between them. In July 1879 Lady Wolseley wrote of her meeting Madame Canrobert and their long discussion, most of which centred around Brackenbury, or 'Brack' as Lady Wolseley referred to him in the letter. It is easy to read too much into what she writes, but one must remember that there is a lot of intrigue and suggestion in the correspondence between the Wolseleys. She wrote that, "We talked of Brack; I with great caution only eulogising his great talent, his fine head, and domestic patience". The last comment obviously refers to his unhappy marriage, but why did Lady Wolseley feel the need to talk with great caution? Why did she also somewhat cryptically write "You can tell Brack I was charmed with her and it will go back".[9] This clearly suggests that there was a great deal of contact between them. Lord Wolseley wrote in July 1878 that Brackenbury disappeared when they passed through Paris, "... to dine with friends. I presume we can guess who she was".[10] The 'she' was underlined. The suggestion that Lady Wolseley would clearly know who it was again supports the suggestion that it was Madame Canrobert. One also wonders if Brackenbury's decision to accept the position of military attaché in Paris had anything to do with Madame Canrobert. Although he never mentions having spent time specifically with her he did spend a lot of time with Marshal Canrobert.[11] Further evidence is lacking and it would be wrong to say on the strength of what has been mentioned that there was definitely a relationship between them, but there is clearly more than a suggestion of one.

The other woman in Brackenbury's life was his second wife Edith. There is a strong likelihood that they had been in a relationship long before their marriage in 1905, the same year as Emilia's death. Edith Desanges was the daughter of Louis Desanges. Although Louis was of French decent he was born in England, but later became a French citizen. Desanges was a talented painter best known for his collection of fifty paintings of Victoria Cross holders, completed between 1859 and 1863. He also painted a number of battlefield scenes, one of which, *Fighting in the Ashantee Forest*, must have included his future son-in-law, although it is difficult to identify Brackenbury clearly. It is clear from what little evidence survives that Edith was

---

9 Lady Wolseley to Lord Wolseley, 21st July 1879, Wolseley Papers.
10 Lord Wolseley to Lady Wolseley, 18th July 1878, Wolseley Papers.
11 Brackenbury, Henry, *Some Memories of My Spare Time* (London: William Blackwood & Sons, 1909), p.299.

deeply in love with Henry. That said there was a considerable age gap between them, a little over twenty-nine years. Their marriage certificate shows that he was sixty-eight and she was thirty-nine when they were married on 14th December 1905.[12] Although they were both happy they enjoyed only eight years of marriage before his death. In a touching move she gathered together all the tributes to her husband that appeared in newspapers, both national and local, along with a telegram from King George V, and several magazine articles, to commemorate his death and placed them in an album, the only copy of which survives in the Brackenbury family to this day. One feels that Henry finally found the married bliss that had eluded him all those years, yet it was so sadly brief. There is also a likelihood that she was more 'acceptable' as a wife for his position and standing in life, and she was certainly much closer to his circle of friends than Emilia had ever been.

His emotional and love life might not appear very important, but there are some things we can gather from it. His unhappy marriage and the various indiscretions that this led to always had the potential to destroy his career and all his hard work. Whilst there were clearly faults on both sides his first marriage did not help his career. That said it had solved his immediate financial problems. Exactly what Emilia was like we shall never know, but she was clearly an emotional and frustrated woman who had her fair share of problems. Although one should not take too much notice of letters that were clearly written in anger, it could be suggested that she was somewhat emotionally unstable. There may also be a point that she was not his equal in intellect, and the fact that the two women we think he might have had affairs with were both noted for their intelligence adds to this belief. We also see that the cold calculating administrator was also capable of strong romantic feelings, be it for Edith or Helen Shepstone. He was clearly a man not merely a machine, and this gives a greater warmth and humanity to his character. It also shows that he was a flawed character and whilst his military career might not always have gone smoothly, neither did his private life.

---

12  A copy of the marriage certificate exists in the Brackenbury family collection of private papers.

CHAPTER 8

# THE FRANCO-PRUSSIAN WAR: WAR CORRESPONDENT

In the summer of 1868 Brackenbury received the appointment as the first Professor of Military History at the Royal Military Academy.[1] Brackenbury had some experience, later writing that "I had felt my feet as a lecturer, having given a lecture on medieval armour and weapons to a full house in the theatre of the Royal Artillery Institution". Brackenbury supported his application with a copy of a certificate from the Royal Artillery Institution attesting to his capability as a lecturer, along with a copy of his article on 'War' from *Brande's Dictionary* and a letter of support from the Governor of the Royal Military Academy Woolwich. Brackenbury was also assisted by the fact that he already had a series of lectures prepared on the 'Campaign of Waterloo'. This clearly played a part in his appointment as he had only five days' notice from his appointment to his first lecture. The appointment was initially temporary but after the Council for Military Education attended one of his lectures it was confirmed and he was formally appointed as Professor.[2]

Brackenbury continued to write and with his new-found appointment as Professor of Military History there was actually an increase in the number of articles he had published as he found that much of the material he gathered for his lectures could be turned very easily into journal articles. To this end he was helped by the fact that he managed to persuade the War Office to give him a small grant of ten shillings a

---

1 Before Brackenbury's appointment a fellow Royal Artillery officer had been presenting a lecture series to the senior class of cadets. However he received criticism from the Council of Military Education, in particular Major-General William Napier and Colonel Edward Hamley, who felt his programme was too ambitious and ordered him to reduce it. He in turn resigned, but before so doing recommended Brackenbury as his success. Brackenbury simply referred to him as a "distinguished brother officer of mine", choosing not to name him. Brackenbury, Henry, *Some Memories of My Spare Time* (London: William Blackwood & Sons, 1909), pp.66-67.
2 Brackenbury, *Some Memories of My Spare Time*, pp.67-69.

day to enable him to conduct battlefield tours during the Royal Military Academy at Woolwich's vacations. There is no record of anyone objecting to his using the visits to gather material for his lectures and for his journalistic career and financial gain, but one cannot help but wonder how the military authorities would have reacted to the knowledge that they were in affect funding his literary career, albeit to a very limited extent.

In July 1870 he was due to visit Belgium, France and Germany, partly to view the frontier defences but also to see the battlefields of the Bohemian campaign of 1866. However his departure was delayed by the death of his mother and by the time he was able to start for the continent war between France and Prussia seemed imminent. Brackenbury used material gathered on previous tours of the continent to write several articles for *The Standard*. On July 12th they published an article of his entitled 'The Armies of France, Prussia, and Spain', followed on the 14th by 'French and Prussian Tactics'. At the same time he proposed a series of articles based on his revised lectures on the Franco-Prussian frontier defences. He was perhaps a little ahead of events and he found no interest for the articles. By the time such interest occurred he was otherwise engaged.

On 16th July the newspapers in London published the communication between the French Government and their army which showed that war was imminent. He was now faced with a dilemma. He still officially had permission to travel to the continent, but on that morning he learnt that his brother and Captain Hozier, both serving officers who had sought permission to travel to the continent as war correspondents for *The Times*, had been refused permission to go abroad. Brackenbury decided to leave immediately and as he later wrote "although within my rights in starting on the strength of my permission previously obtained, I was afraid of an order of recall being sent after me".[3] Thus the speed of his departure and the fact that he left no forwarding address. Here we see an example of how seriously he was taking the study of his profession. The two heavyweight armies of Europe were about to engage and he had no intention of missing it. It appealed to him on many levels. As a military historian he longed to be there at the making of history. When one looks through the lectures he had given already at Woolwich on military campaigns, the detail and depth of such lectures, one appreciates that he would have longed to see the forthcoming campaign close to. His previous lectures had looked at campaigns long ended which he was able to retrace through battlefield visits, maps, and books. Now he had the chance to study such a campaign from the start at close quarters.

It also appealed to him as a military writer, or journalist. As we have already seen he had recently written about the armies and tactics of the combatants for

---

3   Brackenbury, *Some Memories of My Spare Time*, p.87.

*The Standard*. Now he had the chance to see them at close quarters and in campaign conditions and see the tactics put into practice. As a man who had already shown that he had an interest in and flair for military administration he was no doubt intrigued to see how the armies would cope in the field, and as a 'tactician' the situation was full of interest. For here the mighty Prussian General Staff would go up against the highly rated French generals such as Bazaine, MacMahon and Canrobert, all of whom had seen distinguished service in the Crimea. When recalling the incident many years later in 1909 Brackenbury's enthusiasm and keenness to view the war is still apparent. The modern reader would perhaps find this a little anachronistic but one only needs to point to the modern era's delight at twenty-four hour news coverage of world events to see that little has changed. It is not a suggestion that Henry Brackenbury had a deluded or romantic view of war, but he was a professional soldier and thus a chance to study his profession, to see the supposedly leading exponents of his profession go up against each other is understandable if one views it simply in the terms of someone eager to study and advance in his chosen profession.

All in all it was an opportunity too good to pass up, despite being fully aware of the possible repercussions his actions could have on his career if the military authorities or the government felt he had acted inappropriately. Technically he had permission to go abroad, yet his hurried departure and lack of a forwarding address could leave him open to disciplinary action on his return. When he did return to England he found that four days after his departure the Government had published a ban on all officers of the armed forces from serving with either army or acting as newspaper correspondents. It was felt that even the presence of a serving officer in the theatre of war could lead to allegations of a breach of neutrality or an incident that might lead to calls for British involvement.

He had originally travelled to France with the editor of *The Standard*, Captain Hamber, who returned to London on the night of 18th July.[4] As Brackenbury recorded, "I had resolved to take my chance of getting to the front and utilising such days as remained of my vacation in seeing something of the assembly of the army and the preparations for battle". This was despite the fact that he was warned by many in Paris that foreigners, and in particular those suspected of being journalists, would be most unwelcome with the French Army. He travelled to the frontier with Captain John Nolan, also of the Royal Artillery, who was acting as correspondent for *The Daily News*.[5] They found it difficult to get a train as most of the capacity was being

---

[4] Captain Thomas Hamber was not only the editor of *The Standard*, but a veteran of the Crimean War, where he had served in the French Foreign Legion. Why exactly he decided to accompany Brackenbury is unclear and it might simply have been the interest of a former soldier. Hamber left Brackenbury when they reached Paris to return to London.

[5] Captain, later Colonel, Nolan was later well known as the M.P. for Galway and chief whip of the Irish Party in the House of Commons.

used to transport troops to the frontier, and were forced to travel first class. On the train they met soldiers and civilians alike and Brackenbury gave a brief description of the atmosphere. "Neither amongst the soldiers nor the civilians who were our companions on that night's journey was there any sign of enthusiasm. They looked on the war as something that had to be faced, but their hearts were not in it".[6]

Early on the 19th they arrived in Strasbourg and they were immediately viewed with suspicion. Before leaving Paris they had obtained special passports from the British Ambassador Lord Lyons, a precaution which later proved invaluable. Having obtained good rooms at the local inn they walked around the town. At the bridge crossing over the Rhine they saw one of the absurd sights of war. "On the opposite side of the bank the German (Baden) sentries paced up and down within 250 yards or so of the French sentries on our bank". Yet despite the proximity and the fact that they were at war no one fired a shot. Although in clear view of each other no action was taken. Whilst foreigners were treated with suspicion in France at this stage, the levels of security did not meet the level of suspicion. On the 20th Brackenbury, still accompanied by Nolan, visited Polygone, where they had learned that a French division was encamped. With little obstruction, Brackenbury recalls a feeble protest from the single sentry guarding the camp, they were able to walk freely around the camp, visit artillery batteries and inspect the stores of war, along with cooking and sleeping arrangements. The freedom with which two civilians were able to walk around an army division at war seems surprising in our more security-conscious times, but in many ways it was a legacy of the way in which civilians had readily visited armies at war for years. However in only a few days' time Brackenbury and Nolan were to suffer from the suspicion of all foreigners that the war engendered in France.[7]

On the 22nd Brackenbury and his companion followed the division as it broke camp and left in the manner of a full military parade with a band playing at full volume. This was at 5:30a.m. and there would have been hardly a soul within a ten mile radius of the town who did not know that the division was on the move. By process of elimination, based on distance they could march, the nature of French battle plans, and the local towns and geography, Brackenbury worked out that they must be heading for Haguenau. By taking the train Brackenbury and Nolan arrived in Haguenau shortly before the French troops and booked in at the local inn. After breakfast Brackenbury was 'asked' to vacate his room as it was required by the French General's staff. During the day the two men found themselves being watched by the police agent for the division. At first he asked Brackenbury and Nolan to share a glass of wine with him but it soon became apparent that they were suspected of being spies. The suspicion was increased by the action of Captain Nolan

---

6  Brackenbury, *Some Memories of My Spare Time*, pp.89-90.
7  Brackenbury, *Some Memories of My Spare Time*, pp.90-92.

when speaking to the police agent. As Brackenbury later explained "Unfortunately, my companion, seeing the order of Maximillian on his breast, commenced to speak Spanish to him; and nothing is so likely to gain one the credit or discredit of being a spy as the power of speaking three or four languages". Brackenbury attempted to pre-empt any further questions by presenting the documents that Lord Lyons had provided them with. To an extent they worked as "Our suspicious friends were overawed. They dare not go further. They still suspected us, but they dare not arrest us".[8] The French officers still tried to pump both men for information and questions were asked which were designed to test whether or not they really were English, and here Brackenbury's knowledge of English literature was particularly helpful. Yet the suspicions still remained and a guard was placed outside their rooms, ostensibly for their protection, but neither of them were fooled. In the morning they were told they were free to move as they wished and a decision appears to have been reached that they were who they said they were.

It appears that much of the suspicion had been aroused by Brackenbury having figured out exactly where the French division was going. In conversation with the General's aide-de-camp Brackenbury set out the logic which had led to his deduction. "Why, Monsieur Aide-de-Camp, how far do French troops generally march in a day? Which gate of Strasburg did you go out by? Did not your bands notify your start to all the town?".[9] This seemed to final convince them that it had just been logic and an educated guess that had brought them to where the French division decided to camp rather than any means of espionage. The aide-de-camp even went so far as to say they were free to stay on with the division; however Brackenbury and Nolan decided to try to get to Metz. This incident reminds us of the very real danger that Brackenbury was placing himself in. When they arrived at Metz the danger they had been in was brought home to them. Two British officers and two special correspondents had been arrested as spies and badly treated, although they had later been released. With the whole town in the grip of, as Brackenbury called it, 'Spy mania', he decided that he would move on to the comparative calm of independent Luxembourg. Even here there was great anxiety as the country had a great number of French and Germans living there and constant rumours of possible occupation by either of the combatant powers persisted.[10]

With his leave almost over Brackenbury started his journey via Spa and Brussels, and reached London by 1st August. With this his first contact with the Franco-Prussian War came to an end and he returned to his teaching duties at Woolwich. However this was far from his last contact with the conflict. Whilst in France he had written seven "long letters" as he called them to *The Standard* which had been

---

8   Brackenbury, *Some Memories of My Spare Time*, pp.94-95
9   Brackenbury, *Some Memories of My Spare Time*, p.101.
10  Brackenbury, *Some Memories of My Spare Time*, p.102.

published between 19th and 31st July. This led to an offer on his return to write a 'Dairy of the War'. This would be a daily article, written every evening, so as to take full advantage of the latest telegraphs from the front. As Brackenbury later recalled:

> The idea was that I should write every evening a summary of the day's war news, up to the latest hour, explaining its probable bearing on the future of the operations, with such comments as would make the Diary at once intelligible to the general reader and useful to the military student.[11]

He took rooms in the Cannon Street Hotel so as to have a central location where he could receive material. The way it worked was that he prepared his 'copy' for the next day's paper nightly from his hotel room, where he received the latest telegrams from the seat of war and adjusted his article accordingly. A series of messengers were used, presumably paid for by *The Standard*, who would bring the telegrams and take Brackenbury's altered and adjusted diary entry back to the newspaper's office. He was responsible for the 'Diary' from 6th August until 1st September, so for nearly a month he kept this up. The regular routine would see him arrive at his hotel between ten and eleven of the evening, where he would digest the telegrams and news from the seat of war that had come in that day. He would then alter his article as the evening progressed often up until one or two in the morning, when it would finally be sent to the paper to print.

Despite the array of telegrams from the front line many commentators were still very much in the dark over what was actually happening at the front. Brackenbury, using similar military logic to that which had led him to conclude where the French Army division was marching, started to ascertain the actions at the front before others. His 'grand coup' as he later described it was to interpret correctly the strange movements of Marshal MacMahon's Corps. He took great delight in recording many years later that he had been alone amongst British journalists in the morning papers of the 26th August in stating that MacMahon was attempting to manoeuver around the Prussian flank so as to join forces with Marshal Bazaine's force before Metz. *The Standard's* circulation rose dramatically during this period and a degree of that was owed to Brackenbury's 'Diary of the War'. *The Standard* had built its reputation on detailed accounts of foreign news, particularly conflicts. Previously they had covered the American Civil War and the Austro-Prussian War in great detail.[12]

When he had first been asked to write the diary he was asked to sign a formal contract. This he was reluctant to do feeling that as a soldier other duties might make it impossible for him to continue in this work. This might be something as being moved to a new posting away from London, but one also wonders whether this was

---

11   Brackenbury, *Some Memories of My Spare Time*, p.104.
12   Brackenbury, *Some Memories of My Spare Time*, pp.104-107.

partly because he still hoped for further active service overseas. As it happened it was just as well that he did not sign a formal contract as in September 1870 he was asked to take on a position which would see him return to the seat of war and obtain a view of the conflict unparalleled by any other Englishman.

CHAPTER 9

# THE NATIONAL AID SOCIETY

By the year of the outbreak of the Franco-Prussian War in 1870 Henry Brackenbury had been in the Army fourteen years. It had hardly been a meteoric rise. Having been commissioned a Lieutenant, in 1856, by 1870 he was only a Captain. This had much to do with the policy within the Royal Artillery whereby promotion was purely by seniority, thus you had to wait for a 'vacancy'. It is often thought that the Artillery and Engineers had an advantage because they were not bound by the purchase system for commissions. On the other hand promotion was as a consequence slow, and indeed Brackenbury's situation was far from unique or particularly slow for an officer in the Royal Artillery. However when compared with the rest of his career there is a great difference. In the next ten years he would rise to the rank of Colonel and in the next fifteen years he would rise to the rank of Major-General. The relatively rapid promotion that followed had its roots in this period of his career.

It all started with his visit to the Paris Exhibition in 1867 where he was much impressed by the display of ambulances and material aid for the sick and wounded which was demonstrated by the *Société Internationale de Secours aux Blessés*.[1] From this he developed an interest in such matters and began to study the preparations and equipment of other nations, looking at the work done during the American Civil War, the Austro-Prussian War, and Austro-Italian War. He wrote two articles for *The Standard* on such matters entitled 'Help for the Sick and Wounded' and was

---

1   Brackenbury formed a somewhat unfairly favourable view of the French Society. Bertrand Taithe has described it as little more than "a rather informal club of medical men who had personally experienced war, and benevolent aristocrats like Viscount de Melun". The society had no funds and all its views on what could be done were purely theoretical, as nothing had been planned at all. Taithe has also said that as a result it had no purpose. However in fairness it must be added that Britain did not even have this. Taithe, Bertrand 'The Red Cross Flag in the Franco-Prussian War: Civilians, Humanitarians and War in the 'Modern Age'' in Coote, Roger (editor), *War, Medicine and Modernity* (Stroud: Sutton Publishing, 1998), pp.29-32.

generally impressed with what he saw abroad but horrified at the complete unpreparedness at home. In his last article he wrote

> We have seen what other nations have done. What is England doing? We have our Nightingale Fund for training nurses, our Patriotic Fund for the relief of Crimean sufferers. Where is our branch of the 'International Society for the Relief of the Sick and Wounded', and what work is it doing? Where is its shipload of comforts to follow the Abyssinian expedition? There lies before us the catalogue of that most interesting exhibition of objects for the relief of sick and wounded soldiers held in connection with this International Society at Paris, near the chief entrance; and in the midst of the thousands of objects exhibited England sends two books, and one of those is called 'America and its Army'. Surely this is a slur on our national humanity, a blot on our fair escutcheon. In Heaven's name let us be up and doing. We have signed the Convention of Geneva. We are bound in honour to be working in time of peace not for ourselves alone, but for all the other nations, who's wounded may, by even the remotest possibility, ever fall into our hands. We invite discussion and action on a subject affecting both our soldiers' lives and our national honour.[2]

The articles appeared in *The Standard* in January 1868, and it was this which brought him to the attention of John Furley and Captain C.J. Burgess, who both wrote in support of his article. On 4th August 1870 'The British National Society for the Aid to the Sick and Wounded in War' was founded. As a consequence of the articles in *The Standard* Brackenbury had initially been asked to join the committee set up to establish a society to help the sick and wounded of the conflict, and once established he was elected to the executive committee.[3]

A thorough history of the National Aid Society does not exist, and although this is not the place to rectify that, a few comments on the society are necessary. In 1863 the International Red Cross had been established and Britain had signed the charter. One of the resolutions passed at its first conference was the establishment of national relief societies for the relief of wounded soldiers. Yet it was another seven years before any serious attempt was made at creating such a movement in Britain. Even when the National Aid Society was formed in 1870 it was created to meet the

---

2   Brackenbury, Henry, 'Help for the Sick and Wounded' *The Standard* (21st January 1868).
3   Although this is often used as the formal date for the establishment of the society it would be wrong not to acknowledge that a few years previously in 1868 John Furley, Sir Edmund Letchmere, and other members of the Order of St John had set up a provisional committee for the relief of sick and wounded during war. It was only in 1870 that it gained a real purpose and was able to gain much wider support. John Furley later played an important part in the establishment of the St John's Ambulance in 1877 and provided similar service to the sick and wounded of the South African War and the First World War.

need of the moment created by the Franco-Prussian conflict, and there would later be a falling out amongst the members over whether the society should continue after the conflict. In one form or another it survived until 1904 when it formally became the British Red Cross. The National Aid Society owed much to the influence and drive of its chairman Colonel Robert Loyd-Lindsay (later Lord Wantage) M.P. Loyd-Lindsay was far more than a mere soldier or politician. During the Crimean War he was awarded the Victoria Cross whilst serving with the Scots Fusilier Guards at the battles of the Alma and Inkerman. Having been born plain Robert Lindsay he adopted the doubled barrelled name after a very 'good' marriage to Harriet Sarah Jones-Loyd, the only surviving child and heiress to the fortune of Samuel Jones-Loyd, Baron Overstone, who at the time of their marriage in 1858 was said to be one of the richest men in the country. As a consequence he did not feel out of place chairing a committee that contained some of the wealthiest and most powerful people in the land, including his father-in-law, the Earl of Shaftesbury, Baron de Rothschild, Viscount Bury, and many of the leading surgeons of the day. They also received the patronage of the Prince of Wales who accepted the presidency.

On 4th August 1870 the society was formed, and coincidently this was the day the first major battle of the war took place at Wissembourg. The same evening Mr (later Sir John) Furley and Captain C.J. Burgess departed for the continent to visit Geneva, Paris and Berlin to begin preliminary discussion about what the society could do. At the same time Colonel Loyd-Lindsay wrote to *The Times* announcing the formation of the society and stating that he had placed a thousand pounds of his own money in the bank for the use of the society. He encouraged other of a like mind, and bank balance, to do the same. As Lady Wantage later recalled, "After Loyd-Lindsay's letter the Committee made no further appeals for funds: these were given spontaneously, and an overwhelming stream, both of money and material, poured in from every part of England".[4]

Whilst there was on the whole support for the work of the society, which touched upon the growing Victorian notions of philanthropy and help for those less fortunate, there were those who questioned the need for such work. On August 17th 1870 *The Times* published a letter from Lord Sydney Godolphin Osborne which questioned the need for the work of the society. The letter carried a lot of weight due to the fact that Lord Osborne was a known philanthropist. Brackenbury answered this letter, with the blessing of Loyd-Lindsay, and *The Times* published it the following day. A further letter and reply took place before the correspondence ceased. Brackenbury later gave a sense that the correspondence had been in the form of a good natured debate and recorded that Lord Osborne had written to him personally thanking him for his response to his letters in *The Times* and saying that "I cordially accept

---

[4] Baroness Wantage, *Lord Wantage: A Memoir* (London: Smith, Elder & Co, 1907) p.178.

its spirit and its letter". The debate in *The Times* brought the work of the National Society to greater prominence and Brackenbury records that "My letter of 17th had brought me a number of letters enclosing cheques for the fund, among them one for £1,000 from a correspondent who desired to remain anonymous".[5]

It is perhaps understandable that some, even those with a history of philanthropy like Lord Osborne, should question the need for Britain to assist. If one looks back at the previous quotation from Brackenbury's article one sees that such support for the sick and wounded was not even common for operations involving the British Army. It is therefore understandable that some raised questions over why such an effort was being made regarding a conflict that did not even directly involve the British Empire. Brackenbury had his own opinions about the reason why such work was important, which will be looked at later. It is important to reiterate that there was an international movement towards such work and the historian Bertrand Taithe has referred to this period, with the creation of the International Red Cross, the first Geneva Convention, and the humanitarian aid given in conflicts such as the Franco-Prussian War, as the dawn of "new humanitarianism".[6]

Whilst money was not a real concern the logistics and organisation started to become a problem. Within weeks of the society's formation it had forty surgeons working on the continent and by the end of September 1870 sixty-two surgeons and sixteen nurses were working for the society at or near the front lines. All this had been achieved with what at best could be called an *ad hoc* system. Nobody had previous experience of such an undertaking as nothing had been attempted on this scale from Britain. All this was under the wartime problems of communication and transport. One of the biggest problems was trying to guess where the next engagement would be and trying to prepare for it. This, added to the growing scope of the war, was a real problem and it became apparent that the society needed a 'military agent' at the seat of war itself who would conduct its business and organise the communication, logistics and forward planning. There were perhaps many men within in the country who could have been asked to undertake this assignment. However there was one man whose proximity to the National Aid Society, his knowledge of the continent and his knowledge of military affairs and the present conflict made him the obvious candidate.

When Henry Brackenbury arrived for a committee meeting of the National Aid Society on 2nd September 1870, he was taken to one side by Colonel Loyd-Lindsay and asked if he would go to the front as the military agent of the society to organise its work. Brackenbury's immediate reaction was to point out the two main drawbacks to his appointment. First there was his work for *The Standard* and second

---
5   Brackenbury, Henry, *Some Memories of My Spare Time* (London: William Blackwood & Sons, 1909) p.118.
6   Taithe, Bertrand, 'The Red Cross Flag in the Franco-Prussian War' p.25.

there was his professorship at Woolwich. Brackenbury was willing to give up the former but not the latter. He felt that as he had just come back from the summer vacation it was unlikely that he would be allowed the sort of extended leave that such an appointment would require. However as has already been mentioned the National Aid Society had friends in high places. Loyd-Lindsay tried appealing to the Governor of the Academy at Woolwich, Major-General Sir Lintorn Simmons, but to no avail. He then appealed directly to Edward Cardwell, the Secretary of State for War, and it was he who 'ordered' that a month's leave be given to Brackenbury so that he could take up the appointment. The influence of the prominent members of the committee is perhaps only half the reason behind the Secretary of State's decision. If the National Aid Society was to be successful it had become obvious that someone was needed to handle the administration and organisation at the front. Brackenbury was an obvious candidate for this and if he were able to achieve the improvement that was wanted it would do no harm to British prestige and might do much to gain the respect and thanks of the combatant powers.

Brackenbury's initial month's leave was to be paid, but by the time the month was up his work was in full flow and it would have been difficult for him to leave. This time Loyd-Lindsay went to see Lintorn Simmons in person and whilst the latter appreciated that Brackenbury was doing a good and important job, he wanted him to return. Loyd-Lindsay contacted Brackenbury explaining the situation and saying that if he were prepared to leave the army, or go on half-pay, the National Aid Society were prepared to pay Brackenbury a salary of £1,000 a year. However this was not acceptable to Brackenbury who had no desire to leave the army, least of all a posting he thoroughly enjoyed. Loyd-Lindsay appealed to Cardwell for an extension to his leave, stressing that to remove him now would be to the detriment of the Society and to the wounded of the conflict. Again he was successful, and Brackenbury's leave was extended until the end of the year. As Cardwell wrote in a letter to Loyd-Lindsay, a copy of which was latter passed on to Brackenbury, "From your note it appears your affairs are in such a position that Captain Brackenbury cannot leave without risk of serious mischief".[7] The only condition was that this leave was to be unpaid. Colonel Charles Chesney, Professor of Military History at the Staff College, covered for Brackenbury during his leave and as a consequence received Brackenbury's salary. This brings up and interesting point about Brackenbury's service. Although he lost no seniority, which of course was made up by length of service, he lost all his pay both as Professor of History at Woolwich and as a Captain in the Royal Artillery. Besides which he had also given up his earnings from the diary of the war he was writing for *The Standard*, and by giving up his journalism he really was

---

7    The debate regarding the extension of Brackenbury leave is found in three letters - Loyd-Lindsay to Brackenbury, 23rd September 1870, Loyd-Lindsay to Brackenbury, 24th September 1870 and Cardwell to Loyd-Lindsay, 26th September 1870, private collection.

making a financial sacrifice. It may well be that he envisaged returning after a few months with enough material to provide numerous journal articles, but this is not to dismiss the immediate financial difficulties placed upon him. As a man of very limited financial means, indeed his journalism being his main source of income during this period, he was taking a risk. He was also taking a personal risk by being so close to the front lines. Although technically a non-combatant he would still be in 'harm's way', and as we shall see it did not stop him being shot at and nearly killed. There was also a political risk. If he took the wrong course of action and there was a suggestion that an officer of the Crown had breached the laws of neutrality he could be in for a very difficult time on his return to England. So to an extent he was risking his financial security, his life and his career.

At the same time he no doubt saw an opportunity that was far beyond any risk. He would of course be right at the front of a conflict between, theoretically, the two most powerful armies in the world, which would appeal to him as a soldier, tactician and historian. It must be remembered that in the latter capacity he had lectured at Woolwich about all the major conflicts of the nineteenth, and in later years he would lecture on the Franco-Prussian War with a natural air of authority. He would also be presented with an opportunity of unique experiences. He would be one of only a handful of British officers who saw the conflict as it happened which gave him a view that perhaps only one other officer saw, namely Herbert (later Lord) Kitchener. Unlike official observers, who were stationed largely at headquarters, both men got to see the conflict on the front lines. This is why he was able to write to Loyd-Lindsay on the 9th September, that, "It must have been an awful fight here. 129 Bavarian officers and 2000 men killed in and about Balan. Street-fighting in its worst form, and what is worse than street-fighting?". His vivid account continued:

> There they lay side by side together, French and Germans, enemies no longer, all quiet in there common suffering. Floors covered with the poor fellows, with every sort of wound. Some dying with balls through the chest, some with crushed arms or legs from shells. One Frenchman had lain for three days in a ditch, and was brought to have his thigh amputated. He asked for a cigar the moment the amputation was over. Another Bavarian with his thigh smashed to pieces by a shell; and, alas! in such a condition that I could not go near him, though his wounds are dressed with pure carbolic acid. The wounds are now in a state of suppuration, and a cigar was necessary for men who, like myself, are not accustomed to such places.[8]

---

8   Brackenbury, *Some Memories of My Spare Time*, pp.125-126

It was perhaps beneficial that the inexperienced subaltern got his first view of such horrendous sights when there were no troops relying on him. It obviously helped to prepare him for what he would face in his later active service career.

Brackenbury set out for the continent on 3rd September 1870, accompanied by the Hon. Reginald Capel, another agent for the National Aid Society, and an unnamed courier.[9] He had spent the previous day sorting out all the necessary travel documents. Their first stop was Brussels. Here Brackenbury received a letter of introduction from the British Minister Mr Saville Lumley to the Belgium Minister of Foreign Affairs. From the latter he obtained letters of introduction and travel permits to the frontier, which asked the authorities there to give him every assistance. His first task was to find a suitable place for a depot from which the Society's resources could be allocated to hospitals near the front lines. The committee back home had been debating two locations before he left namely Luxembourg and Arlon. A quick visit to Luxembourg showed him that the scarcity of transport, and difficulties with the local customs authority, in the area made in quite impractical as a main depot. The situation was not much better at Arlon but he received every possible help from the authorities there who gave him the ground floor of the Palais de Justice to use as a warehouse. Along with this the local commissary of police also helped to arrange for transport and labour at the depot.

His early days were full of problems, mainly to do with lack of stores, but by 9th September he was able to telegraph Loyd-Lindsay in London to the effect that the Society was now fully at work in Arlon, supplying all the hospitals around Sedan. Once he had set up the depot and started it running smoothly he left Capel in charge so that he could visit the hospitals where the Society's surgeons were at work so he could see the situation for himself, appreciate the problems, and consult the medical staff as to their needs and opinions about future operations. In what must have been a hectic four days he visited Brussels, Luxembourg, Arlon, Douzy, Bazeilles, Balan and Sedan to see the needs of the hospitals at first hand.

In his writing from this period, Brackenbury makes some interesting points about the usefulness of the work the Society did, above the worthy aim of reducing the suffering of the sick and wounded. Whilst recognising the good work of Furley and

---

9 The reason his name was never made public by Brackenbury is probably explained by the fact that his service was short lived and controversial. On their arrival in Luxembourg he was accused by Monsieur Norbert Metz, the leader of the Luxembourg Liberal party who had been assisting Brackenbury and the society, of corruption and had apparently approached Monsieur Metz with a proposal to make money out of the Society's work. According to Brackenbury Metz answered the courier by giving him a black eye and reporting the matter to him. Brackenbury acted quickly and sent him home and reported the matter to Loyd-Lindsay. A new courier called Christian Sonder was sent out, who Brackenbury later called "a dear honest old fellow", and remained with him for the remainder of his service.

others, he now felt that the Society's work had to be raised to another level. Almost as soon as he arrived Brackenbury wrote that:

> It only wants that the individual efforts going on should be completely organised (for which my powers are sufficient) to let it be seen what gigantic efforts England is making to relieve the misery which by all accounts is almost unspeakable.[10]

Brackenbury was obviously keen that the world should see what the Society was doing, not necessarily for any personal glory for himself or the members of the Society but so that Britain could show her humanitarian side to the world. In that sense there was an element of patriotism to his work. On 27th October he wrote to Loyd-Lindsay:

> I cannot tell you with what pleasure I look on our work here; the first to enter Metz, the first to give succour, the first also in liberality, our Society has taken the place which England's generosity entitles us to assume. No one can know the misery we relieve; no one can ever estimate the blessings that are showed upon us for our work.[11]

Whilst this might sound rather grand and patriotic, perhaps even slightly jingoistic, it must be remembered that Brackenbury was the first to give credit to the surgeons and agents who were at the sharp end of the Society's work. More than that, it was an ideal situation for his type of soldier. He was engaged in demanding administrative and organisational work whilst at the same time getting a real sense of wartime and active service conditions. To an extent he lived on the frontlines with the soldiers, and whilst he never deliberately courted danger he did on several occasions come under fire including one incident where he had his hat shot off his head.

The really interesting part in what he writes is about 'England's generosity'. Brackenbury continually makes the argument that Britain's position and reputation in Europe, especially amongst France and Germany, is being enhanced by the work of the Society. A week after the battle of Sedan, Brackenbury wrote to Loyd-Lindsay singling out the work of Dr Frank and Mr Blewitt at the hospital at Balan. Part of this illustrates some of Brackenbury's motivates and his believe in the benefit of the work of the Society to the reputation of Britain. "If England can ever gain kind thoughts from France and Prussia, it is by the work of such men as these".[12] Here

---

10  The original of the letter no longer exists, but it is reproduced in Baroness Wantage, *Lord Wantage: A Memoir*, pp.180-181.
11  Baroness Wantage, *Lord Wantage: A Memoir*, p.182.
12  A large part of the letter is reproduced in *Some Memories of My Spare Time* pp.124-129. The letter is also reproduced in the National Aid Society's official account of its actions. However surviving copies are rare.

is evidence of his desire to show Britain's impartial humanitarianism. Brackenbury tried desperately to avoid the Society becoming anything other than impartial. He found this a problem when asked by the French Société de Secours to distribute stores on their behalf. The reason for this request was that the French Aid agencies were in complete chaos and whilst the mechanisms for them were in place there was no organisation.

This was in stark contrast to the German medical and charitable agencies which were well organised. John F. Hutchinson, in his book about the Red Cross, points out that this had a great deal to do with the fact that the German organisation had been tested in war quite recently with Denmark and Austria, unlike the French organisation which was largely theoretical.[13] This experience had led to many significant changes to the organisation. A year before the war Prince Pless had been appointed as Royal commissioner and Inspector General of Charitable assistance to the military in time of war. During the conflict he took strict control of the work of the German aid societies, who enjoyed no autonomy at all. At one stage the Prussians wanted to take control of the distribution of the Society's stores, as they had done with the stores of the Berlin Society. Brackenbury resisted strongly, and successfully. He pointed out that there had been cases of stores being given to troops that were neither sick nor wounded, and that if the stores under Brackenbury were used in this way he would be guilt of a breach of neutrality and open to the criticism of the British Government. This was no exaggeration, as the case of Herbert Kitchener demonstrated. Kitchener, who was technically a French resident, joined a French Ambulance unit during the war, and later received a severe reprimand from the Commander-in-Chief, who told him that as a serving British Army officer he could have jeopardised British neutrality by his actions.[14]

Such repercussions were obviously in Brackenbury's mind as he resisted Prussian request, but there was also the fact that the National Aid Society had committed itself to providing aid to both sides equally and fairly. After much debate Brackenbury won the argument. "I at last prevailed, and obtained that independence of action which I insisted on as an indispensable condition of further assistance".[15] Although no record exists of his discussion with the Prussian authorities it is likely that he put the case bluntly to them that if they did not allow them independence of action they would be unable to continue, as either the British government or public opinion would not approve of a policy which appeared on the face of it to favour one side over the other.

---

13  Hutchinson, John. F., *Champions of Charity: War and the Rise of the Red Cross* (Colorado: Westview Press, 1996) pp.117-122.
14  Magnus, Phillip, *Kitchener: Portrait of an Imperialist* (London: John Murray, 1958) p.9.
15  Brackenbury, *Some Memories of My Spare Time*, p.136.

The fact that the French wanted the Society to distribute its stores, and the fact that the Germans were sufficiently impressed to want to take over their work illustrates that at the very least the combatant powers were aware and appreciated the work of the Society. The good reputation that was being established was further supported by the comments of the contemporary French journalist M. Thieblin, who wrote to Brackenbury, "I have seldom seen so honest Englishmen. There is nothing but work, hard work, and not a single boast, not even a shade of vanity so natural in men performing so splendid a work".[16] Brackenbury was also invited to dine with the Crown Prince of Prussia (later Kaiser Friedrich (or Frederick) III). During the dinner on 2nd December 1870, Brackenbury sat on the Crown Prince's left, facing General Leonhard Graf von Blumenthal, his chief-of-staff. Brackenbury's account of the dinner gives an interesting portrayal of the two men. Blumenthal continually read out the despatches from the front lines as they were delivered to impress the guests as to the success the Prussians were having. Brackenbury was not fooled and he concluded that, "... the despatches which I heard, though generally favourable, did not record any marked success".[17] It is quite clear from Brackenbury's writing that he saw this as an obvious attempt on the part of Blumenthal to impress his British visitor. This is interesting when compared with Brackenbury's record of his conversation with the Crown Prince. Prince Friedrich told Brackenbury of his admiration for what the society was doing and his hatred of war and assured him that the German states had not set out with the intention to annex parts of France, though he now conceded that such an outcome was inevitable because of national feeling over the Alsace region. Brackenbury late wrote that:

> I left profoundly impressed with the character of this Soldier-Prince, who, fresh from the battles on the frontier and with some of his troops engaged in a hard struggle at that very moment, was not ashamed to avow, in the presence of his whole staff of war-worn soldiers, his hatred of war.[18]

It is interesting that whilst Brackenbury saw through the subterfuge of Blumenthal's attempts to impress him he did not take the same view of the Crown Prince's language towards him. Indeed he seems to have considered him sincere in his views.

The admiration for the work of the society was not only seen in the opinions of the combatant powers. Brackenbury records an incident in September 1870 when a

---

16   Brackenbury, *Some Memories of My Spare Time*, p.130.
17   Brackenbury, *Some Memories of My Spare Time*, pp.159-160. The despatches probably referred to the Battle of Villiers fought from 29th November to 3rd December 1870, which was ultimately a Prussian victory.
18   Brackenbury, *Some Memories of My Spare Time*, p.160. Prince Frederick has been recognised as being rather liberal in his views, this being attributed largely to the influence of his English wife Princess Victoria, daughter of Queen Victoria. Interestingly, von Blumenthal was also married to an Englishwoman, as indeed was von Moltke.

man he referred to in his account simply as 'Mr S' presented himself at the Society's depot in Arlon. He had with him a letter from Loyd-Lindsay stating that he was the representative of Messrs Spiers and Pond, a well-known company of the Victorian era who specialised in hotels and restaurants. Spiers and Pond had offered their services to the Society with a view to taking over much of the administration and running of the hospitals. As a company with great experience of logistical arrangements they had sent their agent, 'Mr S', to investigate the possibility. Brackenbury was asked by Loyd-Lindsay to give the man all the assistance he could. One should not view this anyway as an indictment of the work done to that point or of Brackenbury personally. One must remember that Brackenbury's service was still technically on a part time basis and if the war dragged on indefinitely it was unlikely that, even with all their influence, the Society would be able to get the War Office to agree to a third extension of Brackenbury's leave. Any further extension would have severe repercussions on Brackenbury's career. So if a third party was willing and able to take on the work this would solve a potential problem. 'Mr S' followed Brackenbury for two days as he visited the Society's facilities in Sedan, Bazeilles and Balan. Whilst Brackenbury dealt with the business of the moment the agent was shown around the hospitals and consulted with the surgeons and other staff. At the end of the two days 'Mr S' returned to London. A week later he made a report in which he conclude, according to Brackenbury, that "The work could not, in his opinion, be better done, and that his firm could not undertake it advantageously". He made special mention of Brackenbury's service and his hospitality, although in a rare moment of modesty Brackenbury does not record his words.[19]

Brackenbury had improved the situation regarding the distribution of the Society's stores rapidly. Within only a month of his arrival the system of distribution was running smoothly. He had visited every hospital in the area, particularly around Sedan, to ascertain their needs and had now been able to meet said needs. That this was possible in such a short space of time illustrates the fact that there was clearly no want of supplies and stores made available for the Society. All that had been lacking was the organisation and administration of the system of supply. The Society had taken control of a 100-bed hospital at Saarbruck, a 60-bed hospital at Briey, where they had also set up an advanced depot to supply all the hospitals in the area around Sedan. Arlon was still the main depot supplying the whole area. Depots had also been opened in Saarbruck and Remilly. The whole system was maintained by hired wagons, which transported the stores between depots and to the hospitals themselves.

---

19  Brackenbury did add that Messrs Spiers and Pond made a handsome donation to the Society. Brackenbury was given a letter by them which placed him on the 'free list' at all their restaurants, although he concluded that this was "a privilege of which I never availed myself". Brackenbury, *Some Memories of My Spare Time*, pp.132-133.

When all this had been organised Brackenbury set off for London to make a report to the Society and to consult the committee on its future operations. The main question that he had in mind was how to move into Metz as quickly as possible when the fortress fell. The French forces under Marshal Bazaine had retreated to Metz after defeat at the Battle of Gravelotte on 18th August 1870. Marshal MacMahon's Army of Châlons had attempted to lift the siege but was all but destroyed at the Battle of Sedan on 1st September. From that point on it was just a matter of time before Metz fell and over 170,000 French troops became prisoners. On 4th October Brackenbury returned to the continent, and spent the next three weeks in Brussels. He found information on the conduct of the war far easier to come by there, but he was still close enough to the depots at Arlon and Saarbruck if he was needed. Brackenbury records that during this time he had more than one audience with the King of the Belgians, who did much to help the Society's efforts. His relationship with the French community in Brussels, including both refugees and the French Minister Monsieur Tachard, also helped keep him informed about the situation at Metz. Through them and his own reading of the situation he tried to establish when the fortress was most likely to fall and what the most pressing needs of the inhabitants would be. As a result of this he was able to have such stores as were thought necessary distributed amongst the depots at Arlon, Saarbruck, Briey and Remilly. Whilst much of this sounds quite basic, it is important to point out that because of this planning and forethought the Society was the first to supply materials to the sick and wounded of Metz after its fall, even before the French or the Germans.

When the French forces at Metz finally surrendered on 27th October the plans he had made went into full swing. Brackenbury heard of its demise by late afternoon. He immediately telegraphed this information to the depots that had been prepared for the fall to get ready to move. However he decided that it was too late in the day to start now, as it would be too dangerous to move large numbers of wagons laden with supplies at night. In the early hours of the 28th he went to the national bank in Brussels and withdrew as much gold as he was able to conveniently carry with him. It appears the bank was opened especially for him and this again speaks of the good relations he had developed with the authorities in Belgium. He had a few problems with the French authorities along the way, mainly because news of the fall of Metz had not reached them and they refused to believe the members of the Society, even when they showed them newspapers reporting the event. On his journey he was accompanied by the wife of Marshal Canrobert, who was journeying to be with her husband before he was to leave for captivity in Germany.[20] On the way

---

20  Madame Canrobert was born Leila-Flora MacDonald the daughter of an officer in the British Army Captain Allan MacDonald. She was also the great-granddaughter of the Jacobite heroine Flora MacDonald. He was twenty-nine years her senior, but despite this it was a happy marriage and she bore him three children.

Brackenbury saw many French prisoners, later recounting, "It was a pitiful sight. There were 22,000 men still in the corps, and it had lost 10,800 in the two days about Renzonville and Gravelotte. Half starved, worn and weary, they came out to lie down in the same mud where for so many weary nights the Prussian outposts had lain".[21] Late on the 29th they arrived in Metz, where rooms for the night were scarce. Brackenbury and Madame Canrobert were fortunate to be shown kindness by Captain von Foerster, General von Kummer's aide-de-camp, who was able to get them permission to spend the night in the mansion house that had been the French divisional headquarters before the surrender. It now stood completely empty, and as Brackenbury later wrote, "... in all Metz that night there was nobody so well lodged as ourselves".[22]

Meanwhile stores from the Society poured in to Metz from the depots at Arlon, Remilly and Saarbruck. Mr Bushman, another member of the National Aid Society, had arrived with the stores from Saarbruck and was met by Prince Pless, in charge of the German Aid Society, who offered him a building for a depot. The next day Brackenbury accompanied Mr Bushman to meet with Prince Pless. This was the first of several meeting between the two men, many of which dealt with the future distribution of materials around the Paris area. As a result it was decided that the Society would establish a depot at Chateau Thierry, later moved to Meaux, so as to meet the future demand around Paris. It was not just in Metz itself that the Society helped the relief of the troops engaged in that zone of the conflict. At Forbach, on the railway line between Metz and Saarbruck, a 'restaurant' was established that helped not only the German sick and wounded but, as it was on the line back to Germany, many French Prisoners on their way to captivity. Along with supplying food, coffee and wine, it also gave out warm clothing. Brackenbury estimated that this 'restaurant' helped 19,500 men. The care of prisoners was something that was very much in Brackenbury's mind. He wrote several times about the 'pitiful' sights of these men. He even visited Mainz to see the treatment of the prisoners in the large camp that had been set up there. "I was convinced that the Germans were doing all they could for them, but their conditions left much to be desired, as there was a great want of warm clothing".[23] Brackenbury even persuaded the Society to place £1000 at the disposal of Madame Canrobert to be used to help French prisoners.

He decided to make Metz his headquarters for the foreseeable future and rented a house to use as an office. This was a considerable risk to his own person as typhus and smallpox were rife in the town, but again illustrates his devotion to the work. He stayed in Metz because it was the best place for him to be. Indeed it was where the demand of the moment was. Although the work was extremely demanding he

---

21  Brackenbury, *Some Memories of My Spare Time*, p.142.
22  Brackenbury, *Some Memories of My Spare Time*, p.144.
23  Brackenbury, *Some Memories of My Spare Time*, p.162.

also took the opportunity to visit the frontlines. It appears that this was more out of personal interest than related to his work. This was a dangerous pastime. Whilst working in France he would wear the undress uniform of a Royal Artillery officer adorned with the armlet of the Red Cross signed by both the French and German authorities. One wonders exactly how, given their concerns about neutrality, the British authorities would have reacted to this, but there is no evidence that they were ever aware of it. Whilst the sense of wearing his uniform can be understood, in that it made him look more official rather than simply another civilian, there was clearly a danger. Whilst visiting the German lines around Thionville Brackenbury had his hat shot off his head by a French marksman. Obviously the marksman had no way of seeing the armlet, but even if he had been able to there was no guarantee that it would have made any difference. As John F. Hutchinson points out, "No attempt had been made to familiarise French soldiers with the terms of the Geneva Convention or with the meaning of the Red Cross flag and armband". The situation was hindered further by the fact that French medical staff, on the whole, refused to wear such armlets. "French army surgeons were evidently still wedded to the idea that they were combatants first and physicians second and believed that wearing the badge of neutrality would be seen as a confession of weakness or cowardice".[24] This made the work of Brackenbury and other Society representatives near the front even more hazardous.

At the end of January 1871 Brackenbury returned to England to resume his teaching duties at Woolwich. His last report for the Society, written in February 1871, makes for interesting reading. "Our aid, given most impartially to the French and Germans, has saved lives and relieved suffering to an extent difficult to realise". He goes on to record the thanks that both the French and Germans had given to the society and praises the people who worked for it.

> In spite of this strange mixture of classes and professions, so well has the staff been selected, that among all those sent out by your committee – amounting to considerably more than 100 in my district – there has not been one case of dishonesty, and scarcely one failure of any kind. And I must not omit here to speak of the noble self-sacrificing exertions of the medical staff of our various hospitals, and the English ladies who have acted as nurses.[25]

He stated that everyone, even down to the drivers of the wagons, had done well. "It is not to be wondered at that, as Captain Nevill writes, the people who see the work can only slowly believe that it is done without some deep ulterior motive".

---

24  Hutchinson, John. F., *Champions of Charity: War and the Rise of the Red Cross*, pp.115-116.
25  The report is reproduced in Brackenbury, *Some Memories of My Spare Time*, pp.165-166.

Throughout the war there were comments and accusations that the Society had been acting in breach of its neutrality. Brackenbury answered these critics in unequivocally fashion.

> I have been very much grieved to see persistent statements that we have done more for the Germans than the French, and that we have only been relieving the Germans from doing for their own and the French wounded what otherwise they must have done. Both these statements are very wrong, and the last argues entire ignorance of the terrible strain under which Germany is carrying out this war. Germany is making enormous efforts on behalf of the sick and wounded but do all she can, she cannot meet the wants.

He later went on to say that,

> In regard to our aid not being given equally to the French, I have often been accused abroad of doing more for them than the Germans. I have honestly striven to keep the balance even, but the spectacle of destitution and humiliation, mental and bodily suffering which the invaded districts of France afford, compel the sympathies of most men rather towards weak France than towards strong Germany, proud in her consciousness of power.[26]

After the submission of this report he received a semi-official letter from Loyd-Lindsay thanking him for his efforts, both personally and on behalf of the committee, noting that he had served with the utmost "... zeal and self-devotion, combined with great practical ability ..."[27]

---

26  Brackenbury, *Some Memories of My Spare Time*, pp.166-167.
27  The letter is reproduced in Brackenbury, *Some Memories of My Spare Time*, p.169.

# Chapter 10

# Aftermath of the Franco-Prussian War

The work Brackenbury had done for the National Aid Society had turned him into something of a minor celebrity. Praise and recognition for his work continued to come his way. The French Government issued a decree on 25th January 1871 making Brackenbury an officer of the Legion of Honour, although Brackenbury did not receive the decree officially until 4th March, as protocol demanded that it be sent to him via the War Office. In February the King of Bavaria conferred upon him the Order of St Michael (1st Class), along with a letter praising his work, and in early March, Brackenbury heard through the British Minister in Berlin that the Crown Prince wanted to award him the Iron Cross.[1] There was, however, a snag. The award would only be made if Brackenbury was given official leave to wear it. There were two main problems with this. Firstly Queen Victoria was renowned for her antipathy towards 'her' officers wearing foreign decorations, and secondly the government took the view that as he had not been involved in this work on behalf of Her Majesty's Government they could not give permission for him to wear it. Brackenbury, now to his horror, found that a similar decision applied to his French and Bavarian awards. Mr Eastwick M.P. asked parliament to approve that an exception to be made for those who had served for the Red Cross, and this was originally passed. However, Gladstone objected to it and on calling for another vote the motion was defeated, with five of the Liberal MPs who had originally voted in favour being persuaded to change their minds. Gladstone did give an undertaking that the Foreign Secretary would look into the matter but nothing was ever done. Fortunately for Brackenbury the awards were still sent to him one by one. The Bavarians had sent their award to him long before the matter had been raised in

---

1   The correspondence that Brackenbury had with the British Minister in Berlin, Odo William Leopold Russell, on this matter can be found in WO33/50 (also marked FO918/68) at the National Archives, Kew.

Parliament. Not long after the debate the German and French awards arrived. Later on he received the cross of the French Société de Secours and the cross of the Order of St John. The awarding of the Legion of Honour and the Iron Cross to the same individual is, to the best of the author's knowledge, a unique double.

In January 1871 Brackenbury had ended his service on the continent for the National Aid Society, and at the beginning of February he returned to his appointment as Professor of Military History at Woolwich. His series of lectures for that term covered 'The Campaign of 1809 in Germany' and one cannot help but wonder how his recent close quarters access to the Prussian, now German, Army influenced this series. At that moment it was perhaps too current to look at the recent campaign on the continent, but in the second term of 1873 his lecture programme looked at 'The Campaign of 1870 in France to the Battle of Sedan'. Although he settled back down into the routine of life as a lecturer at Woolwich his contact with the Franco-Prussian War, its leading characters, and its consequences were not yet at an end.

Shortly after the commencement of the new term at Woolwich he received a message from the Empress Eugénie who since the fall of the regime of her husband Napoleon III was living in exile in Chiselhurst, southeast London. According to Brackenbury she had written that "She would like to see me at Chiselhurst", although one imagines the language probably made it sound more like a Royal command even if she was in no such position to make such a request. It appears that the reason she wanted to see him was to thank him for his efforts not merely with regards to help for the sick and wounded but also for the kindness and protection he had offered to Madame Canrobert, who alone amongst her former counsellors still held favour. Brackenbury's account of the interview is interesting. One gets the idea that she remained, even at this stage, in something of a state of shock at the speed at which events had taken place. This is understandable if one remembers that only six months previous the position of her husband as Emperor of France had seemed secure. She spoke of the shock at the fall of Sedan and her decision to flee Paris. According to Brackenbury she said regarding this decision that "I am only a woman, and I had the fate of Marie Antoinette in mind". She asked of his work for the National Aid Society along with his account of the conduct and actions of Marshal and Madame Canrobert.[2]

At the time of Brackenbury's visit to the Empress the Emperor Napoleon III was still a prisoner in Germany. He later joined his wife in exile in England. Just after his return from the Easter vacation at Woolwich, Brackenbury received an invitation from the Emperor Napoleon III to call on him at Chiselhurst. Brackenbury recalls that he found him playing 'Patience' and waited until he had finished the game. A more cynical man might have made the comment that had he shown more

---

2    Brackenbury, Henry, *Some Memories of My Spare Time* (London: William Blackwood & Sons, 1909) pp177-179.

patience whilst Emperor he might still be the Emperor, although Brackenbury made no mention of such thoughts. They then proceeded to have a lengthy and detailed conversation mostly regarding military matters. They discussed the battle of Sedan, the strategy of the French Army, Brackenbury's friends in the French Army and in particular one imagines Marshal Canrobert. They then discussed Brackenbury's own studies and the Emperor was familiar with his work on 'Ancient cannon in Europe'.[3] After the discussion was over and Brackenbury took his leave he noticed that the Emperor returned to his game of cards and he paints the picture of the rather sad existence of the former ruler of France. This was not quite the end of his contact with the Emperor. In June 1872 he received a book from Dulau & Co of Soho Square entitled *Les Forces militaires de la France en 1870*, ostensibly written by the Comte de la Chapelle, but in actuality written by the Emperor himself. The book was signed by the Emperor and had the following inscription, "A. M. le Capitaine Brackenbury de la part de l'Empereur Napoleon, Camden Place, le 1 Juin 1872".[4]

In between his visit to the Empress Eugeine and the Emperor Napoleon III Brackenbury had once again witnessed the fallout from the Franco-Prussian War. At the end of the conflict the terms of surrender of the French Army had insisted that all French troops save one division must lay down their arms. The only other exception to this was the Paris National Guard as the new French Government thought it politically dangerous to disarm them. At the same time they rather foolishly stopped the daily pay of the National Guard. With the French army virtually abolished this made the Paris National Guard the strongest military force in France. When the Government decided to send elements of what remained of the French Army to take possession of the cannon held at Montmartre the National Guard refused and elements of the French Army sided with the National Guard. The army commanders General Thomas and General Lecomte were murdered and the French Government removed to Versailles. By the evening of March 18th 1871 Paris was under mob rule in what would become known to history as the Paris Commune. A detailed analysis of the Commune is not required but it has to be stated that the situation was extremely delicate due to the presence on the outskirts of Paris of elements of the German Army. In short the German authorities warned the French that if they did not get hold of the situation in Paris they would. Had such an event been necessary one cannot imagine that the French Government could have survived and a country struggling to come to terms with the humiliating defeat of the recent conflict would have been plunged into further chaos.

Once again Brackenbury was eager to see what was going on. "The situation was full of interest for a soldier, and I determined to take advantage of the short Easter

---

[3] The Emperor Napoleon had himself written a book on the subject of early artillery entitled *Du passé et de l'avenir de l'artillerie 1328-1638* (Paris, 1846).
[4] Brackenbury, *Some Memories of My Spare Time*, pp.205-207.

vacation to see it with my own eyes".⁵ Again, he took advantage of his existing permission to visit the continent to gather material for the coming terms lectures. On 4th April 1871 he arrived at St Germain on the outskirts of Paris. The following day he met with Lord Lyons the British Ambassador to France who it will be recalled had provided assistance to him in terms of permissions and passports when he was working for the Society. A similar passport was provided along with a letter to the French authorities. Armed with this, and his friends in the French army, he was able to obtain what he thought was a unique document which allowed him to visit and inspect the French lines around Paris. By this stage the French army was gaining in strength as officers and men returned from captivity in Germany, and indeed the speed with which such men were being repatriated was increased to help the French authorities to crush the Commune. Brackenbury's friend Marshal Canrobert was in Brussels on the way back from his captivity in Germany and it was urged that he should return to take up command of the increasing numbers of French troops. It was decided that Brackenbury would escort him from the station at St Denis to Versailles. Exactly who asked him to do this is unclear but it was obviously felt that had the rebels stopped them the technically 'neutral' Brackenbury with his British passport would have more chance of passing unmolested. They also took the precaution of travelling at night and made it safely to Versailles.⁶

Brackenbury made St Germain his base and from there he would travel each day to a selected vantage point to inspect the lines, witness the fighting and get a general picture of events as they unfolded. He was with Lord Lyons one day at Meudon as they witness the artillery duel that was ongoing. Suddenly a shell hit the house from which they were observing and exploded in the garden below. Brackenbury later recorded that Lord Lyons commented "Perhaps I had better retire. It would be a diplomatic blunder if Her Majesty's Ambassador were to be killed". Whilst recording this comment it does not seem to have dawned on Brackenbury that it would have been a similar diplomatic blunder if an officer of the Royal Artillery had also met his end in such a manner.⁷

By now the Commune was operating purely on the defensive as the government forces advanced to retake the city. However progress was slow and bloody. At Neuilly the communists were removed from their positions at the bridge after a determined resistance.⁸ Twenty-two officers alone fell that day, including two generals. Brackenbury later told the poignant story of one of the two unnamed

---

5   Brackenbury, *Some Memories of My Spare Time*, p.180.
6   Brackenbury, *Some Memories of My Spare Time*, pp.181-182.
7   Brackenbury, *Some Memories of My Spare Time*, p.183.
8   Throughout his book *Some Memories of My Spare Time*, Brackenbury uses the term 'communist' compared to the more frequently-encountered 'communard'. To retain the flavour of the man it has been decided to retain it. Brackenbury was writing in 1909, a time when the term would have been more familiar perhaps than in 1870.

generals. During the Franco-Prussian War when the unnamed officer was still a Colonel he had been serving at Metz when it fell. As it had been difficult to get news in and out during the siege Brackenbury was asked to pass on the message that the aforementioned officer was now a father. At Neuilly that morning they had reminisced about that day, but later in the day he was killed. As Brackenbury later recalled, "His regiment was engaged in the hottest fight at the battles of Rezonville and Gravelotte, yet he fell at Neuilly by the hands of his own countrymen".

The next day Brackenbury's own life was at risk when visiting a battery of French field guns at Neuilly. Whilst talking to a French General of Artillery a shell from a communist battery on the other side of the bridge burst in the sandbags of the barricade blowing both men off their feet and covering them in sand. Whilst a languid Brackenbury would later call this "a baptism of sand" we do see yet another illustration of the risks he was taking. One could have understood if after this he had decided to leave the battery, but he instead chose to remain and witnessed being showered with biscuits as a waggon containing the aforementioned item was hit by an artillery shell, much to the delight of the men who much preferred being showered with biscuits rather than sand. He witnessed another example of the strange nature of this conflict when he saw French artillery shells hitting the Arc de Triomphe in their attempts to force back the communists. Brackenbury took and kept a photograph of the monument pitted by French shells. This was particularly ironic given that the Prussians/Germans had deliberately avoided firing on it during the war as they had not wished to enrage French public opinion with what could be construed as a national insult.[9]

He was not the only English visitor to the scene. On occasions he was accompanied by Augustus Anson M.P. and his old friend Colonel Valentine Baker. At times they went so far into harm's way that Brackenbury had to drive his own carriage as his courier refused to take such risks. Brackenbury was very matter-of-fact about the risks taken and almost dismissive of them. It has to be said that his recollections were made many years after the event, so perhaps it was easier to be dismissive. On one occasion when under fire Brackenbury made an interesting observation about others regarding this but it could equally be applied to him. When sheltering one day from the shells of the communist batteries Brackenbury witnessed to small boys, who he estimated to be about ten or twelve, playing in the street dodging the shells as if it were a game. When one shell burst near by the two boys they dropped to the ground. When they stood up they were unharmed and proceeded to pick up the fragments of the shell passing them from hand to hand as they were still too hot to be handled continuously. Speaking of the two boys he stated "No better example could be given of the way in which constant exposure to any form

---

9   Brackenbury, *Some Memories of My Spare Time*, pp.185-186.

of danger deadens the sense of fear of that danger. These urchins had gone through the siege by the Germans, and the previous days' fighting at Neuilly, and they had no fear".[10] The same could equally be applied to Brackenbury. However there seems to be more to it than that. The boys lived in the area and had little choice, whereas Brackenbury had travelled many miles to place himself in harms' way.

In his book *Some Memories of My Spare Time* Brackenbury recorded further incidents that occurred during the commune and gives an interesting insight into the situation in France. Obviously he is writing from an interesting perspective. Although he is an outsider he had previously witness the Franco-Prussian at first hand and knew much of French life, culture and politics. As a professional solider he also brings an interesting perspective and understanding to proceedings. All in all he provides an interesting account of a tumultuous period in French history from a detached yet knowledgeable perspective. Brackenbury and Valentine Baker started to realise that they were taking a risk, being serving officers on full pay, and the fear existed that they might somehow be forced into a breach of neutrality. Brackenbury recalled the experience of an officer friend of his, whom he failed to name for obvious reasons, who had been forced into such a breach. Having been 'captured' by the communists he was put to work on a gun crew despite pleading that he was English. Had such a case ever become public it would have meant serious repercussions for the officer concerned, a position Brackenbury could easily have found himself in. [11]

In April Brackenbury had written a long letter to *The Times* that described what he had seen. This was published in the edition of 17th April and Brackenbury later recalled it created much interest in Britain. He vividly compared the sights he had seen with what history recalled of the period immediately after the French Revolution, and he urged in the strongest possible terms that the French Government must get hold on the situation as soon as possible. He recalled the sights he had seen, the horrors and the comedies, the bravery and the cowardice, the good and the evil, and concluded the letter with the simple words "It is monstrous".[12]

At the end of the vacation he once again returned to Woolwich where the lectures for that term dealt with the 'Austro-Prussian War of 1866'. At this time he wrote little for the press as he devoted a lot of time to his lecture series, no doubt realising that questions about his commitment to his position still hung over him after the events of the Franco-Prussian War. Although the National Aid Society had been able to secure his initial appointment and then two extensions to his leave

---

10    Brackenbury, *Some Memories of My Spare Time*, pp.188-189.
11    Brackenbury, *Some Memories of My Spare Time*, pp.179-205. This section deals with Brackenbury's experiences of the Paris Commune.
12    Brackenbury, *Some Memories of My Spare Time*, pp.204-205. A considerable portion of the letter to *The Times* is reprinted here.

it had not been popular and had only been possible due to political intervention. So it was perhaps understandable that he wanted to show that his outside commitments were not affecting his work. At the same time he was being encouraged to place on record some account of the war. Now working as a military historian he combined the lecture notes he had planned for a forthcoming series of lectures with his knowledge of French accounts of the conflict. Indeed during the summer vacation from Woolwich in 1871 he returned to the battlefields of the Franco-Prussian War to continue his research along with talking to his friends in the French Army, and although he never explicitly mentions it one would presume that he talked to Marshal Canrobert.[13]

His studies made him particularly interested in the operations and conduct of the French Army. Thus he decided to write a book looking specifically at this. He therefore felt it best to write the book in French, and it is suggested that he intended it as a potential study aid for the French Army. Although a cynic might suggest it could be entitled 'how not to fight a war' Brackenbury decided to entitle it *Les Maréchaux de France, Etude de leur Conduite de la Guerre en 1870*. Throughout the autumn and winter of 1871 he spent most of his spare time in writing his book. The problem arose regarding the actions of Marshal Bazaine. Brackenbury had commenced his task under the impression that Bazaine had acted correctly during the siege of Metz. There had been some suggestions already that he had 'betrayed' the army, but this was largely thought to be sour grapes. However as Brackenbury continued to look at the facts and the comments and arguments amongst the high command it soon became clear to him that there was more to it than first met the eye. It became clear that Bazaine had failed to break out of Metz due to his personal arguments with the Emperor and Marshal MacMahon. Bazaine had stated, according to those there at the time, that he would never again serve under the Emperor's direct command. So rather than continue his march to Verdun where he would have been under the command of the Emperor he halted at Metz. He later concealed from his staff signals from Marshal MacMahon urging him to attempt to break out and join him at Montmédy, and argued against any attempt to break out. Brackenbury was convinced from his investigations that it was the petty bickering and politics of the French Army that had led to the trapping of Bazaine's army in Metz and the loss of a large portion of the French army.[14] Brackenbury discussed the matter with his friend Marshal Canrobert who revealed that he had already confronted Bazaine regarding this matter, but had Bazaine's word of honour that he had not concealed any orders. However the evidence made clear that he had. Brackenbury speculated that the reason for this was that Bazaine had foreseen the defeat at Sedan and realised that this would leave him with France's last army in the field. Once the

---

13   Brackenbury, *Some Memories of My Spare Time*, pp.207-208.
14   Brackenbury, *Some Memories of My Spare Time*, pp.208-210.

realisation of what Bazaine had done dawned on Brackenbury he suddenly felt he could make sense of so much of the war. The book in its final form was an indictment of so many of the leading lights of the French army, but in particular Bazaine.

Brackenbury had received a contract from Lachaud to produce a book in French. Just as the book was about to be published Brackenbury heard the news that Marshal Bazaine was to be placed on trial, along with other officers, for his conduct during the War and in particularly the surrender of Metz. There were added political problems to Bazaine's conduct. After the declaration of the Third Republic, during the conflict, Bazaine, as an ardent Monarchist, refused to accept the Government's authority and started to negotiate with the Prussians. There was clearly a political agenda to the decision to place General's on trial, and it appeared that Bazaine was the main target. As soon as he heard of the forthcoming trial Brackenbury felt honour bound to suppress his own book. He immediately sought the assistance of Lord Lyons the British Minister in Paris. Lord Lyons instructed his Private Secretary Mr Sheffield to do all he could to help him in this regard. As Brackenbury recalled "The matter of Bazaine's conduct was now *sub judice*, and I could not reconcile it to my conscience to make public this strong indictment. I asked Sheffield to get the Embassy lawyer to see Lachaud and get the book suppressed".[15] The publisher was willing, under pressure, to agree to this but only on the grounds that Brackenbury would compensate him for the entire edition. Exactly how many books were in the edition is unclear but it appears to have been at considerable personal cost to Brackenbury. Apart from a few copies the entire edition was destroyed. As far as we know only eight copies survived, with Brackenbury keeping two for himself. The others went to Sir Lintorn Simmons the Governor of Woolwich, the Emperor Napoleon III, Marshal Canrobert, the Crown Prince of Prussia, later Emperor Frederick III of Germany, one copy to the French journal *Republique Francaise*, and finally one copy to the Staff College Library.

One sees here an illustration of the problem of writing 'history' so soon after the event. How many books over the years have had to have the final chapter re-written or additional chapters added as events changed? It appears simply to have been his sense of honour that led him to suppress his book. It would be expected that as it dealt with an ongoing trial that the publishers might have wished to delay publication, but this does not appear to have been the case. Although he never doubted that he had done the right thing Brackenbury understandably regretted what he had done writing that, "It is rather sad to think that all the results of my elaborate studies of that war lie buried in the grave of this still-born book".[16]

Brackenbury continued to lecture at Woolwich throughout 1872, and spent the vacations of that year visiting battlefields in Italy, the Tyrol, Bavaria and Venice. His

---

15   Brackenbury, *Some Memories of My Spare Time*, p.214.
16   Brackenbury, *Some Memories of My Spare Time*, p.215.

reputation continued to develop as a military writer and lecturer. He was invited to the manoeuvres on Salisbury plain, and later gave a lecture to Volunteer officers on 'Defensive Positions'. Here he stressed the important of courage and discipline in the defence and argued, perhaps somewhat against the grain, that this was more important than the natural advantages of position. His growing reputation as a lecturer led to an interesting opportunity. In November 1872 he received a letter from Sir Howard Elphinstone, Comptroller of the Household of Prince Arthur. Later the Duke of Connaught and Strathearn, Prince Arthur was Queen Victoria's third son and at that time an officer in the Rifle Brigade. Brackenbury recalled that "H.R.H. had desired him (Elphinstone) to ascertain whether I had the leisure and the inclination to assist him in the study of military history", although one imagines it was worded differently so that it sounded more like a command than a request.[17] Brackenbury was keen to carry out the lectures and Elphinstone sought permission from the Commandant of Woolwich Sir Lintorn Simmons. Brackenbury was later sent a copy of Simmons reply to Elphinstone that included the words, "He (Brackenbury) is a very good lecturer. I don't think you could have hit upon a better man for the purpose".[18] Thus Brackenbury delivered a series of military history lectures to Prince Arthur given in the ballroom of the Lord Warden Hotel Dover, where Prince Arthur was currently stationed. As a consequence a large number of the officers of the garrison were also in attendance, and as Brackenbury remarked it made for "a most interesting audience". The lectures were clearly appreciated by Prince Arthur who presented him with a silver parcel-gilt jug, a copy of a design by Cellini, in gratitude for his work.[19] There seems to have been a friendship between the two, or as much as there ever could be given their positions. After his first visit Brackenbury stayed at the hotel, but on each subsequent visit he stayed with Prince Arthur in his house. It can be imagine that they had much to talk about given Brackenbury's current appointment and Prince Arthur's obvious interest in military history.[20] The lectures were clearly appreciated by Prince Arthur and Queen Victoria. A letter from Elphinstone to Brackenbury remarked that, "It will be gratifying to you to know that Her Majesty was very much pleased to hear that the lectures had been so successful and had so deeply interested the Prince".[21]

Their 'relationship' was such that Brackenbury felt secure enough to ask Prince Arthur to preside over a lecture he was to give at the Royal United Service Institute on the tactical changes introduced as a result of the Franco-Prussian War. With

---

17   Brackenbury, *Some Memories of My Spare Time*, pp.216-217.
18   Lintorn Simmons to Elphinstone, 5th November 1872, private collection.
19   Although referred to by Brackenbury in *Some Memories of My Spare Time* as a 'jug' it is called a 'Silver Cup' in his will, which also mentions a stand presented at the same time.
20   Brackenbury, *Some Memories of My Spare Time*, pp.216-217. This gives Brackenbury's account of the events.
21   Elphinstone to Brackenbury, 3rd January 1873, private collection.

uncharacteristic modesty Brackenbury had originally declined to give this lecture, feeling that there were others better qualified. It might be the case that he feared treading on his brother's toes, as Charles was an expert on European warfare. Whatever the reasons for Henry Brackenbury's initial reluctance he finally agreed to give the lecture. The decision to ask Prince Arthur to preside was partly done to encourage officers to attend, as was the decision to hold the event on 31st May 1873, the Saturday of Derby week. It was felt that this would assure the presence of a large number of officers in London, and thus guarantee a large audience.[22] After the lecture Prince Arthur chaired a debate on the subject matter. It is sad that little record of this exists as many of the best minds and most articulate personalities of the era had their say. It would have been fascinating not only to have heard Brackenbury's opinions on the tactical changes that had occurred and their impact of warfare, but also to have heard such people as George Colley, professor of strategy and tactics at the Staff College, Edward Hamley, a soldier and writer whose work *The Operations of War* was a hugely influential text for the Army of that era, Patrick MacDougall, a soldier, writer and at that time Head of the Intelligence Branch, Colonel C.H. Owen Professor of Artillery at Woolwich and a noted writer on artillery, and Charles Brackenbury, debate the subject.

The lecture was later published in the *Royal United Service Institute Journal* as 'The Tactics of the Three Arms as modified to meet the requirements of the Present day'. The lecture was also important in his relationship with Garnet Wolseley, at that time Assistant Adjutant-General at the War Office. It was not the first time they had met as in December 1872 they had both been part of a committee set up to establish a military periodical entitled the *Military Quarterly Review*. As it happened this never came to fruition at this time. What contact Brackenbury and Wolseley actually had is unknown, however it was at the lecture that Wolseley first saw Brackenbury in 'action'. Although Wolseley took no part in the debate himself the fact that Brackenbury had successfully debated the matter with some of the most notably 'minds' of the army must have stayed in Wolseley mind. A few months later Brackenbury would write to Wolseley and, in his own words, an "event occurred which changed the whole current of my life".[23]

---

22 Brackenbury, *Some Memories of My Spare Time*, pp.219-220. The lecture would later be published as 'The Tactics of the Three Arms as modified to meet the requirements of the Present Day', already mentioned in a previous chapter looking at Brackenbury's work on Army Reform.

23 Brackenbury, *Some Memories of My Spare Time*, p.223.

CHAPTER 11

# THE ASHANTI WAR

Sir Garnet (later Lord) Wolseley was an extremely important figure within the late Victorian British Army. Whilst his legacy was somewhat lost due to his decline in health, both physically and mentally, in the later years of his life, when he became something of an embarrassment, there is no doubt that for large periods of this era he was the most important man in the army. He had first risen to prominence when leading the Red River Expedition in Canada. A minor rebellion had broken out in the Red River region over its entry into the new dominion of Canada. Although there was no fighting the expedition was a logistical triumph that saw the movement of 1,200 troops some 1,118 miles from Toronto to Fort Gary.[1] Through good organisation, planning and successful use of river transport the force had moved the distance in a little over three months through difficult terrain and climatic conditions. Astonished that the British had been able to achieve this, the rebels faded away. This was the foundation of Wolseley's reputation. He also established his credentials as a reformer and acting as Assistant Adjutant-General at the War office he was a key supporter of Edward Cardwell in his attempts to reform the British Army.

When Wolseley was appointed to lead an expedition against the Ashanti in the Gold Coast region of West Africa, Brackenbury had written to him in the hope that he might be given an appointment on the staff. To his surprise he was, and so he embarked on a period of his life and career that would be the making of him. Until this point he had achieved prominence as a writer, lecturer, and administrator within the army. It is likely that he would have remained in similar postings, possibly even ending up as Commandant of Woolwich, had it not been for Wolseley's decision to take him with him to Ashantiland on the first of several overseas 'adventures'.

---

1   Little has been written about this campaign specifically. A good, but basic, account can be found in Haythornthwaite, Philip *The Colonial Wars Source Book* (London: Caxton Publishing Group, 2000) p.264. Obviously any of the biographies of Wolseley will have some detail regarding it.

## The founding of the 'Ashanti Ring'

The Ashanti Campaign of 1873–1874 was one in a long line of punitive expeditions which were undertaken by the British Army, usually assisted by native and local forces, during the Victorian era. What made the Ashanti campaign different was the level of planning and skill that went into organising it. This campaign also saw the foundation of a group of officers, many of whom were considered the brightest and best that the British Army had to offer, around the personage of Garnet Wolseley. Thereafter they followed him from campaign to campaign. These men were called the 'Ashanti Ring', the 'Wolseley Ring' and the 'Wolseley Gang', the latter normally being reserved for use by those who were jealous and envious of them.[2]

The Ashanti were a warrior tribe on Africa's Gold Coast. Europeans had garrisoned the once precious coastline since the 1600s.[3] The British trading posts had long lost their importance by the time the British Africa Company went bankrupt in 1821 and the British government took over its assets. Where the company had been happy to bribe the Ashanti to stay away from their trading posts and to leave the Fanti tribe alone, the British government refused to take such action. The first Crown Governor, Sir Charles McCarthy, refused to pay tribute to the Ashanti and along with the white settlers and the Fanti went out to meet the subsequent Ashanti invasion in December 1823. The settlers' guns should have proved decisive but unfortunately the Fanti, not for the first or the last time, deserted during the battle and Sir Charles and his supporters were defeated near the village of Bonsaso on the 21st January 1824. The Ashanti cut off his head and turned his skull into the Royal drinking cup. The British response was to see it as an act of barbarism, although to the Ashanti it was perceived as a compliment for the way in which Sir Charles had fought so bravely.

The Ashanti continued to dominate until August 1826 when the British Governor, Hope Smith, defeated them near Dodowa. The battle was fought in open ground where British firepower proved decisive and the Ashanti suffered a heavy defeat. This battle does seem to have deterred the Ashanti somewhat. There were some minor attacks in 1863, but it was not until 1873 that they launched the next serious attack. This time it was repelled by a detachment of a hundred Royal Marines from nearby ships. This occurred in January, and by June the marines were still there and had suffered no problems. Then the rainy season began in earnest and by July

---

[2] A detailed account of the campaign is not necessary. For more detail on the Ashanti Ring and the men who made it, see Maxwell, Leigh, *The Ashanti Ring* (London: Leo Cooper, 1985) and Harvie, Ian, 'The Wolseley Ring: A Case Study in the Exercise of Patronage in The Late Victorian Army', M.A. Thesis, Buckingham University, 1993.

[3] A detailed account of the history of the Ashanti land and the build-up to the war can be found in Brackenbury, Henry, *The Ashanti War of 1873-74* Volume I & II (London: William Blackwood & Sons, 1874). A simpler version of events can be found in Maxwell, *The Ashanti Ring*. Wolseley's handwritten campaign journals still exist in WO147/3 and WO147/4 at the National Archives, Kew.

Lord Wolseley – an extremely important influence upon Brackenbury's life and career. Although their relationship had its ups and downs Brackenbury had good reason to be grateful to Wolseley for his patronage, particularly in the early days. (*Illustrated London News*)

the garrison had been decimated by dysentery and smallpox. Ten marines died and a further fifty-eight had to be sent home for hospital treatment.[4] The problems that the marines suffered were no more than was expected. The Gold Coast was renowned as a 'white man's graveyard'. The story is told, perhaps apocryphally, that an officer posted to the Gold Coast asked an officer who had seen previous service there what kit he should take with him. The answer he received was, "Take a coffin, that's all you will need".[5] Whilst the British Government recognised the need for action against the Ashanti, largely to restore British pride, they were reluctant to commit 'white' troops' because of the obvious health risks. Garnet Wolseley was given command of the expedition and was charged with bringing the campaign to a successful conclusion with the use of West African Hausas and the West Indian Regiment. It was felt that they would be better able to stand up to the conditions, and it must be said that they were also considered expendable in a way that even the much-abused British soldier was not.

The evidence suggests that there was in fact tacit agreement between the Secretary of State for War, Edward Cardwell and the Colonial Secretary, Lord Kimberley, that British regulars would be needed to bring the campaign to a successful and decisive

---

4  It has been stated that the situation would have been much worse had it not been for the excellent work of Dr A.D. Home.
5  Farwell, Byron, *Queen Victoria's Little Wars* (London: Allen Lane, 1973), p.191.

conclusion.[6] It was also suggested that if handled properly the Government would agree to such an action. This was partly why Wolseley was selected, despite being officially only a colonel. His conduct when commander of the Red River expedition in Canada had demonstrated both his organisational skills and his attention to detail. Just as important was the fact that he had been able to achieve success in Canada quickly and cheaply, both in terms of casualties and money. The aim of this campaign was simply to restore British pride and hopefully demonstrate British military superiority to such an extent that there would be no more Ashanti raids into British territory. It was made clear to Wolseley by the Government that this had to be done quickly and cheaply and with a small loss of life, at least for the British. This was why he was determined to use what he thought of as the brightest and best of the British officer corps to help him achieve this end. He was criticised for what some saw as an unnecessary use of officers of such calibre, and was accused of, "using the finest steel in our Army to cut brushwood".[7] Yet this was to ignore the fact that such calibre of men were needed if the campaign were to be handled in the way the Government wanted. He needed men who were intelligent, good administrators and who understood fully the constraints under which he was expected to operate. This is not to say that they were not good 'fighting' men, as two had already won the Victoria Cross.[8] It was not usual for a commander of an expedition to be given such a free hand in selecting his officers. It was to be a constant complaint levelled against him, mostly by the Duke of Cambridge, that he picked the same officers each time and objected to those who were 'forced' on him by the War Office. The fact that he was allowed such a free hand illustrates not only the confidence but also the close cooperation he had from the government.

Wolseley and his officers left England on 12th September 1873 and arrived off Cape Coast Castle on 2nd October. It was this group of officers who became known as the 'Ashanti ring', and later the 'Wolseley ring'. In the years ahead they would serve together on many occasions under his leadership, and over time others would be added to this group. They were of a different style of officer from that which was commonly found in the British army during this period, and perhaps nothing illustrates this better than the voyage to Africa. The normal sea-borne entertainments were replaced by hard study of the material concerning the area and the Ashanti themselves that had been provided by the War Office and through private means. Brackenbury and Captain George Huyshe gave a series of lectures on the Ashanti and Fanti and the whole approach was of a level of sophistication that was

---

6    Maxwell, Leigh, *The Ashanti Ring*, Chapter 4.
7    This statement is attributed to Lieutenant-Colonel Sir Augustus Anson V.C., who at the time was M.P. for Bewdley.
8    John Castairs McNeill and Henry Evelyn Wood had already won the V.C. and Redvers Buller would go on to win it in the Zulu War. Lord (later 3rd Baron) Gifford, who would go on to serve with Wolseley in Natal, Cyprus and Zululand was awarded the V.C. for the Ashanti campaign.

largely alien to the British Army.[9] It was in fact a professional campaign at a time when the professional soldier was looked upon with suspicion. 'Officership' was in many quarters essentially a reflection of social status. It was therefore not an occupation demanding hard study. Those who did take their military careers seriously and studied their profession were somewhat outcast. Wolseley fell into this category, as did the majority of his officers on this campaign. The difference was that on this campaign they were amongst like-minded officers.

Brackenbury's own appointment had been something of a surprise, not least to himself. On hearing of the proposed expedition he, like countless others who were keen to see action, wrote immediately to Wolseley offering his services in whatever capacity the commander thought best. Brackenbury did have a slightly better chance than many because his writing had made him well known and had brought him into contact with Wolseley, as mentioned in the previous chapter. Brackenbury hoped that he might get a position concerning transport, given his experiences in the Franco-Prussian War, although he seems to have been doubtful of even this. He felt that he would be "looked upon as only a theorist a writer and a teacher".[10] He was genuinely surprised to receive Wolseley's offer to be his Military Secretary. The reasons for this can be found in Brackenbury's career to date, so now is a good moment to reconsider this. He had seen some, rather limited, active service during the Indian Mutiny and had served at the battle of Banda. He was therefore not completely untested in battle. Perhaps more importantly he had recently witnessed at first hand the Franco-Prussian War, and had probably got the best 'view' of any serving British officer. His service for the National Aid Society had demonstrated his skills as an administrator, and his writing and lecturing exploits had shown him to have the intellectual capacity to think, consider and analyse military history and tactics. His writing would also have appealed to Wolseley, as a large part of it had been devoted to military reform, a subject close to Wolseley's heart and one on which he and Brackenbury shared the same general outlook. It is likely, and indeed logical, that as Brackenbury was currently employed as a Professor of Military History at Woolwich Wolseley would have had him in mind to give the lectures, as he subsequently did, to his officers regarding the forthcoming campaign. Whatever the reason his appointment was the start of an association that would see him rise and benefit from the patronage of Wolseley.

The level to which he was dependent upon his favour is impossible to gauge. If he owed his subsequent success to Wolseley he was far from being the only one. It

---

9   The papers were later published by Blackwoods - Brackenbury, Henry & Huyshe, George Lightfoot, *Fanti and Ashanti: Three papers read on board the S.S. Ambriz on the voyage to the Gold Coast* (London: William Blackwood, 1873).
10  The whole story is told in Brackenbury, Henry, *Some Memories of My Spare Time* (London: William Blackwood and Sons, 1909), pp.223-224.

would be nice to think that an officer of Brackenbury's undoubted ability would have been successful without patronage from one source or another, but it is unlikely. What Wolseley saw as Brackenbury's strengths many would have seen as his weaknesses. As Joseph H. Lehmann wrote, "Most commanders would have passed over the bookish soldier in organising a staff for active service", but he "proved tireless and thorough, and soon demonstrated that he was a superb staff officer and an ideal military secretary, thereby vindicating his chief's estimate".[11] Lehmann also referred to Brackenbury as a "scholastic soldier", a comment which he undoubtedly meant as a compliment but which many of Brackenbury's contemporaries may well have used as an insult. This says a lot about the way in which staff work, particularly in this era, was viewed. For a campaign as complex as the Gold Coast involving issues of time, geographical, medical, financial and political considerations, a smooth running staff system was vital. This required a number of top class administrators and organisers, indeed 'managers' rather than pure and simple fighting men, who were forced into doing staff work. Wolseley understood the importance of staff work in a successful campaign and the Ashanti campaign illustrates this more than most. Attention to detail was seen on a scale unknown for a colonial campaign of this nature and this was the key for the quick and relatively easy success. The Ashanti were a fearsome warrior nation and whilst the modern equipment of the British should have proved enough to defeat the Ashanti on its own, the quality of planning and staff work made victory assured. There were many occasions when failure to pay attention to such things caused embarrassing setbacks for the British in other campaigns, most notably the Zulu War, and meant that more troops, and therefore further expenditure, became necessary.

Yet whilst Brackenbury appreciated the importance of such work, and had a flair for it, he constantly wanted to prove himself as a fighting soldier. Brackenbury's comments, looked at earlier in this chapter, about the way he felt he would be perceived say a lot about the way he felt he had to prove himself in this capacity. He constantly pushed himself to forward positions where he could engage in the attack. During the campaign Brackenbury persuaded Wolseley to send him forward during the action at Essaman to assist Captain Crease and his Marines. Crease led the attack on the hill whilst Brackenbury, supported by another of Wolseley's staff officers keen for action, Lieutenant Charteris, led the frontal assault on the village. It is perhaps worth noting here that the Ashanti marksmanship surprised everyone with its accuracy and rapidity of fire, despite the age of their flintlock weapons. So such an attack was a far from easy one, and leading it illustrated his fighting qualities.

Brackenbury played a key role in what seemed a meticulous campaign. Extraordinary lengths were undertaken to maintain the health of the British troops that arrived in

---

11   Lehmann, Joseph H., *All Sir Garnet: A Life of Field Marshal Lord Wolseley* (London: Jonathan Cape, 1964), p.167.

December 1873. Whilst many of these precautions might seem very logical, such as lightweight clothing, protection from the sun and medical precautions, they were far from common on such campaigns. By the time British troops arrived Wolseley had already had several clashes with the Ashanti, but the poor conduct of the locally raised soldiers had given him the justification he wanted to call for British troops. By the time they arrived preparation to ease their suffering had been put into effect, mostly by the work of Major Robert Home. He had constructed seven 'way-stations' at ten-mile intervals between Cape Coast and Prasu, which was to operate as the forward base for the attacking force. The 'way-stations' had accommodation for 400 men, hospital facilities, water purifiers, ablutions and stores. Some even had fully equipped bakeries and abattoirs. Further precautions were taken for the march itself. A native carrier was assigned to every three soldiers to assist in the carrying of equipment, which included respirators, veils and cholera belts, and a dose of quinine was given to each man in his tea before the start of the march. Even the uniforms were made especially for the campaign, a suit of Elcho Grey Tweed with a cork and canvas helmet, as Wolseley had felt that both the home and colonial service uniforms were unsuitable to the peculiar conditions of the region.

As a result of these precautions the casualties caused by disease and fever were enormously reduced. During the campaign the enemy killed 18 men and 55 were killed by disease out of a force of a little over 1,500 Europeans. Compare such results with the earlier despatch of 100 Royal Marines of whom 10 were killed and 58 had to be invalided home, and Wolseley's precautions to preserve the health of his troops are dramatically justified. More importantly for the British government the whole expedition had cost only £800,000, which was slightly less than they had budgeted for.[12] Everything the government wanted had been achieved. British honour was restored without too much trouble. It is no wonder that a good deal of praise was heaped on the leadership and men who had achieved it. They had gone into an area which was largely thought to be a 'white man's graveyard' and despite difficult conditions and terrain, unreliable allies, and a far from easy opponent who greatly outnumbered them, had met with complete success. British technological superiority was obviously a crucial factor. Although it was never used in action this was the first campaign the British undertook with the use of the Gatling Gun. The fact that it was attached to an artillery carriage made it difficult to transport and so it was never use in battle, although there was a notable demonstration of the gun before Ashanti envoys, which allegedly led to one of them committing suicide. However there were many other campaigns where similar superiority counted for

---

12  Lehmann, *All Sir Garnet: A Life of Field Marshal Lord Wolseley*, p.87. The figures for casualties are sometimes placed somewhat higher, however this was caused after the campaign, and was due to a failure to remove the troops from Ashantiland quick enough. Consequently almost a thousand troops were invalided home sick. This was largely due to a shortage of suitable transport ships.

little because preparations had been inadequate. The campaign showed quite clearly the advantages of having a properly functioning staff that understood its work and did it efficiently and effectively. Wolseley was later to attribute most of the political success of the campaign to Brackenbury.[13] Of course the campaign did take its toll on members of Wolseley's staff, partly because of the sheer volume of work, but also because they had been in the region longer than any other Europeans. By the end of the campaign Brackenbury alone amongst the staff had not succumbed to fever at one point or another.

Perhaps the most appropriate way to conclude this chapter is to quote directly from Wolseley's despatch to London on the conclusion of the conflict.

> To my personal staff I am deeply indebted for the manner in which they have performed their duties. Captain H. Brackenbury, my Assistant Military Secretary, a highly educated officer, has shown much practical ability in the field, and only requires opportunity for the development of great military talents ... Both Captain Brackenbury and Lieutenant Maurice have been with me from the first and have worked indefatigably.[14]

Here Wolseley sums up perfectly the reason why Brackenbury would always have cause to be grateful to him; simply, opportunity. Rightly or wrongly it was active service that brought you quickly to the attention of the military and civil authorities. It was successful active service overseas that obtained your next promotion and your next posting. Without this progress could be very slow. Brackenbury is a good illustration of this. In 1873 Brackenbury, after almost seventeen years' service, had been promoted once from Lieutenant to Captain. In the next fifteen years he would rise from Captain to the rank of Lieutenant-General. That was the difference that active service, an opportunity to illustrate your skills and get noticed, could have upon a career. Joseph H. Lehmann's comment, mentioned previously, that most commanders would have looked past Brackenbury when selecting a staff for active service, is quite true. Not only did Wolseley give him this opportunity but it led to others, fellow soldiers and politicians, recognising his ability and being prepared to give him further opportunity to advance his career.

---

13 Lehmann, *All Sir Garnet: A Life of Field Marshall Lord Wolseley*, p.191.
14 Brackenbury, *The Ashanti War of 1873-74* Volume II, p.355. Appendix No 1 is a reproduction of Wolseley's report. A copy can also be found in WO147/4 at the National Archives, Kew.

CHAPTER 12

# RETURN FROM ASHANTILAND AND EXPERIENCES IN NATAL AND CYPRUS

Brackenbury returned home from the Ashanti campaign in March 1874 along with Wolseley and the remainder of his staff. Once back in England he undertook an immense task. He had suggested to Wolseley that he write a narrative of the campaign. Wolseley, who was keen that officers should read about, debate, and learn from campaigns, agreed enthusiastically. Cynically it could also be suggested that this would enhance the Wolseley 'legend', especially when written by one who had been so close to him during the campaign and took a share in either the success or the blame of the expedition. That would perhaps be a little unfair as it was in many ways a textbook campaign of how to deal with difficult conditions by good administration and preparation which held a lot of lessons for the rest of the army.

On his return Brackenbury put his proposal to publisher John Blackwood who recommended that if such a book was to be a success it would have to be published as soon as possible whilst public interest was still aroused. Brackenbury also felt obliged to produce it speedily as Blackwood had agreed to meet any loss that the book made. There were slight delays over obtaining official papers, which Wolseley overcame on his behalf. The ensuing writing, editing and publishing was a Herculean effort, and in only six weeks the book, 795 pages in length, was completed![1] He worked between twelve and fourteen hours a day, assisted by two

---

1   Brackenbury, Henry, *Some Memories of My Spare Time*, pp.232-235. The Blackwood Papers at the National Library of Scotland show that he was paid £300 for this book. Brackenbury to Blackwood, 27th November 1874, Blackwood Papers, National Library of Scotland, MS 4315.

shorthand writers, to whom he would dictate for around two hours a day. *The Ashanti War*, first published in 1874 in two volumes, was a contemporary success and has remained the best account of the campaign. The reason for its success was probably best summed up by W.B. Cheadle's review in *The Academy*.[2] He noted that by the end of 1874 five works on the Ashanti Campaign had been published. With the exception of Brackenbury's they had all been written by special correspondents. The strength of Brackenbury's work was that it was the only one to concentrate on the military operations, rather than being a recollection of personal experiences. Obviously Brackenbury had the advantage of having been closely involved in the planning and organisation of the campaign and he also had access to the official papers from the War Office. This made his account uniquely authoritative. Whilst generally a glowing review, Cheadle did make two criticisms. Firstly, he felt that in some cases there was evidence of Brackenbury being too close to the events, and secondly, that he failed to make the necessary criticisms of certain mistakes and 'disasters', although perhaps the latter criticism is unfair as it was largely a faultless campaign. Cheadle undoubtedly had a point but it is very understandable that Brackenbury should not want to alienate Wolseley by an overly critical account. At a time when Brackenbury was trying to advance his military career such an account would have been far from helpful. It does perhaps highlight the dilemma faced by a man who was both a soldier and a writer about military matters. Whilst wanting to produce an 'exciting' factual and descriptive account he also had to consider his own career and the consequences of being too analytical or critical. He would also have felt loyalty towards his comrades in the Wolseley 'ring' and would have undoubtedly hoped to see further service with them.

Unsurprisingly, the effort of writing this book in such a short space of time led to a serious deterioration in Brackenbury's health. As he later recalled, "During the preparation of this book I was unable to take any exercise or recreation, and in consequence suffered, after the first three weeks, from insomnia, and for the last fortnight took chloral every night. Yet the book never left my mind even in my sleep. I consulted a doctor, who advised me strongly to take a rest, saying I was running a serious risk of brain fever".[3] Despite the medical advice Brackenbury carried on until it was finished and then rushed off to Switzerland to recover. His holiday, along with the first uninterrupted sleep he had been able to enjoy for many months, helped him recover from the hard months of campaigning and then the strain of writing a book in such a short space of time

Despite his success, both in Ashantiland and with the book, by the end of 1874 Brackenbury's career had stalled. He had hoped that his service in Ashanti would see

---

2    Cheadle, W.B., 'The Ashanti War' (book review), *The Academy* 6 (July/December 1874), 3rd October 1874, pp.365-366.

3    Brackenbury, *Some Memories of My Spare Time*, p.235.

him promoted to more interesting work but instead he found himself back with the Royal Artillery and posted to Sheerness, which he described as "one of the dullest quarters".[4] He was unhappy with his appointment and his failure to be promoted a brevet Lieutenant-Colonel, which he believed had been promised to him. At this point he was considering leaving the army, and had received some offers of work in the City. He consulted Wolseley who asked him to wait before making a decision.[5] A few days later Wolseley informed him that he had been asked to go to Natal as Governor and General Officer Commanding, and wanted Brackenbury to go with him.

## Natal

Although the first 'white' settlers in Natal had been British they were soon outnumbered by the Boer settlers, largely of Dutch origin, who were leaving the British controlled cape colony to seek independence in what would become known at the 'Great Trek'. About three thousand, of approximately 14,000 'trekkers', settled in Natal. However they still found themselves depended upon the British both for supplies and ultimately protection. The mighty Zulu nation clashed with the Natal Boers at regular intervals. This prompted many of the Boers to move on further into what would become the Transvaal and the Orange Free State. In time the number of British settlers grew. However there was a delicate balance to be maintained between the British, the Boers and the indigenous tribes.

Wolseley was sent because it was felt he could handle the delicate political situation, but also the growing unrest amongst the African tribes. Wolseley's role ended up being almost entirely political. Brackenbury became his private secretary and clerk of the executive council. This was not really a demanding job, and he filled his time by helping to run the government newspaper *The Times of Natal* and by giving a series of public lectures in Pietermaritzburg on 'Incidents of the Ashanti War'.[6] He did, along with Colonel Sir George Colley and Sir Napier Broome, play a major part in the reform, and in some cases creation, of public services in Natal. However his time there was remembered more for his social life rather than his professional duties. He socialised with the high and mighty of Natal society and records meeting the controversial Bishop Colenso, who somewhat surprisingly Brackenbury seems to have admired, Theophilus Shepstone, a powerful figure in Natal and Rider Haggard who would gain lasting fame as an author.[7] Brackenbury also records riding a lot and playing tennis and cricket amongst his leisure activities at this time. This social activity reflected the lack of work. As one historian put it he was "As active

---

4 Brackenbury, *Some Memories of My Spare Time*, pp.235-236.
5 Brackenbury, *Some Memories of My Spare Time*, p.236.
6 Brackenbury, *Some Memories of My Spare Time*, pp.237-238.
7 Brackenbury, *Some Memories of My Spare Time*, pp.238-239.

in the drawing-rooms as on the battlefield".[8] According to Wolseley, Brackenbury, a married man, was involved in a rather passionate affair whilst in Natal. What made the position even more delicate was that it was alleged to be with the wife of Theophilus Shepstone Jnr. He was a distinguished politician and volunteer soldier, whose father was the unofficial leader of Natal. What worried Wolseley was that he was said to be an extremely jealous man and a 'crack shot'. Wolseley resolved to get Brackenbury away from temptation as soon as possible, and took the opportunity to move his staff 'up country'.

Although another useful period of service overseas the posting in Natal was for Brackenbury, and Wolseley, only a brief interlude. In October 1875 Brackenbury returned to England with Wolseley and received the promotion to brevet Lieutenant-Colonel that he had hoped for the year before. He was given command of a field battery at Woolwich, an appointment that he seemed to find far more acceptable than Sheerness.[9] The main task was to train recruits to be sent to India each autumn. Woolwich seemed to be where he was at his happiest, particularly when he was in either a training or teaching role. Before his major administrative appointments the only time he talked of happiness in his work was when he was teaching military history and during this second period at Woolwich. The fact that he was busy and enjoying his work is supported by the fact that during this period he wrote very little for the press. There was always a correlation between the level of work and enjoyment of it and the amount Brackenbury wrote for publication.

## Egypt and Crete

During the winter of 1875–1876 Brackenbury accompanied Sir Patrick MacDougall and Major Alexander Tulloch on a tour of Egypt and then travelled on with Tulloch to Crete and Athens.[10] MacDougall was at that time Head of the Intelligence Branch of the War Office. The timing was interesting as it was just after the British Government's purchase of the Khedive's shares in the Suez Canal for £4,000,000 in November 1875. Indeed the timing was more than interesting it was downright suspicious, and the Egyptians knew as much. Although MacDougall was ostensibly travelling for his health, the real reason was obvious. Now that Britain 'owned' the Suez Canal she needed to know everything she could about the country and in particularly its military and its defences. MacDougall and Tulloch would later prepare confidential reports for the Government.[11] Exactly what Brackenbury's role

---

8     Maxwell, Leigh, *The Ashanti Ring* (London: Leo Cooper, 1985) p.91.
9     Brackenbury, *Some Memories of My Spare Time*, pp.242-243.
10   Tulloch, later General Sir Alexander, should not be confused with his uncle of the same name, rank and title, who died in 1864.
11   Indeed Tulloch's knowledge would be put to good use by Wolseley during the 1882 invasion of

was is unclear. He had no prior knowledge of the area, nor was he attached to the Intelligence Branch. There are perhaps several reasons. As someone knowledgeable about artillery he might have been useful. Also he was known as a writer and as an officer of the army who had regularly travelled abroad before. MacDougall and Wolseley were close and it might be that Brackenbury was recommended by him or possibly even going on his behalf. Sadly Brackenbury made no comment other than to confirm that he travelled with the party, but does not even make mention of the purpose or record anything about the tour itself, other than when he and Tulloch get to Crete minus MacDougall.[12] Presumably the 'secret' part of their mission was over by now and Brackenbury felt free to make comment. Whatever Brackenbury's role in the mission was, it is clear that it was another interesting experience and one which would serve him well in the future.

### Writing and Regimental duty

In the summer of 1876 he accompanied the Surgeon-General (later Sir) Thomas Longmore to an exhibition in Brussels that covered ambulance material and other forms of life saving equipment. His reputation from the Franco-Prussian War remained and he had been asked to offer his knowledge of recent practical experience to Longmore. On his return he put his visit to good use for himself and wrote an article for Blackwood's entitled 'Philanthropy in War' which looked at the material he had seen in Brussels whilst examining the preparations of European nations in this direction. He took the opportunity to once again put forward his case that the National Aid Society should be using some of the £73,000 held in its account to plan for its use in the next conflict, wherever that might be. He also suggested that the interest from this account could be used to support British troops with comforts during the many colonial campaigns that the army faced. He later recorded that "My efforts in this direction were not successful. I have always thought that this was due to the conservative influence of the financial element on the committee, my membership of which I had previously resigned when I failed to get them to move in this direction".[13]

In the winter of 1876–1877 Brackenbury found he had a lot of time on his hands for a period. Although he gives no details he does confirm that during this period he had to undergo a series of surgical operations in London. It is unclear what this was for but he had been struggling with his back for some time, an affliction which would return later in his life, and it is likely that it may have been related to this.

---

Egypt, and he would lead the landing party at Alexandria, winning the Victoria Cross in the process.
12   Brackenbury, *Some Memories of My Spare Time*, p.242.
13   Brackenbury, *Some Memories of My Spare Time*, pp.243-245.

As a result he had several months of recuperation where he had little to do and as a consequence he once more 'took up his pen'. During this period he wrote articles for *The World* and *The Daily Telegraph* on a fairly regular basis. His contributions to *The Daily Telegraph* were in many ways highly political and had to do with the current crisis in the Balkans which would lead to the Russo-Turkish War. Brackenbury was looking not only at the crisis itself but the possibility of British involvement. In November 1876 Brackenbury contributed two articles, written under the pseudonym 'Anglophile', entitled 'Russia at Constantinople', and 'Diplomatic Parallels'. The first predicted the events of early 1878 when Russia would be on the verge of capturing the city, and looked at the obvious consequences that Russian control of the Dardanelles could have on the British passage to India through the Mediterranean and the Suez canal in the event of war with Russia. Brackenbury later recorded that "The object of the articles was to ensure the defence of English interests, if necessary, even by war".[14] In a two part article for the paper published on 18th and 20th February 1877, Brackenbury discussed the possibility of an alliance against Russia with Austria and Germany. Throughout the crisis and the Russo-Turkish War he continued to write regular contributions for *The Daily Telegraph*, such as 'England's Threatened Interests', 'Why do we Hesitate?', 'The Russian Advance through Roumania', 'The passage of the Danube', 'The Lines of Gallipoli' and many others. He continued to use the name 'Anglophile' thus allowing him the freedom to write whatever he thought without fear of the repercussions of being a serving officer being openly critical of the government of the day. Interestingly Brackenbury found himself under the strict control of the political editor of the paper, Edwin Arnold, who gave him clear instructions on what he should write and the policy of the paper which he was to advocate at all times. There was no problem in this regard as Brackenbury's 'policy' regarding the crisis was entirely in accord with that of *The Daily Telegraph*.[15]

His work for *The World* was based on occasional articles. Interestingly his first article was beyond his usual range and was entitled 'Five French Plays and a Moral'. This was one of the few times that Brackenbury ventured beyond the military or international politics that was the norm for his work. During his association with that paper Brackenbury developed a lasting friendship with T.H.S. Escott, at that time political editor for the paper. The friendship would last beyond Brackenbury's association with the paper and was sufficiently close that Brackenbury felt comfortable writing to him regarding quite private matters later in his career.[16]

Although Brackenbury had previously had great success as a writer in terms of the effects his work had on his own career, it was at this stage that his literary work was proving to be at its most lucrative financially. A good example of this is shown

---

14  Brackenbury, *Some Memories of My Spare Time*, p.248.
15  Brackenbury, *Some Memories of My Spare Time*, pp.249-250.
16  His correspondence with Escott can be found at the British Library, Add MSS 58775.

in the events of May 1877, when he was visited one evening by a junior editor of *The Illustrated London News*. At this time the Russo-Turkish War was in progress and his visitor said that he was empowered by the proprietor to ask Brackenbury to write an article for a special edition of the paper looking at the war and the armies of the contending powers. They wanted twenty-five columns and must be ready in five days. Brackenbury was not inclined to take the work. "I thought the terms offered insufficient, and was not anxious for the work, as I had plenty to do". He therefore said that he was only willing to take on the work for a fee of a hundred guineas, providing that the *Illustrated London News* also provide a shorthand writer to take down his article. The next morning he was surprised to find a shorthand writer on his doorstep with a letter accepting his terms. His article 'The Armies of the Contending Powers, and a Description of the Theatre of War' was one of a series of articles for the special edition which looked at various angles of the conflict. The edition was a success and sold over 100,000 copies, which when one thinks of the standards of the 1870s was very high. As Brackenbury later remarked "My military duties were not interrupted; and this was the best payment I ever got for five days employment of my spare time".[17]

In the summer of 1877 Brackenbury attended the French Army manoeuvres as the guest of Marshal Canrobert and Brackenbury concluded that he got a better view than most. Indeed on one occasion perhaps a little too close when a battery of horse artillery broke loose and hit Brackenbury's horse throwing him from it. Surprisingly Brackenbury escaped without a scratch but the horse had to be shot. It is unusual to note that Brackenbury did not write anything as a consequence of his visit to the army manoeuvres. Perhaps this was due to the fact that he had been given an up-close view far beyond what most 'foreign' officers had seen, due to his personal friendship with Marshal Canrobert. Brackenbury may not have wished to embarrass or be seen to have taken advantage of his relationship with Canrobert. However he continued to write for *The Daily Telegraph*, *The World* and *Blackwood's* throughout 1877 and 1878 covering such varied subjects as 'The South African Question', looking at the problems of confederation in that area and the threat from the 'Zulu Empire', to 'The Troubles of a Scots Traveller', a review of an 1623 book by William Lithgow connected with Crete.[18]

In late 1877 Brackenbury was disappointed when moved to the command of a garrison battery at Dover, which next year moved on to Newhaven. Both postings met with the same level of enthusiasm as Sheerness. Undoubtedly part of the problem was location which in all three instances he described as 'dreary', largely because a lack of 'society' in which he could ingratiate himself, but he also disliked the appointments

---

17  Brackenbury, *Some Memories of My Spare Time*, pp.254-256. The fee equates to a little over £5,000 in modern money.
18  Brackenbury, *Some Memories of My Spare Time*, pp.256-258.

because he had too little to do.[19] There was nothing in his work to tax him, no problems of organisation, strategy or supply that he had to solve. His dislike of such appointments highlights three things. Firstly, there was his liking for the social trappings of high society, which was often missing in these appointments. His reputation as a writer and the minor 'celebrity' status he had attained as a consequence of the Franco-Prussian War and the Ashanti campaign meant that he was invited to parties and dinners where many of the biggest 'stars' were present. He mixed socially with the likes of Arthur Sullivan, William Russell, and Henry Irving, to name but three. Secondly, his general dislike of regimental duty, but more than that there was his desire to serve beyond and above the Royal Artillery. Thirdly, it is an illustration of his genuine enjoyment of hard and demanding administrative work be that in terms of organisation, strategy or supply. This is also further illustrated by the fact that he found his previous appointment of commanding a depot more interesting than commanding a battery, a preference that few in the army would share.

## Cyprus

In July 1878 he was saved from the tedium of Newhaven. Wolseley had been appointed Lord High Commissioner of the newly acquired 'colony' of Cyprus, granted to Britain as a base from which to counter any Russian attempt to dominate or break out of the Black Sea. Brackenbury had already written an article on the need for a British base in the area, but he had suggested Crete as a more suitable location.[20] Initially a detachment of the Indian Army was deployed to Cyprus at the height of the crisis with Russia.[21] The way in which Brackenbury was asked was interesting and points to the somewhat rushed nature of occupation of the island. Late in the evening Brackenbury received a telegram from Wolseley which simply said "I go in two or three days to Cyprus. Will you come?" The prospect of further experience overseas, and his desire to get away from the tedium of commanding a garrison battery, meant he did not have to think twice and immediately arranged to set off for London early the next morning.

On arrival Brackenbury was appointed Assistant Adjutant and Quarter Master General to this force, but within only a few weeks the crisis had abated and the

---

19  Brackenbury, *Some Memories of My Spare Time*, p.263.
20  Brackenbury, Henry, 'Crete', *Blackwood's Magazine*, Volume 121 (April 1877), pp.428-455.
21  An excellent account of this period is found in Cavendish, Anne, *Cyprus 1878: The Journal of Sir Garnet Wolseley* (Nicosia: Cultural Centre of the Cyprus Popular Bank, 1991). This is an edited version of his journal, which unfortunately has never, to the best of my knowledge, been published in the U.K. However a copy is held, along with the Wolseley papers, at the Central Library Hove. The original journal survives at the National Archives at Kew WO147/6. See also Preston, Adrian, 'Sir Garnet Wolseley and the Cyprus Expedition 1878', *The Journal of The Society for Army Historical Research*, Volume XLV (1967).

Indian troops were removed. It is worth noting that had it come to war with Russia the plan was for Wolseley to be second in command of the expeditionary force, with the veteran general Robert Napier, by now Baron Napier of Magdala, in overall command. This combination was planned to work so that the younger man, Wolseley, would be the main field commander acting under Napier's overall direction. This would have placed Brackenbury at the very heart of the conflict, as he was designated Quartermaster General of the force to be sent to Constantinople. However after the Indian, and the majority of British troops, were withdrawn Wolseley and his staff remained and Brackenbury was now without a position. He was also prepared to leave Cyprus but was asked by Wolseley to become Chief Commandant of Police and Inspector of Prisons. Wolseley needed Brackenbury's organisational skills and his main task was to enlarge and reorganise the Zaptieths, who were a military police force of Turkish origin. This force consisted of 200 mounted and 400 foot. Certain parts of the island were particularly lawless, and Brackenbury and his police were sent by Wolseley to "bring order". To this end Brackenbury made a point of regularly visiting every town and village on the island with a small detachment of mounted police so that the people could see a visible presence of law and order. He was also given the task of reforming and remodelling the prison system.

During this time he was also involved in an interesting yet controversial legal case. Brackenbury, despite the fact that his entire legal career consisted of just two years in a notary's office in Quebec, was chief prosecutor in the case against Mr Cesnola who was accused of breaking into the ancient tombs on the island, something that was illegal under the Turkish law which the British authorities upheld, and of taking artefacts from the country without government permission.[22] The complication came, as Lord Wolseley explained in his journal, because despite being an Italian, Mr Cesnola was also a United States citizen. The possible diplomatic repercussions were obviously a major concern for Wolseley, but in the end the U.S. government was unsympathetic towards Mr Cesnola. Brackenbury disliked Cyprus, again because of its lack of 'society' and the living conditions, but this time he had no complaint about the work, which he later wrote he had enjoyed and found challenging.[23]

In April 1879 Brackenbury returned to England, and whilst on leave was approached by the Foreign Office as to whether he would consider returning to Cyprus as Chief Secretary.[24] Technically this was a civilian position, but at the time the majority of the administration of the island was under military rule. In short he would have been the senior administrator on Cyprus, and *de facto* deputy to

---

22  Brackenbury, *Some Memories of My Spare Time*, pp.265-266 and Cavendish, *Cyprus 1878*, pp.116-117.
23  Brackenbury complained that the lack of society left him living like a monk. Wolseley felt this was a pleasant change from his time in Natal.
24  Brackenbury, *Some Memories of My Spare Time*, p.267.

the High Commissioner. Whilst interested in the offer he was reluctant to accept as he thought it might restrict his chances of further active service. This decision was arrived at after consultation with Wolseley who pointed out that both the High Commissioner and Chief Secretary could not be absent from the island at the same time, and Wolseley assured him that if he were to obtain a further active service command then he would want Brackenbury with him. With the agreement of the Foreign Office the offer was refused. Almost immediately after this Wolseley called upon Brackenbury to accompany him overseas as his military secretary and another period of active service loomed.

# Chapter 13

# The Zulu War, the Sekiiukhune Expedition and Beyond

## The Zulu War

Within a short while the wisdom of Brackenbury's decision to refuse the position as Chief Secretary of Cyprus was proved. After Lord Chelmsford's failure to bring the Zulu War to a successful conclusion, not to mention the disaster of Isandlwana, the British government decided, on 21st May 1879, to send Wolseley to take command. The usual officers would be with him. Maurice, McCalmont, Baker Russell and Brackenbury all travelling with him, with Colley coming from India, and with Buller and Wood already in South Africa. The decision to replace Chelmsford unleashed the wrath of the Queen and the Commander-in-Chief in the direction of Wolseley and his staff. The Queen called Wolseley an 'egotist and a braggart', to which her Prime Minister, Disraeli reminded her 'so was Nelson'.[1] The Duke took the opportunity to attack Wolseley's selection of the same old staff. The Duke of Cambridge actually tried to block the appointment of Wolseley's staff, and it was only after the direct intervention of the Secretary of State for War that the appointments were eventually confirmed. Part of the Duke of Cambridge's objection was based on the fact that Wolseley had appointed the staff without consulting him first. In that sense one can understand why the Commander-in-Chief would feel a little aggrieved.[2]

---

1   Farwell, Byron, *Queen Victoria's Little Wars*, p.228.
2   Lehmann, Joseph H., *All Sir Garnet*, p.246.

Wolseley and his staff departed on 29th May, arriving in Cape Town on 23rd June 1879. He then sailed for Port Durnford to join up with General Crealock's column, and from there to join Chelmsford and take over command. Unfortunately bad weather made it impossible to land and because of this Wolseley was unable to reach Chelmsford before the latter fought the decisive battle of Ulundi. The sea was particularly rough and one feels for Brackenbury as he experienced seasickness at the best of times. Eventually, on the advice of the ship's Captain, they decided it was not only unsafe to land but even to remain off the coast such were the weather conditions. As a result they returned to Durban and entered Zulu territory by land. With Ulundi having ended Zulu military power all that was left for Wolseley to do was to capture the Zulu King Cetewayo and settle the political division of Zululand. Wolseley later became greatly agitated when the government decided that the formal end of the war was to be 4th July, the date of the battle of Ulundi, and that the clasp to the South Africa medal would only be given for service up to that period. Wolseley was furious and told the government that "I and I alone brought the Zulu war to an end". He also threatened to resign if the dates were not changed. Thus the official date of the end of the war was changed to 28th August, the day of King Cetshwayo's capture.[3]

## Sekhukhune Expedition

Brackenbury and Wolseley stayed on after most of the troops had returned to Britain and India. With Colonel Colley returning to his appointment in India, Brackenbury was appointed Wolseley's Chief of Staff. It was during this appointment that the campaign against Chief Sekhukhune was organised and executed. Sekhukhune was a Pedi chief who had taken advantage of British preoccupation with the Zulus to defy colonial rule. He operated from a mountain top camp which had proved too much for several colonial and Boer attacks. The campaign against him was brilliantly organised and triumphed where others had failed. Wolseley initially offered command of the expedition to Wood and then Buller, but both were in desperate need of a rest, and in Buller's case serious medical attention, and in no fit condition to take to the saddle once more for what could be a difficult operation. Eventually Baker Russell was given command with Brackenbury as second in command and Chief of Staff. The success of the campaign was, according to Wolseley, largely down to the meticulous attention to detail that Brackenbury had once more lavished on the plans.[4] This enabled Wolseley to confidently report to the War Office exactly how long and how much the campaign would cost, which was much to their delight

---

3   Kochanski, Halik, *Sir Garnet Wolseley: Victorian Hero* (London: Hambeldon Press, 1999), p.101.
4   Lord Wolseley to Lady Wolseley, 7th November 1879, Wolseley Papers, Central Library Hove.

as in the wake of the Zulu War the last thing they wanted was a potential disaster or another expensive operation. Wolseley had boasted to the War Office before the campaign began that he would have occupied Sekhukhune's capital by 28th November. The fact that he was able to achieve this was largely down to the excellent planning of his Chief of Staff. This led to Brackenbury being described, by Wolseley, as "without question the most able administrator in the army".[5] Brackenbury again wrote of his experiences, although he waited twenty years, in supplying one of the few accounts of the campaign.[6] The operation was overshadowed at the time by the campaign of Lord Roberts in Afghanistan. The only other point of note during this campaign was that Brackenbury again took the opportunity to prove his fighting credentials by joining Lieutenant Colonel Baker Russell and his men in the final charge against Sekhukhune's mountain fortress.

The organisation of the campaign was also hampered by the fact that there was growing unrest in the Transvaal as relations between the British and Boers deteriorated. Once bound together by the need for mutual protection against the Zulus, it was already becoming clear that their defeat would have ramifications for the Anglo-Boer relationship. As a consequence Wolseley, and Brackenbury, had to balance the need to maintain a forceful presence in the Transvaal and particularly Pretoria, with the need to divert troops for the expedition against Sekhukhune. Some of this was obvious such as the decision not to take the King's Dragoon Guards or the Royal Artillery. Brackenbury explained that in mountainous country the heavy guns of the Royal Artillery would be cumbersome and of little use. Also the big horses of the Dragoon's were not suitable either for the cartography or the climate. Indeed a previous British expedition against Sekhukhune had failed largely due to the high level of horse sickness. To compensate for the lack of these units a force of 450 irregular horse mounted on local 'ponies' that were better acclimatised and hardier were employed, and a force of Transvaal artillery equipped with 7-pounder mountain guns and two Krupp-designed 4 cm breech-loading guns made up the artillery. The infantry force consisted of six companies of the 2$^{nd}$ Battalion 21st Regiment, seven companies of the 94th Regiment, and was later supported by a detachment of the 80th Regiment. Medical arrangements were made and each company organised a bearer detail of four stretchers to deal with wounded. A postal service was organised using native runners and considerable numbers of wagons and pack oxen were purchased to enable the transport of supplies and water over the route. In a similar vein to the Ashanti campaign everything possible was done to reduce the carrying weight of each soldier. Some local Pedi chiefs having witness the destruction of the Zulus and wishing to prove their usefulness to the British offered warriors in support. It was

---

5   Wolseley's Zulu War Campaign Journal, National Archives, WO147/7.
6   Brackenbury, Henry 'The Transvaal twenty years ago', *Blackwood's Magazine*, Volume 166 (November 1899), pp.731-752.

agreed that 7,000 warriors would join the British force, but Brackenbury doubted that they ever turned out in the numbers they had promised.[7]

The column advanced into the Lulu Mountains and Wolseley decided that the enemy base not only had to be attacked but destroyed as a warning to other chiefs. To this end he sent out messengers to all the other Pedi chiefs in the area. This stated that Sekhukhune was about to be punished for his raids on the British and the Boers. To that end, the Pedi had better remain within in their own territory whilst this was done. The message was clear: stay out of the way and behave yourself or you might be next. It was also intended to be a reminder to those Boer's with rebellion on their mind of the power of the British Army. One can see why Wolseley was well suited to the task of retaining order. He was illustrating that he was a firm and decisive leader who would stand no nonsense. At the same time he was not a complete dictator and showed that he was prepared to listen to the concerns of the Boers and local tribes. Indeed, one wonders whether the 1881 Boer War would have occurred had Wolseley remained in South Africa.

After a series of pitched battles a final assault was led on Sekhukhune's stronghold, and it was at this point that Brackenbury detached himself from his duties as Chief of Staff to take his place on the front lines for the assault.[8] Although this was a largely unknown and somewhat minor campaign it was another important milestone of the development of Brackenbury's career. To be appointed Chief of Staff for a campaign, and to be given almost sole control of its organisation was a mark of the faith Wolseley had in him but also a measure of how far he had risen. In November 1899 there appeared in *Blackwood's Edinburgh Magazine* an article by Brackenbury entitled 'The Transvaal Twenty Years ago'. This dealt with the aftermath of the Zulu War in 1879 and the subsequent campaign against the Pedi Chief, Sekhukhune. Despite Brackenbury's key role as Chief of Staff during the campaign he makes little mention of his part in the proceedings. Again this illustrates a pertinent point about Brackenbury's writing. Whereas other writers would have made much of their personal contribution Brackenbury choses largely to ignore it or, at the very least, downplay it. Partly this was a stylistic matter, as his narrative style of writing did not allow for this to the same extent that a more personal account of the campaigns would. Both this campaign and the Ashanti campaign were 'textbook' operations for this style of warfare. On each occasion Brackenbury had played a key part in their success. His own failure to comment on this may partly have been a recognition, or even acceptance, of an age that had yet to fully realise the importance of such matters, as he did not usually suffer from modesty. Brackenbury's own attempt to lead battlefield charges illustrates the point that this was where it was perceived that 'glory' lay rather than making the arrangements and plans that would allow

---

7   Brackenbury, 'The Transvaal twenty years ago' *Blackwood's Magazine*, pp.734-735.
8   Brackenbury, 'The Transvaal twenty years ago' *Blackwood's Magazine*, p.738.

a successful campaign. Many a campaign 'failed' during this period for want of adequate preparation and organisation, or more importantly because of a failure to recognise the vital necessity of such matters. It cannot be said that he used his writing as a way of seeking personal glory or to enhance his role in events, as often his role was unmentioned other than as a witness.

After the campaign and the tensions with the Boers had settled down, Brackenbury accompanied Wolseley on his return to Durban. Wolseley was to return home and Colley had been appointed in his place as Governor of Natal. Brackenbury was willing to carry on as Chief of Staff to Colley but received a telegram from Lord Lytton, the Governor-General, more commonly called the Viceroy, of India who offered Brackenbury the appointment as his Private Secretary. As with the appointment as Wolseley's Chief of Staff he replaced Colley in the position. After consulting with Wolseley, who urged him to accept the offer, he telegraphed back his acceptance and within a few days Brackenbury took passage on a troopship conveying a battalion from Durban to Bombay.

Robert Bulwer-Lytton, 1st Earl of Lytton, Governor General of India 1876–1880. Brackenbury served as his private secretary for a short period, however a friendship was established that lasted until Lytton's death in 1891. Brackenbury often sought his advice on matters ranging from his career to his personal financial concerns. (Private collection)

## India

Brackenbury left South Africa to take up an appointment as private secretary to Lord Lytton. Again Brackenbury worked tirelessly at his duties, usually only completely taking a break during mealtimes when he ordered that he was not to be disturbed with telegrams or work of any kind. This is an interesting insight into his working practice. Brackenbury believed in working late at night and into the small hours of the morning. He later wrote, "My experience has always been that the early morning is the best time for study and taking in ideas, night the best time for giving out thoughts".[9] His friend, the novelist and civil servant Anthony Trollope, was critical. Trollope preferred to get up early in the morning and work for several hours before breakfast. He told Brackenbury that whilst, "I give the freshest hours of the day to my work; you give the fag end of the day to yours".[10] Brackenbury's demanding practice of work undoubtedly contributed to his continuing poor health. We have already seen that after the Ashanti campaign he worked himself to the point of collapse and had to spend several weeks recuperating. This seems to have been his usual pattern. After the Gordon Relief Expedition, and again the pressure of writing a book in the immediate aftermath, his health failed him, and he spent several weeks staying with friends at Taplow, Buckinghamshire, in an effort to recover.[11]

**This photograph of Henry Brackenbury was taken in March 1885, when he was commanding the River Column during the Gordon Relief Expedition.**
(Private collection)

---

9  Brackenbury, *Some Memories of My Spare Time*, p.51.
10 Brackenbury, *Some Memories of My Spare Time*, pp.51-52.
11 His friends were Alan and Anna Louisa Egerton. At the time he was the M.P. for Mid-Cheshire, later Knutsford, and in 1907 he succeeded his brother as Baron Egerton of Tatton .

During his appointment he and Lytton became good friends and Brackenbury enjoyed his work. Unfortunately his appointment was brief. When the Conservative Government of Lord Beaconsfield left office Lord Lytton also resigned as the Liberal opposition had been highly critical of the government's policies in India. Although Brackenbury was not obliged to resign with him he felt honour bound to do so and in the late summer of 1880 returned home. However that was not the end of the relationship between the two men and a large amount of correspondence between them survives. This continued right up until Lytton's death in 1891. Brackenbury valued Lytton's advice, and many of the letters are of that nature ranging from such matters as Brackenbury's personal finances to career choices. Brackenbury assessed this short period thus: "Professionally or pecuniarily I had gained nothing by my short time of service under him (Lord Lytton), but I had gained a most valuable experience, and that which was better than money or advancement, the priceless boon of his friendship".[12]

### Military Attaché in Paris

When Brackenbury returned from India there was no work for him and he was placed on half-pay until December when he was offered the appointment of Military Attaché to the British Embassy in Paris. In the past he had turned down similar appointments, most notably to Vienna.[13] The fact that he was on half-pay played an important part in his acceptance of the position, but he was also motivated by the thought that with his friends and contacts in the French Army he would be able to achieve a great deal.[14] A particular advantage was his friendship with Marshal and Madame Canrobert. The role of Military Attaché is easiest described as an 'open spy'. He was part of the diplomatic mission to the country in question, charged with military matters that arose. The attaché represented the military of his nation in the host country, but he had no negotiating authority. His job was in short to find out as much as he could and to get as close as he could to the French military.

He began work on 1st January 1881 with great expectations, but soon found that his contacts and friends were not as much use as he had hoped. His friends were mostly of the Imperialist faction of the army who were much out of favour since the end of the Franco-Prussian War. Not only did this mean that he was unable to gain much assistance from them but that he was treated with suspicion by a considerable section of the French army because of his associations. Yet his contacts were able to gain him access to the French army's manoeuvres in 1881, and this included the whole of the manoeuvres rather than the final corps against corps action, which was all that most attaches

---

12  Brackenbury, *Some Memories of My Spare Time*, p.282
13  Brackenbury, *Some Memories of My Spare Time*, p.285. There are unsubstantiated claims that he also refused the appointment to Berlin and Madrid.
14  Brackenbury, *Some Memories of My Spare Time*, p.286.

ever got to see. He had more success with his political contacts via the Waddington family.[15] Brackenbury had been at Woolwich with Richard Waddington, who had later left the army and entered the family business, which included several cotton mills in Rouen. Through him Brackenbury was introduced to his brother William Waddington, a prominent French politician who later became Prime Minister of France. As a result of this friendship Brackenbury was invited to occasions that would not normally have been open to a Military Attaché. He later wrote, "I particularly remember a dejeuner given by Richard Waddington where I was not only the only foreigner present, but the only man who was not either a Depute or a Sénateur".[16] Despite not being of high birth or particularly wealthy, Brackenbury seemed to have an endless supply of contacts and friends in high places that throughout his career were able to assist him. In this way he was never solely reliant on Wolseley patronage, as one might imagine. Undoubtedly his military career benefited from this assistance immensely but had he not received it he may well have been one of the many eminent Victorians who started off in the army and later made their name in another profession. Wolseley himself had no doubt that Brackenbury could have reached "a very high position" had he made politics his career.[17]

It was also during his appointment in France that he first met Sir Henry Campbell-Bannerman, later Secretary of State for War, and even later Prime Minister.[18] Brackenbury was able to obtain leave for Campbell-Bannerman to visit some French military establishments, which he wanted to see in connection with his work as Financial Secretary to the War Office. Brackenbury also took the opportunity of learning much from Marshal Canrobert about his campaigns and his ideas on military planning. His professional interest in most aspects of soldiering also led him to take a tour of the Franco-Italian border where the political tensions between the two nations had led to significant military preparations being undertaken along both sides of the border. Obviously, if there was to be war between the two nations, as did seem quite possible at one stage, the War Office would want to know all it could. It must be added that he was working under his own initiative here and not on instructions from London. He also sent information to Wolseley through private channels along with anything else he felt the latter should know about. Another example of this is the information that he gained from French Intelligence concerning the situation in Egypt. It was based on this intelligence that Wolseley concluded, correctly, that a British expedition was imminent.[19] Brackenbury continued to hold the position until May 1882 when he was to make another move that was to very nearly end his military career.

---

15   Brackenbury, *Some Memories of My Spare Time*, pp.288-290.
16   Brackenbury, *Some Memories of My Spare Time*, p.290.
17   Wolseley, Sir Garnet, *A Soldier's Life* (London: Archibald, Constable and Co Ltd, 1903), p.281.
18   Brackenbury, *Some Memories of My Spare Time*, pp.293-294.
19   Maurice, Sir Frederick and Arthur, Sir George *The Life of Lord Wolseley* (London: William Heinemann Ltd, 1924), p.142.

# Chapter 14

# Ireland: Disappointment and Near Disaster

### Ireland and disappointment

In May 1882 Brackenbury returned home from Paris on a few days leave. The first news he heard when he returned to England on 7th May was of the murder of Lord Frederick Cavendish, Chief Secretary to the Viceroy of Ireland, in Phoenix Park, Dublin. It had been carried out by a Fenian assassination squad called the Irish National Invincibles, which had been born out of the insistence of the Fenian's American backers that more aggressive means were needed to fight the cause of a free Ireland. The murder had several political ramifications. Not only was Cavendish the son of the Seventh Duke of Devonshire and brother to the influential politician Lord Hartington but he was also married to the niece of the then Prime Minister, Gladstone. It is believed that his murder was due to bad luck, as the real target had been Thomas Henry Burke, the Permanent Under-Secretary for Ireland and the senior civil servant in Ireland.[1] Cavendish had only just arrived in Ireland, literally that morning. Whilst his arrival was known in advance, his movements could not be known. Indeed there was no plan for him to be in that part of Phoenix Park at that time. He had simply met Burke in the Park and decided to walk with him.[2]

---

[1] Jackson, Patrick, *The Last of the Whigs: A Political Biography of Lord Hartington* (Cranbury NJ: New Jersey Associated University Presses, 1994).
[2] One interesting historical note to add is that Cavendish had not been the first choice of the House of Commons for the position. The House was of the view that although Cavendish was an able administrator the situation in Ireland required someone a little tougher. A strong movement in the House had recommended the appointment of Joseph Chamberlain, although the government had clearly made up its mind. One cannot help but wonder as to the historical consequences if Chamberlain had fallen in Phoenix Park rather than Cavendish.

Burke had been selected as the target not only because of the importance of his office, but also because he was a Roman Catholic and viewed by the Fenians as a traitor. It was unfortunate timing that Cavendish happened to be walking across Phoenix Park with him at that moment, something that was unplanned and was therefore the main reason for concluding that Burke was the actual target. They had nearly reached the Viceregal lodge when four men jumped from a cab and attacked them. The murder came as a great shock to the British government and establishment in general, unused as they were to political assassinations. Moreover, the murders were particularly gruesome. Rather than being simply stabbed the men were 'slashed', the weapon being something similar to a surgical knife, and thus suffered greatly before death. In fairness it does have to be stated that the murders were condemned by the majority of other Fenian Groups and by Irish Nationalists in general. Charles Stewart Parnell, the leader of the Irish Nationalists at Westminster, publicly condemned what he called "these vile murders".[3] They occurred at a some-

**Henry Brackenbury. Undated but likely to have been taken around 1882. (Private collection)**

---

3   There are several books and articles on the fallout from the Phoenix Park Murders. The most recent is Senan, Moloney, *The Phoenix Park Murders: Conspiracy, Betrayal and Retribution* (Dublin: Mercier Press, 2006). Although an interesting account of the incident this concentrates mainly on the investigation led by Superintendent John Mallon. See also Corfe, Tom, 'The Phoenix Park Murders' *History Today*, 11(12) (1961), pp.828-835 and *The Phoenix Park Murders: Conflict, Compromise and Tragedy in Ireland 1879-1882* (London: Hodder & Stoughton, 1968); McEldowney, John, 'Miscarriages of Justice? The Phoenix Park Murders 1882', *Journal of Criminal Justice History* 14 (1993), pp.143-149; Cooke, A.B. and Vincent, J.R. 'Lord Spencer and the Phoenix Park Murders', *Journal of Irish Historical Studies*, 18 (72) (1973), pp.583-591. However the best accounts of the intelligence/secret service and police response to the murders and the aftermath remains K.R.M Short's *The Dynamite War: Irish-American Bombers in Victorian Britain* (Dublin: Gill & Macmillan, 1979).

what surprising time. Only four days before the so-called Kilmainham Treaty had been agreed. This had done much to solve the land issue in Ireland and resolve rent problems faced by Irish tenant farmers. Both sides hoped that this would resolve much of the violence.

Brackenbury had sent word of his arrival in London from Paris saying that he would be busy on Monday but would call at the War Office on Tuesday in case the Commander-in-Chief or the Adjutant-General wished to see him.[4] Late on Monday evening he was informed that the War Office had been trying to contact him all day. Early on Tuesday morning he met with Hugh Childers, the Secretary of State for War who informed him that the Government wanted Brackenbury to go to Ireland as the head of police. It must be remembered that at this time it was common for soldiers to be employed in such capacities at home and in the empire. Brackenbury was reluctant to take the job. He was happy in Paris and believed that war would soon come in Egypt and that Wolseley was bound to take him with him. According to Brackenbury he tried to refuse but was told by Childers that, "It is war in Ireland, the Government have selected you, and I do not think you can refuse".[5] Brackenbury later wrote that because of this he felt he had to accept. More likely is the fact that Childers appealed to his ego. In a letter written by Brackenbury to Wolseley three days after his appointment there is nothing about his reluctance to take the job. Instead he wrote of how, "When I was first offered this post I don't think I quite realised its importance".[6] It was obvious that he had been persuaded that this job was a great honour and promotion. Also, given Brackenbury's snobbishness, he would have been greatly honoured to know that Gladstone, Lord Spencer and Lord Hartington had recommended him for this position.

Why was Brackenbury considered to be the best man for the job? Both Gladstone and Lord Spencer had been advised by Wolseley that Brackenbury would be ideally suited to it.[7] Lord Hartington was more likely to have been motivated by his family friendship with Brackenbury. The two men were friends and Brackenbury stayed at the family home of Chatsworth House on several occasions as the guest of the 6th, 7th and 8th Dukes of Devonshire. Lord Hartington was an important figure within the Liberal Party and seen as the leader of the Liberal Unionists, who were later to break with the Liberal Party and support the Conservatives. This, along with Wolseley's recommendation, probably did much to influence Gladstone's decision, perhaps hoping that the appointment of a close friend of the family would appease the Cavendish family or at least convince them the government was acting. The

---

4   Brackenbury, Henry, *Some Memories of My Spare Time*, p.311. The Commander-in-Chief was still the Duke of Cambridge and the Adjutant-General was Wolseley.
5   Brackenbury, *Some Memories of My Spare Time*, pp.311-312.
6   Brackenbury to Wolseley, 13th May 1882, Wolseley Papers, Central Library Hove.
7   Brackenbury to Wolseley, 13th May 1882, Wolseley Papers Central Library Hove and Short, *The Dynamite War: Irish-American Bombers in Victorian Britain*, pp.79-81.

political balance had a further role to play as the murder of his brother had turned Hartington against Home Rule for Ireland, which was Gladstone's great crusade. The Viceroy of Ireland Lord Spencer had wanted to replace the head of the Royal Irish Constabulary, Colonel George Hillier, and had asked Wolseley whom he recommended. Wolseley replied Brackenbury, and thus Lord Spencer asked Gladstone to obtain his services.[8] There were of course other reasons why his appointment was appropriate other than political expediency. Brackenbury's career to date had highlighted him as a top class administrator who would be able to organise the Irish police forces into a unit that could fight the Fenian threat. He also had his experience in Cyprus. The similarities were greater than might at first be thought. They were both in a sense 'occupying' police forces. The Cyprus police force he led was largely made up of Turks and was in effect the same force that had represented the Porte. Although largely Irish in composition the Royal Irish Constabulary was seen as the force of the 'occupying' power in a very similar way to that in Cyprus. They were also both a military style of police, and thus it was perhaps no surprise that a soldier should be its commander.

**Spencer Cavendish, 8th Duke of Devonshire (Lord Hartington), a friend and ally of Brackenbury's since their days together at Woolwich. Cavendish was one of the most important politicians of his generation, but is now largely forgotten.**
(*Illustrated London News*)

Brackenbury arrived in Dublin on 13th May, but as yet without an official position. The government had asked him to "take charge of the police" but there was no

---

8    Spencer to Gladstone, 9th May 1882. Gladstone Papers, British Library Add MSS 44308/234.

further detail on what this meant as at that time both the Royal Irish Constabulary (R.I.C.) and the Dublin Metropolitan Police (D.M.P.) were without a commander. It was not until the 17th May that Lord Spencer confirmed that Brackenbury was to be Chief Special Commissioner, although this was later changed to Assistant Under Secretary for Police and Crime with the main task of organising a force to counter the Fenian threat. Confusion seems to have reigned at this time. Lord Spencer had asked for, and obtained the resignation of the commanders of the R.I.C. and the D.M.P. It had been presumed that as the R.I.C. was a quasi-military organisation that this would be the best place for Brackenbury. With the resignation of Colonel George Hillier from this position it had been explained to his deputy, Colonel Robert Bruce, that he would not be promoted. However ten days later there was a change yet again. Spencer decided that Brackenbury should have an overseeing view of both institutions. Thus Bruce, who ten days previously had been informed by Lord Spencer that he was not considered up to the job, was promoted commander of the R.I.C. This helps to illustrate the chaos and confusion, mostly caused by political indecision, which greeted Brackenbury in Ireland.[9]

Even before he arrived Brackenbury had set about obtaining all the information available on the Fenian organisations. He had already talked at length with Robert Anderson at the Home Office, along with Inspector Williamson and members of the detection force who were responsible for such matters.[10] He also visited the Chief of Detection police in Paris, and found that at the present time this was the most active centre for the Fenian organisations. Paris was where most of their finance was coming from, albeit via a number of other countries, most notably the United States. He discovered that Chicago, Philadelphia and New York were the main areas of support and organisation in the United States. Shortly after his appointment he wrote a long, confidential, memorandum to Lord Spencer, setting out what he had found and giving a series of recommendations.[11] Whilst noting that the majority of support was coming from overseas, he stressed the importance of keeping a close watch on Liverpool, where its large Irish community and geographical proximity to Ireland made it an ideal base for Fenian groups. Brackenbury's investigations led him to believe that an order had been given for the Fenian groups to remain quiet for the moment for fear of further British action, but that in the meantime they were continuing to organise "small secret assassination gangs" for use in Ireland and England.[12]

In terms of combating the Fenian groups Brackenbury did not believe that the forces then available were sufficient for the task. Whilst praising the police for what

---

9   A good account of all the political events and the reorganisation of the police forces can be found in Short, *The Dynamite War*, Chapter 3 in particular.
10  Brackenbury to Lord Spencer, 31st May 1882, Spencer Papers, British Library Add MSS 77088, p.1.
11  Brackenbury to Lord Spencer, 31st May 1882, Spencer Papers, British Library Add MSS 77088, p.1.
12  Brackenbury to Lord Spencer, 31st May 1882, Spencer Papers, British Library Add MSS 77088, p.2.

they had done, he felt that they needed strengthening to act against such powerful secret organisations. Brackenbury also proposed the creation of a new organisation. "To combat them (the Fenian terrorists), there must be a secret organisation formed, whose agents must work their way into its most important seats of administration and of action. Informers must be brought, and men must be paid to enter these societies, work into the confidence of their leaders and betray them".[13] Such an organisation had to be separate from the police and Brackenbury felt he knew of enough appropriate people to operate it. By 22nd May Lord Spencer had received Treasury permission to create such a group which would be above the normal duties of the police and would coordinate all the various groups with responsibility for security. It was in short an intelligence branch for Ireland. It is not surprising that the creation of such a group led to Brackenbury being called Ireland's first 'Spymaster-General'.[14]

Despite the government, and in particular the Treasury, agreeing to the creation of such a group they were still reluctant to pay for it. Brackenbury did not help matters by putting his 'conditions' in terms that sounded like demands. He insisted upon total autonomy for the new organisation and that it be left entirely in his hands to employ agents as he saw fit. The Government were not happy with this but might have been persuaded to go along with it, but they flatly refused the £20,000 a year that Brackenbury wanted for the organisation. Nor would they accept his request that all informers be pardoned for their criminal offences, which Brackenbury later withdrew on the understanding that their assistance would be taken into account at any trial. The Government in turn offered £5,000, with further money dependent on results, but Brackenbury refused to start the work unless the Government pledged to support him to the amount he had requested. He suggested that it was possible that he might at any point,

> ... hook a big fish, and if the money required to land him is dependent upon my explaining the measure of success I have obtained, and setting to work the slow machinery of the Treasury, I should only have wasted my time and the Government's money. The matter is of such a serious nature that I can only attempt it upon the conditions I have myself laid down.[15]

In effect he was saying that the needs of the moment could not be met by having to go through a mountain of red tape and bureaucracy. This would mean him having to have autonomy of expenditure as well as of action. This is always a lot to ask of any government. The Viceroy supported Brackenbury and argued his case with Gladstone, stating that the amount that he was asking for was about the same as the money that

---

13  Brackenbury to Lord Spencer, 31st May 1882, Spencer Papers, British Library Add MSS 77088, p.5.
14  Short, *The Dynamite War*. Chapter 3, about Brackenbury's time in Ireland, is entitled 'Spymaster-general'. On page 81 he refers to Brackenbury's appointment saying, "Ireland had its first 'spymaster-general'".
15  Brackenbury to Lord Spencer, 16th June 1882, British Library Add MSS 77088.

the government had offered in rewards for information leading to the conviction of Fenian terrorists. Lord Spencer wrote to Gladstone, "I feel the absolute necessity of dealing a vigorous blow at the societies which exist in Ireland ... His proposals should I think be adopted".[16] This highlights the difference in opinion there was between London and Dublin on the seriousness of the current situation. There is an obvious correlation between the respective geographical distances of the individuals.

In fact Brackenbury was critical of the somewhat overdramatic measures that certain members of the Dublin government took to protect themselves after the Phoenix Park murders. Brackenbury recorded in a letter to Wolseley that, "There is rather a panic here. The Permanent Secretary carries a loaded revolver in his dispatch box!". Brackenbury compared the situation with that of Lord Chelmsford after Isandlwana, where caution prevailed only after disaster had availed. Brackenbury viewed this as a case of "shutting the stable door after the horse has bolted". Yet the government in London seemed to have already lost interest. Brackenbury wrote of the importance of what he was proposing saying that, "If we can break up one secret society, if we can only make the leaders feel that there is no safety, that they are being betrayed, their terrible confederations will fall to pieces".[17] The aim was to infiltrate the organisations, to set them against one another and create distrust. This is surely the basis of most anti-terrorism operations. Perhaps Brackenbury's plans both in terms of scale and money were a little ahead of their time.

Brackenbury was frustrated with the position in which he had been placed. He had been reluctant to take the position but had been persuaded to take it by the same government who were now blocking his efforts. Brackenbury could not understand why they had been so insistent on him taking the job if they would not allow him to do it the way he wanted. The answer was simple. Gladstone's government would have liked to do nothing about the Phoenix Park murders but party politics made this impossible. They came just after the Kilmainham Treaty, which seemed to suggest that Ireland's problems could be resolved by negotiation. However the political situation within the Liberal Party meant that something had to be seen to be done. Parallels, although on a lesser scale, can be drawn with the same government's handling of the crisis in the Sudan a few years later. Again the government's response was to send one man, in that case Charles Gordon. Both appointments were largely due to pressure that was being placed on them by the press, parliament and the public. Neither man was given specific instructions nor any help or suggestion as to how to accomplish their task. In fact Brackenbury's position was even worse. When Gordon arrived in the Sudan he was Governor General, when Brackenbury arrived in Ireland he still had no specific posting.

---

16  Lord Spencer to W.E. Gladstone, 7th June 1882, Spencer Papers, British Library Add MSS 77088.
17  Brackenbury to Lord Spencer, 31st May 1882, Spencer Papers, British Library Add MSS 77088, p.6.

Brackenbury was not happy. He had made his recommendations and had outlined the establishment of a scheme which he felt would deal with the Fenian threat. The very government which had insisted upon his appointment were now unwilling to assist him. Money now seemed to be the main problem with Brackenbury refusing to undertake the work unless he knew the money had been committed, and the government unwilling to fund the project unless they had evidence of results. Both views have their merit, but it does once again raise the question over what the government expected Brackenbury to achieve. If no new money was being provided for his work, it could be argued that they expected him simply to reorganise and develop existing forces and resources. However, this was clearly not what the Viceroy Lord Spencer and Prime Minister Gladstone had agreed.

Brackenbury's disenchantment with Ireland grew as news of the expedition to Egypt became public. Wolseley was to lead and Brackenbury felt sure he would be called upon. Confusion reigned as each man expected the other to ask him. Wolseley took Brackenbury's silence as evidence that the latter felt his work in Ireland too important to relinquish.[18] As a result the official list of officers was compiled minus Brackenbury's name. Wolseley was keen to obtain his service and tried to have his name added to the list but met with the objection of the Commander-in-Chief, the Duke of Cambridge, who replied that no names could be added.[19] What he really meant was that Brackenbury's name could not be added. The Duke of Cambridge was partly motivated by a dislike of Brackenbury and also because he resented Wolseley's appointment of the same staff time after time. Brackenbury sought Lord Spencer's permission to resign to join the expedition, hoping that if he travelled to Egypt he would be able to serve in one capacity or another. Lord Spencer was reluctant to let Brackenbury go for two reasons. Firstly, he had already lost several members of his staff to this expedition and secondly, he felt that the work Brackenbury was doing was more important than that of the expedition. As a result Lord Spencer insisted that Brackenbury must resign if he wanted to go which Brackenbury did.[20]

The government took grave offence and he was refused permission to even travel to Egypt. Brackenbury's actions were seen as disloyalty. The Home Secretary, William Harcourt, described Brackenbury's behaviour as 'infamous' and 'deceitful'.[21] The government had asked him to perform a task, albeit not one which he joined the army to perform, and he had let them down. They now used the argument that the situation in Ireland was far more important and dangerous than Egypt, which was different to the view they had taken when they were arguing against providing the money Brackenbury had requested. At that point Gladstone himself

---

18  Brackenbury to Lord Spencer, 14th July 1882, Spencer Papers, British Library Add MSS 77088, p.6.
19  Brackenbury to Boyle, 18th July 1882, Spencer Papers, British Library Add MSS 77088.
20  Brackenbury to Boyle, 17th July 1882, Spencer Papers, British Library Add MSS 77088.
21  Short, *The Dynamite War*, p.87.

had written that Brackenbury was exaggerating the danger and that the situation was not as bad as it had been thirty-five years ago when he had been responsible for Ireland.[22] This illustrates how Brackenbury was caught up in a political web. Firstly the Government told him the situation was extremely serious, indeed he was told it was 'War in Ireland'; then when he asked for money to perform his duties, duties which they had asked him to undertake against his better judgement, the Prime Minister declared that the situation was not as serious as it had been thirty five years ago and that Brackenbury was exaggerating. Finally, they went back to their starting position declaring that the situation was extremely serious. It is not surprising that Brackenbury lost patience and longed to get away from Ireland, especially when there was the added incentive of another campaign with Wolseley and the obvious implications that could have upon his career advancement.

There does seem to be genuine surprise at Brackenbury's decision, which is hard to understand, given that it had been difficult to persuade him to take the job in the first place. He had then been frustrated that the Government had rejected his proposals, on grounds of cost when they were already 'wasting' this amount of money on rewards that were never collected. Brackenbury was now being expected to sit back and watch as the other members of Wolseley's staff undertook a campaign, which as Brackenbury himself pointed out was why he was in the army. His views were expressed in a letter to Lord Spencer. "I am above all things a soldier, and on no consideration, and for no inducements would I give up the profession that has been my life's work. While thoroughly willing to help the Government in any way in time of peace, in war I think I should be released for my proper work".[23]

The problem was perhaps a much wider one than would first appear. The lack of any properly trained general staff meant that for every campaign such things were organised on a very *ad hoc* basis. Someone like Brackenbury was an ideal staff officer yet because there was no permanent staff arrangement he had to be found various positions during times of peace. Only so many of these appointments could be found within the Army itself. Consequently Brackenbury found himself in such positions as in Ireland or Paris or Cyprus, whereas in the continental armies he would have certainly been a member of the general staff where his skills could have been put to better use. Brackenbury had a different view of soldiering from that widely prevalent in Britain at the time. He was fully aware of the importance of the planning and administration of any campaign, especially as more often than not during the period of colonial campaigning they were fighting the elements and conditions as much as the enemy. Brackenbury knew that this was where his talents lay. In a letter to Wolseley, that is taken slightly out of context and is often used to criticise him as a non-fighting soldier, Brackenbury complained that his ambitions

---

22   W.E. Gladstone to Lord Spencer, 14th June 1882, Spencer Papers, British Library Add MSS 77088.
23   Brackenbury to Spencer, 14th July 1882, Spencer Papers, British Library Add MSS 77088.

were not being fulfilled as, "Never once have I been asked to serve on a committee or a commission, or in any way whatever to help in the work of organisation or administration of the Army".[24] This may sound a strange complaint for a soldier to make but it makes a pleasant change from the norm. It must be remembered that many of the 'disasters' that the army suffered were as a result of poor planning and administration: very rarely, if ever, were they because of the poor fighting quality of the troops. Wolseley, who understood the importance of administration for a campaign, was always keen to use Brackenbury's services and often praised him as the best administrator and most intelligent thinker in the army. Yet the British army of this period was not one that looked kindly upon such officers.

Brackenbury had tried to withdraw his resignation when it became clear that his decision was extremely unpopular with the government and also that his chances of service in Egypt appeared nil. However, Lord Spencer understandably insisted upon him resigning. As he told Gladstone, "I felt I would have no real confidence in a man ready to throw up duties of such vast importance as these which he did undertake to carry out after so short a time, and for purely selfish reasons".[25] Whilst a fair comment it does ignore the fact that Brackenbury had been prepared to miss the Egyptian Campaign for the sake of his work in Ireland. Shortly after taking up his position Brackenbury wrote to Wolseley, "The Egyptian Crisis coming at this moment makes me feel unhappy but I have put my hand to this plough now, and I will not look back – I cannot be in two places at once; and I am sure there is work of real difficulty, if not actual danger, here, now. Work that will tax all my powers".[26] It was only the attitude of the government and their reluctance to back his ideas that changed his mind. Whilst many officers would have either accepted this or tried to work the system to their advantage that was not Brackenbury's way. He considered himself to be the expert, which was why he was employed; if they did not agree with him them get rid of him. As he said to Lord Spencer, "use me or send me away".[27] In modern parlance 'back me or sack me'. There was undoubtedly an air of arrogance regarding Brackenbury's view and through this experience in Ireland we see the poor way in which Brackenbury dealt with politicians, although it must be added that this was largely when they were of the Liberal Party.[28]

---

24 Brackenbury's remarks were written in the context of expressing that in the administration of the Army he felt most comfortable and useful. Brackenbury to Wolseley, 4th February 1883, Wolseley Papers, Central Library Hove.
25 Lord Spencer to W.E. Gladstone, 2nd July 1882, Gladstone Papers, British Library Add MSS 44309/74
26 Brackenbury to Wolseley, 13th May 1882, Wolseley Papers, Central Library Hove.
27 Brackenbury to Wolseley, 16th May 1882, Wolseley Papers, Central Library Hove.
28 This was not the last time that Ireland would come up in his career. In August 1886, just after he had entered the Intelligence Branch, Brackenbury was asked by the new Secretary of state for War, W.H. Smith to once again go to Ireland, this time as Special Commissioner for Police and Intelligence. Brackenbury was obviously reluctant, but there must have been part of him that was tempted to return, as W.H. Smith was offering him the tools to do the job. However he refused and Redvers Buller

Brackenbury not only missed the Egyptian campaign of 1882, but was also now out of work. He was placed on half-pay and was returned to his regiment, the Royal Artillery, where he only held the rank of Major. So whilst he had been serving as a Colonel he was now drawing the half-pay of a Major. This period saw a recommencement of his literary career as this was the only way he had of supporting himself. The position Brackenbury now faced appeared bleak. "I had lost my appointment in Paris, I was in disgrace at the War Office, and the future was black for me".[29] The position was made worse by the actions of others. The Home Secretary, William Harcourt, who had been particularly strong in his criticism of Brackenbury's actions, now urged the Secretary of State for War, Hugh Childers, that "on no condition shall he be employed at present in any post of distinction".[30] Childers, the man who had done much to persuade him in the first place, felt the same way. He also found that he had enemies at the War Office who took this as *carte blanche* to keep him out of any appointment for as long as they could, clearly in the hope that he would become sufficiently disenchanted as to leave the army. Brackenbury later found out that chief amongst them was Lieutenant-General Sir E.A. Whitmore, the Military Secretary to the Commander-in-Chief, who was obviously motivated by his chief's dislike of Brackenbury, if not his direct prompting.[31]

The Government was also keen to make it clear that Brackenbury had resigned for 'selfish personal' reasons. This was due to the fact that *The Daily News* suggested that Brackenbury's resignation was due to his disagreement with the Government's policy on Ireland. Had Brackenbury ever taken it upon himself to make it publically known that he had been blocked by the Government from doing his job it could have proved embarrassing for the Government. However it would almost certainly have been the end of his military career. In reply to a question in the House of Commons regarding Brackenbury's resignation, asked by a Dublin M.P. Mr Edward Gibson, Mr George Trevelyan the Chief Secretary for Ireland stated;

> It is true that Colonel Brackenbury has resigned, but not for the reason alluded to in *The Daily News*. The resignation has nothing to do with anything relating to the Irish policy of the Government. In questions of employment there are always two parties. In this instance the Government is one, and Colonel Brackenbury is the other. As Colonel Brackenbury has resigned, but on no public grounds whatever, I think the Government are not only absolved from making a statement, but they have no right to make a statement. We are actively engaged in making the arrangements arising from this resignation.[32]

---

was sent in his place. See Brackenbury, *Some Memories of My Spare Time*, pp.352-353.
29  Brackenbury, *Some Memories of My Spare Time*, pp.313-314.
30  Short, *The Dynamite War*, p.87.
31  Brackenbury to T.H.S. Escott, 6th September 1885, Escott Papers, British Library Add MSS 58775.
32  *Hansard*, House of Commons debate 20 July 1882, Vol 272 cc1099.

Indeed the House of Commons was the scene of further wild speculation as to the reasons for Brackenbury's resignation. The notable Irish Nationalist M.P. Mr Thomas Sexton made a speech in which he concluded that the reason for this was due to Brackenbury having urged "for the employment of Belgian and French detectives, for instance, in the use of lady spies, and in the adoption of all the features of the Continental police system". Mr Sexton was also informed that Brackenbury's resignation had nothing to do with policy but was for a 'personal' reason. It is interesting to note that whilst at this stage Sexton's attitude towards Brackenbury appeared quite hostile it changed somewhat over the years. In March 1885 he referred to Brackenbury in the House saying, "Colonel Brackenbury was a soldier—he was a man with a soldier's nature—he was a frank and honourable gentleman, and there was a growing suspicion in Ireland that Colonel Brackenbury wiped the dust of Dublin Castle from his shoes, because he found that pliancy to the ruling Powers there meant degradation and self-abasement".[33] By this stage Brackenbury had long ceased to care about Ireland: he had moved on to bigger things.

Further questions were asked in Parliament regarding Brackenbury's successor, and as to whether Brackenbury had ever been paid during his time in Ireland. To the latter point it is interesting to note that he does not seem to have drawn any pay other than that as a Colonel in the army. The matter of his successor was also an embarrassment to the government. They selected a little known civil servant from the government of India, a Mr E.G. Jenkinson. This infuriated Irish Nationalist M.P.'s who questioned the wisdom of appointing a man who had acted as a magistrate in the aftermath of the Indian Mutiny and who had made some disparaging remarks about the Irish peasants and had compared them with those in the Oude in British India. It was another example of the continued chaotic nature of the Government's response to the situation in Ireland.[34]

There was perhaps an overreaction from the Government towards Brackenbury's actions. Brackenbury's friend George Villiers wrote to him that he had heard he had committed "... Cardinal Sins in Ireland" but that when he actually found out what had happened he recorded that "I though them larger than they are".[35] If one puts it simply he had resigned from a job he had been reluctant to take, and he had been blocked from doing the way he wanted, so that he could return to his real work as a soldier. The whole incident in Ireland illustrated Brackenbury's impatience, his inability to play the political game, or even to understand it and a failure to understand the realities of the situation in which he had been placed. He was a diversion, a sop to public opinion, by a government under pressure. They had appealed to his

---

33  For both Mr Sexton's comments on Brackenbury see *Hansard*, House of Commons debate 31st July 1882, Vol 273 cc311-27 and 30th March 1885, Vol 296 cc1018-53.
34  *Hansard*, House of Commons debate, 3rd August 1882, Vol 273 cc650-707.
35  George Villiers to Brackenbury, 7th July 1882, private collection.

vanity by telling him how important the work was and that he had been asked for personally as the man best suited to the job. However it was not just ego that made Brackenbury take the job as the idea of hard and challenging work would have appealed to him. The problem was this was not what he saw his job as being, and his comment that he was happy to help out in this way during peacetime but not in time of war was something that a civilian government could not grasp. He had entered the murky world of politics and been unable to cope with it.

Examples of this are the statements of the M.P. Thomas Sexton. As was politically expedient he described Brackenbury as both a man who wanted to turn Ireland into a dictatorial police state and then as an honourable man who resigned on a matter of principle because of such matters. Neither statement was correct, but Brackenbury was in a position where his every word and action could be used by one side or another for political gain. This was the nature of Anglo-Irish politics. Clifford Lloyd, an infamous magistrate in Ireland, wrote to Brackenbury regarding his resignation stating, "To us it is a stunning blow, to you I should imagine extrication from an impossible position". Indeed he went further and illustrated the difficult situation Brackenbury had been in. "The fact is that what is right is made subservient to party considerations. This is the rock I suspect which has forced you to alter your course in life and upon which I fear my career will someday be wrecked".[36] This was not something Brackenbury had ever experienced on this sort of scale before. Indeed in the past he had been sheltered from many of the 'political games' by Wolseley. It was a painful but useful experience for him. He was more careful the next time he was exposed to the political domain.

It is worth noting in conclusion that in early 1883 a series of Fenian terrorist attacks started against targets in Britain. This would become known as the 'Dynamite War' and would see attacks in Whitehall, including the Houses of Parliament, on Scotland Yard, several railway stations including the underground, and the offices of *The Times*. This started about six months after Brackenbury's resignation and in many ways can be seen as a vindication of Brackenbury's plans to combat the Fenian threat. Once again the Government changed its mind regarding the situation and the words of the Home Secretary William Harcourt are particularly ironic when in April he wrote to Gladstone saying:

> This is not a temporary emergency requiring a momentary remedy. Fenianism is a permanent conspiracy against English rule which will last far beyond the term of my life and must be met by a permanent organisation to detect and to control it.[37]

---

36  Clifford Lloyd to Brackenbury, 23 July 1882, private collection.
37  Andrew, Christopher, *Secret Service* (London: William Heinemann Ltd, 1985).

This was exactly what Brackenbury had been proposing. As a consequence of the attacks the Special Irish Branch, later simply known as Special Branch, was founded to operate against the Fenian threat. This was established at far greater expense than Brackenbury's scheme and simply dealt with protection and detection matters rather than the preventative scheme that Brackenbury had presented. One cannot help but wonder whether any of the politicians wished, with the benefit of hindsight, that they had listened to Brackenbury.

CHAPTER 15

# REDEMPTION IN THE SUDAN

### BACK FROM IRELAND

Brackenbury recorded that "The remainder of that year (1882) seems like a bad dream. I had lost my appointment in Paris, I was in disgrace at the War Office, and the future looked black before me. But this was nothing compared with the misery of seeing my chief in four expeditions and my old comrades start for Egypt without me".[1] Brackenbury was eventually returned to regimental duties at Portsmouth and in April 1883 was appointed to the garrison artillery at Gibraltar. Brackenbury seemed to enjoy his new appointment. There was plenty to do because, as he told his friend T.H.S. Escott, "the command had fallen somewhat out of order".[2] He also had plenty of spare time in which to write, and for the first time in several years he started to play cricket and tennis regularly. Despite this, and the fact that a posting in Gibraltar was more in keeping with his financial means, he was keen to gain more 'useful' employment. He was desperate to put his career back on course, having now resolved to stay in the army despite an offer from Edward Stanhope to become Chief Agent for the Conservative Party. Although this must have been a tempting offer, particularly with the chance to take a modicum of revenge upon the Liberal Party, it does not appear that he ever gave the offer any serious consideration. In later years he made an interesting remark about the offer when he wrote that "I do not think I should have suited the Party, and they arrived at the same conclusion". It would be interesting to know whether this was because of views he expressed or simply a matter of Brackenbury's idea of administrative practice not fitting with that of the Conservative Party, or indeed party politics in general. Brackenbury himself took

---

1    Brackenbury, Henry, *Some Memories of My Spare Time* (London: William Blackwood & Sons, 1909) pp.313-314.
2    Brackenbury to T.H.S. Escott, 22nd July 1883, Escott Papers, British Library Add MSS 58775.

an apolitical stance in public due to his position as a serving soldier; indeed he later revealed that he had never even cast his vote whilst serving in the army.[3]

Wolseley, as Adjutant-General, tried to get Brackenbury appointed Assistant Adjutant-General, but was thwarted in his efforts by the Secretary of State and the Commander-in-Chief. Brackenbury also pressed his case to be appointed the new Assistant Director of Military Education which as a former Professor of Military History at Woolwich he felt he was a strong candidate for.[4] Despite all his effort, and those that others undertook on his behalf, it soon became obvious to him that the coalition against him would keep him out of any important position at home for the foreseeable future. With hindsight this was perhaps fortunate as such positions as he was considering could have seen him confined to the backwaters of the War Office.

He started to look overseas, he hoped for a command in India, which was not forthcoming. He thought he had found his opportunity when it was announced that his old friend Valentine Baker was to be the commander of the newly constituted Egyptian Army. Brackenbury wrote offering his services and was sounded out about becoming Chief of Staff with the rank of Major-General. The War Office gave their approval, doubtless pleased to get rid of him. Unfortunately Valentine Baker was still under something of a cloud in Britain for the scandal that had led him to be dismissed from the British Army.[5] Baker had been convicted of indecent assault, but cleared of rape, upon Miss Rebecca Dickinson in a railway carriage between Woking and Esher. He was fined £500 and imprisoned for a year. There were many holes in Miss Dickinson's story which were never tested in court as Baker's sense of 'honour' meant that he refused to put his side of the story and would not allow his barrister to cross-examine Miss Dickinson. 'Cashiered' from the British Army he found service in the Ottoman Army fighting against the Russians and quickly emerged as a fine commander, particularly praised for leading a rear-guard action at the Battle of Tashkessen. It was this command of 'Arab' troops that saw him recommended as the commander of the reconstituted Egyptian Army after British success in the 1882 campaign. However his past still haunted him. Queen Victoria, in particular, refused to forgive and she let it be known that she would strongly object to his appointment. That was all it took to make sure that Baker did not get the post. As a result Brackenbury missed what would have been a great appointment for him. He would have excelled at the opportunity to oversee the organisation of a whole army. Also, it would have helped him from a pecuniary point of view as his salary would have been £1,200 a year, about £58,000 in modern money,

---

3   Brackenbury, *Some Memories of My Spare Time*, p.314.
4   Brackenbury to T.H.S. Escott, 28th April 1883, Escott Papers, British Library Add MSS 58775.
5   See Beckett, Ian, *The Victorians at War* (London: Hambeldon & London, 2003). Chapter 8, entitled 'The Excitement of Railway Carriages' (pp.76-82) is clearly a reference to Baker and tells the story of his fall from grace.

whilst his expenses would have been greatly reduced by service in Egypt.[6] Baker wrote to Brackenbury in December 1882, just after the decision not to appoint him that, "I had looked forward to our working together. I had fondly imagined what a first rate force we could have made of it".[7] It is interesting to note that there is no evidence to suggest that Brackenbury was offered any position when Evelyn Wood, another member of the 'Ashanti ring', was appointed to command the Egyptian Army. Wood and Brackenbury had a good personal relationship so one wonders why Brackenbury did not write to him offering his services again.

Edward Stanhope, who valued Brackenbury's ability and advice. As Secretary of State for War Stanhope did a lot of good. (*Illustrated London News*)

## The Gordon Relief Expedition

In the early summer of 1884 Brackenbury received a letter from Lord Wolseley urging him to obtain leave from Gibraltar and to go to England as an expedition to the Sudan was imminent. Wolseley was certain that he would be asked to lead it and wanted Brackenbury to go with him.[8] This time there was no problem obtaining permission to go, as the Governor of Gibraltar was General Sir John Adye, himself a distinguished soldier and fellow Royal Artillery man who could understand Brackenbury's desire for

---

6   Whilst this might sound quite reasonable it is worth pointing out by way of comparison that a newly appointed Lieutenant-Colonel in the modern British Army is paid £67,000 a year or that a Major after eight years in the rank would be on £57,000 a year.
7   Valentine Baker to Brackenbury, 12th December 1882, private collection.
8   Brackenbury, *Some Memories of My Spare Time*, pp.334-335.

active service far more than the civilian administration in Dublin or London had been able to in 1882. Brackenbury arrived in Cairo in September 1884 and was appointed Deputy Adjutant General and Quartermaster General under General Sir Redvers Buller who was Chief of Staff for the expedition. Brackenbury played an active part in the planning and preparation for the forthcoming expedition which would attempt to reach and relieve the besieged General Gordon at Khartoum.

It does appear that his 'sins' had not been completely forgiven by the government or the War Office. According to Wolseley both the government and the Commander-in-Chief raised objections to Brackenbury's appointment.[9] The Duke of Cambridge was said to be furious, but again how much of this was down to Ireland is unclear, as he was also known to object to Wolseley's decision to pick the same staff time and again and by his personal dislike of Brackenbury. Wolseley's response was that he sought to employ only the best men for the public good saying that "H.R.H. would prefer nonentities belonging to his own club, men socially agreeable to him and his own set".[10] This is an important point as there was bound to be favouritism from whoever commanded an expedition. If the Duke of Cambridge had been in command he would have appointed men, as Wolseley put it, of "his own club". In Wolseley's case they were men who had proven themselves with him in the past, and it would be wrong to say that he did not take 'new' officers with him. However, it did cause some bitterness in the army, and not just with the Duke of Cambridge, as certain elements, particularly those who had seen considerable service with the Indian army, perceived such expeditions as being closed to them. Also by this time many of the Wolseley 'ring' felt they had outgrown the patronage of Lord Wolseley and there was much discord amongst the various officers.

Brackenbury continued to serve as Deputy Adjutant General to the force until he arrived at Wolseley's headquarters at Korti on 24th December 1884, some 250 km from Khartoum. At this time he was informed that he was to be appointed as Chief of Staff of the River Column. The aim of the campaign was to relieve General Gordon, locked up in Khartoum and by this stage surrounded by the Mahdi's Army. Gordon had been sent by the government to evacuate the Sudan of all Egyptians and Europeans, as the Mahdi, a Muslim prophet named Muhammad Ahmed, had rallied the Sudan in a revolt against Egyptian rule but also in a much wider Holy War to 'purify Islam'. He had gone largely unnoticed by the wider world until an Egyptian army commanded by a former British Indian Army officer named William Hicks, and armed with modern rifles and artillery, had been massacred. British influence

---

9   Lord Wolseley Campaign Journal for the Sudan, 22nd August 1884 to 13 July 1885, National Archives, WO147/8.
10  Preston, Adrian, *In Relief of Gordon: Lord Wolseley's Campaign Journal of the Khartoum Relief Expedition 1884-1885* (London: Hutchinson & Co, 1967), p.61.

and unofficial control in Egypt had brought with it the burden of the Sudan.[11] Gladstone's government was prepared to abandon the Sudan, and Gordon, who had previous experience there, was sent to organise the evacuation. The problem was that Gordon disobeyed his orders and refused to leave. From the beginning he had been prepared to recognise the status of the Mahdi and allow him to rule a large part of the Sudan. Gordon was convinced that he could save the Sudan and given the awe in which he was held in that part of the world it was an understandable mistake. The problem now facing the British Government was what to do about him. It is impossible to explain to the modern reader the status that Gordon held in Victorian society. He was the epitome of the concept of the 'Christian Soldier', a powerful image in the Victorian Era, and his heroics in China and the Sudan had made him into a legend. The government tried to ignore him and hoped he would leave Khartoum of his own accord but when it became clear that he could no longer do this a military expedition had to be formed.[12]

Wolseley had originally intended to move his entire force of about 6,000–7,000 men down the Nile.[13] This soon became impractical, not only from the logistical point of view but also from the point of view of time. The expected time of arrival was longer than it was presumed, from the correspondence with Gordon, that Khartoum would be able to hold out. Consequently Wolseley decided to despatch a column of approximately 2,500 men across the desert, made up almost exclusively of mounted troops: in other words a flying column. They were to move from Korti to Metemmeh and form a secure base there. The next part of the plan would see a small force of infantry move down the river from Metemmeh under the command of Sir Charles Wilson to reach Gordon and communicate with him. On Wilson's return Wolseley would them make his next move. It was hoped that by this time the remainder of the army would have made their way down the Nile so that the entire force could move as one under the direct command of Wolseley. The Desert Column could take a direct route to Metemmeh, however to travel via the Nile from

---

11  It is worth remembering that at this point the British-organised and led Egyptian Army was designed for use purely within Egypt. Therefore the Egyptian Army massacred in the Sudan had been especially raised for that purpose.

12  There were in fact two expeditionary forces sent to the Sudan. Wolseley commanded between 6,000-7,000 men who were intended to relive Gordon in Khartoum. Another force, largely from India and consisting of British and Indian troops, was despatched to the port of Suakin in March 1884. This was commanded by Lieutenant-General Sir Gerald Graham and consisted of about 4,000-6,000 men. They successfully fought the battles of El-Teb and Tamai. They opened the road from Suakin to Berber and there was an opportunity to relieve Gordon at this point. Graham offered to advance but the Government refused. He was ordered to leave two battalions at Suakin and then embark the rest of his force. Graham was later ordered to return to Suakin with a force of about 13,000 men in March 1885 and fought the battles of Hasin and Tofrik.

13  It is interesting to note as an aside that the initial passage of the army down the Nile as far as the second cataract and Wadi Halfa was contracted to the travel agent Thomas Cook. Thus the entire army was transported in boats towed by the paddle steamers of the aforementioned company.

Korti to Metemmeh required the River Column to head north-east for a time before making the journey south as there is a bend in the river from Korti to Abu Hamed.

Wolseley hoped – and with some justification – that if he could reach Gordon and relieve the siege the Mahdi's power base would start to crumble. The Desert Column would theoretically have the more difficult route and thus the majority of equipment went to them. Initially the River Column was considered as a back-up plan, and it was never envisaged that the River Column would have to advance on Khartoum by itself. General Earle, a man of proven fighting quality, commanded this column, though Wolseley had a low opinion of his ability to organise an independent command. Compelled to use Earle because of his seniority, Wolseley decided to send Brackenbury to support him. The idea was that the qualities of the two men would complement each other. Earle would be competent to lead the column in battle, but it was envisaged that the biggest obstacle would be the journey itself rather than the enemy. Wolseley was renowned for taking the issue of second-in-command seriously and it was a vote of confidence in Brackenbury's fighting abilities that Wolseley had confidence in him to command such a force if necessary.[14]

**Major-General William Earle, the commander of the River Column. Although Wolseley had a low opinion of him he seems to have been a good commander with a degree of tactical nous. (Private collection)**

Wolseley's decision to send a column down the Nile has been criticised as unnecessarily complicated, but was in many ways a necessity if he was to move his entire army into place. He was undoubtedly partially motivated by his success in the Red River expedition in Canada in 1870, even going so far as to have Canadian-style

---

14 Born in Liverpool in 1833, William Earle had seen service in the Crimean War and in India. A bronze statue of him can be seen outside St George's Hall, Liverpool.

whaler boats built and shipped to Egypt along with employing Canadian boatmen, known as voyagers, who used such boats. Brackenbury faced many problems. By the time he arrived with the column much of the equipment and stores had been either stolen or lost. The Canadians' contracts were also due to run out soon due to the delay in starting the campaign and very few were keen to sign on again, due partly to their treatment but also their dislike of military discipline. There were virtually no camels available to carry baggage and to accompany the column along the banks of the Nile. It was later found that much of the tinned food and biscuit was inedible.[15] Another problem came with the 'local' troops that were meant to be supporting them. Many were stealing and looting all they could, and their discipline, and even their loyalty, was indifferent to say the least. The column also suffered from a lack of adequate maps for that part of the Nile, to the extent where Brackenbury commissioned one of his officers to travel the route and make a sketch of the area.[16] However neither map correctly marked the cataract of Sherrari, which led to damage to many of the boats and caused a significant delay in the progress of the force. Consequently they were delayed by not knowing the type of conditions ahead, which made a mockery of the timetable for advancement, which Earle had given to Wolseley. It is not necessary to go into a detailed account of the progress and passage of the River Column during this period. The main reason for this is that Brackenbury himself left an excellent and extremely detailed account in his book *The River Column*, which goes into far greater detail than it would be possible to do here. Therefore anyone wishing to examine the detail of an extremely interesting military and logistical exercise has only to read that book. Yet it is interesting to look at some of the aspects of the column's movements and the way in which Brackenbury exercised control.

Progress along the Nile was slow but steady. Stores were in very short supply and even before the advance had begun Brackenbury had issued orders to his officers that, "You must impress upon your men the necessity of economy. They have many weeks, probably some months, of work yet before them, and all supplies are limited in quantity". Things got a little better when they reached Birti, an area of fertile land, but until recently this area had been occupied by the Mahdi's troops and was not as bountiful as it might otherwise have been. On 4th February Brackenbury received a ciphered telegram from Wood, now acting as Chief of Staff to Wolseley, which informed the River Column of the fateful news about Gordon. Brackenbury recalled the telegram as simply saying "I am ordered by Lord Wolseley to inform

---

15   Kochanski, Halik, *Sir Garnet Wolseley, Victorian Hero* (London: Hambeldon Press, 1999), p.170.
16   This officer was Captain, later Major-General, Lord Edward Gleichen. Gleichen was convinced that it was this incident that led Brackenbury to form a high opinion of him and later arrange his appoint to serve under him at the Intelligence Branch. Gleichen, Edward, *A Guardsman's Memories* (London: William Blackwood, 1932), p.140.

you that, to his deep regret, Khartoum was found by Wilson to be in possession of enemy. Wilson in returning was wrecked, but steamer has gone for him, and there is no apparent danger for him. You are to halt where you are until further orders".[17] For the time being Earle and Brackenbury decided that the reason for the orders should be kept to themselves. By this time the column was suffering from the conditions and the difficult of the journey. The rough water had taken its toll on the boats and Brackenbury telegraphed for urgent supplies of boat repairing material along with further food supplies, horseshoes and nails. A slightly amusing part of the telegraph illustrates the severity of the conditions faced by the column; "Men's and many officers' trousers in rags; not sufficient for decency!".[18] This illustrates the difficulty of the task facing the advancing column and in particular the difficult conditions they faced. In August 1885 Brackenbury had an article published in the *Fortnightly Review* entitled 'Midsummer in the Soudan' where he went into further details about the difficulty of terrain, wildlife, supplies and the climate. The route was hard. An example of this is given in the fact that it took the column four days to move seven miles through a cataract in the river, and at times the boats literally had to be man handled, emptied and pushed, through the river to make progress.

The significance of this should not be lost. It would be easy to deride Brackenbury's complaints as that of a staff officer unused to hard campaigning, but this was not the case. This was a man who had spent several months in Ashantiland, who knew the difficulties of colonial campaigning first hand. It is easy to deride the relief expedition for being 'too late' to save Gordon, without fully understanding the mammoth task which they were undertaking. As a purely logistical exercise, without railway or roads worthy of the name, this was difficult. To move thousands of men, supplies, and animals down the River Nile or through barren desert was quite an accomplishment, but one which could never be done quickly. The reason it was attempted and the reason that speed was essential were due to circumstances beyond Wolseley's control. The initial delay was caused by a reluctant government. It is easy to forget the pressure Wolseley was under. His task was to relive Gordon, to bring him out alive, not to conquer the Sudan, not even to destroy the Mahdi's Army. It was also difficult for him personally. Gordon was his hero and his friend. If Wolseley acted imprudently during this campaign this was clearly the reason. Wolseley still keenly felt the death of Colonel Colley at Majuba. Colley had been his protégé, the man who he trusted most out of his 'ring' of officers. His death and betrayal, as Wolseley saw it, by the same Government who had now placed Gordon in jeopardy made his emotions raw. He was also suffering from ill heath at this stage, which did not help his judgement.[19]

---

17  Brackenbury, Henry, *The River Column* (Nashville: The Battery Press, 1993) p.127. First published in 1885 by Blackwood's, London.
18  Brackenbury, *The River Column*, p.131.
19  Wolseley was suffering from dysentery during much of the campaign.

The order to halt gave the column a much-needed period of rest. They had been constantly on the move for about a month. It gave them chance to wash and mend their clothes, to eat properly and to rest physically. It also gave Brackenbury a chance to improve the supply system. Extra grain and camels were found in the locality. The column now stood at 2,966 officers and men, but the supplies were insufficient for this number. Brackenbury sent a telegram to the Chief of Staff asking for extra supplies to be sent to enable the column to move on. There was an urgent need for soap, as lice were become a real problem. On 8th February they received a telegram from Wood which read "Lord Wolseley is communicating with Government as to future operations but he wishes you to push on to Abu Hamed, and await further orders there". This would see the two columns join up again and Wolseley would then have all of his force united for any further action. The problem that faced Earle and Brackenbury was that they knew an enemy force, of what they believed to be a thousand men, lay ahead of them. They had continued to scout the area as best they could and had identified the enemy at a place called Kirbekan, where they had taken up a defensive position on the ridge.[20]

General Earle decided to attack the enemy and whilst feigning a frontal attack, led by Lieutenant-Colonel Alleyne and two companies of the Staffords, he personally led six companies of the Staffords and six companies of the Black Watch along with a squadron of the 19th Hussars to out flank the enemy on the left and attack them from behind. Although the plan was clearly that of General Earle it was put into operation by Brackenbury. He took care of the detail, ordering that all troops should be breakfasted and ready by seven o'clock. Each man was to have sixty rounds of ammunition, a full water bottle and a day's ration of meat and biscuit. Each battalion had two camels carrying four boxes of reserve ammunition each. He also made the preparations for the inevitable casualties having each battalion prepare eight stretchers and sixteen stretcher bearers, and four in reserve, all of whom were to be unarmed. A detachment of the field hospital and three camels carrying surgical equipment and supplies was to accompany the force as it left camp. Finally two camels were loaded with water to accompany the force.[21]

Brackenbury recalled that not a shot was fired at them as they advanced, despite the fact that he was sure they were visible from the ridge. By now they could hear Alleyne's troops firing. It was only when they were actually behind the enemy that they were fired upon, at around 0915hrs. Earle despatched two companies to high ground so they could fire on the enemy and cover the advance of the rest of the force.

---
20  Brackenbury, *The River Column*, pp.136-138.
21  It is also interesting to note that just before the battle the Black Watch and South Staffords changed into their red tunics. Up to that point they, like the majority of the army, had been wearing the grey tunic common for service in Egypt and Sudan. This change was due to the presumed psychological effect upon the enemy of seeing the famous 'redcoat'. Whether this was Earle's idea or Brackenbury's or the officers commanding the battalions is unclear.

Continuing to advance two companies at a time General Earle was about to order a general assault when the enemy left their defensive position and advanced upon the furthest forward part of the British force which consisted of two companies of the Black Watch commanded by Colonel Green. The witheringly accurate fire of the Black Watch soon saw the enemy in full flight, few of them ever actually reaching the British lines. At this point in the battle Brackenbury himself carried the orders to each company for a general advance. The Black Watch led the way with pipes playing and the enemy was soon despatched. The battle was over apart from a few stone huts where it was believed some of the enemy had taken refuge. Earle ordered the roofs to be pulled down to clear the huts. Brackenbury later recalled that he called out to General Earle "Take care sir" as Earle started to approach one of the huts where the soldiers were pulling down the roof. Just at that moment Brackenbury's attention was distracted as an enemy warrior rushed out from another hut, but he was quickly bayonetted by a British soldier. As Brackenbury turned back he heard a shot and saw Earle fall to the ground. He had been shot through the head and lived only a few minutes.[22]

Command of the column now devolved upon Brackenbury. He quickly started to issue orders. The Black Watch were to continue to clear the area of enemy whilst the Staffords, who had become separated during the battle, were reassembled. However this was easier said than done. Two companies of the Staffords were still engaged with the enemy, who had taken refuge amongst the rocks. Worse still Colonel Eyre had been killed and several other officers were severely wounded. Brackenbury took prompt action and ordered four companies of the Black Watch to stand by to reinforce if necessary whilst sending the second in command Lieutenant-Colonel Beale with the remainder of the Staffords to clear the enemy from the rocks. With this done Brackenbury started to re-gather his force together and attend to the wounded. The day had been a success but had taken its toll of the leadership of the column. There were only twelve dead, but three of them were senior officers – General Earle, Colonel Eyre and Colonel Coveney. Amongst the forty-eight wounded were another four officers, so it was not simply the command of the column which now fell upon the second in command. It is interesting to note that Wolseley made no attempt to replace Brackenbury as he did with the Desert Column when their commander was killed. In the case of the latter he despatched Buller to take over. Part of this may be down to the fact that the Desert column was more important to the success of the operation. Another reason was that he was glad to get rid of Buller who he had found disappointing as a Chief of Staff. However it must also be seen as a vote of confidence in Brackenbury.

---

22   Brackenbury, *The River Column*, pp.161-162.

The battle of Kirbekan was a success and a relatively cheap one at that. Admittedly the death toll had included three senior officers but it did not seriously affect the column. Indeed Brackenbury hoped to continue the advance with fresh troops. The battle had been fought simply using the Staffords and the Black Watch. A half battalion of the Cornwalls arrived at the column's camp during the battle and a similarly sized force of the Gordon Highlanders was on its way, although the falling Nile was slowing their progress. Brackenbury was unsure how many men they had faced at Kirbekan but believed it to be between 800 and 1000. Brackenbury estimated the enemy's casualties at over 200, but believed that the effect on their morale would be even more significant. The enemy had been in a strong position, Brackenbury later called it "an impregnable position", and had been waiting for the attack. The flanking movement had been successful and had seen the enemy facing the wrong way. They had been thoroughly beaten not just with greater firepower and superior tactics but by some quite ferocious bayonet charges. The effect upon British morale was, in Brackenbury's view, equally significant. The idea had been built up that the British soldier could only successfully meet the enemy when formed up in square. As Brackenbury recorded, "Today the troops had learnt that they could beat the enemy in hand-to-hand combats in the rocks, fighting in lose order".[23]

The problem that Brackenbury faced was that ahead lay the Shukook Pass, which he described as a position that a few men could hold against a thousand.[24] After the battle Colonel Butler, commanding the squadron of the 19th Hussars, harried the retreating enemy to their camp at the mouth of the pass. Whilst capturing some enemy camels they came under fire from the surrounding hills and were forced to retreat. Brackenbury considered despatching the small detachment of the Egyptian Camel Corps within the column, under Major Marriot, but decided that as the time was now 1300hrs and they had been engaged since dawn it would be ill-advised. According to Brackenbury Butler shared his view. Brackenbury later admitted that he could have seized the pass after the battle of Kirbekan whilst the enemy was still in disarray but for his lack of mounted troops. Sending sufficient troops to take and hold it would have left the column without any mounted troops at all, even for patrols. The lack of mounted troops was part of a much wider problem. Wolseley had been critical of Earle and Brackenbury for their lack of reconnaissance and their failure to provide him with sufficient intelligence.[25] However with only one squadron of the 19th Hussars and a small detachment of the Egyptian Camel Corps there was little more they could have done. In the end the column moved through the pass with little trouble, taking only two days, rather than the week that Wolseley

---

23   Brackenbury, *The River Column*, p. 171.
24   Brackenbury, *The River Column*, pp. 169-170.
25   Lord Wolseley to Lady Wolseley, 20th January 1885, Wolseley Papers, Central Library Hove.

had expected. The column continued to make good progress and Brackenbury was confident they could defeat the enemy that lay ahead.

However events elsewhere changed the picture. Khartoum had fallen and Gordon was dead. The Desert Column was struggling, through casualties and a transport system that was near to collapse. Both columns were short of supplies and no-one knew what the aim of the campaign was anymore. Brackenbury was ordered to proceed and make contact with the Desert Column. However Buller, who had taken command of it, decided to withdraw without reference to Wolseley. Subsequently, on 24th February, Brackenbury received an order from Wolseley to retire with the column.

There have been many who have been critical of Brackenbury's decision to withdraw, but it was clearly an order.[26] Even if it had not been an order it would have been foolhardy to continue. The column was short of supplies and was not equipped for a major battle. The lack of mounted troops was a problem, as was the fact that the command structure had been weakened after Kirbekan. Brackenbury was not only acting commander but still having to do most of his previous work as chief of staff, added to which two of the regiments were now commanded by the second-in-command. Without the hope of joining up with the Desert Column there was no point to their progress. Had Brackenbury ignored the order and pressed ahead he might well be remembered today in the same way as Hicks. The only thing he was instructed to do before withdrawing was to avenge the death of Colonel J.D.H. Stewart and the European civilians who had been murdered when the river steamers they had escaped from Khartoum in had run aground. They had been offered refuge by Sheikh Suleiman Wad Gamr. Stewart had entered his home and in keeping with custom was unarmed. As they drank coffee warriors burst in and killed them. The brutality and deceit with which this had been done had sickened Wolseley. Brackenbury was ordered to make a careful study of which property belonged to the Sheikh and destroy it.[27]

After this Brackenbury withdrew without incident and acted as commander of the rearguard for the whole army. Early in August 1885 he returned to England. He was mentioned in despatches for his part in the campaign and promoted to the rank of Major-General. Whilst still in Sudan Wolseley had said that he would have

---

26  The source of much of this criticism came from Lt Col, later General Sir, Ian Hamilton who was part of the River Column. It is his views that are repeated by many historians in criticism. Hamilton had a strange relationship with Brackenbury. They were friends but Hamilton would often criticise Brackenbury as a way of attacking Wolseley, whom he detested. However the suggestion by Julian Symonds that Brackenbury, like Charles Wilson, was responsible for the death of Gordon because neither were experienced combat soldiers, both being primarily administrators, is extremely unfair. These comments not only show ignorance of Brackenbury's career, but also ignore the fact that Brackenbury did not take over command of the column until 10th February. Gordon was killed, and Khartoum fell, on 26th January.

27  Brackenbury, *The River Column*, pp.206-207.

Brackenbury made a General. Writing in his campaign journal Wolseley emphasised that Brackenbury was

> ... an Excellent Officer and now on the high road to advancement. Indeed unless he be shot in the autumn even the hatred of H.R.H. (Duke of Cambridge) cannot keep him back any longer. I shall have him made a Major General whether H.R.H. likes it or not.[28]

Wolseley's official despatch mentioned Brackenbury in glowing terms.

> It is very desirable to utilise to the full the opportunity which active service affords of gauging the military ability of our officers. Every campaign enables a selection to be made among those whose proved skill in the field and thorough knowledge of their profession mark them out as fitted for higher rank. Brigadier-General Brackenbury, R.A., comes, I consider, prominently under this category, and, in the interests of the army and the state, I would strongly recommend him to your favourable consideration. When Major General Earle was killed at Kirbekan, Brigadier-General Brackenbury assumed command of the Nile Column, and led its advance towards Abu-Hamed. In this, and throughout the operations in the Soudan, he proved himself to be one of the ablest officers in Her Majesty's Army, and he would be a most valuable addition to our present list of General Officers.[29]

The list of promotions and awards for the campaign included, "For distinguished service in the Field: Lieutenant Colonel and Colonel Henry Brackenbury C.B., Royal Artillery to be Major General".[30] The original draft of the dispatch had been even stronger in its recommendation for Brackenbury's promotion but Wolseley had toned the whole document down somewhat in the second draft obviously conscious of objections from the Commander-in-Chief and accusations of favouritism within the 'ring'. There is a question as to how much Wolseley's drive for Brackenbury's promotion was down to his performance in the field and how much it had to do with Wolseley's feeling that he had 'lost' other more senior members of the 'ring'. He had fallen out with Wood before the campaign in the Sudan, and his opinion of him deteriorated during the campaign.[31] He had already started to find Buller

---
28  Lord Wolseley's Campaign Journal for the Sudan, 22nd August 1884 to 13th July 1885, National Archives, WO147/8.
29  Lord Wolseley's Sudan Campaign Despatch, 'Supplement to *The London Gazette* of Tuesday the 25th of August 1885', National Archives, WO32/6136.
30  Lord Wolseley's Sudan Campaign Despatch, 'Supplement to *The London Gazette* of Tuesday the 25th of August 1885', National Archives, WO32/6136. Brackenbury was only a Lieutenant Colonel in his Regiment, the Royal Artillery, but was a Colonel in the army as a whole, hence the two ranks.
31  Wolseley blamed Wood for signing the peace treaty with the Boers in 1881 after the Battle of Ma-

impossible to work with. In fact Wolseley had written to his wife on 22nd December 1884 that if he was to have a field command again he would want Brackenbury as his Chief of Staff.[32] As it happened the Sudan was the last time either man went on active service, and Brackenbury never got the opportunity to prove himself in this position. So at the age of forty-eight his field service career was over. It had been an interesting and varied career covering twelve years. Not only had he shown himself to be the most able administrator in the Army, who knew the importance of careful planning for a campaign, he had also proved he could fight. He proved his courage, which it appears he felt he needed to, in leading a number of charges against the enemy in various campaigns. Perhaps most importantly he proved that he could handle a large body of men. The advance of the River Column was as good as it could have been given the circumstances and the necessity of the retreat was out of his hands. Brackenbury had done all he could. Although he never said it there was undoubtedly a great deal of regret that he did not get the chance to command again, as evidenced by the fact that he continually kept himself ready for appointment during the war scares of the 1880s and 1890s. Given that at forty-eight, he could be considered quite young to be a general when he returned from the Sudan, he could have legitimately hoped to see further service. The problem was that few others recognised in him the talents that Wolseley saw and so the end of Wolseley's active service career was always likely to be the end of Brackenbury's. It was now that Brackenbury got the chance he had wanted: to undertake staff appointments at the highest level. His greatest achievements were still to come.

---

juba Hill, in which Wolseley's favourite member of the 'ring', Sir George Colley, was killed. This was despite the fact that Wood was following a direct order from the Government. Wolseley believed he should have resigned rather than sign such a treaty.

32  Lord Wolseley to Lady Wolseley, 22nd December 1884, Wolseley Papers, Central Library Hove. It is interesting to note that this is before Brackenbury had 'distinguished himself in the field' on this campaign.

CHAPTER 16

# THE INTELLIGENCE BRANCH

Although he could be considered to be at the height of his profession Brackenbury now worried about his future. Although promoted to Major-General he had not been given an appointment. He wrote to Wolseley that he could not believe that they could "... promote me for distinguished service, and then leave me unemployed". Once again he hoped that he would receive an appointment in India, and had been in correspondence with Lord Roberts. According to Brackenbury Roberts was anxious to have him appointed to his staff, particularly as war with Russia seemed a distinct probability. However before Roberts was able to find him an appointment Brackenbury was offered the position as the new head of the Intelligence Branch of the War Office.[1]

The Intelligence Branch of the War Office was a fairly new organisation, having been formally established in 1873. Yet by 1885 it had reached its lowest ebb and could, with some justification, be said to have virtually ceased to exist. Whilst the office and administration was still there most of the section heads, including the head of the branch itself, had moved away. In a bizarre example of military 'logic', the head of the branch, Major-General Sir Archibald Allison, was sent on active service in Egypt in 1882 and remained there for three years. Whilst slightly unusual it would have been understandable if he had been placed in charge of intelligence for the army in the field. Yet his appointments were as military governor of Alexandria and commander of the Highland Brigade. So whilst the senior officer for intelligence in the British Army was "living in a tent in Egypt", he had only limited contact with intelligence, even though he was still charged with gathering and presenting intelligence to the senior commanders of the Army and the Cabinet.[2] This meant

---

1   During Henry Brackenbury's time, and indeed from 1884 to 1901, the Intelligence Branch of the War Office was not actually based in the War Office itself but across St James's Park in Queen Anne's Gate. It occupied numbers 16 and 18, two large townhouses which had been knocked through.
2   Parritt, Lt-Colonel B.A.H., *The Intelligencers: The Story of British Military Intelligence up to 1914* (Ashford: The Intelligence Corps, 1971), p.151.

the deputy of the Intelligence Branch took control during this period: firstly Colonel East, then Colonel Cameron. Both men tried their best but were hampered by the same practice that had taken their head away. During the Gordon Relief Expedition four of the six section heads at the Intelligence Branch were away on active service.[3] Added to the head of the branch being away, it is not surprising that by the end of the war the branch was in serious trouble. To say the branch had completely collapsed would be unfair. That would suggest that it had been unable to cope with the demands of war, which was simply not the case. Under the difficult situation the intelligence necessary had continued to be produced. What had happened was that the branch had been considerably weakened at the point at which it would, in a larger conflict, need to be at its strongest. The war in the Sudan further highlighted the administrative and staff problems that were rife in the branch, and it could be argued, the army in general.

On his return from the Sudan, and his promotion to Major-General, Henry Brackenbury was offered the position as Head of the Intelligence Branch. Brackenbury was undoubtedly chosen because of his proven administrative ability but the appointment owed something to the intervention of Lord Wolseley, by now Adjutant-General. Sir Frederick Maurice and Sir George Arthur support this view in their biography of Lord Wolseley by giving him credit for Brackenbury's appointment.[4] Brackenbury had also been in contact with W.H. Smith, the Secretary of State for War, between June 1885 and February 1886 and then again between August 1886 and January 1887. In the short intervening period the Liberal politician Henry Campbell-Bannerman was Secretary of State for War. It will be recalled that Brackenbury had contact with the latter during his time as Military Attaché in Paris where he had given assistance to Campbell-Bannerman. Whilst Wolseley might have taken the lead in putting Brackenbury's name forward for the position his recommendation would have met with a positive reception.

Brackenbury himself had an interesting view on his appointment and in a letter to T.H.S. Escott stated that the Duke of Cambridge had himself originated the idea. This seems hard to believe but Brackenbury must have had good reason for writing this. Unfortunately the letter does not give any further detail.[5] Yet whilst patronage had undoubtedly played a significant part in getting him the position, there was little doubt that he was capable and perhaps one of the best-qualified men in the British Army for the position. He was also fresh from a successful spell in charge of the River Column in the Sudan. Although there was to be criticism of some of his decisions in later years, at that time his star was most certainly in the ascendant.

---

3 Parritt, *The Intelligencers*, p.152.
4 Maurice, Maj-General Sir F. and Arthur, Sir George, *The Life of Lord Wolseley* (London: William Heinemann, 1924), p.224.
5 Brackenbury to T.H.S. Escott, 6th December 1885, Escott Papers, British Library Add MSS 58775.

The degree to which he was suited for the post was best answered by Thomas G. Fergusson, who wrote that:

> In addition to his considerable talents as an administrator, staff officer, and writer, he was not without experience in military intelligence. Most notably, Brackenbury had served as military attaché in Paris in 1881–82 and so played a vital role in the collection of strategic intelligence on the armed forces of France.[6]

He goes on to stress the importance of Brackenbury's service in colonial campaigns, his first hand witnessing of the Franco-Prussian War, and his 'educational' career both in his writing and his previous spell as teacher at the Royal Military Academy, Woolwich. It was usual practice for the head of the department to have served in it previously at some point in his career. The fact that Brackenbury had not was perhaps an advantage. He was not set in the ways of the Intelligence Branch, which gave him the freedom to undertake the necessary reform. The branch had got into a bad way, and perhaps needed a new 'broom' to sweep away the old ideas. However, at the same time it could not be said that Brackenbury was in any way unqualified or unsuited for the position. Brackenbury took an Intelligence Branch that had virtually ceased to exist and turned it into an important part of the War Office machine that gained much praise from soldiers and civilians alike.[7] Although his time during the South African War, which will be looked at later, was of great importance, Brackenbury would probably have considered his time at the Intelligence Branch to be his greatest period of achievement.

## Background to the Intelligence Branch

The Intelligence Branch had its roots in the Topographical Branch of the Quartermaster-General's Department.[8] The Topographical Branch had been created

---

6   Fergusson, Thomas G., *British Military Intelligence 1870-1914* (Frederick, Maryland: University Publications of America, 1984), p.82.
7   There is a slight problem in terms of researching the Intelligence Branch, in that the War Office/ Ministry of Defence Library that held the materials that Fergusson and Parritt used no longer exists. Some of its material still survives, but no record was kept of where the archives went. Some naturally ended up at the Intelligence Corps Museum at Chicksands and the National Archives at Kew (and I have found some material at both the National Army Museum and the Royal Artillery Museum at Woolwich). However a great deal of material appears to have been lost. In 2012 William Beaver's book *Under Every Leaf* (London: Biteback Publishing, 2012) was published. This examines the actions of the Intelligence Branch during the Victorian era. Although a new publication, William Beaver did his initial research some years ago at a time when the Ministry of Defence Library still existed.
8   The best accounts of the Intelligence Branch during this period are Fergusson, *British Military Intelligence 1870-1914* and Parritt, *The Intelligencers*. See also Haswell, Jock, *British Military Intelligence*

as a response to the lessons of the Crimean War where a lack of maps and knowledge of the area caused extensive problems for the British Army. The lessons of another war, although this time one in which the British took no part, led to the decision by Secretary of State for War Cardwell to expand the Topographical Branch into the Intelligence Branch.[9] The Franco-Prussian War had highlighted that the War Office lacked any detailed knowledge of either the French or Prussian armies and that because of its small size and limited resources there were not even any satisfactory military maps of either country. As a result, on 24th February 1873, the Intelligence Branch of the War Office was formally created with Major-General Sir Patrick MacDougall as its first head. The branch grew in both size and importance under him, largely due to the presence of political will that Prussian victories had created. In 1878 MacDougall left to take up command in Canada and Major-General Sir Archibald Allison replaced him. The branch lost direction under Allison, largely due to the fact that by now the 'panics', which both the Crimean and Franco-Prussian War had created, had lost their political impetus. Moreover there was the continued practice of sending officers from the Branch on active service, and at the height of the Sudan expedition four out of the six Major's in the Branch were on active service along with Allison himself. This could perhaps have been excused if the officers were taken on active service to perform intelligence duties, but even this was not the case. Most simply performed their regimental duties. This would continue to be a problem until sufficient funding for the department allowed more officers to be permanently on the establishment.

## Brackenbury's arrival at the Intelligence Branch

One of the biggest problems facing Brackenbury when he took up his new appointment in January 1886 was that many of the officers serving at the Intelligence Branch were only 'attached'. This meant that the majority of them were still expected to carry out their regimental duties along with their intelligence work. A good example of this is found in the experiences of the then Captain Edward Gleichen.[10] As an officer in the Grenadier Guards he was still expected to carry out his duties in that capacity along with his work at the Intelligence Branch. This included every fourth night being on guard duty at the Bank of England. This continued for eighteen months, until his regiment went to Ireland. As Parritt remarks when writing of

---

(London: Weidenfeld & Nicolson, 1973), Beaver, W.C .,'The Development of the Intelligence Division and its role in aspects of Imperial Policy making, 1854-1901: The Military Mind of Imperialism' DPhil diss. Oxford University, 1976.
9  For the best accounts of the development of the Intelligence Branch in its early days see Fergusson, *British Military Intelligence 1870-1914* and Parritt, *The Intelligencers*.
10  Gleichen, Edward, *A Guardsman's Memories* (London: William Blackwood, 1932), p.77.

Gleichen, "One wonders how staff officers in the Ministry of Defence today, would react to doing regimental guard duties every fourth night!"[11]

Brackenbury immediately identified this as a major problem. He needed a permanent and established staff if he was to enable the department to produce the volume and quality of material that was needed. The whole operation was at present conducted in a very unprofessional way and Brackenbury intended to turn the branch into a professional organisation, therefore the situation had to change. The point was further illustrated in the early days of his tenure, when three officers of the Royal Artillery attached to the branch were recalled to their regiment on the same day.[12] It would be difficult for him to continue at the same level with three senior officers absent. Of further concern was the fact that this was happening in peacetime. The branch knew only too well from recent experience that if a major campaign was launched all the attached officers would likely be required by their Regiments. The branch would be denuded of officers at the very time it needed them most. Brackenbury's argument succeeded, despite Treasury opposition. In October 1887 the branch was increased to a strength of seven staff captains, six of whom were serving long terms at the Branch. This was achieved by the transfer of the branch back to the Adjutant General's Department on 1st June 1887.[13] It had originally been in the Adjutant General's Department, but in 1874 had been transferred to the Quarter-Master General's Department. The transfer back brought more prestige to the branch, as the Adjutant-General's Department was seen as the real hub of the War Office due to it being much larger than the Quarter-Master General's Department and the fact that the Adjutant General was seen as the 'deputy' to the Commander-in-Chief. Whilst six permanent officers might still seem insufficient it was a major triumph for Brackenbury to get any improvement and perhaps marks the start of the branch starting to be taken seriously under his leadership. At the same time Brackenbury was given the authority to report straight to the Commander-in-Chief and the relevant members of the cabinet, without having to go through laborious official channels.[14]

His other immediate decision was to set up a 'Ways and Means Committee' which was unusual in the fact that it only had two members, Brackenbury and the Permanent Under Secretary at the War Office, Sir Ralph Thompson. Brackenbury's aim was to obtain a complete picture of how the branch operated and what it was required for. This meant that when the results were known he was able to undertake a full and

---

11   Parritt, *The Intelligencers*, p.155.
12   Parritt, *The Intelligencers*, p.156.
13   To save confusion the term Intelligence Branch is used throughout. On 1st June 1887 the title was changed to The Intelligence Department and Brackenbury became the first Director of Military Intelligence. On 1st April 1888 Brackenbury was promoted to Lieutenant-General and the Department was thus raised to a Division.
14   Fergusson, Thomas G., *British Military Intelligence 1870-1914*, pp.85-87.

thorough reform of the branch and not be just "... 'tinkering' with the organisation rather than making any radical improvement".[15] This investigation led Brackenbury to the conclusion that the most likely threat came from an aggressive European power, possibly leading to invasion of British territories overseas and conceivably the British Isles. He therefore wanted to make the branch use the intelligence it had gathered to prepare the Army to meet these perceived threats. He therefore began a process of considering and planning for the mobilisation of the army in time of war. His aim was to make the intelligence gathered relevant to the perceived threats to the Empire.

Although the invasion scares that occurred periodically throughout the late nineteenth century might seem rather fanciful, and were often fuelled by works of fiction such as *The Battle of Dorking*, they were taken extremely seriously at the time by both military and civilians alike. Often this was due to political concerns and a furore in the 'press'. Large-scale fortifications and coastal defences were being built and enhanced. Brackenbury, however, rather than merely responding to public concern believed strongly that the possibility of invasion existed. A continuing fear that he expressed throughout much of his career was the possibility of a Franco-Russian alliance that was hostile towards Britain.[16] Britain had clashed with Russia over their intervention in Afghanistan, and the fear of a Russian invasion of India, no matter how unlikely that event actually was, continued to be a constant anxiety expressed in the press and wider literature. In 1885 there had been tension between the two nations during the Bulgarian crisis and the Royal Navy and the army had been readied for war. There was also continual tension with France around the world regarding trade, the most recent example of which concerned British operations in Egypt. This, when added to the existence of some rather bellicose French politicians, most notably the War Minister General Boulanger, meant that the possibility of invasion could not be ignored. Whilst believing that such an invasion would be unsuccessful, Brackenbury feared it would be used as a gambit to hold British forces in India in check whilst France attacked the British Isles. There was some logic to this in the fact that in the aforementioned Bulgarian crisis it was largely the Indian Army that had been moved into position to reply to Russian aggression. If all British and Indian troops had to be kept in India it would rob Britain of a very large part of its trained manpower. This view was supported by the intelligence gathered by his department that found that plans for an invasion of India by Russia did exist.[17] It was also known that the proposed commander of such a force would be the highly

---

15    Parritt, *The Intelligencers*, p.152.
16    General Sketch of the Situation Abroad and at Home from a Military Standpoint by Major-General H. Brackenbury, 3rd August 1886'. National Archives, WO33/46, pp.12-15. Also see Memorandum by Lt-General Brackenbury and Maj-General Newmark, National Archives, WO32/6349.
17    General Sketch of the Situation Abroad and at Home from a Military Standpoint, National Archives, WO33/46. Brackenbury also discusses the invasion plans in a letter to Lord Roberts, 22nd July 1886, Roberts Papers, National Army Museum, Chelsea.

regarded General Kuropatkin, a general in his late thirties who had created quite a reputation in command of the Russian conquest of Central Asia.[18] Brackenbury's fear was that he would keep British forces tied down to the extent that the already thinly spread British Army would be unable to gather sufficient strength in Britain to repel any possible invasion. This was also based on the assumption, supported by Lord Roberts, the Commander-in-Chief in India, that the large majority of the Indian Army would be unable to match the Russian forces. It was therefore being argued that rather than taking troops from India in the event of war with Russia, extra British troops may well be needed there to deal with any such threat.[19]

The obvious reply to this was the strength of the Royal Navy, but it must be remembered that France and Russia had the next two biggest fleets and that eighty years of unchallenged British naval supremacy had led to complacency within the service. Questions were being asked about the real strength of the Royal Navy, given that many of its ships could be regarded as obsolescent. The debate concerning the Royal Navy was widened by W.T. Stead's series of articles 'What is the Truth about the Navy?', written in 1884, which commented on the large shipbuilding programme of the French Navy and suggested that it had nearly reached parity with the Royal Navy as a result.[20] It was the strength of this argument and the debate that it caused that once again raised the question of invasion and the plans for dealing with such an event. It was with this in mind that the continuing question of the need for fixed mobilisation plans resurfaced and this would occupy a great deal of Brackenbury's time. Whatever the likelihood of such an invasion of either India or Britain, Brackenbury felt it his duty and responsibility to plan for such eventualities. In this sense he had already started to act like a Chief of Staff, sensing out potential problems and attempting to prepare for them. As we shall see later, Brackenbury was extremely sceptical that either Russia or France had the capability to launch such an attack, but he now set about trying to use the Intelligence Branch to prepare for such potential threats.

---

18  General Alexei Nikolaievitch Kuropatkin was highly regarded in military circles at the time but was later to take the blame, slightly unfairly, for the Russian disasters in Russo-Japanese War in 1904.
19  This matter and the views of Lord Roberts are looked at in more detail later.
20  Stead, W.T., 'What is the Truth about the Navy?' *Pall Mall Gazette* (15th September 1884).

# Chapter 17

# The Mobilisation Plans

The idea that the drawing up of mobilisation plans was the responsibility of the Intelligence Branch might seem rather anachronistic to the modern reader. It was perhaps slightly unusual but it must be remembered that at this time the British Army lacked any form of General Staff. This presented a major problem as there existed no body of soldiers able to prepare and plan schemes for the future that was devoid of any other organisational and administrative duties. There were many within the Army who saw the Intelligence Branch as the organisation best placed to fill this void. Brackenbury was amongst this number – in fact as a member of the Hartington Commission he was to press the case for the creation of a General Staff – but the Hartington Commission will be looked at in more detail later. Whilst the Intelligence Branch was able to undertake these duties in the absence of a General Staff this was on top of their already quite considerable workload. It was therefore not just a problem of who would do the work, but also what amount of time could be devoted to it.

One of the duties that Brackenbury was charged with was the "preparation and maintenance of information relative to the defence of the Empire and mobilisation of the Army".[1] Brackenbury found it difficult to make such preparations without any form of mobilisation scheme being in place. He therefore decided to undertake the planning of mobilisation. The problem was what operations was he planning to mobilise the army for? There were no fixed duties for the British army. As we have seen, it spent most its time engaged in colonial campaigning. It was becoming likely that there may well be a need for the Army to fight a European foe either on the continent or in repelling an invasion of the British Isles or the Empire. Brackenbury resurrected Wolseley's demands for the formal setting out of the duties, which the

---

1   Memorandum on Mobilisation Scheme 19th April 1886 by Major-General Henry Brackenbury to Quarter Master General Arthur Herbert, and Adjutant General Garnet Wolseley, National Archives, WO33/46, p.1.

army was expected to undertake.² The added pressure was enough and the Stanhope Memorandum, whist semi-unofficial in nature, clarified the situation listing as it did the priorities of the army.

However this was not officially arrived at until December 1888. In the meantime Brackenbury had been advised to plan mobilisation on the basis of two army corps for service at home, and two army corps for possible service overseas. The basic instructions that Brackenbury received from the War Office were that he was to organise a scheme for the mobilisation of one army corps, with line of communication troops, for service outside of Britain and Ireland. He was also to produce a scheme along similar lines for the mobilisation of two army corps for service outside Britain and Ireland. Finally, he was to produce a scheme for the mobilisation of "all forces of the Crown", so as to dispatch two army corps overseas and mobilise the rest for the defence of Britain and Ireland and to support the forces overseas.³

In a memorandum to Arthur Herbert, the Quartermaster-General, and Lord Wolseley, the Adjutant General, Brackenbury set out the dismal picture.⁴ He had found that whilst there was plenty of infantry and cavalry for two, and even four, army corps there was a severe lack of support for them. In terms of the commissariat, transport, and medical staff, the ordnance store department, and the veterinary corps there were insufficient men available at home for the mobilisation of even one army corps. He also found that to mobilise one corps 8,000 horses would have to be purchased. If that were not bad enough he found that for a second army corps 800 extra men were needed for the artillery alone and even this was after exhausting the depot batteries, the riding troop, and the army and militia reserve. Moreover, the second corps would be completely without commissariat, transport or medical support. He did suggest that by using the militia and volunteers there might be sufficient veterinary and ordnance department support, but of course these men could not be used outside the British Isles. In addition 11,000 further horses would have to be bought for a second army corps.

The situation looked bad, but as Brackenbury pointed out it was in fact even worse than it looked.

> Yet this is after withdrawing from every part of the United Kingdom every field gun, every field engineer, and Commissariat and Transport man over one year's service; and after withdrawing from the hospitals every medical officer and trained man of the Medical Staff Corps.⁵

2   Beckett, Ian, 'Edward Stanhope at the War Office 1887-92' *Journal of Strategic Studies* (June 1982), p.299.
3   Memorandum on Mobilisation Scheme 19th April 1886, National Archives, WO33/46, p.8.
4   All the following figures are taken from Brackenbury's Memorandum to the Quarter Master General and the Adjutant General, National Archives WO33/46, which was subsequently circulated to the Secretary of State for War.
5   Memorandum on Mobilisation Scheme 19th April, 1886 National Archives, WO33/46, p.1.

In effect there would be plenty of fighting men of the infantry and cavalry left in the British Isles, but there would be no support for the movement of such a force. They would therefore be largely confined to defending and operating close to their fortresses which, as Brackenbury had seen in the Franco-Prussian War, could prove disastrous. There is a very pertinent point to make from the fact that there were sufficient fighting men but insufficient support services. It illustrates the lack of understanding and appreciation that existed within the army and government of the importance of such things. In the same way that the administrative skills of Brackenbury were largely ignored, so was the vital work of support services that enabled the troops to take the field fully equipped and supplied, and cared for their needs after the battle. Brackenbury placed the blame for this squarely on civilian government, who were not cognisant of the fact that battles and wars were not won by holding defensive positions alone and that there was more to the make-up of an army than infantry, cavalry and artillery. An army's "... very existence depends upon it containing a due proportion of the three arms, and being complete in those auxiliary services, without which neither infantry, cavalry, nor artillery, can live, march, or fight". As a result of this lack of support troops, Brackenbury wrote, "It is useless to attempt to carry out my instructions beyond the point to which troops are available".[6] This was an understandable soldier's response but ignored the fact that many soldiers were equally unappreciative of this work. If nothing else this lent weight to Brackenbury's argument for a General Staff who, being responsible for planning, would do their best to make such forces available.

Brackenbury would have been forgiven for abandoning the exercise there and then, as others had done in the past, but he believed deeply that the country needed to prepare itself better for the prospect of war. Brackenbury would have been as well informed as any man of the dangers that were facing the country and the Empire at that time. There was considered to be a very real danger of a major continental war and possible invasion of the British Isles. Whilst the possibility of invasion is open to question, the situation was potentially full of peril. If Britain was unable to place even two army corps in the field there was a serious threat. To put the lack of even two army corps into a continental context, Brackenbury also published in his report the number of army corps "exclusive of garrisons and troops of the second line, the principal continental nations can place in the field complete in every detail, immediately after the order of mobilisation has been given".[7] Whilst this showed the obvious superiority of France, and Germany, being able to place nineteen, and eighteen Army corps in the field respectively, and that Russia could place seventeen and a half in the field in Europe, it also highlighted Britain's position behind even the lesser of the great powers. The Austro-Hungarian Empire could place thirteen army corps in the field,

---

6 Memorandum on Mobilisation Scheme 19th April, 1886 National Archives, WO33/46, pp.2-3.
7 Memorandum on Mobilisation Scheme 19th April 1886, National Archives, WO33/46, p.3.

the Italians twelve, and perhaps most embarrassing of all Belgium could place two army corps in the field. The figures are perhaps slightly misleading, as the other great powers had some form of compulsory service and all had land borders needing protection. Britain's lack of any land frontiers, the absence of conscription and the supposed superiority of the Royal Navy, always made her vulnerable to complacency regarding the size of army it required. Yet this did not change the fact that the state of affairs should have been of great concern.

Brackenbury's language became quite extreme. It could be argued that there was even a veiled threat, though more probably a warning, towards the government. He wrote about his experiences in the Franco-Prussian War, and the consequences that were visited upon the French government for failure to have sufficiently prepared the Army for it.

> Then a great nation turned and rent those who had governed it, and whom it rightly and justly accused of having deceived it as to the state of its army, and, by their neglect to make the army an efficient weapon, betrayed the trust that the nation had placed in their hands.

Brackenbury could in no way be called an alarmist, nor did he really have a significant personal agenda, any more than a member of the Armed forces has ever had. However it is strange to find such direct language in an official report, and it shows the clear influence of his literary career. The final paragraph in his report underlined the point.

> If now I venture to press this matter in stronger language than is customary in official documents, it is because I am convinced that to leave our Army in its present state is to court national disaster, and because I have seen with my own eyes what such national disaster brings in its train.[8]

Despite the deficiencies he produced a mobilisation plan in three parts in December 1886.[9] The first dealt with mobilising the army for home defence and the wider implications of that. The second looked at the despatch of a single army corps abroad. The fact that Brackenbury produced the scheme for one corps rather than the two he had initially been instructed to plan for was simply down to the lack of support services. No doubt Brackenbury hoped that the fact he had done it this way would support the case for greater emphasis to be given to such services. At the same time it has to be said that a mobilisation plan for one corps could easily be duplicated for a second, a third, or however many was required. The third report dealt with the poor way in

---

8  Memorandum on Mobilisation Scheme 19th April 1886, National Archives, WO33/46, p.4.
9  Mobilisation Scheme Memorandum and Plans, prepared in the Intelligence Branch of the War Office, 14th April and 1st December 1886, National Archives, WO33/46.

which the army was organised at home. The three reports formed the basis of the mobilisation scheme, which was to work so successfully, much to the surprise of the War Office, during the South African War. Problems only occurred, like so much concerning the South African War, after the numbers got beyond that which anyone within the army had ever anticipated, and even then it was more a case of supply rather than mobilisation and transport.

The main problem was how to make the despatch of two army corps a reality, and this had to be sorted out with the civilian side of the War Office. This would take too much of his and his staff's time at the expense of their real purpose of gathering and collating intelligence. In November 1887 a separate mobilisation section was formed at Brackenbury's request so as to free the Intelligence Branch to concentrate on its primary duties. Brackenbury argued for this by stating that since his arrival the post of Deputy Assistant Adjutant General had been vacant.[10] This position was the *de facto* deputy to the head of the Intelligence Branch, and because of his desire to be more hands on he had not filled the vacancy. He argued that he was not asking for an addition to his staff but filling an already vacant post, albeit with slightly different responsibilities. On the 15th August 1887 Brackenbury wrote to Colonel John Ardagh asking if he would accept the position, stating that whilst official approval was still waiting he had the support of both Wolseley and Sir Ralph Thompson, the Permanent Under Secretary for the War Office.[11] Ardagh had previously worked in the Intelligence Branch and his administrative skills had been demonstrated on active service in Egypt and the Sudan, where Brackenbury had established a high opinion of him.[12] Although not one of the Wolseley 'ring' he was highly thought of by the great man and in the years that followed their service in the Sudan together a great deal of private correspondence passed between Wolseley and Ardagh. On the 13th October 1887 Brackenbury wrote confirming that official sanction had been given for his appointment and asking him to do all he could to return with speed from Egypt.

> The more I think the matter over, the more I feel that although we have, in our mobilisation scheme, laid the foundation of a great national work, we have only laid the foundations and that the whole super-structure has got to be built.[13]

---

10   Brackenbury to Ardagh, 15th August 1887, National Archives, WO30/40/2.
11   Brackenbury to Ardagh, 15th August 1887, National Archives, WO30/40/2.
12   The relationship between Brackenbury and Ardagh predated their active service, or any relationship with Wolseley. When Brackenbury had been Professor of Military History at Woolwich Ardagh, according to T.H.S. Escott, had been a student he had taken "special interest" in and in some ways Brackenbury viewed him as his protégé. Ardagh was Brackenbury's companion on several of his European battlefield tours.
13   Brackenbury to Ardagh, 15th October 1887, National Archives, WO30/40/2.

He also confirmed that Ardagh would be his deputy and replace him in his absence. With this appointment the detail of the scheme began to be put in place. By early 1888 the mobilisation section became independent of the Intelligence Branch, and the branch was able to concentrate fully on its main task of gathering, collating and distributing intelligence product.

# Chapter 18

# Intelligence Work

### Producing Intelligence

A conversation Brackenbury had with the future Major-General Sir Charles Callwell, when the latter was a staff captain in the Intelligence Branch, sums up Brackenbury's views on the way in which he perceived the operation of the Branch. Callwell records the conversation as follows:

> I shan't expect you to be able to answer every question that may arise in respect to your particular work, right off the reel; I shan't even expect the information necessarily to be actually available in the department. But I shall expect you not to be helpless, but to find means of getting that information somehow within a reasonable time. If you keep your wits about you, if you look ahead, if, whenever anything crops up that you do not know all about you set yourself to find out all about it, if you keep sucking in information into the place and if you see that the information you suck into the place is properly registered and so made available when required, your particular section will in course of time become a real going concern.[1]

This is a perfect example of Brackenbury's professional and business approach to his military work. Added to that, this statement clearly highlights that he knew his department's limitations, due largely to finance, and was not expecting miracles from his officers, but to perform in an equally professional and business like-manner. This concept of constantly 'sucking' in information was to prove its worth. As a consequence it amassed a series of archives of military intelligence. The intelligence library and archive was a great asset and was referred to by the Treasury as "...

---

1   Callwell, Maj-General Sir Charles E., *Stray Recollections* (London: Edward Arnold & Co, 1923), p.305.

the best military library in the world". When Brackenbury entered the intelligence branch the library already contained some 40,000 books and grew by an average of 5,500 a year.[2] The other key aspect he brought to the position was an insistence on getting the right officers for the branch. This clearly shows that he realised it was not merely a case of acquiring the information and storing it but having men who understood it and were able to appreciate its significance. In the days before computers this made having intelligent and resourceful officers in the branch essential. This was illustrated some years later when he was advising on the establishment of the Indian Army's Intelligence Branch. In a letter to Roberts he advised, "So much depends upon getting the very best men for the Intelligence Department".[3]

One of the best sources of information about Brackenbury's time and achievements as Head of the Intelligence Branch, and the way in which he worked, is to be found in the biographies, memoirs and autobiographies of those who served under him. Callwell has already been mentioned. Another of these was Captain, later Lieutenant-General Sir James Grierson, who was given command of II Corps of the British Expeditionary Force (B.E.F.) in 1914.[4] Grierson and Brackenbury were very much alike. They were both intellectual soldiers, or as Grierson's biographer put it, they were, "scientific soldiers in the dawn of scientific soldiering".[5] They were both able to combine active service with administrative appointments, for which their intellectual capabilities suited them. Grierson admired Brackenbury and saw him as proof that officers of their unusual abilities could be successful. It appears that Grierson was even more committed to his work than Brackenbury, the latter once commenting that, "I always thought I was a hard worker, but you quite put me to shame".[6] One of the keys to Brackenbury's success in building up the branch was the fact that he obtained the appointment of several good workers. Their, and his, sheer industry made it possible for him to achieve much with a relatively small staff. This hard work seems to have been something that Brackenbury demanded from his staff. Mention has already been made of Gleichen who combined his work at the Intelligence Branch with regimental duties. Many of his other officers were men of equal drive and determination. It is worth considering the subsequent careers of some of those who served under Brackenbury during this period or who were

---

2   Only one real work has looked at these archives specifically - Beaver, William C., 'The Intelligence Division Library 1854-1902'. See also Andrew, Christopher, *Secret Service: The Making of the British Intelligence Community* (London: William Heineman, 1985) pp.51-53.

3   Brackenbury to Roberts 12th March 1892, Roberts Papers, National Army Museum, R11/42.

4   Although he was given command of II Corps he died of a heart attack before he had chance to lead them in battle. Grierson left considerable private papers and diaries. They were acquired by his biographer D.S. Macdiarmid, but were unfortunately destroyed upon his death. All that remains is Macdiarmid's book, which quotes widely from the diaries.

5   Macdiarmid, D.S., *The Life of Lieut. General Sir James Moncrieff Grierson* (London: Constable & Co Ltd, 1923), p.63.

6   Macdiarmid, *The Life of Lieut. General Sir James Moncrieff Grierson*, p.82.

appointed on his recommendation after he had actually left the Intelligence Branch. Two of them, Sir Henry Wilson and Sir William Robertson, reached the rank of Field Marshal. Sir James Wolfe Murray was Chief of the Imperial General Staff for a period during the First World War. Five of them, Aston, Callwell, Dalton, Trotter and Gleichen attained the rank of Major-General. It is also worth noting the background of those who served in the Intelligence Branch. When Callwell entered in 1887 he brought the total number of Staff College graduates to thirteen.[7] It will be remembered that Brackenbury himself never attended the Staff College, so rather than being seen as championing the cause of the Staff College it was more to do with the practicalities of the situation. The absence of a General Staff meant that the obvious destination for the brightest and best of the Staff College graduates was unavailable. In its absence the Intelligence Branch attracted those graduates and in many ways began to take on the appearance of a General Staff. It was certainly the case that during Brackenbury's time in command the overwhelming majority of his officers were graduates of the Staff College.

Brackenbury seems to have developed a good relationship with those who worked under him. They were full of respect and praise for him; he also seems to have developed good personal relationships with those under his command, which goes against the 'unfriendly' and 'loner' image that Wolseley suggested. According to Callwell he made it a point to get to know his staff outside of office hours. "Of the many officers who served under 'Brack' in Queen Anne's Gate during the following four years, there was not one who did not simply swear by him nor part from him full of respect for his gifts".[8] Gleichen in similar vein also noted that, "We were zealous, and worked hard under the masterful supervision of Brackenbury, whom we both admired and respected".[9] To a large extent it was a meeting of likeminded soldiers, but it was also the respect they gained through seeing him at work. The amount of material that the branch began to collect was large, and the collation of it a laborious business. As Callwell recalled, "One could have occupied one's office chair for twenty-four hours each day and never have been at a loose end for something to be at".[10] One gets the feeling from, reading these comments that they all considered it an important experience from which they learnt a great deal. It was almost as if the intelligence branch became the training ground for the future leaders of the army. Perhaps that is a slight exaggeration and their subsequent careers had more to

---

7  Bond, Brian, *The Victorian Army and the Staff College 1854-1914* (London: Eyre Methuen, 1972), p.171. During Brackenbury's time in charge there were few who had not qualified from the Staff College. It is difficult to say for certain, as attached officers were not officially on the Army List for the Intelligence Branch. Of approximately twenty-eight officers who served under Brackenbury, only five had not attended the Staff College.
8  Callwell, *Stray Recollections*, p.306.
9  Gleichen, Maj-General Lord Edward, *A Guardsman's Memories*, p.143.
10 Callwell, *Stray Recollections*, p.308.

do with natural ability than training, but it would certainly be fair to say that this was the first experience of the War Office for many of them. Added to which they had the opportunity to learn from the greatest administrator, and one of the hardest workers, in the army.

The majority of the intelligence gathered was by overt means. Callwell gave a good description of what the process of the branch entailed:

1. Collection of information by means of special reports, newspapers, periodicals, volumes reaching the daily growing War Office Library, which was under charge of the department and enquires addressed to individuals known to, possess knowledge
2. Methodical registration of the information for further use.
3. Collation into reports. The first and second headings were in reality the most important, although the third took up most of one's time, and the second required the greatest care of all.[11]

Reports came in from various sources and were added to the information kept on various subjects and countries. Much would come through official publications, newspapers, and translations of foreign military journals. The latter was another reason why Brackenbury encouraged the appointment to the Intelligence Branch of officers who were at the very least bilingual, as they could translate the material themselves, and for which they were paid extra.[12] Whilst this was hardly sophisticated it meant that large folders of information were established that gave a well-balanced account of the various countries politically, socially and militarily. When added to the small amount of material that was obtained by covert means, it added to quality intelligence reports. The department was split into six sections.[13] Sections A to E dealt with the various areas of the world, but there was also a Topographical Section (F) and a Central Section, charged with the collation, filing and distribution of the reports from the other sections. The Central Section was commanded by the deputy of the Intelligence Branch, but when Brackenbury arrived the post was vacant. It was for this position originally that he sought the services of Colonel Ardagh, who did become deputy, but he was so busy with the mobilisation scheme that the Central Section ceased to exist and the duties were taken over by Brackenbury himself. The shortage of staff, and more importantly money, meant that the size and areas covered by the sections were large. Where

---

11   Callwell, *Stray Recollections*, p.312.
12   Translating Russian was charged at 3 to 5 shillings per 72 words, and French and German at 1 to 2 shillings per 72 words. The rates could vary depending on the technicality of the work.
13   Parritt, Lt-Colonel B.A.H., *The Intelligencers*, p.154, has a table showing the organisation of the Intelligence Branch. Similar tables can be found at the back of Fergusson's *British Military Intelligence 1870-1914*.

possible it was organised on a geographical basis so that section D covered Russia, India, Afghanistan, Burma, Siberia, China, Japan, Siam, Central Asia and Persia. However, in other sections the geographical element was not so logical with section A covering France, Belgium, Italy, Spain and Portugal but also being responsible for Central and South America and Mexico. Section F was responsible for maps and the library. Brackenbury encouraged his officers to visit, as much as possible, the countries for which they were responsible. For this he was able to wheedle out of the Treasury a travel grant of £600 a year.[14] Whilst not much it was better than the previous situation whereby officers had to pay their own expenses. Visiting the areas under their surveillance was one obvious way of obtaining information. Whilst some of this was covert, much was gathered by invitation. Foreign manoeuvres were a good place to gain intelligence. Brackenbury issued instructions that:

> Officers attending manoeuvres in all foreign countries will find it adds much to the usefulness and pleasure of their visit if they take the trouble to get themselves duly presented to as many of the Officers as possible of the army to which they are sent, especially those of high rank. Two hundred visiting cards should be taken by each officer.[15]

It was also less risky than other means of gathering intelligence, as there was little need for subterfuge. For example, Captain Repington visited the French Army manoeuvres in 1891 by official invitation.[16] It would be interesting to know whether the French knew that he was head of the section responsible for gathering intelligence on them. It may well be that they saw him merely as an interested fellow soldier. This was certainly the case with Grierson, who was often invited to visit the General Staff in Berlin.[17] He spoke fluent German and had built up friendships with many German Staff Officers over the years. He used such visits to gather intelligence from them on the Russians, which they had gathered through being prepared to, as Grierson said, "put down the necessary roubles".[18] At the same time his easy access to the General Staff, which was freely given, enabled him to gather intelligence on the Germans. This relationship worked both ways and was openly encouraged by Brackenbury. Indeed, the intelligence gathered by Captain Waters mission to Russia in 1891 was shared with the Germans; in fact his report was read by the chief of the intelligence staff in Germany before Brackenbury saw it.[19] It must be

---

14  Fergusson, Thomas G., *British Military Intelligence 1870-1914*, p.85.
15  Brackenbury, Lt General H., DMI, *Notes for the Information of Officers attending Foreign Manoeuvres*, Intelligence Division, 1890. Intelligence Corps Museum, Chicksands.
16  Repington, Lieut-General Charles à Court, *Vestigia* (London: Constable & Co Ltd, 1919), p.83. From 1903 onwards he was known as Charles à Court Repington.
17  Macdiarmid, *The Life of Lieut. General Sir James Moncrieff Grierson*, pp.86-96.
18  Macdiarmid, *The Life of Lieut. General Sir James Moncrieff Grierson*, p.100.
19  Waters, Brig-General W.H.H., *Secret and Confidential* (London: John Murray, 1926), pp.27-28.

remembered that this was at a time when Anglo-German relations were still good, and as Brackenbury's intelligence reports show, Russia was considered the most likely enemy, and Germany was seen as a potential ally. Under such circumstances intelligence on Russia was freely exchanged between the Intelligence Branch and its German counterpart on a practical if not official level. Grierson was ideally suited for this, as Brackenbury knew full well, because, as a member of the German General Staff wrote, "Grierson, that excellent comrade, is almost as well known at Berlin as at Woolwich, and the whole General Staff of our Army knows him and highly values and appreciates his thorough knowledge".[20]

Whilst a great deal of intelligence could be gathered like this it failed to provide the detailed knowledge that was sometimes necessary. There was also a limited amount that those in the Intelligence Branch could do themselves. They also took a very great risk, as it was harder for them to deny spying if they were detained and it was discovered they worked at the War Office. The same was true for military attachés, as in many countries they were usually followed. The answer was found in a large number of 'volunteer spies', who undertook missions. Many were soldiers who on leave would visit the continent and gather what they could for the branch, though Brackenbury was reluctant to accept such offers, fearing that it might endanger his more legitimate intelligence gathering and lead to unfortunate clashes with foreign powers. Many were motivated by a desire for adventure and a rather jingoistic type of patriotism.[21] A leading example of this, and a man whose success convinced Brackenbury of the usefulness of such individuals, was Robert Baden-Powell. Baden-Powell believed that "The best spies are unpaid men who are doing it for the love of the thing".[22] Although a soldier he undertook such missions privately, originally without the knowledge of Brackenbury, and would present his information on his return. He managed to get himself access to the German Army manoeuvres and was thus able to get far closer than official guests to a new German machine gun that was being tested. He also found ingenious ways of smuggling out his information, such as hiding the details of fortifications in detailed drawings of butterfly wings. On another occasion he posed as a painter, and in watercolours of Algerian coastal scenes he hid in a code of dots and dashes the position of fixed defences, along with his opinion of the calibre of gun at the naval base at Bizerta.[23]

---

20 Macdiarmid, *The Life of Lieut. General Sir James Moncrieff Grierson*, p.87. The slight irony of this was that it was Grierson who undertook the negotiations with the French General Staff in 1906 about the prosecution of a war against Germany.
21 For a more detailed account of these exploits than this study allows see Fisher, John, *Gentleman Spies: Intelligence Agents in the British Empire* (Stroud: Sutton Publishing, 2002).
22 Baden-Powell, Robert, *My Adventures as a Spy* (London: C.A. Pearson, 1915) pp.11-12; Fergusson, Thomas, *British Military Intelligence 1870-1914*, pp.89-91 and Haswell, Jock, *British Military Intelligence*, pp.44-46. One of Baden Powell's more recent biographers also includes details of his work for Brackenbury - Jeal, Tim, *Baden-Powell* (London: Pimlico Press, 1995), pp.123-126.
23 Haswell, Jock, *British Military Intelligence*, p.44.

Such information was greatly appreciated by Brackenbury.[24] It is strange that such an usual mixture as the highly professional approach of Brackenbury and the 'gentleman amateur' so clearly embodied in Baden-Powell worked together so well.

However not all were as effective as Baden-Powell, and there were those whose incompetence caused problems for the Intelligence Branch. Gleichen tells the story of an officer who when on such a 'mission' was approached by two gendarmes. In a panic he started to try to eat the pages of his notebook, which contained the intelligence he had gathered. He was arrested, and it turned out that the two gendarmes had merely approached him for a light for their cigarettes.[25] In an attempt to try and avert such embarrassments Brackenbury issued his 'Rules to be observed by Officers travelling who are endeavouring to obtain Information for the Intelligence Division'.[26] He made it clear that such individuals:

> ... were not to consider themselves as employed by the Intelligence Division, and are, on no account whatever, to represent themselves to any person as being so employed, or as being engaged on any official work, or as having any official mission, unless they have received especial authority to do so from His Royal Highness, the Commander-in-Chief.[27]

The rest of his rules made it clear to the individuals concerned that they were on their own if they were caught, and that the penalties for being caught could be severe. Whilst he had his doubts about the motives and competence of many of these volunteers, he did appreciate their efforts. Later, when in India, he recommended to Lord Roberts that a similar course be taken to gather intelligence on Madagascar. Roberts was concerned about their lack of knowledge regarding French defences and forces in Madagascar, and with some justification as the forces there could have harassed British interests in the Indian Ocean in the event of war. There was a possibility that in the future an operation might need to be mounted from India against it but intelligence was lacking. Brackenbury wrote that:

---

24    Jeal, Tim, *Baden-Powell*, pp.123-126 and Haswell, Jock *British Military Intelligence*, p.45. The usefulness of such missions was not lost on Brackenbury's successors, and were continued. Brackenbury's successor would obtain intelligence on Cuba and the United States via a young Winston Churchill. For details see Stafford, David, *Churchill and Secret Service* (London: John Murray Ltd, 1997), pp.13-15.
25    Gleichen, Maj-General Lord Edward, *A Guardsman's Memories*, pp.138-139.
26    Brackenbury, Lieut-General H., DMI, 'Rules to be observed by Officers Travelling, who are endeavouring to obtain Information for the Intelligence Division', Intelligence Corps Museum, Chicksands. No date exists for this document, but due to the fact that Brackenbury is a Lieut-General we know it is after 1st April 1888 and before he left the Branch in April 1891. There is a date of 1890 on the document but it is not clear whether this is actually for the whole document or just the accompanying note.
27    Brackenbury, 'Rules to be observed by Officers Travelling, who are endeavouring to obtain Information for the Intelligence Division', Intelligence Corps Museum, Chicksands.

I should suggest following the plan which I found success with. Let your Intelligence Department do the thing quietly, by leave of absence being given to some officer who speaks French fluently, and is a cool hand. Let him go without any official mission, or any written instructions, but with the verbal information as to the points to be reported on ... It is difficult work and dangerous work, but it can be done. No one except Woodthorpe, should know about it. Even you and I should have our hands clean, if any official representations are made by the French government.[28]

Another success of Brackenbury's time in office was the development of relations with other departments. The Admiralty had established its own Foreign Intelligence Committee only in 1882, with the role of collecting and producing intelligence and coordinating the work of the various naval attaches but it was not until 1887 that this became the Naval Intelligence Department. Like its army counterpart it was small, under-staffed and under-funded. Cooperation between the two was logical but did not occur until Brackenbury's arrival. Partly this was due to the chaos that the Intelligence Branch had been in, but it was also partly due to the parochial views of Brackenbury's predecessors. Brackenbury himself began the system of cooperation and coordination, and was able to build a close working relationship with his naval counterpart, Captain William H. Hall R.N.[29] The relationship between the two departments was largely based on the exchange of information though there were times that they undertook intelligence-gathering missions together.[30]

The other key relationship that Brackenbury built up was with the Foreign Office. Before Brackenbury's arrival there was little contact between the two. In fact the only contact appears to have been the passing on of military attaché reports and it was understood that despite the fact that they were military officers their reports were for the Foreign Office. One key reason for Brackenbury's keenness was the fact that the Foreign Office had a budget for intelligence that was approximately six times the size of his. The main element of this was the Secret Intelligence Service (S.I.S.), which spent most of its budget on coping with the threat of Irish terrorists but the Foreign Office did use some of it for work overseas, most notably in Persia and Afghanistan, where it was able to 'buy' the plans for a Russian invasion of

---

28  Brackenbury to Roberts, 5th August 1891, Roberts Papers, National Army Museum, R11/42.
29  Fergusson, *British Military Intelligence 1870-1914*, pp.87-88. Captain William H. Hall also served on the Hartington Commission, as one of the two Secretaries. He should not be confused with his son William Reginald Hall who also served as Director of Naval Intelligence. For further information on development of Naval Intelligence see Andrew, Christopher, *Secret Service: The Making of the British Intelligence Community* (London: William Heinemann Ltd, 1985), for a general view, and Beresford, Lord Charles, *The Memoirs of Lord Charles Beresford* (London: Methuen, 1914, 2 volumes), who was involved in its creation and development.
30  Fergusson, *British Military Intelligence 1870-1914*, p.91.

Afghanistan.[31] It appears, from the testimony of officers who served in the branch during this period that from time to time some of the Foreign Office's secret service money was used by the Intelligence Branch to fund overseas missions.[32] A large amount of Foreign Office intelligence came from its ambassadors and military attachés, and like the Intelligence Branch much of this came freely from legitimate sources without recourse to financial inducement. Problems occurred when they tried to gather intelligence themselves, given that they were often followed, as were other embassy staff. It was therefore much easier for a visiting officer from the Intelligence Branch, who would only be in the country for a few weeks, to move freely without arousing suspicion. It was partly for this reason, and also to save any potential embarrassment, that Brackenbury ordered his staff not to meet publicly with any embassy staff when they were on intelligence work. [33]

An interesting insight into how Brackenbury built these relationships is found in a letter he wrote to Lord Lansdowne in 1892. By this time Brackenbury had left the department and was working in India. Speaking of the relationship with other departments he said:

> There was, at first, some little jealously and suspicion both in the Foreign, Colonial and War offices of this (the quality of the Intelligence Branch reports). But when they grew to see how useful we could be, and how much trouble we often saved them, it all ceased. I made them understand we wanted to work for them and with them, and we all became fast friends.[34]

This shows a skill in diplomacy and man-management that many have ignored regarding Brackenbury. Throughout his career he endeavoured to illustrate that his work was important and useful to others. In an atmosphere of inter-departmental rivalry Brackenbury was able to get them to work together by showing that they could serve each other's interests. Brackenbury knew that there was still hostility within other departments towards the work of the Intelligence Branch, in particular, within the Foreign Office, but he chose to ignore this and continued to work well with them. Another reason he made the branch important was by pre-empting events. In the same letter to Lansdowne he wrote that:

> When I knew that any subject was engaging the attention of government, I used to prepare a paper showing the state of the question from one point of view, and send it either to all the cabinet ministers, or as to such only as

---

31  Fergusson, *British Military Intelligence 1870-1914*, p.88.
32  Callwell, *Stray Recollections*, pp.327.
33  Brackenbury, 'Rules to be observed by Officers Travelling, who are endeavouring to obtain Information for the Intelligence Division'. Intelligence Corps Museum, Chicksands.
34  Brackenbury to Lansdowne, 17th October 1892, Brackenbury letter books, Royal Artillery Museum Woolwich.

I thought would be interested in it, and I have over and over again received their personal thanks for the papers sent.

Such an attitude, of providing material before being asked about such matters, was to a large extent a new departure for the Branch. Brackenbury was certainly right when he suggested that the material was greatly appreciated. A good example of this can be seen during the Anglo-Portuguese crisis of 1890. Portuguese aggression saw the arrest of British railway engineers, the hauling down of British Flags and the massacre of the British-protected Makalolo tribe by the Portuguese Army. Brackenbury sent a paper to the Prime Minister and senior members of the cabinet on the military capability of Portugal and the defensive measures taken for their homeland and empire. Salisbury was clearly impressed and asked Brackenbury to prepare a report on what operations could be conducted against Portugal and her Empire in the event of war.[35] This not only illustrates how Brackenbury made himself and his department useful but the way in which he had developed its reputation, and that the branch had grown in significance and responsibility. The fact that he was asked to prepare a report on what operations could be undertaken in the event of war shows why it can be argued that the Intelligence Branch had become a General Staff in all but name. It also demonstrates the importance and the confidence which was placed in Brackenbury. This is further illustrated by correspondence between Brackenbury and the Secretary of State for War Edward Stanhope, via his Military Secretary Sir Coleridge Grove, in 1888. A Cabinet Memorandum on the possibility of French Invasion of the British Isles had been prepared in light of material sent by Brackenbury to the Cabinet. Brackenbury asked permission to show the memorandum to Wolseley to gain his opinion. Stanhope responded that he had no authority to give this permission.[36] We see here that Brackenbury was dealing with the Cabinet on a personal level regarding material that not even Wolseley as Adjutant General was allowed to see. This is a clear illustration of how Brackenbury had turned the Intelligence Branch from being seen as a "harmless but rather useless appendage to the War Office" into a highly regarded and useful organisation.

---

35   For further information on this and the Anglo-Portuguese Crisis see Roberts, Andrew, *Salisbury: Victorian Titan* (London: Phoenix, 1999), pp.520–523. William Beaver's book *Under Every Leaf* gives similar examples for the usefulness of the intelligence provided by the branch during the crisis with Russia during the late 1880s.
36   Grove to Brackenbury, 2nd and 3rd July 1888, Stanhope Papers, Centre for Kentish Studies, Maidstone.

CHAPTER 19

# THE HARTINGTON COMMISSION

Although it had little to do directly with the work of the Intelligence Branch, Brackenbury's membership of the Hartington Commission deserves comment, especially as it came about partly because he was Head of the Intelligence Branch. The setting up of the committee was an attempt by the government to defuse the hysteria caused by the invasion scares of the late 1880s and wider political considerations. Much of the debate had been caused by the mobilisation plans of Brackenbury and Ardagh, and in particular the latter's report, supported by Brackenbury, that London lay completely undefended.[1] A Royal Commission was established under Lord Hartington, who had served as Secretary of State for War from December 1882 to June 1885. By limiting the terms of reference to looking at the administration rather than a detailed account of what was perceived to be 'wrong' with the army and navy, the government hoped to limit its scope and avoid a report that suggested the need for a large-scale overhaul of the armed forces. It has also been suggested that the appointment of three former Secretaries of State for War, Hartington, W.H. Smith and Henry Campbell-Bannerman, was a clear attempt to avoid criticism of the War Office administration and the idea of civilian control of the War Office.[2] Added to this, another key member was Lord Randolph Churchill, a former Chancellor of the Exchequer, who had been an ardent campaigner for the reduction of military spending on the army.

Indeed the appointing of the commission in the first place owed much to Churchill.[3] In December 1886 Churchill had resigned as Chancellor of the Exchequer

---

1   Memorandum on Mobilisation scheme, National Archives, WO33/46.
2   Spiers, Edward, *The Late Victorian Army* (Manchester: Manchester University Press, 1992), p.46.
3   See Hamer, W.S., *The British Army Civil Military Relations 1885-1905* (Oxford: Clarendon Press, 1970) Chapter IV for information on the background and history of the Hartington Commission.

ostensibly over military expenditure. Churchill believed there was considerable military inefficiency and waste. The real reason for his resignation had much more to do with internal Conservative Party politics and Churchill's ambition. In the aftermath Churchill chaired the Select Committee on the Army estimates. After taking evidence from many witnesses Churchill had been genuinely surprised to find that there was a severe lack of funding, and that what waste and inefficiency there was came largely from the civilian side. To this end Churchill supported his argument with the evidence of Brackenbury's mobilisation scheme, which had illustrated great deficiencies in various areas of the army. Brackenbury gave evidence before the select committee in both 1886 and 1887. The latter was the more interesting and when looking at the questions asked it is clear that the politically shrewd Churchill already knew the answers. He simply wanted a senior member of the War Office staff to publically state them. Brackenbury answered that the army was largely denied the money that would make it efficient, that there was a lack of understanding of the military requirements by the civilian administration, and he even made the case for the creation of a Chief of Staff and General Staff. This was all supported by the evidence of his mobilisation scheme, and nobody seems to have questioned his findings. One of Brackenbury's most interesting statements illustrates all three points.

> Our Army has not been built up with a view to the relative proportions of the various areas of the service; it has not got the horses and to the best of my belief, it has not got the equipment and stores sufficient to enable it to take the field immediately. That defective organisation is largely due to the money not having been spent upon ... horses, and, secondly, on stores.[4]

Churchill continued to highlight civilian inefficiency within the War Office. It is ironic that what started as a campaign for economy and greater civilian control became a movement for increased expenditure and an indictment of civilian administration. The pressure continued to build upon the government and on 15th November 1888 the Secretary of State for War announced the intention to appoint a commission to investigate the matter.

Brackenbury's presence on the Commission was partly recognition of him as an army reformer but also because it was his report that had highlighted many of the problems. It was undoubtedly hoped that with his name attached to a report, which, with the background of the other members was likely to support the government and the principle of civilian control, would help to defuse the public argument. There was also a more practical reason in that one of the questions that the Hartington Commission asked was whether there was any link between Naval and

---

[4] *Second Report from the Select Committee on Army and Navy Estimates 1887*, Volume VIII, no.3668.

Military Intelligence Departments, and also whether this should be enhanced: there was even a suggestion that they might be combined.

The commission was first appointed on 15th May 1888, but it took till July 1889 before the first part of the report was published, with the second following in February 1890. The minutes of evidence were never published.[5] The report commented on four areas. Firstly the measures required to secure full and sufficient administrative harmony between the two intelligence and planning departments; secondly, the internal administration of the Admiralty; thirdly the internal administration of the War Office; and fourthly the relation of the Treasury to the War Office and the Admiralty and matters of financial control generally. The evidence was in two parts. Firstly there was a list of written questions that were sent to various officials, both civilian and military, and secondly a number of people were interviewed directly by the Commission. Many senior politicians including, Gladstone, Lord Salisbury, Lord Ripon, the Earl of Grey, Campbell-Bannerman, Hugh Childers, Stanhope and Hartington himself gave evidence to the commission. Admiral Hay, Admiral Hornby, Admiral Hood, Admiral Mends, Vice-Admiral Hoskins, and Captain Beresford represented the Naval viewpoint, whilst the Duke of Cambridge, Wolseley, General Adye, General Simmons, and Sir Ralph Thompson, the Permanent Secretary to the War Office, represented the Army. There were two main questions, although each had various sub-sections. The first was concerned with the defence of the Empire and matters of cooperation between the two services. The second question dealt with the relationship between the civilian and military side of both services. Given the diversity of those questioned it is not surprising that there was little agreement on any of the subjects brought before the Commission.[6]

The second section of the evidence was taken in front of the commission itself. The commission sat for 16 days, between 16th November 1888 and 11th April 1889, including a gap of nearly three months between December 1888 and March 1889. Very few of the commissioners sat for all 16 days. In fact Hartington, as chairman, was virtually the only one present throughout. Brackenbury attended 13 days, which was better than most, whilst Sir Randolph Churchill, though by political weight one of the most important members, was only present for 3 days. Other leading members, such as W.H. Smith and Campbell-Bannerman, were also missing most of the time. It meant that in the end the report became largely the work of Hartington, Brackenbury, Sir Richard Temple M.P., T.H. Ismay and Vice-Admiral

---

5  The non-publication of the minutes was largely an attempt to prevent any further debate on the subject, which would undoubtedly have happened given the diverging opinions expressed by the various soldiers, sailors and civilians. The Minutes of Evidence taken and received by the Hartington Commission do survive and are held under National Archives, HO73/35/3.

6  The Minutes of Evidence included a document which declared who supported which of the recommendations, both amongst the Commission and those who gave evidence.

Sir F.W. Richards. This probably goes a long way to explaining why Churchill and Campbell-Bannerman dissented from the final report.

The basic differences between the two services in administrative terms were in relation to professionalism and royal influence. The commission asserted that unlike the Navy, the Army, through the Commander-in-Chief, had the right of direct approach to the Crown on military matters. The case was made by Lord Esher that:

> The Navy is a constitutional force. Every Commission is signed by the (Admiralty) Board. The Army is a Royal force and, while the Queen never interferes with the Navy, she interferes very much with the Army.[7]

The other problem with administration was the status of the Commander-in-Chief. Unlike the Navy he was, in the words of the Royal Commission, "the only officer who had any direct responsibility to the Secretary of State". He had far too much responsibility, and the Royal Commission reported that:

> This system appears to us to involve excessive centralisation of responsibility in the person of the Commander-in-Chief on whom the whole executive command, administration and supply of the Army now devolve.

It was in the light of this that the Hartington Commission recommended that the office of Commander-in-Chief should be abolished. In the hope of avoiding royal disapproval it added the proviso that the change was to happen on the retirement of the current Commander-in-Chief, the Duke of Cambridge, who it will be remembered, was the Queen's cousin. It was recommended that the new position of Chief of Staff be created, who would be the senior of five senior military officers who would form a War Office Council. Under the new system the five heads would be responsible to the Secretary of State for the administration of their departments. The Chief of Staff would be given responsibility for military planning, mobilisation, consulting with the Admiralty, intelligence and the defence of the United Kingdom. The idea was to free such an individual from the more executive duties of the Commander-in-Chief and make him:

> ... responsible for preparing plans of military operations, collecting and co-ordinating information of all kinds, and generally tendering advice upon all matters of organisation and the preparation of the army for war.[8]

Whilst this was one suggested scheme there was another, drawn up by Churchill, who wanted the creation of a Ministry of Defence. The Minister would be a senior

---
[7] Brett, M. V., *The Journals and Letters of Viscount Esher* (London: Ivor Nicolson & Watson, 1934), Volume I p.269.
[8] Report of the Hartington Commission, 1889. National Archives, HO73/36/4.

member of the Cabinet. He would be advised by two professional heads at the army and navy, who would take over the duties of the Secretary of State for War and the First Lord of the Admiralty. The two military men would be members of the cabinet, but only when matters of a military consequence were being discussed. Such a policy was unpopular with most politicians, because it diminished their control, as the professional heads of the army and navy would run their departments largely independently of the government. It was also unpopular with many soldiers, sailors and politicians because it would leave the services without an individual representative at cabinet level that would represent their interests alone. The scheme did have its supporters, including Brackenbury, Childers, the Duke of Cambridge, Wolseley and Stanhope.[9] This system also included a Chief of Staff for the Army, who would be the direct subordinate and deputy for the new professional head of the Army. Under Churchill's suggestion this appeared to be an acceptable idea to Wolseley, as in this form the Chief of Staff would not be the senior soldier.

The proposed creation of a General Staff, as envisaged by the Hartington Commission, caused a great deal of controversy, and outside of the Commission itself was very unpopular. The Duke of Cambridge and Lord Wolseley were for once united in their opposition. The Queen opposed it as she continued to hope that her son, the Duke of Connaught, would succeed as Commander-in-Chief. The hope of members of the Hartington Commission was that the Duke of Cambridge could be persuaded to step down immediately so the recommendations could be implemented, but they phrased it so as to avoid royal anger at the suggestion saying it could be done on his retirement or any favourable opportunity. It failed to work and Her Majesty referred to it as "this really abominable report". It was largely the Queen's response that led to the report being ignored. She saw it as a personal attack on her authority. "One of the greatest prerogatives of the Sovereign is the direct communication with an immovable and non-political officer of high rank about the army ..."[10] Another problem was the objection of Campbell-Bannerman. He was the only member of the commission to object to this idea in principle. However his objection was enough to give a somewhat sceptical government the excuse they needed to avoid the conflict with the Royal Family that creating a Chief of Staff would cause. The eventual death knell for the Hartington Commission was the arrival of a Liberal Government in 1892 and in particular Campbell-Bannerman's appointment as Secretary of State for War. He held a typical Liberal aversion to anything that was remotely militaristic. To him the creation of a Chief of Staff, a truly professional senior soldier, would make the possibility of war more, not less, likely. As Brian Bond has written, "To such a mind the Duke

---

9   The Minutes of Evidence of the Hartington Commission. National Archives, HO73/35/3.
10  Bond, Brian, 'The Retirement of the Duke of Cambridge', *Journal of the Royal United Service Institution* 106, (1961), pp.546-7. Queen Victoria's anger seems to have had more to do with the fact that this had emanated from a Conservative Government.

of Cambridge, although an obstacle to important internal reforms, was at least safer than a General Staff". Ironically it was Campbell-Bannerman who would successfully negotiate the retirement of the Duke of Cambridge in 1895.[11] In the end a War Office Council was established with the Commander-in-Chief as the senior member. It looked like a reform but in fact nothing happened, and the Royal Commission on the War in South Africa heard evidence that the Council rarely met and was never called upon to vote on any matter.[12] The attempt to create a body similar to the Admiralty Board had failed.

There is no doubt that Wolseley believed that Brackenbury was responsible for the Hartington Commission's recommendation for the creation of a Chief of Staff. He believed that the new post had been suggested so that Brackenbury himself would be the ideal choice for the position. This caused a cooling in the relations between the two men, as Wolseley knew he was the obvious choice to be the next Commander-in-Chief but would not necessarily be for the position of Chief-of-Staff. The belief that the Chief of Staff would be Brackenbury was not just held by Wolseley. Grierson wrote in his diary on the day he read the Hartington Commission's report: "Very good, especially creation of Chief of Staff. Sure to be Brackenbury".[13] Callwell agreed with Wolseley's opinion that Brackenbury, and to a lesser extent Major George Clarke, had been the driving force behind the commission's recommendation, but did not see this as a necessarily bad thing.[14] Brackenbury's case for the appointment was supported by the fact that the proposed General Staff was to be made up largely of his existing Intelligence Branch.[15] The Government was also reluctant to accept it. Largely it was the age-old fear that such a 'professional' appointment could give rise to a disturbing level of militarism; the idea being that the more you prepared for war the more likely it would be. The other fear was that if they accepted this one part of the commission's report they would be under pressure to accept the rest.

Whilst Brackenbury obviously wanted the Chief of Staff appointment, he may not have intended it to be at the expense of Wolseley. The evidence shows that Brackenbury supported Churchill's scheme for a national Ministry of Defence.[16] Brackenbury may have had a hand in Lord Randolph Churchill's drawing up of the scheme for a National Minister of Defence. Charles Callwell, an officer serving under Brackenbury in the Intelligence Branch, claims that during this period Churchill was often at Queen Anne's Gate to discuss matters with Brackenbury. A

---

11  Bond, Brian, 'The Retirement of the Duke of Cambridge', p.549. A further irony was that it was the Liberal Government of Campbell-Bannerman who would create the first Chief of Staff for the army in 1904.
12  *Royal Commission on the War in South Africa* (Elgin Commission) (London: H.M.S.O., 1903).
13  Macdiarmid, D.S., *The Life of Lieut. General Sir James Moncrieff Grierson* p.82.
14  Callwell, Maj-General Sir Charles, *Stray Recollections*, p.327.
15  Report of the Hartington Commission. National Archives, HO73/36/4.
16  Callwell, Maj-General Sir Charles *Stray Recollections*, pp.327-8.

letter between Churchill and Brackenbury referrers to a private meeting they had at the Carlton Club to discuss the Hartington Commission.[17] The date is interesting as it is just after the Commission has finished taking evidence and is now considering its final report. Randolph Churchill's scheme provided for a professional head of the Army, which would have suited Wolseley. It is more than likely that Brackenbury saw himself fulfilling a Chief of Staff's role under him as he had done throughout their service overseas together. Unfortunately there is no direct evidence to support this, other than the fact that Brackenbury supported Randolph Churchill's scheme.

The duties of the Chief of Staff were considered to be the same under either proposal. If Churchill's scheme had been accepted it would have pleased both Wolseley and Brackenbury. The problem was that Hartington was opposed to Churchill's scheme, largely on the grounds that he knew it would never win political support. The report was uncommitted on the creation of a Minister of Defence, but strong in its support of the post of Chief of Staff. Brackenbury was naturally ambitious, but the creation of a Chief of Staff was not a new idea of his to attain high office, as Wolseley later suggested. Brackenbury had first publicly urged the creation of such a post in 1867 in his series of articles on Military Reform.[18] This was obviously at a time when he was in no position to be considered for the position, nor did his career to date suggest that he ever would, as this was prior to his association with Wolseley. If this suggestion is read in the light of his 1867 article then it is obvious that the proposal was one that was thought important for the modernisation of the army, rather than for personal advantage. The creation of a General Staff would fit in nicely with Brackenbury's constant theme: the improved efficiency of the army. A General Staff would improve the efficiency by planning, preparation and improved organisation throughout the army and it could be argued that such a body was a logical next step from mobilisation plans. It would have taken on the duties of the mobilisation and intelligence departments in a much more efficient way. It will be remembered that whilst Brackenbury saw the desirability of having both departments together he had insisted that the mobilisation section become separate as he had insufficient funds and manpower to do both duties effectively. A General Staff would have allowed him to do this. However, whatever his reasons, there was no creation of a Chief of Staff, nor was there until shortly after Brackenbury's retirement.[19]

Brackenbury's appointment to the commission caused him a number of problems. On 12th December 1888 he was sent for by the Duke of Cambridge, "and he expressed to me in very strong terms his disapproval of the appointment of a Chief of Staff", even if this appointment were to be under the Commander-in-Chief. It was

---

17  Randolph Churchill to Brackenbury, 15th May 1889, private collection.
18  Brackenbury, Henry, 'Military Reform', Part V *Fraser's Magazine* Volume 76 (August 1867), pp.214-215.
19  Ironically the position of Chief of Staff was created by the Government of Sir Henry Campbell-Bannerman, whose lone dissension to such a post being created gave the Government of the day the justification it needed.

the Duke of Cambridge's view that this would "destroy the connection between the Crown and the army, and that neither H.R.H. (Cambridge) nor any good man would hold office under these conditions". This placed Brackenbury in a difficult position, and he consulted Stanhope on this matter. Brackenbury declared that his view on the creation of a Chief of Staff had not been altered by the Duke's position, but he asked Stanhope: "Am I, an officer on the staff of H.R.H., to advocate on the Royal Commission a course which H.R.H. has strongly condemned?". Brackenbury offered two possible solutions, that either he resign from the Hartington Commission or from the War Office.

> The former would, I think have an unfortunate affect, as it would be misinterpreted by the public and the press. The latter would impugn no one but myself, and I am quite prepared to sacrifice myself to carry through what I consider a most necessary reform. But I am unwilling to take a step, which will probably attract some attention, without ascertaining what the views of Her Majesty's Government are, by whom I was placed on the Royal Commission.[20]

Although the language is a little melodramatic this really was a dilemma for Brackenbury, and one that only the government could solve. As Brackenbury pointed out, he had been placed on this commission by the government, but the normal military discipline meant that it was unconventional, to say the least, for a Lieutenant-General to publicly, and before a Royal Commission at that, disagree with the Commander-in-Chief. This perhaps illustrates once again the slightly precarious position that Brackenbury was in. Had it been Wolseley in this position it is hard to believe that he would have hesitated to contradict the Duke, but Brackenbury did not have that security of position. Wolseley could not be disposed of easily, yet Brackenbury could simply not be re-employed when his tenure as Head of the Intelligence Branch expired. This may explain his anxiety about his future appointment a few years later when his tenure at the Intelligence Branch was due to expire.[21]

Stanhope replied that he had discussed the matter with his cabinet colleagues and that they all agreed that whilst his position was difficult there should be no question of him resigning. Stanhope went on to say that being appointed to the Royal Commission gave Brackenbury, "absolute and entire freedom to follow and express

---

20  All quotations taken from Brackenbury to Stanhope, 27th February 1889, Stanhope Papers, Centre for Kentish Studies, Maidstone.
21  In another example of his insecurity about his career, despite the fact that he was now a Lieutenant-General, Brackenbury used all his contacts to gain his appointment in India. Stanhope, Lord Salisbury, W.H. Smith and Lord Knutsford were all asked to speak to Lord Cross, the Secretary of State for India, on his behalf.

his opinion on all the matters referred to the Commission". Stanhope tried to make the case that no one would object if Brackenbury were to criticise the policy of the Secretary of State, and that therefore he should be free to criticise the policy of the Commander-in-Chief if necessary.

> But in this you are asked to be a member of the commission in order that you might join in telling the country irrespective of the views of the Secretary of State or the Commander in Chief, what you think wanting in the organisation of the War Office; as if you were to hold that your position precluded you from doing so, it would render any enquiry of this sort, which may be essential to the public service, nugatory. We therefore are strongly of opinion, and I venture to express it to you, that you are fully justified in going on to the end with the work you have undertaken on the Commission.[22]

The significance of Brackenbury's problems should not be overlooked. It would be naive to think that he acted "solely upon grounds of public duty", as Stanhope stated. He undoubtedly had private motivation, some of which we may never know.[23] However, that he was driving to improve the efficiency of the army cannot be doubted, and it was in this way that he was acting "upon grounds of public duty", as he had always endeavoured to do. His career, his writing and his service had constantly demonstrated a determination to improve the efficiency, and therefore the capability, of the army. It was to this end that both he and Stanhope believed that the creation of a Chief of Staff was necessary. It is likely that Brackenbury had convinced Stanhope of the need for this appointment, but he would not have needed much persuading. Programmes like mobilisation plans, the so-called 'Stanhope Storehouses' and similar projects did really require a Chief of Staff to operate them efficiently. As Stanhope was committed to these programmes a Chief of Staff would have seemed an obvious and appropriate next step.

The Hartington Commission report was, by the standards of the day, small in size. Yet its findings could have had a profound effect on the military forces of Britain and the Empire. A Chief of Staff and more general cooperation and planning between the two services would have improved efficiency and effectiveness considerably. Indeed The War Office Reconstitution Committee of 1904 (commonly called the Esher Committee), which came in the wake of the disaster of the South African War, remarked that:

---

22  All quotations from Stanhope's reply to Brackenbury's of 27th February 1889 - Stanhope to Brackenbury, 2nd March 1889, Stanhope Papers, Centre for Kentish Studies, Maidstone.
23  Stanhope to Brackenbury, 2nd March 1889, Stanhope Papers, Centre for Kentish Studies, Maidstone.

We unhesitatingly assert that if the recommendations of the majority of the Hartington Commission had not been ignored, the country would have been saved the loss of many thousands of lives, and of many millions of pounds, subsequently sacrificed in the South African War ... Upon many material points we have done no more than adopt and develop the principles laid down by the Hartington Commission, especially as regards the creation of the branch of a Chief of the General Staff.[24]

---

24  *Report of the War Office Reconstitution Committee* (Esher Committee). (London, H.M.S.O., 1904), Part I p.161.

# Chapter 20

# Legacy of Intelligence Work

During his appointment Brackenbury did much to improve the Intelligence Branch. As well as enlarging it he also increased both the quantity and quality of the work. It was well collated and its use to the government was proved by the rise in importance of the Intelligence Branch, which was driven by the civilian side of the War Office. This is also illustrated by the fact that Brackenbury was given authority to present reports direct to the Secretary of State for War, and other members of the cabinet rather than having to go through the usual War Office channels of either the Commander in Chief, the Adjutant General or the Quarter Master General. This led to occasions when Brackenbury saw cabinet papers that had not been shown to anyone else in the Army, including Cambridge and Wolseley.[1] This surely illustrates the importance that was now attached to the Intelligence Branch. This had come about due to Brackenbury's hard work and his ability to make the branch both relevant and useful.

The Foreign Office became very interested in the product of the Intelligence Branch, as it seemed able to gain more accurate information than they did by their own efforts. Nevertheless, despite recognising the benefit of their work the Foreign Office viewed the Intelligence Branch with suspicion largely because they saw them as inexperienced amateurs whereas they were the professionals.[2] This started to change during Brackenbury's era because of his professional approach and because he made sure his agents did not tread on the toes of their Foreign Office counterparts. Brackenbury was given permission by the Secretary of State, and reluctantly, the Commander-in-Chief to correspond directly, if necessary, with the Foreign

---

[1] Colleridge Grove (Stanhope's Military Secretary) to Brackenbury, 3rd July 1888, Stanhope Papers, Centre for Kentish Studies, Maidstone.
[2] Parritt, Lieut-Colonel B.A.H., *The Intelligencers*, pp.160-161.

Office and the Private Under Secretary for the Colonies. This was on the strict understanding that he was merely to provide information and not to touch upon matters of policy. Clearly they did not want a soldier interfering in politics. In light of Brackenbury's exposure to political intrigue whilst in Ireland he was no doubt happy to oblige in this regard. It was a big jump in prestige for the branch, and one that had only come about because it had proved its worth through the quality of intelligence they were providing.

The biggest step forward was that Brackenbury had now established the principle that the Head of the Intelligence Branch should be consulted on military matters concerning foreign powers. This was a significant advance from the position when Brackenbury had first been appointed, when it was considered, "a harmless but rather useless appendage to the War Office".[3] Brackenbury had changed this not only by improving the amount and quality of intelligence, but by also making those who received the intelligence appreciate it. Given the size of the Branch the results were little short of amazing. This was due partly to its reorganisation, but also because of the presence of the brightest and best of the army. From Brackenbury down every man was hand-picked to be the best for the post. It was their hard work and commitment that enabled them to produce and collate such vast quantities of intelligence, so much so that the quality of the work they produced was on a par with that of the vast general staffs of Europe. Grierson recalled that Count von Schlieffen, Chief of the General Staff in Berlin, once told him that he was amazed that such a small staff could produce such work and do such a good job.[4] With only 18 permanent staff and a budget of £11,000 a year the Intelligence Branch was producing material on a par with the German General Staff that numbered over 300 and had a budget of £270,000 a year simply for intelligence work.[5] It was truly a remarkable reorganisation that had caused this: achieved by enlarging the department and having handpicked men for the positions. It was not just the selection, but also the guidance Brackenbury provided in techniques and manners of intelligence gathering that were so impressive. His rules for officers travelling to gather intelligence continued to be used for many years to come.

## Brackenbury's Legacy

Brackenbury's five year term as Head of the Intelligence Branch came to an end in 1891, and he was replaced by Major-General Edward F. Chapman, who arrived from India. Brackenbury left to take up the appointment of Military Member of

---

3   Maurice, Maj-General Sir F. and Arthur, Sir George, *The Life of Lord Wolseley*, p.224.
4   Macdiarmid, D.S., *The Life of Lieut. General Sir James Moncrieff Grierson*, pp.89-90.
5   Amery, Leopold, *The Times History of the War in South Africa 1899-1902* (London: Sampson Low, 1909), pp.39-40.

the Governor-General's (Viceroy's) Council in India. Chapman's time in charge, though largely through no fault of his own, was something of a backwards step for the Intelligence Branch. His major problem was that he had never served outside of India and was only returning home through ill-health. It has been suggested that Lord Roberts largely engineered this appointment in a desire to have someone with vast experience of India and who understood the Russian threat within the War Office. Chapman seems to have been liked personally by his staff but they all quickly recognised his limitations.[6] He later confided in Brackenbury that he had little idea of what was going on in his department and asked for his help.[7] Whilst in India Brackenbury continued to keep in touch with many of his former officers who were still in the Intelligence Branch. Most notable among these was Grierson who continued to keep Brackenbury supplied with documents from the Intelligence Branch.[8] During Chapman's time the relationship with the Foreign Office soured. Unlike Brackenbury, who had worked for them when he was a military attaché, Chapman had no previous experience of the Foreign Office. Also unlike Brackenbury, Chapman failed to keep close control of officers travelling abroad and was notably embarrassed by an officer who, on a mission to Russia, threw his weight around in the British Embassy, leading to an official complaint by the ambassador and the Foreign Office.[9] This incident led to a reissuing of Brackenbury's 'rules'.

Chapman was succeeded in 1896 by Ardagh who was able to restore the branch to the level Brackenbury had left, and renew good relations with the Foreign and Colonial Offices. The Intelligence Branch was much criticised during the South African War for not having foreseen the capabilities of the Boers.[10] However, the Royal Commission and numerous enquiries found that the Intelligence Branch had provided accurate and relevant information to the necessary authorities. It had partly been ignored and some important documents never got further than the Commander-in-Chief's office. Despite its limited numbers and finance the Branch proved itself successful during the South African War. Brackenbury's legacy was actually long lasting. The system he created, except for minor changes, lasted intact until 1965. Whilst partly saying something about the lethargy of the War Office it

---

6  Repington, Lieut-Colonel Charles à Court, *Vestigia*, p.89 and Gleichen, Maj-General Lord Edward, *A Guardsman's Memories*, p.177.
7  Chapman to Brackenbury, 21st October 1892, Chapman Papers, National Archives, WO106/16.
8  Letter books of Lieutenant General Sir Henry Brackenbury. Royal Artillery Museum, Woolwich. They include numerous letters between the two.
9  This account is told by both Fergusson, p.107 and Parritt, pp.162-163.
10 The major fault of the Intelligence Department was that they expected the Boers to use small raiding parties rather than a full-scale invasion. That is why the figure of 9,000 men is sometimes quoted from the Intelligence Branch as the number they believed the Boers would place in the field. They believed that this force would be used to raid, and the rest of the Boer force would defend the frontier from a British strike.

is perhaps partial proof of the soundness of what Brackenbury was able to achieve during his five years in charge of the Intelligence Branch.

The other great legacy of Brackenbury's time in the Intelligence Branch was the start of the mobilisation scheme. His own view on the importance of these schemes was later set out in a personal letter to Sir George White.

> I was for five years teaching military history, and few men have studied the big problems of war more closely than I have done. All my study impressed firmly on my mind the conviction that no country was ever yet saved by fortifications, and that nothing can enable us to beat our enemies but a strong army for field fighting, and a strong Navy to sweep the seas.[11]

This was to prove vital during the South African War where the smoothness and ease of mobilisation shocked even the War Office, who appointed extra staff to deal with expected problems. To everyone's surprise the problems never materialised. Although a great deal of credit needs to go to Sir John Ardagh, who organised and fine-tuned Brackenbury's plans, and Colonel John Cowans, who put the plans into practice, it has to be remembered that it was Brackenbury who drew them up. They were deliberately open-ended so that they would suit all purposes and they also had the effect of creating the impetus for a formal declaration of what the Army's duties were. Although the significance of the Stanhope Memorandum has been overplayed, and has been rightly questioned in more recent times, it was significant, if for no other reason, that it formally set down the duties of the Army for the first time.[12] It thus allowed for more formal planning, such as mobilisation schemes, to take place and be effective. As Howard Bailes has commented:

> In an almost flawless mobilisation, 112,000 regular troops were equipped and sent to South Africa between 7th October 1899 and 30th January 1900. This was an unprecedented achievement for Britain and a tribute to the work of mobilisation begun by Sir Henry Brackenbury fourteen years previously.[13]

---

11  Brackenbury to White, 5th December 1892, Brackenbury letter books, Royal Artillery Museum Woolwich. There is a certain historical irony in Brackenbury's remarks given that during the South African War Sir George White was to retreat behind fortifications with a field army, and gain much criticism for so doing.
12  Beckett, Ian, *The Victorians at War* (London: Hambeldon & London, 2003), Chapter 16 'The Improbable Probability'. In many ways this is a slightly updated version of Beckett's own article 'The Stanhope Memorandum of 1888: A Reinterpretation', *Bulletin of the Institute of Historical Research*, 57 (1984), pp.240-47.
13  Bailes, Howard, 'Technology and Imperialism: A case study of the Victorian Army in Africa', *Journal of Victorian Studies*, Volume XXIV (Autumn 1980), pp.82-104.

CHAPTER 21

# THE CHALLENGE OF INDIA

## INTRODUCTION

During the years 1891 to 1896 Brackenbury held the rather grandiose title of Military Member of the Council of the Governor-General (Viceroy) of India.[1] The period that Brackenbury spent in India can all too easily be viewed as little more than an interlude between the two very significant appointments he held at the War Office. We have already seen how important his time as Head of the Intelligence Branch was, and whilst his success there is plain to see, it is harder to see what lasting effect Brackenbury had in India. Perhaps this is not surprising. Being able to change and leave a mark on a department at the War Office, despite its obvious difficulties, was far easier than making an impact on the government of a huge country such as Imperial India. However it is possible to see improvements in administration and logistics which owed much to Brackenbury. It is first necessary to look at some of the background to the British position in, and governance of, India to understand Brackenbury's time there.

## BRITISH POWER IN INDIA

Whilst it is not necessary to outline in detail the history of British influence in India, a brief outline of the machinery of government will prove useful in terms of understanding the situation in which Brackenbury found himself. British power in India was initially developed not by the British Government but by the

---

[1] In November 1858 Lord Canning was declared 'Viceroy of India' and he and his successors continued to use the title, but it had no official standing. So whilst the reader might recognise the term Viceroy more than Governor-General, it is technically incorrect. For the sake of simplicity the term Viceroy will be used in the main for the rest of this book.

Honourable East India Company. It was only after the Indian Mutiny in 1858 that control of India passed to Her Majesty's Government. Rather than the twenty-four strong Court of Directors of the East India Company, India was to be governed by a Governor-General, commonly known as the Viceroy, who was in turn responsible to the Secretary of State for India who as a member of the British Government was responsible to both the Cabinet and Parliament. A council, whose members were chosen by the British government, advised the Governor-General. The Governor-General, himself chosen by the British government, had the theoretical power to overrule the council, but it was seldom used.[2] The members of the council served for a fixed five-year period, and this was why Brackenbury spent only five years in India as the military representative on the council. More will be said about the status of his position later.

## The Military in India

A single Indian Army did not strictly exist until 1895. Before that date four main forces made up the available military strength; the three Presidency Armies of Bengal, Bombay and Madras, and the Punjab Frontier Force. Each Army had its own Commander-in-Chief, and in practice the Commander-in-Chief of the Bengal Army was also Commander-in-Chief India. The military system in India had an unnecessarily complex organisation. The Punjab Frontier Force, for example, was actually under the control of the Government of India, not the Commander-in-Chief. As a result if the army Commander in the Punjab wanted to move an element of the force from its current deployment he had to ask the Commander-in-Chief India. He in turn had to ask the Governor-General, who then had to tell the Lieutenant Governor of the Punjab to order the Commander of the Frontier force to do what it was he had wanted to do in the first place.

The Commander-in-Chief in India played an important part in Brackenbury's time there, and a good relationship between the Military Member and the Commander-in-Chief was vital. The Commander-in-Chief was usually an officer of General rank taken from the British Army; very few came from the Indian Army.[3] Yet despite being a British Army officer he was not subordinate to the Commander-in-Chief of the British Army. The Secretary of State for India appointed him, although normally with the recommendation or support of the Governor-General. More will be said of the Commander-in-Chief later when looking at the relationship between him and the Military Member of the Council.

---

2   Heathcote, T.A., *The Indian Army: The Garrison of British Imperial India, 1822-1922* (Vancouver: David and Charles, 1974), p.20.
3   Heathcote, *The Indian Army*, pp.24-35.

## 'THE GREAT GAME'

One of the major imperial concerns, in some cases bordering on obsession, of this period was the threat of a Russian invasion of India through Afghanistan and the Northwest Frontier. These anxieties started when the Russians began to fight their way down through the Caucasus, thereby expanding the Russian empire in Central Asia. In 1865 Tashkent fell to the Russians, followed by Samarkand and Bokhara in 1868, and in 1873 Khiva. Peter Hopkirk writes that:

> As the gap between the two front lines gradually narrowed, the Great Game intensified. Despite the dangers, principally from hostile rulers, there was no shortage of intrepid young officers eager to risk their lives beyond the frontier ...[4]

The Cold War that this created was commonly referred to as the 'Great Game'. There is some doubt as to who first used the phrase, but the term the 'Great Game' was popularised by Rudyard Kipling in his novel Kim.

A great deal of the 'game' was played out in Afghanistan, the country that lay between the two expanding empires. Between 1839 and 1842 Britain had first ventured into Afghanistan and fought the First Afghan War.[5] Although the details of the war need not concern us here, it has to be stated that the war was a disaster. Of the initial force of 4,500 British and Indian Troops and 12,000 camp followers that withdrew from Kabul, only one European made it back through his own means. Pride was partially restored during General Robert Sale's defence of Jellalabad (or Jalalabad). Not only did his troops lift the siege by themselves, but they also defeated the main Afghan force.

Events took a significant turn in 1878 when the Russians signed a treaty with the Afghan Amir Sher Ali, whilst at the same time refusing to hear representations from British officials. The possibility of Russian troops being based in Afghanistan, and training an Afghan Army in European methods, was unthinkable to the British, some of whom thought it a prelude to invasion. The response was a British invasion force of three columns, totalling 35,000 men and 144 guns, being sent into Afghanistan. This action was ultimately a complete success, although there were a few setbacks along the way. Frederick Sleigh Roberts, later Lord Roberts, came to fame during this campaign for his defeat of a numerically superior force by use of guile and cunning. This was the making of his reputation and special mention is made of it here because he was Commander-in-Chief in India during the first two years of Brackenbury's appointment there.

---

[4] Hopkirk, Peter, *The Great Game* (Oxford: Oxford University Press, 1990), pp.4-5.

[5] For detail of Afghan Wars see Farwell, Byron, *Queen Victoria's Little Wars* (London: Penguin Books Ltd, 1973) or Haythornthwaite, Philip J., *The Colonial Wars Source Book* (London: Caxton Publishing Group, 2000). Both give concise and basic understanding of the campaigns in Afghanistan.

As a result of the invasion the Treaty of Gandamuk was signed on 26th May 1879. This stated that the Afghans would agree to live "... in perfect peace and friendship"[6] with the British, as well as ceding Kurram Pishin and Sibi to Britain. Sher Ali was replaced by Yakub Khan as Amir. There were other elements to this treaty, such as the establishment of a permanent residency in Kabul, an agreement to allow British subjects to trade freely in Afghanistan, the building of a telegraph line from Kabul to India, and the stipulation that Britain would control the foreign policy of Afghanistan, thus making sure that Russian influence was officially kept to a minimum. With the signing of this treaty the British thought hostilities were over, and consequently most of the Army left. Only a small force under Roberts remained to control the newly acquired provinces.

This force became vital when in September 1879 Afghan soldiers mutinied and supported a mob in attacking the British Residency in Kabul, killing the Resident and his staff. Roberts was reinforced and his force was renamed the Kabul Field Force and ordered to advance on that town. After bitter fighting Kabul fell and Yakub Khan was replaced by Abdul al-Rahaman. However, another Afghan Prince, Ayub Khan, had started a popular uprising in Kandahar supported by many of the old regiments of Sher Ali's Army. The British force in Kandahar supported the local ruler, the Wali, and along with his forces set out to stop Ayub Khan. The British and the Wali were defeated at the battle of Maiwand and retreated to Kandahar where they were besieged. It was Roberts again who came to the rescue and added to his growing reputation by relieving Kandahar and defeating the Afghan Army. As a result of this war the Amir Abdul al-Rahaman agreed to have no dealings with the Russians, as a show of gratitude for Britain's support. In return the British agreed to abandon the idea of a permanent residency in Kabul, and by May 1881 the British and Indian troops had withdrawn.

Despite all this the fear of Russian expansion into Afghanistan did not go away. In March 1885 Russian and Afghan troops clashed at the border town of Pendjeh. In India the fear spread that Russia would use this as a pretext for an invasion of Afghanistan and that then it would only be a matter of time before India was threatened. In Britain the incident was used by Gladstone and the Liberal government as an excuse to withdraw British troops from the Sudan in the wake of the embarrassment of Gordon's death at Khartoum.[7] In India, the Governor-General, Lord Dufferin, assured the Amir of Afghanistan that if Russia attacked Herat, which was near the border, it would be met by a British declaration of war.[8] It must be added that the Afghans treated the Russians with the same suspicion as the British. British

---

6   Farwell, *Queen Victoria's Little Wars*, p.205.
7   Farwell, *Queen Victoria's Little Wars*, pp.293-294.
8   Fergusson, Thomas G., *British Military Intelligence, 1870-1914* (Maryland: University Publications of America, 1984), p.79.

involvement in Afghanistan had proved costly, in terms of lives, money and prestige. There was little prospect of financial gain there and the lengths to which the British had gone further illustrate the magnitude of the threat that was perceived to be posed by the Russians. Sometimes British involvement in Afghanistan was renewed to restore the prestige that a military defeat in that country had cost but more often than not it was designed to keep Russia out and to create a buffer between Russian territory and India. Nothing ever came of this 'Cold War' but when Brackenbury arrived in India tensions had risen yet again.[9]

---

[9] The best account of the 'Great Game' can be found in Hopkirk, *The Great Game*.

# Chapter 22

# Military Member

## Military Member of the Council of the Viceroy of India

As we have already seen Brackenbury had been to India before, having served as part of the reinforcements sent there following the Indian Mutiny and then later he had briefly held an appointment as Private Secretary to Lord Lytton, then Governor-General, but on the latter's resignation returned home with him after only a few months. Obviously this was not enough time for him to gain any meaningful experience of India but it did mean that when he arrived in 1891, he was at least familiar with some of the structures and workings of its government. It also meant that he had some knowledge of how the Governor-General operated, and as his appointment was to be in effect the military representative on the Governor-General's council, this would have proved useful. Given his reputation for organisation it would be very surprising if he had not done preparatory work before embarking for India. Brackenbury would be remembered as one of the finest holders of the office of Military Member. This is not surprising as the position was almost tailor-made for his peculiar qualities.

The position that Brackenbury held had something of an ambiguous nature. The Commander-in-Chief was perceived as being junior only to the Governor-General. However the Commander-in-Chief in India worked very differently to the Commander-in-Chief in Britain.[1] In Britain the job of the Commander-in-Chief in wartime was to put an army in the field and to make sure it was fully supplied and maintained. He also had responsibility for its discipline. In India the Commander-in-Chief was expected to take the field with the Army, and the responsibility for supply, organisation and maintaining the army fell upon the Military Department,

---

1   See Heathcote, T.A., *The Indian Army* (Manchester: Manchester University Press, 1995), pp.24-26, for detail of differences between British and Indian Commander-in-Chiefs.

headed by the Military Member of the Viceroy's Council. This department was in charge of what would commonly be called the 'support services'. Byron Farwell lists its responsibilities as "... military administration, medical stores, supply, transportation, clothing, remounts, military works and military finance".[2] This left the Commander-in-Chief to concentrate on training, discipline and maintaining combat readiness. In effect the Military member was a Chief of Staff with the Military Department close to being a General Staff. The Military Member prepared the army for war, kept it equipped and supplied but had a wider strategic responsibility dealing with political matters.

In practical terms it was actually an efficient division of powers and was in theory a much better system than the one found at home. As the Indian Army spent most of its time involved in one campaign or another this system allowed the Commander-in-Chief to concentrate on combat matters without being snowed under by administration.[3] The system worked well when the Commander-in-Chief was someone who had served in India for a long time and was used to it. It was when the Commander-in-Chief came from a mainly British Army background that problems arose, because it was likely he would want to be a Commander-in-Chief in the British style. This was particularly true when Lord Kitchener arrived as Commander-in-Chief in 1902. He came to India wanting to overhaul the Indian Army to incorporate the lessons of the South African War and because he feared imminent Russian invasion. He had been used to total control, especially when he had commanded the Egyptian Army, and found it impossible to accept the status of the Military Member. He felt his reforms were hampered by the powers of the Military Member and concluded that "... he would have found it easier to accomplish his mission if he had come to India as military member of council instead of as Commander-in-Chief". Although an exaggeration it does illustrate the not inconsiderable powers of the position Brackenbury occupied. It is important to underline the differing roles played by the two positions in the governance of India. The Military Department:

> ... enjoyed a watching brief over expenditure, and its head served as the channel of communication between the Viceroy and the Commander-in-Chief. Because he was expected to advise the civilian Viceroy upon broad aspects of military policy, the Military Member of the Council was entitled to criticise freely the plans and projects of the Commander-in-Chief.[4]

---

2   Farwell, Byron, *Armies of the Raj, 1858-1947* (New York: W.W. Norton and Company, 1989), p.210.
3   For a list of the various campaigns, fought after the mutiny and up to the end of the century, with basic details, see Haythornthwaite, Philip, *The Colonial Wars Source Book* (London: Caxton Editions, 2000), pp.109-116. This lists some thirty-one expeditions and campaign fought within the subcontinent during this period. Many were small campaigns on the Northwest Frontier, but all provided valuable combat experience.
4   Magnus, Phillip, *Kitchener: Portrait of an Imperialist* (London: John Murray, 1958), p.201.

To someone like Kitchener the idea that anyone, let alone someone who was of junior military rank, could freely criticise his plans to the Government of India would have been totally unacceptable. To Lord Roberts, who served as Commander-in-Chief from 1885 to 1893, there never seemed to be such a problem. This was perhaps a consequence of the perception of Roberts as the foremost military expert on India, and certainly it was likely to be a brave man who would dare to criticise him publically. As a result of Kitchener's complaints about the Military Member a committee of inquiry was set up. Two members of this committee defended the current position, namely Lord Roberts and Sir George White.[5] White had followed Roberts, and was the other Commander-in-Chief with whom Brackenbury had worked. Roberts and White were regarded as two of the most successful Commanders-in-Chief and the fact that they supported the current system contradicted Kitchener's assertion that it made it impossible for the Commander-in-Chief to achieve anything.

Although the Military Member was always a serving military officer he held a civilian appointment and worked on a civilian council, and a precedent had been established that he did not wear uniform in his official capacity. Some had been known to wear it on social occasions, but General Sir George Barrow wrote that he never once saw Brackenbury in his uniform the entire time he was in India.[6] Brackenbury's own view was that,

> I only wear uniform when other members of the council wear it. On state occasions I have always refused to inspect troops or to take salutes on parades in uniform, in order to mark the fact that I am here in a civil and not a military capacity.[7]

The fact that Sir Edmond Elles, Military Member from 1901 to 1905, wore his uniform to council meetings was a further source of annoyance to Kitchener. The Military Member sat in on all meetings of the Governing Council regardless of whether military matters were being discussed or not, and had full voting rights. The Commander-in-Chief only sat in on meetings when military matters were being discussed but even then he had no vote. In light of all this the indignation that Kitchener felt is perhaps understandable, but illustrates his total ignorance of the way the Indian Army worked before he entered his appointment. The idea that a junior officer could sit on a civilian council, in a civilian position, wearing military uniform, and criticise and vote against his proposals understandably caused him some consternation. Brackenbury's decision not to wear uniform at all illustrates the tact that he brought to the position. He had previously served as Chief of Police

---

5 Farwell, *Armies of the Raj 1858-1947*, pp.212-213.
6 Barrow, General Sir George, *The Fire of Life* (London: Hutchinson, 1941), p.95.
7 Brackenbury to Brigadier-General Lance, 31st December 1893, Brackenbury letter books Royal Artillery Museum Woolwich.

in both Cyprus and Ireland, although he had disliked these appointments, and as both of these were in effect civilian positions he did have some relevant experience outside military circles, which undoubtedly helped him in the sub-continent. Brackenbury always accepted the idea that in effect he was a civilian whilst serving in India. However he seems to have taken exception to a letter from Sir Ralph Thompson, the Permanent Secretary to the War Office, which suggested he was not an active serving officer. Brackenbury, largely for devilment, replied requesting that in that case he should be drawing half-pay and asked that it be backdated to his appointment in India. On 7th June Thompson replied that Brackenbury could not draw half-pay, but the conciliatory nature of the letter suggests that Brackenbury had made his point, and the unique nature of the position that Brackenbury found himself in was now understood.[8]

**Henry Brackenbury. A photograph taken during his time in India, 1891–1896. It illustrates that whilst Henry never wore his military uniform in public, people looking at him could have been in little doubt that he was an experienced soldier given his campaign medals. (Private collection)**

The Military Member of the Council was usually selected for his knowledge of Indian military affairs. All the members of the council were selected for their expertise in a particular area. It was felt that with Brackenbury's record as an administrator, and Roberts expert knowledge, that this did not matter in his case. Not being an expert on Indian matters, although he could never be called ignorant of

---

8   Ralph Thompson to Brackenbury, 7th June 1895, private collection. A copy of Thompson's original letter is attached, but is undated.

the subject, resulted in him remaining quiet on most of the Commander-in-Chief's proposals.[9] It was only when he thought he could add something to the debate, as a result of his experience elsewhere, that he used his privilege to pass comment and criticise the proposals of the Commander-in-Chief.

## BRACKENBURY AND ROBERTS

During the first two years of Brackenbury's service in India Sir Frederick Sleigh Roberts, who became Lord Roberts in 1892, was Commander-in-Chief. Roberts was a legend in India and could with some justification be called the finest general in British service. The press liked to call Wolseley "Our only General" and some referred to Roberts as "our other only General", but an examination of their tactical careers suggests that Roberts perhaps had the edge. In truth there would be little to choose between them. Despite the fact that Brackenbury was a founder member of the rival 'ring' of Lord Wolseley there appears to be nothing but mutual respect and admiration between the two. It would not have been surprising if Roberts had viewed Brackenbury as a threat, given that he was widely regarded as Wolseley's protégé. This perhaps goes to show that the rivalry between the two 'rings' was not as strong as is sometimes suggested. In fact Roberts actually used Brackenbury's links with the Wolseley 'ring' to try and change a decision. In 1890 Wolseley, then Adjutant-General, had passed an ordnance that would have seen all officers holding certain positions promoted to Major-General. Every eligible officer in Britain and the colonies received this promotion but none of the eligible officers in India did. John Lee wrote that "This was the most blatant piece of 'African' preferment in the on-going 'war between the rings'". There is no doubt that Roberts saw it as such.[10] Roberts had written continually complaining of the injustice but to no avail. In August 1891 he asked for Brackenbury's support in trying to change the decision. He specifically asked for help over Ian Hamilton's promotion, knowing the high regard Brackenbury held him in after their service together in the Sudan, but Brackenbury said he was willing to fight for all of them. He then wrote, not only officially, as Roberts had done, but also privately to Redvers Buller, another of the Wolseley 'ring', who by this time had succeeded Wolseley as Adjutant-General at the War Office.[11] Eventually the promotions were obtained, which probably had as much to do with the Secretary of State for India's intervention as Brackenbury's.

---

9  Even his time as Head of the Intelligence Branch at the War Office had not helped in his knowledge of India, as this was considered off limits. Responsibility for such intelligence was seen to lie with the Indian Army and authorities.
10  Lee, John, *A Soldier's Life, General Sir Ian Hamilton 1853-1947* (London: Macmillan Publishers, 2000), pp.33-34.
11  Brackenbury to Roberts, 14th August 1891. National Army Museum, Roberts Papers R11/42.

However this is another example of the strength of the relationship between the two, if only for the fact that Roberts was prepared to ask Brackenbury for help. This and his willingness to help again casts doubt on the strength of the rivalry between the 'rings' in the British Army, and shows a growing relationship between Roberts and Brackenbury.

This view is further supported by correspondence between Sir Redvers Buller and Brackenbury in May 1894. Buller had written to Brackenbury complaining of Roberts selecting certain 'favoured' officers. Brackenbury replied that the same was said of them regarding the 'Wolseley gang' saying, "Any Commander will want the men whom he has tried and found never to fail him, and will prefer them to those he has not tried". He then went on to quote Roberts, "I think Wolseley has always been perfectly right. He has a great eye for selecting men and he goes on selecting the best out of his previous selections".[12] Whilst this does not have too much to do with Brackenbury's time in India, it does focus on the much wider issue of his involvement with the two competing 'rings' within the army. He never complained of feeling side-lined or in any way unwanted in India because of his association with Wolseley. The relationship he had with Roberts perhaps illustrates both that the rivalry was not as aggressive as had been supposed and that Brackenbury's ability outweighed any rivalry.

In fact their good relationship was nothing new, as two events serve to illustrate. In a letter to the Governor-General in October 1886 Roberts discusses appointments in the Indian Army, in particular the possibility of his needing a new Chief-of-Staff and proposed that "General Brackenbury is, I believe, the officer best fitted for such an important position".[13] At that time Brackenbury was serving as Head of the Intelligence Branch at the War Office. This is perhaps related to events that had happened some months prior to Roberts letter. When Brackenbury had returned from Egypt in August 1885 he had been promoted to Major-General but had also been put on half-pay. He himself records the reasons for this.

> I doubt if it is realised by the public generally how great are the difficulties of a military career to an officer who is not possessed of private means. It would have been impossible for me to take a Major-General's command at home or in the colonies, involving as it would have done furnishing a large house, buying horses and carriages, and setting up an expensive establishment for a maximum period of five years. My only chance was India.[14]

The expenses of such an appointment were far less in India and so Brackenbury appealed to Roberts for a command there. For his part Roberts was only too pleased

---

12  Brackenbury to Buller, 9th May 1894, Brackenbury letter books Royal Artillery Museum Woolwich.
13  Robson, Bryan (ed.), *Roberts in India: The Military Papers of Field Marshal Lord Roberts 1876-1893* (Stroud: Alan Sutton, 1993), p.354.
14  Brackenbury, Henry, *Some Memories of My Spare Time*, pp.349-50.

to try and obtain the services of an officer who had already made quite a name for himself, and along with his good record for management and organisation, had just returned from leading a column in the field. However Roberts was unable to obtain the appointment and within a few months Brackenbury was Head of the Intelligence Branch. Brackenbury believed he failed to get the position, despite Roberts help, because "... the vacancy was wanted for someone else", and that Roberts' "... kind efforts were in vain". The real reason seems to be that there was a fear that Roberts, as an ex-artillery man, was filling all the positions in India with 'gunners'.[15] At that time Charles Arbuthnot, Edward Francis Chapman, Edwin Hayter Collen, and George Pretyman, amongst others, were all ex-artillerymen holding commands in India.

Bryan Robson, in his edition of the Roberts papers, thought that "Roberts clearly regarded some of his [Brackenbury's] views as unsound and found him less congenial than Chesney and his predecessors".[16] He gives no evidence for this judgement, and there seems little to substantiate it. There is no doubt that the two men had differences of opinion, especially when it came to the 'Russian menace'. Brackenbury thought that Russian preparations were a bluff and in this he was supported by the reports of the Intelligence Branch in London but, either because he did not think it his place or because he thought Roberts was too set in his ways, he quickly stopped trying to convince him. When Sir George White succeeded Roberts, Brackenbury made a point of sending him all the material on Russia that he was being supplied with by Grierson.[17] Roberts and Brackenbury also differed on the value and spread of education in the Army. Brackenbury had initially felt that Roberts might be against his appointment and had written to him, "I know that you would rather the post had been given to another man, but none the less I do feel quite confident that you will give me every possible help in carrying out the duties devolving upon me".[18] Roberts replied that he had no objection. It appears that any objections Roberts might have had were due to his preference for a man with more experience of India, rather than fearing any major clashes over policy with Brackenbury. However, there is no doubt that they had differences of opinion; they came from two completely different military backgrounds. Yet there is no evidence of any animosity between them and they worked well together. If anything, it could be argued that it was the different backgrounds of the two men that was the basis of a very good partnership. Their letters were always warm and friendly and their correspondence continued long after they had both retired and almost right up until Brackenbury's death in 1914. Perhaps part of the reason for this is that Brackenbury was careful never

---

15  Speech at Royal Artillery Dinner for Lord Roberts on 21st September 1892. Roberts Papers, National Army Museum.
16  Robson (ed.), *Roberts in India: The Military Papers of Field Marshal Lord Roberts 1876-1893*, p.448n.
17  Brackenbury to White, 12th May 1893, Brackenbury letter books, Royal Artillery Museum Woolwich.
18  Brackenbury to Roberts, 2nd January 1891. Roberts Papers. National Army Museum.

to exceed his authority. An incident that illustrates this was when Brackenbury was asked by Colonel Charles Bromhead to help find employment for his brother Gonville Bromhead V.C., of Rorke's Drift fame. The Bromheads and Brackenburys were both Lincolnshire families and there was a distant relationship via marriage. Brackenbury refused, pointing out that all appointments were the responsibility of the Commander-in-Chief. Bromhead responded that a word from Brackenbury would help. Brackenbury still refused and later wrote, "Bromhead has a higher opinion of what a good word from me will do than I have!" Another interesting example was that of Major Charles Townshend, who would later gain infamy during the Mesopotamia Campaign in the First World War, who wrote to Brackenbury asking for an appointment in the Intelligence Branch. Brackenbury not only told him he was unable to secure this, but that Townshend wasn't qualified for such a position.[19]

In July 1892, with preparations starting to be made for the departure of Lord Roberts, the Governor-General Lord Lansdowne considered the "advantage of the present combination being that Lord Roberts possesses a special knowledge of India and the Indian Army, while General Brackenbury has considerable experience outside India, and knowledge of the views held at home".[20] A good example of this is found in correspondence between Roberts and Brackenbury in July 1891. Roberts wanted to obtain permission from the War Office in London to convert field artillery batteries into horse artillery batteries.[21] Brackenbury responded "Knowing, as I do, that more field batteries and not more horse artillery are wanted for the home mobilisation scheme, I do not think there would be the slightest chance of getting War Office approval". As a result the matter was dropped, preventing any chance of a clash between the British and Indian army and the chance of any further antipathy being created. Lansdowne hoped that a similar relationship could be maintained with Lord Roberts successor, an appointment upon which Brackenbury, when asked for his opinion, said, "I know of only one officer in either the British or the Indian Army of at all sufficient standing, who possesses all the qualities required in Lord Roberts successor. That officer is Major-General Sir George White".[22] It was, in

---

19  Brackenbury to Colonel C.J. Bromhead, 15th October 1891, Brackenbury to Sir Mortimer Durand, 19th October 1891 and Brackenbury to Major C. Townshend, 28th August 1895. All found in Brackenbury letter books, Royal Artillery Museum Woolwich.
20  Brackenbury's Own Memorandum on Correspondence with the Viceroy, 19th July 1892. British Library, Asia, Pacific and Africa Collections, Mss. Eur. D.735, pp.1-2.
21  Brackenbury to Roberts, 20th and 23rd July 1891, Brackenbury letter books, Royal Artillery Woolwich. Permission was needed from London, as all artillery was part of the British Army on loan to the Indian Army. Technically the Indian Army possessed no artillery of its own.
22  Brackenbury's Own Memorandum on Correspondence with the Viceroy, 19th July 1892. British Library Asia, Pacific and Africa Collections, Mss. Eur. D. 735, p.2. Even back in October 1892 Brackenbury was recommending that White be the next Commander-in-Chief, despite at this time White still being a Major General. Brackenbury to Chapman 22 October 1892, Brackenbury letter books, Royal Artillery Museum Woolwich.

fact, White who succeeded Roberts in 1893 and Brackenbury continued a similarly cordial relationship with him.

Despite being in many ways the protégé of Roberts' great rival Wolseley, Brackenbury does seem to have been deeply respected by Roberts. There is a warmth and friendliness in their letters that is missing for much of the Wolseley papers. Perhaps key in this was the fact that Roberts would ask for Brackenbury's advice, something that Wolseley never did. It would have been difficult for Wolseley to have ever seen Brackenbury as anything other than a subordinate, given their history of service together. Roberts, although clearly senior, did not have such baggage in his relationship with Brackenbury. Roberts's correspondence with Brackenbury starts when the latter was at the Intelligence Branch, prior to his appointment in India. Obviously their correspondence is at its greatest during the time they served together in India, but it continues after Roberts is replaced by White, through the South African War and even into Brackenbury's retirement.[23] It is interesting to note that it was Roberts who proposed and then organised the memorial fund in memory of Sir Henry Brackenbury, and this final act of kindness towards Brackenbury illustrates the high regard in which he was held by Lord Roberts.

---

23  Roberts Papers, National Army Museum R11/42. Brackenbury's correspondence with Roberts covers the period from 1886 to 1910.

CHAPTER 23

# BRACKENBURY AND THE 'RUSSIAN MENACE'

As a consequence of his time as Head of the Intelligence Branch the Russian 'threat' was nothing new to Brackenbury. His time in intelligence gave him significant background knowledge of the subject whilst also keeping him aloof from the situation in India. He therefore entered India without any of that obsessive fear of Russian invasion that seemed to grip all those who served there. Indeed, he urged the Governor-General, Lord Lansdowne to "... doubt the wisdom of leading the Afghans and the people of India to suppose that we are afraid of being attacked on this side of the Indus by the Russian".[1] His knowledge of the wider picture brought an element of realism to the invasion scare. This was an alternative viewpoint that Lansdowne appreciated. "The touch with Eastern affairs that I got in my five years in the Intelligence Department is invaluable to me here; and the Viceroy is good enough to keep me in touch by sending me personally early copies of telegrams, and consulting me on questions that arise with Russia, China and Siam".[2]

It was whilst he had been Head of the Intelligence Branch that he and Major-General Newmarch, then Military Secretary at the India Office, had been asked to write a memorandum for the Cabinet on troop deployment and the disposition of a field force in India after troops had been provided for garrisons.[3] It is interesting to note that at the meeting at which the memorandum was agreed upon only two members had served in India for any period of time, namely Sir Donald Stewart and Major-General Newmarch. Yet rather than take the advice from India for discussion

---

1   Brackenbury to Lansdowne, 2nd June 1891, Brackenbury letter books, Royal Artillery Museum Woolwich.
2   Brackenbury to Sanderson, 9th October 1891, Brackenbury letter books, Royal Artillery Museum Woolwich.
3   Memorandum by Lieutenant-General Brackenbury and Major-General Newmarch, 19th August 1889, National Archives, WO32/6349.

by the cabinet, it was this report alone that formed the basis of the debate. To an extent this serves to illustrate the suspicion that existed in Britain that the Indian government and military tended to panic about a possible invasion and their belief that more troops, and in particular British ones, were needed to successfully defend and garrison the country.

The memorandum itself makes interesting reading on the dangers faced within India. "We believe that the conditions now obtaining in India are so different from those which obtained at the time of the mutiny, that a serious military revolt is no longer within the region of probability".[4] This is an interesting comment when it is remembered that the troops in India were still dispersed under schemes designed after the Mutiny to guard against a repeat. Until the reorganisation of 1895 troops were scattered throughout India and every major city had its own garrison. "This made it difficult to assemble troops in large numbers for exercise and the formation staffs had little opportunity of training for their active service duties".[5] Brackenbury and Newmarch made the point that if the conditions of the Mutiny era no longer existed then thousands of troops could be used in a field force in the event of any invasion, thus negating to an extent the need for reinforcements from Britain to guard against such an attack. To a degree this was what Brackenbury did when he produced a mobilisation scheme for India when he was Military Member. The memorandum goes on,

> But we consider that, in the event of the approach of Russian troops to the frontiers of India, or in the event of any serious disaster to the Army of India in the field beyond the frontiers, a state of things might arise which would demand the presence of strong garrisons.[6]

This is an interesting insight. One of the reasons for the dispersal of troops throughout India was the hope that any future mutiny could be isolated to one area and therefore more easily dealt with. The fear was no longer simply of a mutiny in the Indian Army, but the possibility of revolt amongst the general populace. Roberts held this view and "... he expected 'grave unrest' the moment the Russians entered Kabul, with worse to follow if they advanced any further".[7] So to Brackenbury the easiest way to prevent this was to have a field force prepared that could stop an invasion almost before it got started.

---

4    Memorandum by Lieutenant-General Brackenbury and Major-General Newmarch, 19th August 1889, National Archives, WO32/6349, p.1.
5    Heathcote, T.A., *The Indian Army*, p.30.
6    Memorandum by Lieutenant-General Brackenbury and Major-General Newmarch, National Archives, WO32/6349, pp.1-2.
7    James, Lawrence, *Raj: The making and unmaking of British India* (London: Abacus, 1997), p.366.

**Lord Lansdowne. He gained a high opinion of Brackenbury in India and then at the War Office. Their relationship went beyond the professional.**
*(Illustrated London News)*

The idea of Indian revolt in the event of war with Russia began to gain support throughout British India and the Russians helped to build this fear. The Russian Colonel Terentiev wrote a book *Russia and England in the struggle for the Markets of Central Asia*, which was translated into English. "It was designed to make the flesh creep, with the prophecy that if Russia ever mounted a serious military challenge to the Raj, the Indian Army would turn on its masters and the masses would follow suit".[8] That this view was widely held amongst the Russians is evidenced by the testimony of Captain Ralph Cobbold, who was told at a dinner with Russian officers that "... the Cossack would prove no match for the Sepoy who, when put to the test, would refuse to fight for his rulers".[9] The military themselves had doubts over the Indian Army's ability, if not necessarily its willingness, to defeat the Russians. In a rare instance of agreement, both Lord Wolseley and Lord Roberts concluded that the Indian Army would struggle against the Russians. In August 1889 Wolseley wrote in response to the memorandum from Brackenbury and Newmarch that he had seen a lot of the Russian Army in 1883, and that to pit 'native troops' against them, "and risk our hold on India on the issue, would be, according to my notions, a mad crime."[10] His arch-rival wrote similarly in March 1890:

---

8   James, *Raj: The making and unmaking of British India*, p.365.
9   James, *Raj: The making and unmaking of British India*, p.365.
10  Memorandum by Lord Wolseley in response to Memorandum of Lieutenant-General Brackenbury and Major-General Newmarch, 25th August 1889, National Archives, WO32/6349, p.4.

I have no hesitation in stating that except the Gurkhas, Dogrras, Sikhs, the pick of the Punjabi Muhammadans, Hindustanis of the Jay and Ranghur castes (such as enlist in our Cavalry) and certain classes of Pathans, there are no Native soldiers in our service whom we could venture in safety to place in the field against the Russian ... I should be sorry to find myself in front of a European foe unless my forces were composed of as many Europeans as Natives.[11]

These comments were all perhaps a little unfair, and there were clearly racial issues involved. The Indian Army had faced the Afghans and Pathan tribesmen with distinction. Whilst the Russians might have more modern equipment they would not match the ferocity of the Indian Army's previous enemies. The anxiety remained in India that the Indian Army would need reinforcing from Britain. However there was a real possibility that British reinforcements might not be available. In 1887 Lord Stanhope, the Secretary of State for War, responded to a despatch from the Government of India:

It is evidently far from improbable that the same circumstances which necessitated a mobilisation in India might also render it impossible for this country to part with any considerable portion of the small number of regular troops in the United Kingdom.[12]

Stanhope, therefore, implored the Government of India not to calculate reinforcements into any scheme they planned to undertake in the event of war with Russia.

There were many supporters of the so called 'forward' school of thought that wanted to pre-empt any Russian invasion and safeguard India by pushing as far into Central Asia as possible, a view which Brackenbury said, "is one which my judgement condemns as thoroughly unsound".[13] They wanted Britain to secure Kandahar, Kabul and even Herat on the Persian border, as fortresses to stop any Russian invasion. Although not one of the 'forward' school, Brackenbury held the view "that we can never allow Russian troops to occupy or enter either Kabul or Kandahar, and that we must defend the Kabul-Kandahar alignment".[14] Much of his work for a time revolved around the strengthening of garrisons and communications on the Northwest Frontier. In particular he was concerned that there must be a sufficiently good road through the Peshawar Valley to Chitral and that this

---

11   Farwell, Byron, *Armies of the Raj 1858-1947*, pp.118-119.
12   Memorandum by Sir Ralph Thompson in response to Memorandum of Lieutenant-General Brackenbury and Major-General Newmarch, 15th March 1892, National Archives, WO32/6349.
13   Brackenbury to Collen, 28th June 1892, Brackenbury letter books, Royal Artillery Museum, Woolwich.
14   Enclosures of Secret Military Despatch No 180, 15th September 1891, National Archives, WO32/6349, p.5.

must be "maintained, protected and renewed".[15] This would make any response to a Russian invasion much more efficient and effective, without going to the extreme, and costly option, put forward by the forward school. The probability of a speedy British response to any invasion might again help to deter the Russians.

Whilst knowing that it was his job to try and plan for every eventuality, it is clear that Brackenbury had grave doubts about the prospect of a Russian invasion. In a memorandum of August 1889 he wrote, "The Field Force, as distinct from the local or garrison troops, which Russia now has in Transcaspia and Turkestan, is about 34,000 men, 6,500 horses, and 80 guns". This was hardly an invasion force, even if the Russians envisaged support from Afghanistan and a popular uprising in India itself, especially when it is remembered that some of this force would have had to be used to secure the lines of communication, which would have left a field army of approximately 20,000 men. Moreover, any force would have to be supplied through inhospitable country. Obviously there was the possibility of additional troops but Brackenbury was not sure of the likelihood of this. "The numbers by which this army could be reinforced must necessarily depend upon the attitude of other powers whenever Russia and Great Britain may find themselves at war".[16] Almost certainly as a result of his time as Head of the Intelligence Branch, Brackenbury was able to see the broader picture that was perhaps not as clear to those in office in India with more parochial views. Much had been written on Russia within the Intelligence Branch whilst he had been its head, in particular 'Russia's power to concentrate troops in Central Asia', and Captain J. Wolfe Murray's 'Military operations in the event of war with Russia', although the latter was actually published just a few months after Brackenbury had left the branch. Again this shows that although he had never previously served in India for any length of time, he did have substantial knowledge of the major issues. Wolfe Murray's report talked of the inevitability of a war between Russia and Britain expanding into a much broader conflict.[17] He noted the importance of Turkey and discussed the possible scenarios of Turkey being either friend, foe or neutral. This report also considered the likelihood of French support for Russia and in a way, foretold the Franco-Russian Military Convention signed two years later. This was nothing new to Brackenbury as in August 1886 he had revealed to the Cabinet the existence of Russian plans to attack India and discussed the possibility of a Franco-Russian alliance, and its anti-British purpose.[18]

---

15   Memorandum by Hon. Lieutenant-General Sir Henry Brackenbury on the Defence of Chitral, 3rd June 1895, British Library Asia, Pacific and Africa Collections, Mss.Eur.D.735.
16   Memorandum by Lieutenant-General Brackenbury and Major-General Newmarch, National Archives, WO32/6349, p.2.
17   Military Operations in the event of War with Russia, by Captain J. Wolfe Murray, Intelligence Department, 17th November 1892, National Archives, WO106/6157.
18   Deputy Quartermaster-General for Intelligence, 'A General sketch of the Situation Abroad and at Home from a Military Standpoint', 3rd August 1886, National Archives, WO 33/46.

This was one of the reasons why Brackenbury supported the view that Indian preparations for invasion had to concentrate solely on troops already in India. Even if troops could be found from the British Army to send to India, there was a real possibility that their arrival could be delayed until the Royal Navy had achieved supremacy at sea. Brackenbury knew that if this meant war with the French and Russian Navy combined it could take some time before such supremacy could be achieved. He also wrote, in 1891, of the vital role that the Turkish Empire would play in any conflict, supporting the view of Wolfe Murray. Presuming that only Turkey joined Britain in war against Russia, he could not see Russia moving troops to Central Asia.

> In that case we should only have to deal with the forces present in Trans-Caspia and Turkestan. These, inclusive of all local troops, amount to about 50,000, and, as Russia must guard her Chinese and Persian frontiers, and cannot, any more than ourselves, disperse with obligatory garrisons, I estimate the forces available for operations in Afghanistan at not more than 30,000; and I cannot but think that the 30,000 British and 70,000 Native troops, which the Commander-in-Chief admits to be available, would be sufficient to hold the lines of communication and the Kabul-Kandahar alignment against such portion of these 30,000 men as would (for Russia also would have communications to defend) reach that alignment.[19]

In fact, on 27th June 1892 he went further: "... in the event of the war becoming general, it is, in my opinion, certain that Russia would withdraw, rather than reinforce, her troops in Central Asia".[20] Whilst we can never know how accurate Brackenbury was on these matters, the fact that there was no Russian invasion does lend some weight to his argument. His knowledge and experience would have also strengthened his case. There were several periods during this 'cold war' when, if Russia had the ability to invade, the conditions would have been right to do so. Perhaps the most obvious moments would have been after the last Afghan War, the Gordon relief expedition, and perhaps most notably the South African War. This has to be seen as one of Brackenbury's most significant contributions during his time in India. There were too many who saw a Russian invasion of India purely in that context, as a straight fight between the two powers, and were blinded by an Indo-centric view. Brackenbury brought knowledge of affairs outside of India that was invaluable. Some in India would have been aware of potential allies that Britain would have in a war with Russia but Brackenbury not only knew this but was also

---

19 Enclosure of Secret Military Despatch No 180, 15th September 1891, National Archives, WO32/6349, pp.5-6.
20 Memorandum by Brackenbury, 27th June 1892, British Library Asia, Pacific and Africa Collections, Mss.Eur.D.735.

aware of the likelihood of these powers joining Britain in any conflict. It must be remembered that much of Brackenbury's early work at the Intelligence Branch was concerned with the construction of mobilisation plans and the defence of Great Britain. Being the strategist and administrator he was, he will have looked at who these plans were being prepared against and who were potential allies. In terms of home defence the greatest threat was France, and France's strengthening relationship with Russia might cause further problems for Britain.

Whilst Britain had no formal alliances the practicalities of international relations would mean that they would soon have found some in the event of a Franco-Russian war against Britain. Both Brackenbury and Roberts had agreed that the next major war was likely to be one "in which France and Russia would be engaged on the one side, and the Triple Alliance and Great Britain on the other side".[21] Indeed this was the predominant view in the British Army for many years to come. In Brackenbury's own experiences there was evidence to suggest the likelihood of the Triple Alliance supporting Britain. Whilst he was at the Intelligence Branch he would have been aware of the negotiations with Austria, when Britain and Austria joined forces to prevent an enlarged Bulgaria becoming a puppet state of Russia.[22] Keeping Russia in check was not only in Britain's interest. This may well have played an important part in leading Brackenbury to the conclusion that the Austro-Hungarian Empire was a likely ally if Russia invaded India and initiated a wider war. Their support would bring with it Italian, and more importantly, German support under the terms of the Triple Alliance. The writings and thinking of many in the military, and in particular Brackenbury, over the British position in the European Alliance system are fascinating, especially in light of what we know happened in 1914. Whilst Turkey had its problems with Britain they were also aware that, in their war with Russia in 1877–1878, it had only been the presence of the Royal Navy's Mediterranean Fleet in the Dardanelles and Disraeli's threat to use it, that had halted the Russian Army on the outskirts of Constantinople. If war was fought along these lines then the Russians would not be able to support their troops in Central Asia. In fact, the opposite was more likely. With German and Austro-Hungarian armies on her borders, and a possible Anglo-Turkish attack through the Black Sea, Russia would want to recall troops from Central Asia, especially given that these were some of their most experienced soldiers. Although all this goes beyond Brackenbury's role in India that is, in itself, a pertinent point. At this time there was no planning for imperial defence, and thus it was almost inevitable that Indian planning would be devoid of any wider thoughts of international strategy. Indeed, there were no formal

---

21  Enclosure of Secret Military Despatch No 180, 15th September 1891, National Archives, WO32/6349, pp.5-6.
22  Hopkirk, Peter, *The Great Game*, pp.377-381, describes the situation in the context of Anglo-Russian hostility.

links for cooperation between the British and Indian armies and indeed an air of distrust and suspicion existed between the two.

Whilst Brackenbury's responsibility for planning only encompassed India it was inevitable that his views would be influenced by his wider knowledge, especially that gained from his time in intelligence. His former colleagues in the Branch were still, of course, supplying him with material. One such report, received from Grierson, led him to comment:

> What he [Grierson] says as to Russia's attention being directed westwards not eastwards is quite correct. But I find it difficult to get officers who have passed their lives in India to look beyond their own margins. Russia's whole present aim in the east is to keep us constantly guessing, and to so alarm us by her intrigues and her military demonstrations as to make us believe we cannot spare a man from India to act against her farther west; and she has effectually succeeded.[23]

Whilst there were many Russian generals who advocated an invasion of India, and some even drew up plans, these were more often than not just 'war games'. Even the highly rated General Alexei Kuropatkin, who later lost some of his reputation in the Russo-Japanese War, joined in the hysteria and asked for command of the invasion force. The practicalities of the scheme were always likely to make it a non-starter. To have been successful any invasion would have needed support from Afghanistan, if only the promise of free passage, which was unlikely as the Russians were as unpopular as the British in that country, together with a popular uprising in India on a far bigger scale than even the Indian Mutiny. The Russians would also have needed the support of the tribes in Russian-held Central Asia, and British Intelligence saw these as possible British allies. However despite, the difficulties at the Russian end, the main concern of the British was whether the Indian Army, and elements of the British Army stationed in India, could even deal with an invasion of 30,000 men. With the best of the Indian and British troops it was likely that the invasion could be dealt with. Yet one sees in the writings of those in the Government of India the fear that preoccupied many about putting 'native' troops up against Europeans. The British had beaten numerically superior native armies with fewer than the 30,000 Russian troops that could possibly have invaded. Such concerns were rather disparaging to the Indian Army, who were not only trained along European lines and commanded by European officers, but had many in the ranks who came from societies with proud military heritages. It was also an army that was as experienced at warfare as any in the world as it had been involved in

---

23 Brackenbury to Elles, 17th December 1892, Brackenbury letter books, Royal Artillery Museum Woolwich.

almost constant campaigning since the Mutiny. Whilst these campaigns may have been against inferior opponents they were not without their value, if only for the experience of being under fire in combat conditions. All the evidence suggested that a Russian invasion was unlikely, and in any case would be repulsed, though Brackenbury believed that an invasion might be attempted if only as part of a much broader strategy in a conflict against Britain by Russian and France. He suggested that such an invasion might be used in the knowledge that it would tie down large numbers of troops and resources that could otherwise be employed elsewhere. It would have meant all of the Indian and British contingents in India staying there and therefore not being available for any other campaign.

CHAPTER 24

# THE REORGANISATION OF THE INDIAN ARMY AND FAREWELL TO INDIA

### REORGANISATION OF THE INDIAN ARMY

If one wants to find any lasting impact made by Brackenbury in India perhaps one of the easiest ways is to look at his role in the reorganisation of the Indian Army under one command. A scheme for such a reorganisation had been floating around for many years. Yet it was during Brackenbury's time in India that it was actually put in place. The major problem with achieving reorganisation had been the division of powers that existed in India at that time. Reorganisation needed the cooperation of the Governor-General, the Commander-in-Chief and the Military Member. It was only now in the cordial atmosphere that existed between Roberts and Brackenbury and with the willingness of the Governor-General to trust their advice, that the circumstances were right for reform. T.A. Heathcote supports the view that it was the influence of Roberts and Brackenbury together that made it possible to revive the old proposals.[1] As a result the posts of Commander-in-Chief of Madras and Bombay were abolished and, although the army was split into four regional commands, it was now united formally under one Commander-in-Chief. This also had the effect of further expanding the Military Department. "With the centralising of the army administration ... and the abolition of the presidential C-in-C's and military departments in 1895, the Military Department had grown

---

1  Heathcote, T.A., *The Military in British India* (Manchester: Manchester University Press, 1995), p.156.

in responsibilities, importance, and power", and therefore so had the Military Member.[2] Again, as at the Intelligence Branch, it could be argued that Brackenbury was empire building. How much personal ambition and a desire for power was the motivation for Brackenbury's actions is impossible to say and there is no evidence to support such suspicions. What cannot be denied is that the system introduced was an improvement on what had gone before and streamlined the system of command and control in India. Once again it was the happy coincidence that what was good for the efficiency of the army was also good for Brackenbury personally.

Brackenbury also helped in the development of the Intelligence Department of the Indian Army, which had been created in 1890. His experiences at the War Office proved useful here. In a detailed letter to Roberts he outlined the best ways for Intelligence to be carried out and the sort of men who were best suited for this type of work. He believed that a good Intelligence Branch could be obtained for 50,000 rupees a year. The Accountant General thought this too much but Brackenbury assured him, "it will be money well spent if it gives us a really good working Intelligence Department".[3] Brackenbury wanted the branch to be seen as a stepping-stone to advancement, thus encouraging the brightest and best of the Indian Army to join it. The branch was duly established under Lieutenant-Colonel Edmond Elles. It is likely that Elles had been taught by Brackenbury whilst at the Royal Military Academy, Woolwich. There is evidence of a great deal of correspondence between the two on intelligence matters. Elles appears to have been one of the Indian Army officers who panicked over potential Russian invasion. Elles believed that Russia was planning a double strike against India and China. Brackenbury told him that the Intelligence Branch in London had no evidence to support such ideas and warned Elles, "Avoid being an alarmist. There is an immense improvement in this respect in the Intelligence Branch summaries of late". In his correspondence with Brackenbury, Elles does come across as an alarmist, at one point advocating attacking the Afghan army and occupying the country to forestall Russian advancement. This is the same Elles who as Military Member would clash with Lord Kitchener and consequently be the last Military Member.[4]

In some ways Brackenbury's time in India was a good preparation for what he would experience as Director General of Ordnance during the South African War. It gave him experience of large scale military organisation, and in many ways it should be viewed as the most powerful position he ever held. Here he came across what

---

2  Brackenbury to Lansdowne, 15th December 1893, Brackenbury letter books, Royal Artillery Museum Woolwich. Brackenbury had wanted Burma to form a separate fifth command. Brackenbury to Lansdowne, 15th December, 1893 Brackenbury letter books, Royal Artillery Museum Woolwich.
3  Brackenbury to Roberts, 2nd March 1892, Brackenbury letter books, Royal Artillery Museum Woolwich.
4  Brackenbury to Elles, 7th May 1892, Brackenbury letter books, Royal Artillery Museum. Brackenbury to Elles, 25th August 1892, Brackenbury letter books, Royal Artillery Museum Woolwich. Brackenbury replied that he thought negotiation and financial pressure would be more effective.

Lord Roberts. Although Wolseley's great rival, Roberts and Brackenbury developed a good working relationship. Whilst they had their differences there is no doubt that Roberts thought highly of Brackenbury from a professional point of view. (Private collection)

could be termed false economies which were damaging the military machine. In a letter to Lord Roberts, dated 16th May 1891, he highlighted such an issue regarding remounts for cavalry and artillery regiments. Horses were being sent out that were not fit for service for another year for reasons of age or conditioning. This was done largely to save money by keeping the horses a year less at the depots and allowing new ones to be stored there in preparation for future remounts, but it also meant that regiments had to find extra stabling for horses they could not use. Brackenbury felt that:

> Surely it's a false economy to have on the strength of regiments and batteries horses which are not fit for active service. We cannot ensure that our enemies will suit our convenience and wait till the horses have had a year to mature, and if they did, we should have to fill up casualties that had occurred during that year with immature remounts.[5]

Whilst Brackenbury had undoubtedly come across similar problems in his career he was now in a position to do something about it and the situation was changed so that remounts were not dispatched until a year later.

Another key concern of Brackenbury's and "The point to which I first turned my office", was the preparation of what would in modern military language be called

---
5  Brackenbury to Roberts, 16th May 1891, Brackenbury letter books, Royal Artillery Museum Woolwich.

a rapid reaction force. His plan was to prepare a force of 35,000 men that could be placed in the field as and when required. One key aim of this force was to meet any possible Russian invasion of Afghanistan, but Brackenbury admitted that its use was almost universal, and not confined to the subcontinent. He knew that similar ideas had been considered before but nothing had been done. Not only did Brackenbury bring his organisational skills to the problem but he also obtained the support of the Finance Minister of the Government of India, Sir David Barham. As he wrote:

> The troops are told off, the commanders and staff named, railway timetables are being prepared and are nearly complete. But this is only the paper work. The solid preparation is going on rapidly.

Under Brackenbury's instructions, "All the stores, commissariat, ordnance, medical, veterinary, engineering, required for rapid advance are being prepared".[6] Such planning would have been easier for him than that which he had attempted whilst at the Intelligence Branch. In India he had more of a free hand, partly due to the seniority of his position but also because of the different nature of the relationship between military and civilian authority within India. The planning details were impressive even down to the creation of reserve railway lines in case, for whatever reason, existing ones could not be used. Such administrative duties, whilst

**Henry Brackenbury. Another photograph showing Henry in India.**
**(Private collection)**

---

6  As the most likely deployment for such troops within India was to the north Brackenbury had got the agreement for extra railway sidings and communications to be created along the route, right to the edge of what is modern day Pakistan.

disliked by most officers, were 'exciting' to Brackenbury. "The administration of this great Indian Army is a task of immense interest to me".[7] With this basic plan in place he started to work on expanding it. By April 1893 he was writing that, "Our mobilisation scheme for putting four divisions, about 70,000 men and line of communication troops upon the North West Frontier is thoroughly practical and has been worked out in every detail, and is constantly kept up to date".[8] Moreover, because of the level of control he had he was able to have all the non-perishable stores for this force collected and available at advanced points.

His success in India was such that there had been some suggestions that Brackenbury might be the man to succeed Roberts as Commander-in-Chief in India. In a very frank and honest letter to Lord Lansdowne Brackenbury rejected the idea in self-deprecating terms. Speaking of himself he said:

> Lieutenant-General Brackenbury does not possess in a high degree the qualities required in a Commander-in-Chief. He is unknown to the Indian Army. He has not the gift of attaching soldiers to him, which is possessed by Lord Roberts and Sir George White. He has no practical knowledge of the Indian Army. He is an indifferent horseman. He has been for the last seven years dissociated from the command of troops. His appointment could therefore only be considered as affording a possible, though by no means satisfactory solution of a very difficult problem.[9]

He was right to acknowledge his own limitations, but one cannot help but wonder whether it was a position he would have really wanted. Undoubtedly it would be a high honour and a source of great pride, but on a practical level he did not suit the position. Let us remember that the Commander-in-Chief India was expected to lead the army in battle. Whilst it would be unfair to say he could not have done this, as he had never had an opportunity to put the 'theory into practice', it was not where his skills lay. The final sentence is interesting when read in the context of the time. Brackenbury, and Lansdowne, both felt the ideal man to succeed Lord Roberts was George White. Ultimately White did become Commander-in-Chief but it was known that White's lack of seniority was being put forward as an argument by the Duke of Cambridge to block the appointment. Had Brackenbury assumed the role of Commander-in-Chief for a brief period it would have solved the problem,

---

7 Brackenbury to Sanderson, 9th October 1891, Brackenbury letter books, Royal Artillery Museum Woolwich.
8 Brackenbury to Herbert, 24th April 1893, Brackenbury letter books Royal Artillery Museum Woolwich.
9 Brackenbury to Buller, Confidential Memorandum 19th July 1892, Buller Papers, Devon Records Office, Exeter. This includes a copy of the letter to Lansdowne. This is the only copy of the actual letter that I have found, however Brackenbury's papers in the British Library Asia, Pacific and Africa Collections Mss. Eur D.735 have a confidential memorandum written by Brackenbury referring to this letter and its contents.

giving White extra time to gain seniority whilst maintaining the present course on which the Indian Army had been placed. As it happened the objections over White's seniority were overlooked. It may well be the case that White heard something of Brackenbury's comments and perhaps misunderstood them. Sir George White claimed that Brackenbury was an "intriguer" who tried "... to turn everything to his own credit".[10] In a sense it was inevitable that Brackenbury would gain some credit for all things done in the Indian Army, as he was ultimately the senior man, and in theory White's 'boss'. It would be interesting to know if White realised that Brackenbury had championed his claim to be Commander-in-Chief in India, despite his juniority, and had written to both Stanhope, as Secretary of State for War, and Lord Lansdowne as Viceroy, in his favour. Indeed in both letters he said White was the only option. So whatever view White had of Brackenbury it did not affect Brackenbury's view of White.

**Field Marshal Sir George White. White replaced Lord Roberts as Commander-in-Chief India in 1893 and had a difficult relationship with Brackenbury. Ironically, Brackenbury had been largely responsible for White's appointment. (Private collection)**

## Legacy

In a letter dated 4th May 1895 Brackenbury wrote to his old friend Sir John Ardagh that: "I have entered upon my last year in India, and shall not be sorry when it is over. I am nearly worn out".[11] In similar vein he wrote to Sir Edwin Markham: "It is

---
10   Sir George White to John White, 7th April 1898, White papers, British Library P3/132.
11   Brackenbury to Ardagh, 4th May 1895, Ardagh Papers, National Archives, 30/40/2.

by far the hardest work I have ever had, and I sometimes feel played out, and long for rest".[12] Brackenbury's 'workaholic' nature and his practice of regularly working into the early hours of the morning made it unsurprising that his four years up to that point had left him in such a condition. He had a demanding job, virtually controlling the entire administrative machine for the Indian Army. It must be remembered that the climate in the sub-continent was not conducive to the health of the average 'European'. As early as August 1893 he was complaining to Grierson about the effect it was having on his health. Whilst in India he experienced gout, sciatica and malaria. Despite this he seems to have enjoyed the work, and some of the privileges that went with the post. Brackenbury took a great delight in having his own railway carriage, and even more delight in asking for 'his' special carriage to be made ready for him. He also enjoyed the comfort of two splendid houses, but disliked having to accept a bodyguard of Gurkhas.

Mention has already been made of the fact that there had been some consideration to him staying on in India as Commander-in-Chief. Whilst that was never very likely there were other attempts to persuade him to stay in India in a different appointment. Indeed Lord George Hamilton, Secretary of State for India, wrote to him in September 1895 offering him Sir Donald Stewart's place on the Viceroy's Council. Hamilton wrote "I am so impressed with the conditions and administration of the Indian Army, that I should be very sorry to see one who has contributed so efficiently to that work, out of military or public employment in India". This was quite a compliment for a man who had little working knowledge of India before he arrived. It could be argued cynically, but perhaps with a degree of truth, that the real reason the Government wanted him to stay was that he was not one of the Indian 'crowd' with their pre-conceived ideas and worries, and he had knowledge of the wider picture within which events in India took place. In this way it could be argued that Hamilton wanted Brackenbury to stay to make his own job easier. This time, unlike Ireland, flattery did not work and Brackenbury refused the offer. His reasons were quite clear as he would virtually have to retire from the Army. It would be the end of any hopes of further employment in the army, except perhaps in the exceptional circumstances of a major conflict.[13]

Brackenbury left India in April 1896, as his appointment was for five years. His organisational skills had quickly been put to good effect. Fresh from the drawing up of mobilisation plans at home, he set about reorganising those of the Indian Army. In September 1891 he wrote that he had been able to make the mobilisation plans more efficient and reduce the cost "... without excluding anything the absence of

---

12   Brackenbury to Markham, 1st May 1895, Brackenbury letter books, Royal Artillery Museum Woolwich.
13   Correspondence with Lord George Hamilton on this subject is found in Lord George Hamilton to Brackenbury, 25th September 1895, and Brackenbury to Lord George Hamilton, 19th October 1895, Private Collection.

which would delay taking the field".[14] He had also played a key part in the reorganisation of the command structure which also helped to streamline and strengthen the Indian Army. It is not too strong to say that the Indian Army was in better condition because of the time spent by Brackenbury in India. The whole system of supply, transport, communications, disposition and mobilisation had improved under his administration. He also brought useful knowledge of the strategic situation outside of India and his realisation that Russian invasion would be part of a much wider conflict between the great powers brought some much needed reality to the concerns of those in power there. Brackenbury showed that not only were there numerous problems with a Russian invasion but also that the size of such a force was not likely to be the horde of Russians streaming over the border that was the common misconception, and as an ex-head of the Intelligence Branch of the British Army, he took a keen interest in the setting up and development of the Indian Army's Intelligence Service.[15] He wrote at length to Roberts and Lord Lansdowne on the subject, giving advice that varied from how best to carry out intelligence gathering missions to the best sort of men for the job.

This highlights another interesting facet of Brackenbury's time in India. Although having a direct line of communication with the Governor-General, he continually writes to Roberts and later Sir George White when he was Commander-in-Chief, before presenting his ideas to the Governor-General. Perhaps this is one of the reasons for the success of the relationship between Commander-in-Chief and Military Member during these years. It perhaps reflects his respect for Roberts but may also be admission of his own relative lack of experience on Indian matters. The appointment of Military Member usually went to someone on the basis of their knowledge on Indian issues. This obviously was not the case with Brackenbury, but the partnership worked well, as Lansdowne said, because of Roberts' expert knowledge of India, which made up for Brackenbury's limitations in this area, and Brackenbury's knowledge and experience of military and political matters outside of India. Brackenbury's skill as an administrator would have proved invaluable anywhere and his recent appointments commanding troops in Sudan and being in charge of the Intelligence Branch meant that he had very useful recent experience that was put to good effect in India.

Although much of what he had achieved has been forgotten, as so much related to the Indian Army has been, there is no doubt that at the time his work was highly significant and appreciated by those who had observed his work closely. Whatever they might have thought of Brackenbury personally, and perhaps he was not the easiest person to get to know or like, there was great praise for his work. Even White, who had been critical of him previously, conceded that he was, "such a capable judge

---

14   Brackenbury to Roberts, 23rd September 1891, Roberts Papers, National Army Museum R11/42.
15   Brackenbury to Lord Lansdowne, 19th July 1892, Brackenbury letter books, Royal Artillery Museum, Woolwich. This fully describes Brackenbury's ideas for the Intelligence Service.

and so thoroughly master of every detail". He went further and stated that "... all who watch the administration of the country (India) testify to the excellent work you have done during your tenure of office".

In light of this his time in India has to be seen as a success. Despite the fact that he could never be called one of the 'Indian' crowd of the British Army this brought to an end almost seven years, in total, of service in India. He returned with an increased reputation as a man with experience not just in Africa, Britain and the War Office, but now also India. There were few who had his all-round experience. Perhaps the only other man in this period who ever achieved this was Lord Roberts himself. Brackenbury returned to England in 1896 and took up his new appointment as President of the Ordnance Committee, which stood him in good stead when, at the pinnacle of his career, he took on the appointment of Director-General of the Ordnance, at a time when the South African War stretched the department to breaking point. There can be little doubt that his experience in the Military Department in India proved useful. By 1896 Brackenbury had served in two important administrative appointments. In each he had met with success. More importantly others had recognised that. As we have seen Lord Lansdowne had praised his work, and they had developed a close working and personal relationship. This was to prove important for Brackenbury's future prospects. Lansdowne's time as Viceroy ended in January 1894 and by June 1895 he had been appointed Secretary of State for War.

CHAPTER 25

# PRESIDENT OF THE ORDNANCE BOARD: THE CALM BEFORE THE STORM

Brackenbury had returned from India in April 1896 and in May of that year he was appointed to the post of President of the Ordnance Committee (or Board) by the Secretary of State for War Lord Lansdowne who, it will be remembered, Brackenbury had served under in India. Brackenbury himself whilst giving evidence to the Royal Commission on the war in South Africa explained his duties.

> The Ordnance Committee is a consultative body, which is appointed to take up such questions as may be referred to them by the Director General of Ordnance. It is not an initiative body; it is a consultative body. It is a body which has upon it as President a General of Artillery, the Vice President is an Admiral of the Navy, and the members are two Artillery officers, an Engineer officer, two Naval officers, a consulting officer from India, two civil engineers, Sir Frederick Bramwell, and Sir Benjamin Barker; and the other members are members for special purposes, for instance, the chemist of the War Department and Dr Dupre, the chemist of the Home Department, and such other associate members as are required from time to time.[1]

It can therefore be seen that alongside his knowledge as a serving artillery officer who had experience of active service Brackenbury also brought to the position knowledge of the workings of military administration and his recent experience in

---

1   *Royal Commission on the War in South Africa* (Elgin Commission) Minutes of Evidence (London H.M.S.O, 1903), p.83.

India where he had been responsible to a very large degree for the administration of the whole army.

One gets the impression from reading his letters of the time that Brackenbury, and many others, saw his Presidency of the Ordnance Board merely as an interlude before his next major appointment. That was certainly what Brackenbury hoped. The Presidency of the Ordnance Board, whilst appealing to his enquiring mind, did not have either the level of work or seniority to keep him engaged for long. It must be remember that he had just returned from India where he had fulfilled a role on a par, at least in terms of duties and responsibilities, with that of a Chief of Staff and in some respects a Secretary of State for War. To now have to chair a committee, and in particular one which could be said to have responsibility without authority, would be an anti-climax to say the least. A good example of this difficulty is found in a letter to Lord Lansdowne in December 1897. The Ordnance Board had produced a report urging in the strongest possible terms that a 6 inch quick firing gun produced by Vickers be adopted by the Royal Navy, having been asked to look into the matter. Despite being given a long and detailed explanation of their choice the Director of Naval Ordnance decided to go with a non-quick firing gun produced by an unnamed company. Brackenbury believed that the Director had already made his choice and simply wanted the Ordnance Board to 'rubber stamp' the decision.[2] This had never been Brackenbury's way, and must have been rather galling after having had such authority whilst in India. Brackenbury was now fifty-nine years old and must have been aware that he was on the last lap of his career, and this was clearly not the way he wanted it to end.

At this time one of his closest confidents was Lord Lansdowne, who had been Viceroy in India whilst Brackenbury was Military Member and was now, somewhat fortuitously for Brackenbury, Secretary of State for War. The relationship between the two was by this stage extremely close and a friendship above their work together had developed. Through their correspondence of the time one reads of many occasions when they met together socially. One also gets a sense, reading between the lines, that Lansdowne was trying to tell Brackenbury to be patient and that a job more suited to his talents would be found for him before too long. Lansdowne assures him that "Your friends have not forgotten you" and that he understood "... your feeling that such a comparative holiday might not last too long".[3] On Brackenbury's part there was understandably a fear that he might have reached the end of his career. His membership of the Hartington Commission had, as we have seen, made him new enemies, and his time in India had further alienated him for Wolseley. Neither proved decisive and his career soon moved on to what could be regarded as its pinnacle, but it is interesting to note that even now he felt insecure

---

2    Brackenbury to Lansdowne, 3rd December 1897, private collection.
3    Lansdowne to Brackenbury, 12th December 1896, private collection.

and worried about his future. Partly this was due to his financial insecurity. It is also another example of the way in which he had always had to 'earn' or 'ask' for things throughout his life. In short, he had no wealth or influence of his own and instead had to rely on what he earned or was given in both respects.

He continued as President of the Ordnance Committee until February 1899 when he was offered the position of Director General of the Ordnance. Whilst Wolseley had pushed for Brackenbury's appointment, it must be added that his decision had the full support of Lansdowne. Lansdowne stated that he felt Brackenbury was "head and shoulders above all competitors" for the position.[4] Whilst historians have seen this as simply another case of Wolseley appointing members of the ring there is perhaps more to it than that. Indeed it could be argued that the appointment had much more to do with Lansdowne than Wolseley, and the former's appreciation of Brackenbury's ability from their time together in India and a realisation on Lansdowne's part that it would need a first rate experienced administrator if he was to sort out the Ordnance Department with all its various responsibilities. This was in many ways the driving force behind Brackenbury's appointment. In short they were looking for a repeat of his performance in reforming the Intelligence Department. With the backing of the Commander-in-Chief and the Secretary of State for War Brackenbury would have the support he needed to undertake such changes as were deemed necessary. However, this was a much greater challenge than the Intelligence Department, if only because of the size of his new responsibility. The Ordnance Department was one of the major appointments at the War Office, giving him a seat on the Army Board, and it was, in this respect, on a par with the Adjutant General and the Quartermaster General. It had also recently gained added responsibilities.

Brackenbury was appointed to the position of Director General of Ordnance in February 1899. As on his arrival at the Intelligence Branch, he was given a reforming brief. Lord Wolseley, now Commander-in-Chief, had argued with the previous Director General, Sir Edwin Markham, over the necessity of the complete rearming of all types of artillery. Perhaps surprisingly it was Wolseley and not the artillery officer who saw the necessity for this. In response to Wolseley's pressure to modernise, particularly coastal artillery, Markham set up a series of trials designed to prove the ability of existing guns.[5] Wolseley decided at this point that a new Director General of Ordnance was needed, and with the support of the Secretary of State for War, Lord Lansdowne, the position was offered to Brackenbury.

The accusation that Wolseley was once again promoting the same old members of the 'ring' is not without foundation and it is doubtful that Brackenbury would have

---

4 Dunlop, Colonel John, *The Development of the British Army 1899-1914* (London: Methuen Press, 1938), p.84.
5 Kochanski, Halik, *Sir Garnet Wolseley: Victorian Hero* (London: Hambeldon Press, 1999), p.209. Markham is often mistakenly referred to as Edward rather than Edwin.

been the first choice of many of the other leading generals of the day. It is worth taking a few moments just to understand the state of the relationship between Wolseley and Brackenbury at this time. It must be remembered that by this stage the 'ring' had all but collapsed. The members of it were now all so senior that they no longer felt the need for Wolseley's patronage, added to which they had fallen out amongst themselves, as the Gordon Relief expedition had illustrated. Wolseley had in fact had a major falling-out with Brackenbury, although it is doubtful that Brackenbury realised this. Wolseley had taken offence at Brackenbury's part in the Hartington Commission's recommendation that the office of Commander-in-Chief be abolished and replaced with a Chief-of-Staff. Wolseley saw this as an attempt by Brackenbury to become the first Chief-of-Staff. The second reason for their falling out was Brackenbury's service in India, where he had become too close to Lord Roberts for Wolseley's liking. Brackenbury had used his considerable knowledge to help advance Roberts' position in various debates with the home government. Despite the aforementioned difficulties Wolseley recommended Brackenbury's appointment, which perhaps is further evidence for the reputation Brackenbury had made for himself. Just as important in Brackenbury's appointment was the relationship he had built with Lord Lansdowne. As we saw in the previous chapter, Lansdowne held him in high regard. That Brackenbury was able to achieve what he did was thanks to him being in the enviable position of having the full backing and cooperation, not to mention trust and confidence, of both the Commander-in-Chief and the Secretary of State.

Brackenbury set about a thorough investigation of his department and its responsibilities and he reached the conclusion that the rearmament of coastal artillery was the first priority.[6] He clearly investigated this matter himself but he was under pressure from Lansdowne to rearm the coastal artillery first. Lansdowne was himself under pressure after revelations in the press about the antiquated nature of coastal armaments which were considered completely insufficient to deal with modern warships. However it is unlikely that Brackenbury would simply have yielded to pressure; he had not in Ireland. It can therefore be presumed that Brackenbury's own findings reached the same conclusion and that he considered coastal armament to be the most pressing concern. If anything this illustrates the serious state his department was in, as the war would highlight many serious problems within the Ordnance Department.

When war came in South Africa in October 1899 Brackenbury had started the rearmament of the coastal artillery and had nearly finished his assessment of the department. Brackenbury faced a very difficult situation during the South African War and in the following chapters we will look at the difficulties he faced and the

---

6    A copy of his findings are found in the Appendices to the *Royal Commission on the War in South Africa* (Elgin Commission) and are quoted from later in this chapter.

ways in which he responded to the strenuous demands of the conflict. A major source to this end is the evidence he gave to the Royal Commission on the War in South Africa, commonly called the Elgin Commission after its chairman, the Earl of Elgin and Kincardine.[7] Brackenbury was in a strong position. He could not reasonably be held responsible for the state the department was in having only taken command eight months previously. It was obvious that the problems went back much further than that. He was also the recipient of much praise for the way he had dealt with the crisis in the department and had initiated large-scale reforms whilst continuing to meet ever-increasing demands for arms, ammunition, equipment and supplies. His reputation preceded him and as a result the commission, and in particular one of its leading members Viscount Esher, dealt with him much more gently than many of the others who came before it. Indeed a remarkable letter exists from Lord Elgin to Brackenbury, dated the day before Brackenbury first gave evidence on 21st October 1902. Elgin informs Brackenbury as to what the Commission wants to hear from him, also suggesting possible questions. Elgin even goes so far as to suggest how best Brackenbury could express his evidence. This clearly illustrates that they saw Brackenbury as a potentially helpful witness.[8] The result was that he left a fascinating insight into the working of the Ordnance Department, and his evidence shows the working of a vital but sometimes ignored part of any military campaign.

---

[7] Officially known as the *Report of His Majesty's Commissioners appointed to inquire into the military preparations and other matters connected with the War in South Africa* (London: H.M.S.O, 1903). It is often confused with Lord Esher's *War Office Reconstitution Committee* (London: H.M.S.O, 1904). The confusion is not helped by the fact that many contemporary authors referred to the Royal Commission as the Esher Commission. Lord Elgin was at least third choice for chairman, after Lord Spencer and Mr Herbert Asquith, had both declined. Unsurprisingly therefore Elgin very much played second fiddle to Lord Esher. This suited Esher, as he liked to work behind the scenes, and later turned down the appointment of Secretary of State for War for that reason.

[8] For an example of this see the evidence of Lord Wolseley and Lord Lansdowne. Also, see any commander with field experience i.e. Buller, Kelly-Kenny, White, etc. The Commission is hostile towards them, questioning their every action. Lord Elgin to Brackenbury, 20th October 1902, private collection.

# Chapter 26

# Director General of the Ordnance

The position as Director General of Ordnance, particularly given the demands of the South African War, was in many ways a fitting way for a first rate military administrator to bow out. This was a greater challenge than the Intelligence Department, if only because of the size of his new responsibility. Indeed it was more demanding than his time as Military Member in India because the British Army, and its civilian administration, was a more complex machine than the Indian Army. Added to which Brackenbury soon found himself managing a department during an ever expanding conflict. The Ordnance Department was one of the major appointments at the War Office, on a par with the Adjutant General and the Quartermaster General, and thus made him a member of the Army Board. It had also recently gained added responsibilities. The name changed slightly as his predecessor had actually been entitled the Inspector General of Ordnance. Perhaps this illustrates a change in emphasis. Whereas Markham had simply been expected to 'inspect' Brackenbury was now charged to 'direct' and was required to manage the department.

## The South African War

A detailed account of the South African War is not necessary, but it might be useful to explain a few points and provide a little background. The original white settlers in South Africa had largely been of Dutch descent. In 1793 the Dutch colony had been captured by the British but subsequently returned in 1802 under the Treaty of Amiens. In 1806 it was recaptured and after this the British presence remained. The Dutch settlers, commonly referred to as Boers, disliked the imposition of British laws and in 1835 this led to what has become known as The Great Trek, when

14,000 Boers left British territory in the hopes of establishing their own state. Such Boer states were small and highly vulnerable to native attack. The British eventually started to colonise other parts of southern Africa and by 1877 the Boer settler state of Transvaal had been annexed by the British. Although not welcomed by the Boers this was largely accepted because of military protection and the fact that the Boer state was put back on a sound financial footing after having gone bankrupt.

The British were removing the threat that native tribes posed to the Boers and it is no coincidence that the first major Boer rebellion against British rule came shortly after the last and most powerful of the tribes, the Zulus, had been defeated. The Boer revolt of 1881 was something of a shock to the British and culminated in defeat at the battle of Majuba Hill, where General Colley, the British commander, was killed. The Boers were granted independence but the British retained 'suzerainty' over them: something the Boers denied and which nobody really seemed to understand. The peace had been concluded quickly by the Gladstone government, who had opposed the annexation of the Transvaal in the first place. However there were many within Britain, particularly the army, who were not satisfied and the cry of 'avenge Majuba!' was a common rallying call in the subsequent South African War. Relations between the Boers and the British never really recovered from the 1881 conflict. The situation altered with the discovery of large gold reserves in the Transvaal, which led to a large number of foreign workers, or Uitlanders as the Boers called them, moving into the Transvaal. Soon they outnumbered the Boers but they had no say in the running of the country and very limited rights. This gave a kind moral justification to attempts to reassert British control over the Transvaal, led by the business community and industrialists, which disguised the financial motives. The situation was exacerbated by the so-called Jameson Raid of December 1895, when a private army, financed by the businessman Cecil Rhodes, attempted to invade the Transvaal with 500 men in the hope that this would lead to a further uprising of the 'Uitlanders' now working and living in the vicinity. The hoped-for uprising never took place and Jameson's force was ambushed and either killed or captured. Politically it was a disaster for the British, and debate still rages to this day as to whether the Colonial Secretary Joseph Chamberlain was aware of the raid or even colluded with Rhodes. The likeliest conclusion is that Chamberlain was aware of the impending raid and gave his unofficial support. As a consequence he was reluctant to take severe action against Rhodes for fear of what might come out.

Attempts were made to repair relations with the Boers and a new High Commissioner was despatched, but to no avail, and relations continued to deteriorate to the point that the Transvaal declared war on 11th October 1899. At the beginning of the war the British were outnumbered as 10,000 British troops faced an estimated 30,000 Boers. The early setbacks could seemingly be put down to this, and Britain was convinced that once the 50,000 men of I Army Corps, a cavalry division and line of communication troops arrived victory would be a foregone conclusion. Yet this was not the case and a war that was thought would be over in months dragged on until 1902 and required the despatch of almost half a million men from Britain and the Empire. The war was a great blow to British prestige and had far-reaching political consequences. To the British Army, and civilian administration, it was a much-needed wakeup call and gave the opportunity to rectify many of the problems inherent in the military system. The war caused severe problems for the military machine. In an era when the largest force the army had planned to place in the field was 40,000 to 50,000 men it was not surprising that the surge to almost half a million caused an already creaking military machine to almost collapse. Brackenbury found himself at the heart of this crisis, as the Ordnance Department struggled to deal with demands far beyond anything it had ever anticipated before.

## The Ordnance Department

The department that Brackenbury entered had a wider set of responsibilities than the mere name suggests. Under the Order in Council of 7th March 1899,

> The Director General of Ordnance is charged with supplying the Army with warlike stores, equipment and clothing; with the direction of the Ordnance Committee and the manufacturing departments of the Army; with dealing with questions of armament, patterns, inventions, and designs; and with the inspection of all stores, whether supplied by the manufacturing departments or by contractors.[1]

Many of these responsibilities were fairly new to the department never mind Brackenbury. The clothing side had been taken over by the Ordnance Department in December 1898, and Brackenbury had made it a condition of accepting the position that the ordnance factories were also placed under his command.

## The Transfer of the Ordnance Factories

The subject of the ordnance factories deserves further comment as it caused much controversy.[2] The ordnance factories were a major source of arms and equipment for the army, but they had been allowed to get into a poor condition. Relations between

---

1   *Elgin Commission Minutes of Evidence*, p.71.
2   The Ordnance Factories consisted of six factories - The Royal Laboratory, The Royal Carriage Factory, The Royal Gun Factory (all based at Woolwich), The Gunpowder Factory at Waltham Abbey, and the two Small Arms factories at Enfield and Birmingham.

the Financial Department of the War Office and the factories were not good and there was little consultation, nor any mechanism for it. After the transfer of control the Director of Ordnance Factories was made directly responsible to Brackenbury, rather than the Financial Department. Added to this was the antiquated equipment with which the factories were working. There were two main reasons for this. Firstly, reasons of economy meant that new investment had not been undertaken. Secondly, the civilian side of the War Office seems to have operated a policy of not wanting to step on the toes of 'the trade', that is the private arms firms who provided the remainder of the army and navy munitions. The power of British industry was considered to be such that the trade could cover any deficiencies in the ordnance factories. This was a bubble that the South African War would burst.[3]

Brackenbury's time as President of the Ordnance Committee, from his return from India in 1896 until his appointment as Director General of Ordnance in 1899, had alerted him to this deficiency and the South African War was to demonstrate further the antiquated machinery and practices of the ordnance factories. The main problem that Brackenbury saw was that the factories were under the direction of the Financial Secretary at the War Office, Mr Powell-Williams, who was a civilian. Brackenbury told the Royal Commission that, as a result, the management of the factories had become divorced from the needs and requirements of the army.[4] Brackenbury's belief in the necessity of this section being under control of the Director General of Ordnance was justified by the events of the South African War. As he said before the Royal Commission:

> If the Director General of Ordnance, instead of being able to go direct to his head of the factories, and turn him off from his work on to that work, to suit the exigencies of the moment, had had to go with his hat in his hand to the Financial Secretary and ask that this, that, and the other might be done, I do not think we could have supplied the Army during the war ...[5]

Although Brackenbury made a valid point, it must be pointed out that a large amount of the material for South Africa, especially clothing and stores, still had to be supplied largely by the 'trade', but the change undoubtedly made things easier for him.

Brackenbury's demand that the ordnance factories be placed under his control as a condition of his acceptance of the position prompted an interesting political debate. The Financial Secretary of the War Office, who, despite Lansdowne's assurances to the contrary, saw the removal as a comment on his abilities, naturally

---

3 Brackenbury used the phrase in evidence to the *Elgin Commission*, p.84, and in a letter to Colonel Clarke quoted at the Committee of Inquiry into Ordnance Officers in South Africa, NA WO32/7026.
4 *Elgin Commission Minutes of Evidence*, p.71.
5 *Elgin Commission Minutes of Evidence*, p.72.

opposed the removal of the ordnance factories from his control. To an extent he was correct that the action was a comment on his abilities, as Brackenbury and Lansdowne both clashed with him over matters of inspection and his dealings with the trade. One of St John Brodrick's first duties on becoming Secretary of State for War in October 1900 was to remove Powell-Williams from his job. Like Brackenbury much of Powell-Williams' career had been reliant upon patronage. In the early years his career at the Post Office had been thanks to his second cousin Rowland Hill, the postal reformer and founder of the modern postal service. As a Liberal, later Liberal Unionist, M.P. from Birmingham he was very much part of the Chamberlain faction within the party, and in later years he owed his career to them. However, unlike Brackenbury, he probably was not as deserving of such patronage. The term 'square peg in a round hole' was used by *The Daily Chronicle* to describe his time as Financial Secretary to the War Office and Arthur Balfour wrote of Powell-Williams that, "He would never have got even his present place except as the immediate personal friend and follower of Joe".[6] 'Joe' was Joseph Chamberlain, the Secretary of State for the Colonies and as the unofficial leader of the faction that split from the Liberal Party to join the Conservative Party, a figure of importance. He was a dynamic politician but also controversial, and the role of companies of which his brother was chairman and he himself had an interest in will be touched on later. It is unsurprising then that Chamberlain opposed the transfer of control of the ordnance factories. He complained to Arthur Balfour that Lansdowne was "Brackenbury-ridden".[7] This however missed the point that Lansdowne was also convinced of the necessity of the change, as was evidenced by his defence of the policy in cabinet. It may also illustrate that Chamberlain had a personal dislike of Brackenbury, and it will be remembered that Brackenbury and the Liberal Party had not been on the best of terms. It is also worth pointing out that Gladstone held a grudge many years after Brackenbury's time in Ireland, so it may not be as unrealistic as it sounds that Chamberlain was influenced by past political quarrels.[8]

In the cabinet debate that followed Powell-Williams produced a seven-page memorandum supporting the retention of the existing system. This document drew attention to the poor state that had existed before the present system had been introduced, and received support from members of the cabinet, including St John Brodrick, who had been financial secretary when Stanhope had initially introduced

---

6 Page, Andrew, 'The Supply Services of the British Army in the South African War 1899-1902' PhD Thesis, University of Oxford (1976). Powell left office as Financial Secretary in November 1901 but remained as M.P. for Birmingham South until he suffered a stroke and died in the lobby of the House of Commons in 1904.
7 Chamberlain to Balfour, 2nd February 1899, Balfour Papers, British Library Add MSS 49683.
8 A story telling how Gladstone had not forgiven, or at least not forgotten, Brackenbury by 1892 is told in Brackenbury, Henry, *Some Memories of My Spare Time* (London: William Blackwood & Sons, (1909), pp.347-348.

the present system and could therefore remember better than most the state the factories had been in before transfer to the financial department. Similarly unsurprising was the opposition to the transfer of the Chancellor of the Exchequer, Sir Michael Hicks Beach, who was naturally opposed to anything that would weaken civilian control of military expenditure. The transfer was not without support in cabinet, the most prominent advocate being George Goschen, First Lord of the Admiralty. The Royal Navy also relied on the ordnance factories, and was equally affected by their current poor state. Lord Salisbury also supported the move, but as Prime Minster he was trying his best to maintain cabinet harmony. His suggestion was the establishment of a Cabinet Committee, made up of the Duke of Devonshire (who as Lord Hartington had recommended the transfer of the ordnance factories back to military control as Chairman of the Hartington Commission), Lansdowne, Hicks Beach and Goschen, to investigate the matter. The committee was set up and unsurprisingly, given that three of its members had already announced their support for the transfer, recommended that Lansdowne's plan be introduced.[9] This committee can be seen as Salisbury giving his Chancellor an opportunity to state his case fully, but there can have been little doubt of the outcome.

Lansdowne had defended the transfer by saying that he was following the advice of four separate Commissions that had looked at this matter, and that he was not advocating a return to the old system, as Powell-Williams had suggested.[10] Financial control would still ultimately rest with the Financial Secretary, but the Director General of Ordnance would draw up proposals and calculations and control the day to day running. Lansdowne also took the opportunity to deny another fear that Powell-Williams had raised, namely that military control would lead to discrimination against the 'trade', and to this end Lansdowne was supported by Sir Andrew Noble of the armaments manufacturers Armstrong's.[11] It was also argued that it was dangerous to have the same person responsible for both the department and the means of production, as it was felt that conflicts of interest would be inevitable. Lansdowne rather shrewdly pointed out that this could set a dangerous precedent as the same argument could be applied to the position of the Secretary of State. In the end the cabinet supported Lansdowne and the transfer was approved. What this whole episode illustrated was the continuing exertions of successive governments to establish unequivocally the paramount control of civilian government over the

---

9   The debate surrounding the transfer is covered in greater depth in Page, 'The Supply Services of the British Army in the South African War 1899-1902', pp.172-175.
10  Page, 'The Supply Services of the British Army in the South African War 1899-1902', pp.174-175. The four reports were the Stephen Commission, Ridley Commission, Morley Commission and the Hartington Commission.
11  Page, 'The Supply Services of the British Army in the South African War 1899-1902', p.176. It would be very interesting to know if any of the cabinet were aware that Henry Brackenbury and Sir Andrew Noble were related by marriage. Had they known it might have given them cause to question Noble's impartiality.

military. It has been said that no other transfer in any other department of government would have caused such controversy and division, nor would it have needed a cabinet committee to settle it.[12] It was yet another example of the distrust of soldiers as 'managers', even one as experienced as Brackenbury. It might also be the case that his reputation for 'empire building' had gone before him, and that the fact that it was Brackenbury asking for the transfer might have been the cause of some of the concerns.

The system that the transfer created was not without problems. The main one was the need for the continual reference by the Director General of Ordnance to the Financial Secretary, and when war came such problems were exacerbated. Change was necessary for wartime, and Brackenbury gave an example of that when, one day early in the war, 138 items had to be costed and proposals drawn up, necessitating reference to facilities at Woolwich, Pimlico and Weedon to get the necessary information. The amount of paper work this created did little to help the speed of an already slow process.[13] Such a highly bureaucratic system was troublesome enough in peacetime, but was doomed to failure in war, particularly with the unexpectedly large demands that the South African War placed on the Ordnance Department. Brackenbury was able to obtain verbal, and later written, permission from Lansdowne that 'urgent' demands could be ordered before detailed calculations were given. Brackenbury subsequently took the view that everything connected with the war fell into the category of 'urgent', and thus for the remainder of the war he had near exclusive control of all financial decisions, although he reported to the Army Board how much he had spent each week. Sometimes he pushed his wartime authority to the limit, such as when, on his own authority, he had ten new buildings erected for the cartridge division of the Arsenal at Woolwich.[14] This sort of freedom was rare and would not have been granted had it not been for the fact that Lansdowne had complete confidence in Brackenbury. Although this freedom helped, Brackenbury still faced a difficult task in keeping the army supplied. Without Lansdowne giving him freedom to act on his own initiative it would likely have been impossible.

---

12  Page, 'The Supply Services of the British Army in the South African War 1899-1902', p.179.
13  *Elgin Commission Minutes of Evidence*, p.77.
14  For details of Lord Lansdowne's instructions see *Elgin Commission*, p.77 and for details of new factories and plant see Page, 'The Supply Services of the British Army in the South African War 1899-1902', p.200.

# Chapter 27

# The State of the Ordnance Department

We now move on to look at some of the issues that Brackenbury faced in the department during the South African War. Before doing that it is first necessary to examine the starting point and look at the state of the department on his entry as Director General of the Ordnance. After this the following chapters will look at particular problems and difficulties.

### Brackenbury's Report on the Ordnance Department

Brackenbury decided that his first task should be to undertake a thorough review of his department. Partly this was as a means to the changes he had been brought in to undertake, but also because little was known within the department of the new responsibilities for clothing and the ordnance factories. The completion of his report was delayed by the start of the South African War, but on 15th December 1899 he presented his findings to the Secretary of State and the Commander-in-Chief.[1] Even allowing for the interruption caused by the start of the war, it is clear that Brackenbury had been thorough. The fact that it took him almost ten months should be seen as an indication not only of the size of the department but the variety of equipment, stores, weapons, munitions, and production facilities they were responsible for. The major finding was the department's total unpreparedness for war and,

---

1 Report by Director-General of Ordnance to Commander-in Chief, 15th December 1899. Interestingly this was included as Appendix E of the *Elgin Commission*, pp.278-280. Brackenbury was ordered to send this report direct to Lord Lansdowne, rather than through War Office channels. Technically he had the authority to do this under the existing Order in Council, but the old system of all material going through the Commander-in-Chief still prevailed on the whole. Lansdowne wanted the document so he could take it to the Cabinet to support his case.

in particular, the virtually non-existent reserves of equipment. There was barely enough for the despatch of two army corps which had been the working standard for the mobilisation scheme since the Stanhope Memorandum. It must be remembered that although technically part of the reserves, the stores to equip the two army corps were held separately. The reserves accounted for the equipment to supply the corps once in the field.

Brackenbury's report found that there were numerous deficiencies in the levels of reserves. In fact his report declared that the only items in which the reserves were ample were for rifles, carbines, revolvers and lances. By the end of 1899 14,000 rifles, 850 carbines, 1,400 pistols and 500 lances had been despatched to South Africa from the reserves, and Brackenbury declared that they still had good stocks.[2] Perhaps this is not surprising. Lances were used less as the war went on and cavalry were reluctant to use their carbines, although as the war continued they were forced to change. The large reserves of revolvers is not surprising as many officers continued the practice of using privately purchased small arms rather than the Webley service revolver.[3] The reserve of rifles, especially of older patterns, was vital. As demand grew with the despatch of more soldiers a problem was discovered with the new Lee-Enfield, which was found to be incorrectly sighted, so that it fired 18 inches to the right when firing at 500 yards.[4] In all other areas the reserves were alarmingly below the authorised number. In many cases this was because the forces in South Africa grew so rapidly. Difficulties were identified in clothing, infantry accoutrements, camping equipment, and tents. There were however other items that were insufficient because of the unconventional nature and conditions of the South Africa War. The unprecedented need for mounted infantry meant that saddlery reserves were totally insufficient. At the outbreak of the war there were only 500 sets in reserve. By the end of 1899 Brackenbury had despatched or had on order some 11,525 extra sets. The same was true of mule harnesses, of which 1,700 were in reserve. The need to transport supplies along vast distances without the use of the railways meant that mules played an important role. By the end of 1899 Brackenbury had despatched nearly 25,000 sets. Another problem along similar lines concerned the vehicles of the Army Service Corps. The majority were unsuited for the harsh terrain of South Africa, having been designed for use in European conditions. Brackenbury ordered 600 vehicles from the trade in this country and authorised the buying of many more in South Africa itself.

---

2   All the figures in this section are taken from Report by Director General of Ordnance to Commander-in-Chief, 15th December 1899, pp.278-281.
3   Many of these were still Webley products, just not the service pattern of revolver, although the Mauser C96 was popular with both sides.
4   Brackenbury gave a full account of this incident to the *Elgin Commission*, p.86.

Many of the deficiencies were due to the practice of borrowing from the reserve for overseas expeditions without any thought being given to replacement. For example if a battalion on its way to Sudan during the Gordon relief expedition had been short of tents they would be borrowed from the reserve to bring them up to strength. This only became a problem because replacements were not ordered or they were not returned. There was also a belief in the power of British industry to make good any gaps. It was publically stated that reserves were kept to the bare minimum in the belief that any force sent overseas could be maintained by the output of the ordnance factories and the trade.[5] The key reason for doing this was for the sake of economy but there was a more legitimate reason. It was likely that equipment left in the reserve would be of quite old patterns. To maintain the reserve with the level of equipment for the army corps would require continual, and expensive, maintenance of a large level of stocks. With belief in the power of British industry to be able to provide anything at short notice this would have seemed a much better option. It would mean that any force on active service would be provided with the very latest equipment straight from the factory. Whilst a somewhat naïve approach it would have been very appealing to those responsible, soldiers and civilians alike, as army expenditure was always scrutinised most carefully.

The problem was that the aforementioned practice had denuded the reserves to a level that was completely inadequate for the size of campaign that followed. It is certain that even if the reserves had been up to the expected level they would have proved insufficient to meet the demands of the South African War. The war took the British Army into a position, in terms of numbers in the field, which they had never been in before, and it must be remembered that the South African War saw the despatch of the largest army ever to leave Britain up to that point. The fact is that if the reserves had been up to the required level things would have gone more smoothly for the Ordnance Department and the demands of the situation could have been met more easily. The problem was that even the basic field force that had been envisaged in the mobilisation plans did not have the necessary reserves to bring it up to wartime standard or to keep it at that level for the initially envisaged six months. It is fair to point out that at this point no one could have known how long the conflict would go on for, but when even six months of supplies for two army corps were not held in reserve we can see just how bad things were.

Brackenbury found that by the time he had completed his report he had already despatched the majority of reserves to South Africa, and in most instances he had already sent double what he had originally had in reserve. The fact that this was only two months into the war was not lost on him. Nor was the fact that whilst the

---

5  Sir Ralph Thompson originally made this point in his evidence to the Mowatt Committee and Lord Lansdowne and Sir Ralph Thompson, the Permanent Secretary of the War Office, made this point in their evidence to the Elgin Commission.

reserves were now empty the war was still escalating and the number of troops that had to be equipped was growing steadily. To meet these demands he had to borrow equipment from all over the empire and the Royal Navy. In light of this Brackenbury wrote that his report had:

> ... disclosed a situation as regards armaments, and reserves of guns, ammunition, stores and clothing, and as regards the power of output of material of war in emergency, which is, in my opinion, full of peril for the Empire.[6]

He therefore urged that the report was acted upon as soon as possible. To assist him in his attempts at reform he had been given permission by Lansdowne to send papers to him directly rather than through the normal War Office channels, provided that the papers were also sent to those who would normally have received them. Lansdowne took the report straight to the cabinet and used it as his main tool in trying to get increased expenditure for the maintenance of the army during the war.

There was a wider, longer term, angle that Brackenbury wanted to pursue. He wanted change quickly so that in any future conflict his successor would not have to cope with the same problems that he did. A lot of the modernisation proposals he made were not particularly designed to fight the present conflict. As his report made clear, "The following are absolutely necessary to enable us to carry on a war with a maritime power, in which both Navy and Army might be engaged".[7] He took the opportunity to again emphasise the importance of the rearmament of the coastal defences, probably fearing that the money put aside for this would be transferred to fund his other proposals. He also pressed for the construction of new ordnance store buildings, to be completed as soon as possible. It was one thing to press for increased holdings of reserves but without increased space they could not be stored efficiently. Part of this was development of the buildings of the Army Clothing Department, which he had found to be ill-equipped even for the maintenance of the army in peacetime. Alongside this came the demand that the ordnance factories be completely re-equipped with modern labour-saving machinery, which in Brackenbury's estimation would increase output by 50%.[8]

Brackenbury also took the opportunity to criticise the way in which the War Office did business in general. He pointed out that the cost of the changes would be impossible to achieve through the usual route of the Annual Army Estimates. He criticised the present system:

> ... under which orders cannot be given for any length of time ahead, which cripples the power of output of the trade. They will not, under such a

---

6    Report by Director General of Ordnance to Commander-in-Chief, 15th December 1899, p.279.
7    Report by Director General of Ordnance to Commander-in-Chief, 15th December 1899, p.279.
8    Report by Director General of Ordnance to Commander-in-Chief, 15th December 1899, pp.279-80.

system, invest money in buildings or plant, not knowing from year to year whether they will have further orders.[9]

It was a very pertinent point and one that the events of the war would bear out. A trade that was used to the small annual orders from the War Office could not meet the large-scale demands that the war created. As profit-making concerns they were unlikely to keep plant in reserve for emergencies; it would not be cost effective. In such a case it was essential that the ordnance factories were efficient and modern, so that capability to increase production in time of emergency existed. It also underlined Brackenbury's demand that there should be a reserve of output, in the form of buildings and machinery, which would only be used in time of war.

The word demand is not too strong a word to use when viewing Brackenbury's recommendations in his report, as it was in many ways a series of ultimatums. It is no exaggeration to say that even Brackenbury was shocked at the situation he found in the department. The report on its state was a considered view of what Brackenbury felt was wrong and what needed to be done. No official record exists, but it is known that he told Lord Roberts he was prepared to resign if the necessary money was not made available for the reforms his report outlined, saying "I hope and pray they will be accepted. If not they must find another D.G.O."[10] Given Brackenbury's close working relationship with Lansdowne it is unlikely that ministers would have had no idea of Brackenbury's threat to resign. He was also following a similar course to when he was in Ireland, although a little more tactfully, in that he would not go on if, after being asked to come up with a solution to the problem, his plans were ignored on financial grounds. There was undoubtedly an element of arrogance in his approach towards the government. In this case he was the expert and the government should take his word for it when he said that this was necessary. If, as seems likely, the government were aware of his threat to resign it may well have had a much stronger impact than would normally be expected. His resignation would have come at a time when the government were being strongly criticised for its conduct of the war. Questions were being asked in both parliament and the press about the preparedness of the country. If at this time a senior member of the War Office, in fact a member of the Army Board, had resigned because of the government's failure to back what would have appeared to be essential reform, the ramifications could have been considerable. The damage would have been increased by his reputation as one of the army's leading administrators.

Brackenbury's threat of resignation was made particularly effective because of the course of the South African War. At any other time his resignation might cause slight embarrassment to the government but it would not have received the publicity

---
9    Report by Director General of Ordnance to Commander-in-Chief, 15th December 1899, pp.279–80.
10   Brackenbury to Roberts, 18th January 1900, Roberts Papers, National Army Museum.

that his resignation during the war would likely have caused. The same could be said of the changes that Brackenbury was able to undertake. Whilst there was recognition that reform was needed, both by soldiers and politicians within the War Office, if the war had not created the impetus politically the reform would probably have been only piecemeal. The war highlighted the scale of change that was needed. It opened eyes to the necessity not only of being able to send a force overseas, which the mobilisation plans were equipped to accomplish, but also the need to be able to maintain such a force. In this Britain was fortunate to have the world's largest navy, both militarily and in terms of mercantile shipping. The problem the war highlighted was the 'failure' of the trade to be able to supply a force in the field. This was perhaps an unrealistic aim in the first place, but it was the theory that the War Office entered the South African War believing. The war showed that there was a need to be able to supply a force largely out of reserves and the ordnance factories for at least a significant part of any war, so that the trade had time to catch up in terms of finishing other orders, changing patterns to meet War Office requirements or changing to new equipment and methods of production to produce what was required.

CHAPTER 28

# The Mowatt Committee

The reforms that Brackenbury's report suggested would necessitate a large one-off payment to cover them. Brackenbury himself gave no estimate of the cost of his changes, aside from the £1.3 million he asked for new machinery for the ordnance factories. He felt that a loan of £10 million would be the minimum needed. This would be used for new buildings and machinery for the ordnance factories and the Clothing Department, guns and ammunition for the new coastal defences, and to start establishing a reserve of stores for the future. He realised, and wanted the politicians to realise, that this in itself would not be enough. "I cannot say whether this may cost 10, 15, or 20 millions sterling. I can only say it is necessary to spend whatever it may cost to save us from this situation of peril".[1] The Mowatt Committee, named after its chairman, Sir Francis Mowatt, the Permanent Under Secretary of the Treasury, was established to look into the need for these measures.[2] Apart from Mowatt the committee comprised two other members, the Parliamentary Under Secretary of State for War, Mr George Windham M.P., and the Director General of Stores at the India Office, Mr E. Grant Burls. Its terms of reference were to establish the number of guns needed to form a reserve of 25 per cent for Horse and Field artillery, and for the siege train, and the amount of ammunition needed to maintain a reserve of 6 months supply of 1,000 rounds per gun. It also had a wider reference to look at the reserve of stores needed to maintain three army corps, one cavalry division and line of communication troops overseas for a period of six months. It was argued that if six months of supply could be found from the reserves this would give time for the ordnance factories and the trade to change over to the demands of wartime. The committee was also asked to look at what was needed to complete the number of guns for fortress and coastal artillery and to provide a satisfactory reserve of ammunition for them. It will be remembered that this was

---

1    Report by Director General of Ordnance to Commander-in-Chief, 15th December 1899, p.279.
2    Report of the Inter-Departmental Committee on Reserves of guns, stores for the Army (Mowatt Committee) British Library, Add MSS 50306.

one of Brackenbury's original proposals and, whilst the government had agreed to the expenditure in principle, it had not been forthcoming. Thus Brackenbury used the Mowatt Committee to remind the government of this pressing need.

The committee was established largely at the insistence of the Chancellor of the Exchequer, Sir Michael Hicks Beach. His chief argument was that he objected to relying on the word of a single man, Brackenbury, who himself had a vested interest.[3] Hicks Beach no doubt felt that Mowatt, who it could be argued equally had a vested interest, would share his reluctance to spend the large amount that Brackenbury had requested. He had good cause to believe this as in the build-up to the war Mowatt had supported Hicks Beach's opposition to increased Army spending. Mowatt probably did share his reluctance, yet it seems that his investigation persuaded him that the expenditure was necessary. There was also an economic argument for the one-off expenditure, which Mowatt seems to have grasped but that Hicks Beach did not. The war had pushed up War Office costs and the current arrangements were extremely expensive. Overtime was being paid on a constant basis and the wear and tear on machinery would necessitate complete replacement before too long. Added to this was the inflated cost that the trade was charging for wartime supplies. Brackenbury's scheme would have increased the capacity of the ordnance factories by 50 per cent. More important was one of Brackenbury's other suggestions. He had recommended that new buildings and machinery be established which would be for wartime use only.[4] He had expected that once the reserves had been used up, the additional buildings at the ordnance factories would be up and running and able to meet the increased demand. This was a recognition that the trade could not be so heavily relied upon to do just what the Government wanted suddenly, and rightly so as they were profit-making organisations. It was unrealistic to ask them to drop all other orders or to keep reserve capacity purely for time of emergency under present circumstances.

Hicks Beach obviously regarded Brackenbury with suspicion. If he had ever read or witnessed the proceedings of the Mowatt Committee he would certainly have had grounds for feeling that way. Whilst Mowatt was chairman it was undoubtedly Brackenbury's committee. It sat for nineteen days and examined twenty-five witnesses. Brackenbury was examined extensively himself but was also there when those who served under him were examined and was given leave by the chairman to make comments when he wanted. He was also allowed to cross-examine these witnesses, and he used the committee to make his case. Mowatt's attitude towards Brackenbury was unusual to say the least. Many of Mowatt's questions to Brackenbury could be construed as 'leading' questions as they allowed him to make quite sweeping statements on the state of the department and his remedy for it. The

---

3    Elgin Commission Minutes of Evidence, Evidence of Lord Lansdowne. Question 21280.
4    Report by Director General of Ordnance to Commander-in-Chief, 15th December 1899, pp.279-80.

interviewing was extensive and went beyond those officers within the Ordnance Department. The Adjutant General, Sir Evelyn Wood, and the Storekeeper-General of Naval Ordnance, Colonel Thales Pease, were called. So too were the various civil servants who had responsibility within the War Office. Interestingly enough there was only one M.P. amongst the witnesses, which is slightly strange given that they were responsible for the financial and administrative arrangements of the War Office. Perhaps this illustrates a desire on the part of Lord Lansdowne to keep the committee as one of 'experts' in an attempt to enhance the case for the expenditure. Eight of the witnesses represented the trade, many of whom were keen to defend themselves against the criticism they had received for their role in the war up to that point.[5]

The Mowatt Committee ended up agreeing entirely with Brackenbury and its recommendations were almost exactly the same as those that he had put forward in his report on the state of his department.[6] This included agreement with his suggested levels of reserves for guns and ammunition, more uniformity of dress for wartime and peacetime, maintaining the amounts of reservists equipment up to the same level as regulars, and his proposed keeping of six months supply of stores to maintain an army in the field. They also agreed with his suggestion that mobilisation plans should be based around three army corps, one cavalry division and line of communication troops. Wolseley, who had become obsessed with a three army corps system, undoubtedly influenced this. Whilst criticised as insufficient, as it would take a force larger than this to subdue the Boers never mind defeat a European power, it has been defended as being the best Wolseley believed he could get out of governments who feared a large standing army and a society extremely reluctant to accept conscription. This may well be true but his defence of a three army corps system to the Elgin Commission was on the grounds that this force could match any threat from any power, which was rather an unusual position to take. The committee supported Brackenbury's call for increased storage space and new buildings and machinery for the ordnance factories, adding that they felt no time should be lost in the completion of this. Much to Brackenbury's delight they also criticised the failure to enforce the penalties for late delivery that were written into every contract with the trade. There was also support for his scheme of having 'reserve' factories that would be used only in emergency. Another interesting suggestion

---

5    The only M.P. called was Mr J. Powell-Williams, the Financial Secretary at the War Office. The witnesses from 'the Trade' were: Sir Andrew Noble, Director of Armstrong and Whitworth & Co Ltd, Mr Albert Vickers and Mr Douglas Vickers, Managing Directors of Messrs Vickers & Sons & Maxim, Mr A.T. Dawson, Director and Superintendent of Ordnance at Messrs Vickers & Sons & Maxim, Mr C.T. Cayley, Managing Director of Messrs Hadfield's Steel Foundry Company, Mr Bernard A. Firth, Managing Director Thomas Firth & Sons Ltd, Mr R.A. Hadfield, Chairman and Managing Director of Hadfield's Steel Foundry Company. Mr Arthur Chamberlain, Chairman of Messrs Kynoch & Co.
6    Mowatt Committee, pp.i-xiii.

was the idea of moving so-called 'danger' buildings. The committee acknowledged Brackenbury as the source of this idea, despite the fact that he mentioned it neither in his report or his evidence to the committee. This once again suggests that he had the chairman's ear.[7] In short the idea was that the buildings in which explosives were made and used should be moved from their present location surrounded by other factories and workshops to more isolated areas. The idea was that any explosion in the current location would cause serious damage to other factories and could virtually stop production of all stores at the various ordnance factories.

The Mowatt Committee gave detailed costs of all their recommendations. The first figure they arrived at was £6,482,567. This would cover the reserve of guns and ammunition of fortress, coastal, siege, horse and field guns, and a 25% reserve of machine guns and also the reserve of general stores for three army corps, one cavalry division and line of communications troops and a six-month working stock. This also covered the removal and rebuilding of the 'danger' buildings and the additional storage facilities that had been proposed. In addition to this was £1,586,338 to carry out existing recommendations for improvements to field and horse artillery, and £3,552,965 to complete the rearmament of coastal batteries and buildings, which had already been agreed upon. This brought the total requested by the Mowatt Committee to £11,621,870.[8] This was to be provided over three years. This was a comprehensive report, and whilst small in size its significance was huge. The fact that it reached almost the same conclusions as Brackenbury made it clear that this was no longer simply a soldier with the age old cry of 'we haven't got enough money', it was now supported by the Permanent Secretary of the Treasury. However it needed the impetus of war and impending national crisis to bring the political will to this matter, as many of the findings regarding a lack of funding and support were the same as those discovered by Lord Randolph Churchill when he was examining the Army estimates in the late 1880s.

The Mowatt Committee had the backing of the War Office, both civilian and military, the cabinet, and the trade. Yet despite having called for the committee in the first place Hicks Beach refused to accept its findings, despite the fact that the Permanent Secretary to the Treasury had himself investigated and drawn up the proposed expenditure. Whilst it might be expected that he would oppose such a level of expenditure the way in which Hicks Beach did it, without regard for the opinion of the military, the cabinet and his own Permanent Secretary was quite extraordinary. He made a counter proposal of a little over £3,000,000 that illustrated his failure to grasp the seriousness of the situation both politically and materially. He abrasively stated that even this reduced amount was conditional upon immediate

---

7    Mowatt Committee, p.xiii.
8    Mowatt Committee, p.xiii provides all the calculations and comes at the end of the Committee's recommendations.

acceptance with no further claims being made. This was a misjudgement of the strength of the position of Lansdowne and Brackenbury, especially when supported by the Permanent Secretary of the Treasury. With the cabinet also supporting them, Hicks Beach was forced to take the findings of the Mowatt Committee seriously. The Chancellor was eventually persuaded to agree to expenditure of £10,500,000, over three years from 1901 to 1904 to meet the recommendation of the committee.[9]

The strength of Brackenbury's position is important to understand. Not only did he have the backing of the Secretary of State for War, but also the report of a committee of enquiry chaired by the Permanent Secretary of the Treasury, one of the last men one would expect to recommend such large scale expenditure. The fact that this was the case clearly illustrated just how severe the problem was and just how seriously it was being taken. Brackenbury had also been clever by not placing exact costings before the cabinet or the War Office. He must have had an idea as his estimate of £10 million was not far off the figure that the Mowatt committee arrived at. However he had allowed the committee to examine the matter thoroughly and arrive at a cost slightly higher than he had surmised. This meant there could be no criticism of Brackenbury for having exaggerated the level of expenditure required, or months of ministers and civil servants pouring over every last detail in a critical manner. The figure had been arrived at by a civil servant after a thorough investigation. This time, Brackenbury had played the political game very well. Brackenbury had won a major battle but his problems were far from over.

---

9   See, Page, Andrew, 'The Supply Services of the British Army in the South African War 1899-1902', pp.349-352 for more details of the cabinet wrangling over this issue.

# Chapter 29

# Army Contracts and the Trade

### Over reliance on 'the trade'

During the war significant sectors of the economy became almost entirely committed to the production of equipment for South Africa. This was a limited foretaste of what was to come in the twentieth century. The war in South Africa was on a larger scale than anything seen before. The significance of this is often lost in the light of the subsequent events of the two world wars of the twentieth century. Although the War Office had its own factories it was never the intention that they should be able to supply the army by themselves. It was said that:

> Their function was seen as providing a model for the trade to work from, to check how much items cost to manufacture, to make those items which the trade was unable or unwilling to produce, and to give a certain flexibility in providing for the needs of the moment.[1]

This was an arrangement that was largely due to financial constraints. The Treasury would not allow plant or machinery to be kept merely for expansion in time of war. There was also an element of arrogance about the supposed status of British industry. There was an assumption that British industry could produce anything at any notice, an assumption that was never investigated. It was this assumption of the strength and flexibility of British industry that led the War Office to presume that the day-to-day upkeep of any field force could be maintained by the trade. The South African War showed that such faith in the trade was misplaced.

---

1    Page, Andrew, 'The Supply Services of the British Army in the South African War 1899-1902', p.182.

## Army Contracts

Brackenbury soon found much to complain about in the way that firms treated contracts with the War Office. The Director of Army Contracts drew them up, and from 1895 Mr Alfred Major had held that position. He was a civilian working under the Financial Secretary of the War Office with a staff of twenty-seven, which was increased to thirty-four during the war. The title is slightly misleading, as he also had to act for the Admiralty, the Government of India, the Colonial Office, the Metropolitan Police and the Post Office. Alfred Major comes across as a well-meaning civil servant, somewhat out of his depth. With only twenty-seven staff covering so many different responsibilities it is not surprising that the system was sluggish at best. Brackenbury disliked the contracts system, largely because of its overly bureaucratic nature, and in November 1899 he proposed to the Army Board that for the duration of the war the system of obtaining everything through the Director of Army Contracts be abandoned.[2] The idea had merit as the Director of Army Contracts would on the whole only deal with companies who were on the approved list of War Office firms. It led to supply being dominated by a few firms, such as the Birmingham Small Arms Company and London Small Arms Company who were the only suppliers of service rifles. Webley had a monopoly on service revolvers, although officers did purchase others privately. Only seven companies ever supplied cordite for ammunition, and just three, Kynoch, National Explosives and Nobel Explosives supplied most of it, despite the fact that there were an estimated twenty manufacturers within the country.[3] In peacetime the system perhaps had some limited merit where by using the same firms over and over again got them used to War Office practice and methods, but even this was of questionable value. However in time of war it was ridiculous that when supply was not meeting demand that there was still a reluctance to go outside the approved list. This was something that Brackenbury found very difficult to accept.

With the supply of cordite being a particular problem – so much so that at one point Brackenbury had to send out a consignment of shells filled with gunpowder – the Director of Contracts' refusal to go outside the seven War Office recognised firms appears strange. Brackenbury also felt that at a time where demand was outstripping supply there was much to be gained from approaching foreign manufacturers. Indeed, as the war went on, more material was purchased overseas. Horses and mules were bought from all over the world, as were horseshoes, but largely from Germany and Sweden. It was found that no firm in Britain was geared up to produce mule shoes and these inevitably had to be sought abroad.[4] A major objection to

---

2    Proceedings of the Army Board, 3rd November 1899, NA WO108/79.
3    Page, 'The Supply Services of the British Army in the South African War 1899-1902', p.186.
4    *Elgin Commission Minutes of Evidence*, p.74.

the purchase of overseas goods, and the one which the Financial Secretary and his department used, was the fear of reliance on foreign powers for supplies in time of war. Although a valid concern it overlooked two points. Firstly, the purchase of overseas goods was only designed to get the army through the war, and many of the items were already being used as examples for British designs; it was not intended as a long-term solution. Secondly, a lot of the items purchased were brought with the necessary amount of supplies and spares to last its lifetime. The obvious example for this is the decision to purchase four Austrian made 9.4 inch howitzers, which used a special kind of ammunition. Brackenbury brought sufficient ammunition to last the rather limited lifetime of the guns.[5] He was only ever recommending a temporary process of buying overseas and never contemplated a long-term change. Brackenbury saw it as something that would help deal with the present demand and get the army through the current crisis. By the end of the war he hoped to have the necessary reforms underway to avoid such a crisis in the future. Despite this the Director of Contracts took great offence at his idea and complained to the Financial Secretary who in turn complained to the Secretary of State. Lansdowne prevailed upon Brackenbury to apologize, and a veiled apology was made before the Army Board where Brackenbury expressed his belief in the system, which was not entirely true, but maintained that the present emergency called for temporary measures.[6]

## 'The Trade'

The commercial sector as a whole was commonly referred to at the War Office as 'the trade'. Brackenbury faced constant problems with many suppliers which stemmed from the casual approach of his predecessors. One of the worst culprits was the Birmingham firm of Kynoch, who produced shells and small arms ammunition for the War Office.[7] They were often unable to supply the amounts for which they had been contracted. For the financial year 1898–1899, for example, they had been contracted to supply 10 million rounds of small arms ammunition yet supplied only 6 million.[8] Brackenbury complained to the Financial Secretary and demanded that the financial penalties that were in the contract agreement be imposed in line

---

5 The guns could only fire 250 rounds before they would wear out. Thus a thousand rounds were purchased, but the battery only fired one round in action, at some retreating Boers! They had been bought to besiege Pretoria, but that was not necessary. Two were despatched to China during the Boxer Rebellion, but were never used.
6 Proceedings of the Army Board, 25th November 1899, NA WO108/79.
7 The firm had been established as an engineering works by a Scotsman called George Kynoch. After he hit financial problems other investors joined the company, most notably Arthur Chamberlain. By 1899 he was chairman and many of the other investors had been persuaded to step down from the board and other members of the Chamberlain family joined the board. Arthur Chamberlain concentrated the business on armament manufacturing and succeeded in turning around a £50,000 overdraft.
8 Mowatt Committee, p.10.

with War Office procedures. Such penalties were rarely used and this proved to be half the problem as it allowed a situation to develop whereby firms ignored delivery dates knowing that there would be no consequences. One of the complications surrounding Kynoch, and probably one of the reasons for Powell-Williams reluctance to impose financial sanctions, was the fact that Arthur Chamberlain, the brother of Joseph, was chairman of the firm, having succeeded his brother in that capacity. Mention has already been made of Arthur Balfour's belief that Powell-Williams owed his job to Chamberlain and their relationship obviously played a part in his reluctance to impose the fines which were in the contract.

However, this cannot have been the whole reason, as the system of fines was rarely imposed on other companies. As the Mowatt Committee explained:

> It is true that every contract entered into by the Contract Department contains a clause by which a penalty is imposed for arrears of delivery, but the penalty is very rarely enforced, and has come to be regarded by contractors as a dead letter.[9]

Brackenbury complained to Lansdowne, who decided that a compromise arrangement should be sought and the following year's order was reduced to 6 million rounds. Brackenbury was not pleased as the amount, added to the 4 million outstanding, equalled the amount that Kynoch had already proved they were unable to produce. This was not the end of the conflict with the Chamberlains. Brackenbury later wrote to Arthur Balfour about the failure of the firm in quite aggressive language and pointedly added that; "You can show the letter to (Joseph) Chamberlain".[10] If Brackenbury had mellowed and become more tactful with age, as Lord Wantage believed, the situation with Kynoch and the Chamberlains had altered that and it is clear that Brackenbury was furious with the whole situation. It is surely understandable that a man under pressure to keep an ever-growing army supplied in a time of war found it difficult to deal with a situation where political relationships and family ties were making a difficult job even harder.

Kynoch further annoyed Brackenbury when they took on a financially lucrative contract from the United States, and further delayed deliveries to the War Office that were already in arrears. Arthur Chamberlain was called to give evidence to the Mowatt Committee, and his evidence has justly been described as both arrogant and patronising.[11] There were also moments when, under quite aggressive questioning from the Chairman, his evidence appeared to be contradictory. At one point he claimed that with only a few weeks' notice he could have met Brackenbury's demands for ammunition. He later contradicted this by saying that the reason he

---

9   Mowatt Committee, p.ix.
10  Brackenbury to Balfour, 23rd January 1900, Balfour Papers, British Library Add MSS 49683.
11  Page, 'The Supply Services of the British Army in the South African War 1899-1902', p.188.

could not meet the demands was because of the United States order, which he felt fully entitled to take because there was no arrangement by which British orders were to be given greater priority.[12] His protestations did little to convince anyone that it was anything other than a matter of money. In fact it appears to have been quite common that foreign orders were dealt with first as the delivery of these on time was thought to be especially important. Something of an attitude of 'anything will do' for the War Office seems to have existed. He also gave conflicting evidence when asked if the Director of Army Contracts had approved the order for the United States. He originally answered 'Yes', but changed his mind when read Brackenbury's evidence which contradicted him.[13]

Chamberlain claimed that under Brackenbury's predecessors delivery dates were never taken seriously and were not considered as binding contracts. He felt that Brackenbury's criticism was completely unfair and that the new Director General of Ordnance did not understand the way 'business' was done. "The Director General of Ordnance probably did not know that everybody is more or less behindhand; it is common practice and there has never been any attempt at the War Office to cut out contractors for being in arrears". Chamberlain also made a thinly veiled attack on Brackenbury stating that before war was declared, "We had not become aware of the existence of Sir Henry Brackenbury".[14] He then went on to attack him as a "new broom" that he held personally responsible for the unreasonable suggestion that a fine be imposed. He actually went further and declared that before Brackenbury nobody cared whether deliveries were on time or not. Saving money for Kynoch, he said, was more important than "being bound by time".[15] Whilst Chamberlain's position was in one sense understandable, after all he was a businessman, it did not go down well at a time when the country was at war and facing a very real shortage of ammunition. His evidence not only displayed arrogance but also an ignorance of the world situation. He may have felt that he was dealt with unfairly, but had it not been for the connection with his brother, Brackenbury would surely have had his way and the company would have been blacklisted. Kynoch were not alone, but they were by far and away the worst offender. In fairness it must be added that some firms, most notably Armstrong and Whitworth Ltd, tried to do all they could to help Brackenbury during this period. At one point they were able, after a special request, to make limbers and carriages for six batteries of artillery in a month. Sir Andrew Noble, in evidence, said that he had at one point proposed a plan for the expansion of their plant for times of emergencies, but that the then Inspector General of Ordnance, Sir Frederick Bramwell, had shown no interest in the scheme.[16]

---

12   Mowatt Committee, pp.78-79.
13   Mowatt Committee, p.79.
14   Mowatt Committee, p.80.
15   Mowatt Committee, p.79.
16   Mowatt Committee, pp.68-69.

Also interesting to note is the evidence of Colonel Sir W.D. Richardson to the Elgin Commission after the South African War.[17] Colonel Richardson arrived in South Africa in early October 1899 and took up the appointment of Deputy Adjutant-General for Supplies and Transport. Later on in the war he became Director of Supplies in Cape Town. His evidence showed the stark contrast of American attitudes towards supplying the British Army. Colonel Richardson told how every two to three weeks he would be visited by the American Consul-General at Cape Town, Mr Stowe, who would check to make sure American orders were satisfactory and whether there was anything else they could do to help. One problem Colonel Richardson had was the size of tins of meat. Normally such tins would be in 1lb or 2lb sizes, which could be carried by individual soldiers. During the war, because of the unexpectedly large demands for meat, much of the meat was sent out in 4lb or 6lb tins. Not only were these far heavier, but also there was as a consequence large-scale waste, as what was not eaten had to be thrown away. Colonel Richardson, according to his evidence, mentioned this problem to the Consul-General and was told that despite the fact that American firms did not normally produce them in 1lb or 2lb tins they would have no problem in supplying them. According to Colonel Richardson the Consul-General said "When you are buying tins by the million, you have only to let it be known what you want".[18] Whilst this perhaps says more about the contemporary business practices of the United States and Britain, it does serve to illustrate something of the ways in which parts of British industry could have been more helpful. Many British firms saw the demands of the South African War as problems that would cost them money, whereas many U.S. firms took the opportunity to make money by meeting the demand of the moment.

It is likely that the attitude expressed by many foreign firms was exactly what Brackenbury wanted from all British firms. The situation in South Africa was after all being portrayed as a national crisis and Brackenbury's attitude towards some of the firms seems to suggest that he expected them to do their bit for the war effort. However, with the Financial Secretary unwilling to impose sanctions upon the firms that failed to meet deadlines there was little else that Brackenbury could do. He eventually managed to get Lord Lansdowne's approval that, rather than fine firms, they would be charged the difference in the cost that the War Office undertook to make good the shortfall in their supply. Given that prices in general had risen during the war this was no little expense. It seems to have had little effect

---

17  *Elgin Commission Minutes of Evidence*, pp.146-154. Elements of Colonel Richardson's evidence have been used in, O'Brien, Jim, 'The Anglo-Boer War: Soap and Tinned Meat', *Soldiers of the Queen: The Journal of the Victorian Military Society*, Issue No 125 (June 2006), pp.19-22.
18  *Elgin Commission, Minutes of Evidence*, pp.148-149. This story is supported by Wilson H.W., *After Pretoria: The Guerrilla Campaign* Volume I (London: Amalgamated Press, 1902), p.76.

as the practice of charging the difference to the offending firm became common. However it did improve the situation from Brackenbury's point of view.

It is unlikely that there was any personal agenda in Brackenbury's tough attitude towards Kynoch in particular. They were at that time a major supplier, but also one of the worst offenders. After his original conflict with the firm Brackenbury was amazed when next year's order was again placed largely with them. He made the point to the Mowatt Committee that the treatment of Kynoch was unfair on those suppliers who did meet deadlines. He gave the example of the Birmingham Metal and Munitions Company which, on 6th September 1898, had along with Kynoch, received an order for 10 million rounds of ammunition. By 31st March 1899 the B.M.M.C. had delivered the entire order, whilst Kynoch had failed to deliver almost half theirs, some 4,976,974 rounds still outstanding. Yet in the next set of orders the Director of Contracts awarded 60% of the order to Kynoch rather than the other Birmingham firm. The decision was baffling. Admittedly Kynoch were marginally cheaper, but they had already proved that they were unreliable and there were serious doubts about their quality. Brackenbury felt that the B.M.M.C. should have been rewarded for their performance with an increased order.[19]

The whole situation with Kynoch was also caught up in a much wider public debate about the role of Joseph Chamberlain within the firm, which was the subject of an attack from the Liberal M.P. and 'pro-Boer' campaigner, David Lloyd George. He asked Chamberlain in parliament about his connection with Kynoch. Chamberlain replied that he was no longer a shareholder or had any control over the management of the company. Lloyd-George also asked why Kynoch had been awarded a contract to supply cordite for ammunition when of the seven tenders they were the most expensive.[20] The only logical reason for accepting the highest tender would be if the firm were known for their prompt delivery and reliability or the superior quality of their product and this was obviously not the case. To Brackenbury, that "first rate man of business", as Wolseley called him, it seemed incredible that a firm that so blatantly ignored delivery dates escaped penalty. Brackenbury's relationship with the Chamberlains was not helped by the fact that Lloyd George often quoted from the official reports and evidence of Brackenbury to further embarrass Joseph Chamberlain.[21]

---

19  Mowatt Committee, pp.85-86.
20  Unfortunately for Lloyd-George he did not know the most damaging part of Kynoch's wartime trading, namely that during the South African War Kynoch, through its South African subsidiary, sold twelve million rounds of ammunition to the Boers. Exactly how much control of this Kynoch had is unclear, but it would have proved extremely embarrassing to both Arthur and Joseph Chamberlain, to say the least.
21  Owen, Frank, *Tempestuous Journey: Lloyd-George his life and times* (London: Hutchinson & Co, 1954), p.140.

The evidence of the representatives of other firms to the Mowatt Committee in this context is interesting. Without directly saying so they appear to have taken the example of Kynoch as a warning. Though some firms had tried their best before, there were those like Vickers, Hadfield's and Firth and sons who were now trying to meet deadlines. In fairness it has to be mentioned that there was a potentially embarrassing conflict of interests here as Brackenbury held 600 shares in Hadfield's and Firths. The difference between he and the Chamberlains was that there was nothing in his treatment of that firm to even hint at preferential treatment. Hadfield's were not getting orders for tenders that were the most expensive, nor were they continuing to get orders despite failure to deliver on time nor were there questions over their quality. Most firms did eventually start to act the way in which Brackenbury wished, ultimately realising the seriousness of the situation and the needs of the moment. Whilst this is partly due to a sense of patriotism stirred by war, the example of the way Brackenbury had dealt with Kynoch may have had some impact. However Brackenbury's battles with Kynoch were not over.

# Chapter 30

# Problems of Production

The problems Brackenbury faced as Director General were not simply due to a lack of supply. It was not simply a case of getting equipment. Whilst there were problems with the amount of material that the ordnance factories and the trade could produce, this was largely because the demands of the conflict had initially caught them unawares. Once they had caught up supply problems became manageable. There was however a wider problem with production in terms of quality and control. This caused Brackenbury many problems and reinforced his concerns that production had become divorced from the need of the army. There also appeared to be a real failure to understand the demands and rigours of active service and the strength and endurance that the equipment would need to show. This somewhat surprisingly applied not only to 'the trade' but also the factories under War Office control. Again it reinforced Brackenbury's demand that such factories must be under his direct control.

## Quality and Inspection

There was a much wider problem with the quality of goods provided by the trade, and once again the worst offender was Kynoch. One could be forgiven for wondering if there was a personal agenda on behalf of Brackenbury, or Lansdowne, against the firm, but there genuinely does not appear to have been. They simply were that bad! What made it worse was Arthur Chamberlain's complete surprise and incredible arrogance regarding matters. He clearly had skills as a businessman, as his ability to save a failing company and turn them into a going concern illustrated. However one senses a real naivety in his dealings with the War Office, almost as if he was doing them a 'favour' by simply supplying them.

Not only were they more expensive than many and failed to deliver on time, there were real concerns over their quality. In one week in early 1900 Kynoch had 1,749,000 rounds rejected.[1] This was simply following the War Office system of inspection that applied to all products, and was not special treatment. On completion of any order it was returned with an inspection note stating the pattern and quantity. The goods were then inspected by Lt Colonel C.F. Hadden, the Chief Inspector Army Ordnance Department, and his staff. After the goods had been counted and inspected the note was completed and sent to the Principal Ordnance Officer, Colonel Steevens, who then notified the firms as to the findings. On receiving the news of the large-scale rejection Kynoch sent one of their agents, General Arbuthnot, to inquire as to the reason. Arbuthnot inspected the items and agreed with the rejection and declared that the reason for the fault was too much 'varnish'.[2] This was a serious problem as if the varnish melted in a hot rifle barrel it could remain there. When it cooled and set in the barrel it had the potential to cause a blow-back when the rifle was next used and injure or potentially kill the user of the rifle. This was not just sloppy workmanship, it was potentially criminally negligent. The matter seemed to be closed until Arthur Chamberlain came to see Brackenbury and complained that the reasons for the rejection of his ammunition were wrong, despite the opinion of his own agent. According to Brackenbury Chamberlain's main concern was the fact that as the ammunition was Mark V they could not sell it to anyone else and he therefore felt that the War Office 'had a duty' to buy it rather than leave his firm out of pocket.[3] History does not record Brackenbury's response, but one imagines it would have been interesting to say the least! As it happened Kynoch were left out of pocket, and perhaps Brackenbury had made his point, as there were no further recorded instances of this nature from them.

This illustrates how important inspection was but it was sometimes taken too far. At one stage a whole consignment of uniforms was rejected on the grounds that there was a slight difference in colour.[4] Such high demands led to a clash with the Financial Secretary, Powell-Williams. He believed that a lot of the supply problems that were being faced could be solved if the inspections were less demanding. He did have a point, as the previous example illustrates, but there were other more serious shortcomings. For example Brackenbury demanded straight-grained wood for the spokes on wheels. To Powell-Williams this seemed excessive but as they were to be fitted on artillery and heavy-laden wagons, their strength was all-important.[5] It was a basic conflict between military and civilian viewpoints, with the civilian not understanding the heavy wear and tear that the equipment would undergo. Another objection that Powell-Williams raised was Brackenbury's rejection of wooden picketing and tent

---

1   Brackenbury to Balfour, 23rd January 1900, Balfour Papers, British Library Add MSS 49683.
2   Mowatt Committee, pp.86-88.
3   Mowatt Committee, p.88.
4   Page, Andrew, 'The Supply Services of the British Army in the South African War 1899-1902', pp.202-203.
5   Page, 'The Supply Services of the British Army in the South African War 1899-1902', p.203.

pegs. Brackenbury explained that the pegs would have to be hammered into the dry veldt and removed, on average at least twice a day. If they were to break the tents could become useless, and worse, if a picketing peg went a unit could lose all its horses. The problem also applied to picks, hammers and entrenching tools that were made to commercial patterns. Most were designed for gardening in the soft soil of England not the hard dry veldt of South Africa. In this point the Commander-in-Chief in South Africa, Lord Roberts, supported Brackenbury's objections.[6] Another instance where the standard mattered was horseshoes. Brackenbury initially issued instructions to refuse anything that was not of the highest standard, because the majority of horses were being shod for the first time. Desperation later led him to accept anything that would not lame the animal.

Brackenbury's evidence to the Mowatt Committee shows that he felt that Alfred Major, Director of Army Contracts, and the trade, just wanted to give him what was easiest and cheapest to make. In Major's defence it can be said that this was in reality what was expected of him. At a time when demand was urgent and the cost of the war was escalating the merit of Major's position can be seen, and once again it appears that he had the best of intentions. There were undoubtedly occasions where the inspection process was far too vigorous, and items were refused that would have been satisfactory. Even despite the rigorous inspections there were celebrated cases of defective items being sent to South Africa. Major for his part, in his evidence to the Mowatt Committee, claimed that his main concern was the fear that if commercial patterns were not accepted the army would get no material at all whether, "good, bad or indifferent".[7] On this point he undoubtedly acted out of the best of motives, but once again there was an illustration of the problem of civilian control not understanding the difficulties of military campaigns. Brackenbury was prepared to accept material out of necessity that was below the standards that had been set but he was not prepared to send material that would, as he said, be liable to "breakdown, simply to please the trade".[8] There was a balance to be struck between the two points of view and as the war continued this started to be reached.

## Ammunition

One of the obvious results of the despatching overseas of the largest force ever to leave this country up to that point was the unprecedented demand for ammunition. One event illustrates the surprise of demands and the fact that the army and the War Office were in new territory. When General Sir George White asked for 4 million

---

6   Page, 'The Supply Services of the British Army in the South African War 1899-1902', p.204.
7   Mowatt Committee, pp.32-33.
8   Page, 'The Supply Services of the British Army in the South African War 1899-1902', p.203.

rounds of small arms ammunition to be sent out to South Africa in October 1899, he was cabled back the next day to check that the amount was correct![9] Surely this was a typographical error? If this seemed excessive to the War Office it soon became common, as by the end of November 1899 18 million rounds of ammunition had been sent. This was on top of the ammunition that troops carried with them to South Africa, which by the end of the year 1899 was calculated at some 30 million rounds in total. By the end of November 1899 the weekly supply that the army in South Africa needed was 3.7 million rounds.[10] However Brackenbury had been aware that such demands would be likely, although even he would have been surprised by the scale of demand, and had started to borrow as much ammunition as he could in preparation. As has been seen the trade could not be relied upon to deliver on time, or the correct amount, and the ordnance factories working flat out and including weekends could only produce 1.5 million rounds a week. The reserves of small arms ammunition were in a better state than most. In March 1899 the authorised reserve stood at 151 million rounds, but problems arose just before the war.[11]

The experience of several conflicts, most notably in the Sudanese campaigns and the Chitral Campaign, on the North West Frontier, had shown that the standard Mark II rifle ammunition had insufficient stopping power to halt the more 'fanatical' charges of some of Britain's colonial enemies. Brackenbury, in his evidence to the Elgin Commission, explained that because of this the decision was taken to develop an expanding bullet, which had greater stopping power. The basic principle was that the exit wound was far greater than the entry point and therefore more damage was done to the victim and a greater amount of blood was lost. In short the bullet 'expanded' the wound as it travelled through the body. There were various methods of creating such a bullet. In India what was commonly referred to as the 'Dum Dum' bullet was developed, which had no nickel covering on its tip. Dum Dum has become general terminology for an expanding bullet, but was in fact the name of the factory. This was to cause embarrassment in South Africa when cases of ammunition marked Dum Dum were discovered. They were however not expanding ammunition, but regular ordnance supplied by the Dum Dum factory. In Britain Mark IV ammunition was produced, which had a small hole in the tip of the nickel. Brackenbury told the Elgin Commission that:

> We had every intention of using this bullet and making it, in fact, the bullet for the British Army all over the world, and, I think, about 66,000,000 of

---

[9]  Page, 'The Supply Services of the British Army in the South African War 1899-1902', p.194.
[10] Report by Director General of Ordnance to Commander-in-Chief, pp.279-280. Also see Page, 'The Supply Services of the British Army in the South African War 1899-1902', p.195.
[11] Report by Director General of Ordnance to Commander-in-Chief, pp.278-279.

it up to the 31st March 1899 had been delivered, and formed part of our stock of 172,000,000.[12]

The Hague Convention of 29th July 1899 outlawed the use of such bullets but because of colonial experiences Britain failed to sign the convention. However there was a feeling within the government that there was a moral obligation to abide by this when fighting a civilised 'white' race like the Boers.

After questions were raised in Parliament an official statement was made stating that the ammunition would not be used, using the moral argument. There was actually a more practical reason that caused the abandonment of Mark IV ammunition. It was found that the bullet, in certain circumstances, had a tendency to 'strip', which is for the lead to squirt through the hole in the nickel envelope, and leave the nickel behind. In this scenario the next round fired caused a blow-back. The particular conditions in which this occurred were when the barrel of the rifle was dirty and hot. As Brackenbury stated:

> Those two conditions of great heat and a dirty rifle were exactly the conditions which were likely to occur in war, and, therefore, it seemed to me, and I so advised the Commander in Chief and the Secretary of State, that none of this ammunition should be considered serviceable for war, and, consequently, 66,000,000, or thereabouts, of our reserve was non-effective for purposes of war.[13]

Whilst Brackenbury felt that the Hague Convention had a certain moral impact on the government he maintained that, "The reason why we did not use the expanding bullet in South Africa was not the Hague Convention, however, but because the Mark IV ammunition, our expanding ammunition, had proved unfit to be used in war".[14] This perhaps explains the government's willingness to hide behind the 'moral obligation' of the Hague Convention, rather than admit the failure of production. It is difficult not to attach blame to Brackenbury's predecessor as it is obvious that the ammunition was not tested properly before it was produced on a large scale. It was during peacetime exercises that the problem was found and it is difficult to conclude anything other than the fact that the ammunition cannot have been given sufficient testing as surely such an obvious fault would have been identified.

Such problems made a difficult situation even worse and were just part of the problem Brackenbury had to deal with. Failures of production and inspection had been unexpected. Yet even without them the whole process of ordering, production, inspection and testing seemed to be flawed. Brackenbury started to reform

---

12  *Elgin Commission Minutes of Evidence*, p.74.
13  *Elgin Commission Minutes of Evidence*, p.74.
14  *Elgin Commission Minutes of Evidence*, p.74.

this process even during the war making greater demands on both the ordnance factories and 'the trade' to be more careful at their end of the process. However he could not really improve the inspection process. In the end he did have to accept some products that were at best satisfactory, but he ensured that this had to be the exception not the rule. Even then it was because of necessity and not, as he put it, "simply to please the trade".

CHAPTER 31

# THE EHRHARDT GUN

### ARTILLERY IN THE SOUTH AFRICAN WAR

Much has been written about the role of artillery during the war.[1] In many works that touch briefly on the subject it has been considered sufficient simply to say that the more modern guns of the Boers outclassed the British artillery. There is an element of truth in this as the wealth of the Boer states was such that they could afford to buy the latest French and German weapons. British artillery on the other hand included a number of old guns, and patterns, many of which, for reasons of economy, had modern technology added to them rather than the purchase of completely new models being undertaken. Ironically both sides converted guns to meet the demands of the war. Much of the Boer artillery was made up of converted 'guns of position', that is fortress guns which had a carriage added to make them mobile artillery pieces. The British did a similar thing with Naval artillery, converting ships' guns to act as long range artillery, and the role played by such guns in the defence of Ladysmith is often mentioned.

Whilst the debate on the role of artillery in South Africa and the consequences of modernisation are beyond the scope of this book, Brackenbury's evidence to the Elgin Commission on this matter is of interest and deserves comment. His responsibility for artillery was limited, his main task being to make sure that sufficient ammunition was available. Production of artillery equipment was partly his responsibility but the choice of guns and the number of them were only partly within his

---

[1] Virtually every book on the South African War makes some comment on the quality and performance of the British Artillery. Headlam, Maj-General Sir John, *The History of the Royal Artillery* Volume II (Woolwich: Royal Artillery Institution, 1937), gives a biased British perspective on their performance, but is interesting nonetheless. The best and most detailed accounts of the performance of artillery during the war are to be found in the series of articles that Major Darrell Hall wrote for *The Journal of the South African Military History Society* (see Bibliography).

remit. However he was charged with making sure that there were sufficient guns and during the war he had some notable success in this regard. Sir Henry Evelyn Wood, who had been Adjutant General during the war, praised the way in which Brackenbury had been able to supply guns for the army in South Africa despite the difficulties. He wrote to Brackenbury that, "I shall always look back to the provision of the 108 guns, which you carried through at a critical moment, with immense satisfaction".[2] This was the previously mentioned Armstrong and Whitworth order and, whilst credit must go to the aforementioned company, it was Brackenbury's drive and initiative which had made this possible. Brackenbury had no responsibility for training and tactics, that being the role of the Director of Artillery and the Adjutant-General. He was of course interested as an artilleryman himself and one who had experienced his fair share of combat.

One of the key advantages that Boer artillery had was that it could fire at longer range than British guns. This was a general fault found with British weapons but never before had it been a problem. Even when firing at such distances had been contemplated, it was difficult to practice anywhere in Britain. The conditions of South Africa made such training essential as climatic and geographical conditions made long-range firing a workable concept. Brackenbury felt that the implication of this was singular because it meant that British troops came under fire long before they could respond and thus morale was weakened. In his evidence to the Elgin Commission he made it quite clear that to the best of his knowledge no engagement was won or any attack repulsed because of the longer range and quicker firing guns possessed by the Boers. Brackenbury's view was that heavy artillery, both Boer and the naval guns of the British, did little serious harm to the enemy during the war, and that the main benefit was that of morale. He told the Elgin Commission that, "Nothing was so astonishing to me, and I think to many others among us, as the extraordinary effect which the presence of these big guns had upon our troops especially the Cavalry".[3] He also informed them that they had already started experimenting with heavy artillery such as field guns that could fire a 60lb shell in excess of 10,000 yards. For Brackenbury the effect on morale was the main reason for the development of such guns at the time but he did not rule out the fact that as technology progressed they would become more effective, as the First World War proved. In this regard Brackenbury should be seen as urging caution over adapting British tactics and weapons simply on account of the unique experiences of the South African War.

Much of Brackenbury's evidence is unsurprisingly little more than a defence of his own branch of the army, and there was obviously a sense of injured pride as the conduct of the artillery in general had been much maligned. He went into a long

---

2    Wood to Brackenbury, 24th September 1901, private collection.
3    *Elgin Commission Minutes of Evidence*, p.82.

explanation of the principles with which the field artillery took the field in South Africa. The key reason why Boer guns outranged British was, as mentioned earlier, because they were generally guns of 'position', which had been made mobile, whereas the British guns had been designed to move with the army. The key reason for this was that British artillery was seen largely as being available for a European conflict.[4] Whilst artillery did serve in any number of colonial campaigns, it was never present in large numbers and, as Brackenbury's evidence showed, the tactics and equipment were designed for battle in Europe, or more accurately to fight European opposition. Indeed the topography of most colonial conflicts ensured that only light guns, mountain guns and rockets could be used and operated effectively. He stressed that British artillery tactics were based largely on the lessons of the Austro-Prussian War, the Franco-Prussian War and the Russo-Turkish War. He reminded the Commission that Britain had not fought a major campaign with breech-loading guns, and thus such conflicts were the best guide for the British. These conflicts had proved, in the view of those in authority in the army, that guns needed to be pushed forward and fired as closely as possible to maximise their effect. In short they needed to be mobile. This was the way the Prussians had been successful in 1870, and when the Russians had tried to use their guns at long range they had found that their infantry got little or no support as a consequence.

A wider point must be made that British battle tactics in general saw the engagement ending in an infantry charge. Guns and cavalry were largely there to make this possible and to finish off an enemy once the bayonet charge had won the battle, not to win the battle on their own. As a result the British Army's Artillery Drill Book of 1896 stated that the range for 'distant' fire was 3,500 to 2,500 yards. The Infantry Drill book of 1896 laid down that despite the claims of artillery officers that their guns were effective beyond 3,000 yards, there was no need to practice this as it was beyond the range of support for the infantry. Even the German Field Service Regulations of 1900 stated that 3,300 yards was the range up to which artillery fire became effective and thus fire beyond that range was unnecessary.[5] It was believed that the physical effect would be small and not worth the wastage of ammunition. Again there was the geographical point that in Europe conditions would rarely allow guns to be used at such distances, except in sieges, for which purpose a siege train was maintained. However in the veldt such conditions existed.

Brackenbury continually emphasised in his evidence that the only major effect of long-range fire was on morale.

---

4    Brackenbury gives a detailed account of the development of British tactics in his evidence to the *Elgin Commission*, pp.579-582.

5    The reference to all these regulations is the *Elgin Commission Minutes of Evidence*, p.79.

> In spite of the peculiar features of the Boer gun and of the country, it cannot be said that long range artillery fire was proved to be effective. It did not secure the success of any attack that was seriously resisted; it never repulsed any determined advance. The moderate range-fire of our guns did both, and those who have studied numbers of reports from South Africa can have no doubt whatever of the very great value to our Army of our field artillery fire.[6]

Brackenbury was trying to defend British tactics against knee-jerk reactions to the peculiar and unique conditions of South Africa, and appreciate the value of long-range fire. He refused to enter into any further debate about tactics used by the artillery in South Africa. He correctly pointed out to the Commission that tactics, in the form of the drill book, was the responsibility of the Adjutant-General's Department. One of the key reasons for the Boer success with artillery was their use of indirect fire, that is firing from concealed position or at least from positions where they could not see the target. The British stuck to the principle of direct fire and placed their guns in the open, which with the accurate long range rifle fire of the Boer Mauser rifles proved devastating, most notably at the battle of Colenso. Boer success with artillery was in fact short-lived. Even in the early days of the war they were outnumbered three to one, and British numbers continued to grow whilst the Boers could not replace their guns. However Brackenbury was not arguing that there was no need for improvement in British artillery, simply that it had not been a decisive factor in the war. This makes sense if one remembers that the Royal Commission had been appointed to examine a particular conflict not the general state of the army, although at times it naturally looked at this.

Brackenbury had tried to take action to reform and improve the artillery during the war. For example, as early as November 1899 he had directed the Ordnance Committee, in his words, "to push on with the question of obtaining a satisfactory time fuse effective up to longer ranges than those then in service".[7] By January 1900 4,000 of these fuses were ready for despatch to South Africa. They had a twenty-one second fuse, which would cover 6,400 yards before the explosion, although obviously the full distance was never intended to be used. The other thing that Brackenbury wanted to obtain was an efficient quick-firing gun for the field artillery. The simple definition of a 'quick firer' was a gun where there was a system in place to 'absorb' the recoil, and thus avoid having to relay after each round was fired. In achieving this he was helped by the fact that the majority of artillery officers who had gained experience in South Africa were amongst the first to return home, as their presence was not deemed necessary for the 'guerrilla' phase of the war.

---

6   *Elgin Commission Minutes of Evidence*, p.80.
7   *Elgin Commission Minutes of Evidence*, p.80.

## The Ehrhardt Gun

This was something that Brackenbury had been interested in when President of the Ordnance Board, but acting only in an advisory capacity he had only been able to look at the designs that were sent to him. None of them proved acceptable. A stopgap measure was introduced whereby an axle spade was added to the gun, but this only checked the recoil. It did not make the gun a true quick firer, but it certainly made it considerably quicker in terms of rate of fire. The system was fitted to all the guns that were sent to South Africa. The Boer guns were theoretically capable of firing 10 or 12 rounds a minute, although Brackenbury felt that only 6 or 8 would be possible with aimed fire.[8] The average of the British guns in trials at Okehampton was only 4 rounds of aimed fire. It must be added that there is no evidence to suggest that rapidity of fire had any significant influence in any engagement during the war but had the Boers possessed more guns or had Britain been fighting a European power it may well have proved vital.

Brackenbury attempted to find true quick-firing designs amongst British manufacturers that were satisfactory, but he could not find one complete system to meet his standards. He then took the slightly controversial step of gaining government permission to obtain a quick firing gun from Germany. The deal was kept secret for a variety of reasons. After the war Brackenbury made a brief reference before the Royal Commission on the War in South Africa to the fact that Britain had now joined France as the only nation to operate a truly quick-firing gun. He mentioned that the guns had come from Germany, but this point seems to have caused little comment or surprise so one must presume that eventually details leaked out.[9] We have already seen that there was concern over the dependence of the army on overseas equipment. Added to this was the fact that Germany was increasingly starting to look like a potential enemy. It would also have been a blow to British prestige to admit that British industry was not up to the task of supplying modern equipment to the army. A government that was already under pressure over the conduct of the war and the state of the army would not want questions raised about the 'might' of British industry. The Germans were also keen to keep the deal secret as there was growing anti-British feeling in Germany which was being fuelled by the South African War. In Germany the order caused complaints from the German manufacturer Krupp, who had been pressured by the German Government not to sell further guns to the Boers, or the British for that matter. They were a little annoyed to say the least that another German manufacturer was being given permission to sell guns to the British.[10]

---

8  *Elgin Commission Minutes of Evidence*, pp.84-85.
9  *Elgin Commission Minutes of Evidence*, pp.85-86.
10 For the German point of view regarding the Ehrhardt guns I am indebted to the assistance of Dr Christian Leitzbach, the official historian for Rheimentall AG, who has very kindly provided me with very useful information regarding this issue.

The War Office placed an order with Rheinische Metallwaaren und Maschinenfabrik of Düsseldorf for 108 guns, limbers and ammunition wagons, considered enough to equip eighteen batteries.[11] This was commonly referred to as the Ehrhardt Gun after the founder and owner of the company Henirich Ehrhardt. The company had until that point been unknown as gun manufacturers, yet they produced a gun where the top carriage took up the recoil, so that the wheels remained stationary and thus the gun did not need to be relayed. Brackenbury wrote that the recoil was taken up so well that during firing a coin could be placed on the wheel and not be knocked off by the action of the gun. The new gun never served in South Africa but it equipped the army at Aldershot and meant that invasion fears were alleviated a little by the knowledge that the very latest modern guns were in service, but it had many problems and because it was completely unlike anything the artillery had seen before it took them some time to get used to it. This gun was never meant for long-term service, but it made Britain one of the few nations at that time to have genuine quick-firing field artillery. It also gave the British manufacturers something to work from and, in Brackenbury's words, "... caused them to wake up, and taught them a lesson".[12] Indeed future British guns took many of the design features of the Ehrhardt gun and improved upon them. There is some irony that a German designed gun would be the basis for British artillery going into the First World War.

Lord Roberts wrote that the German-built guns had "advanced us by five if not ten years in our knowledge of what field guns might do".[13] The changes were dramatic in regards to what the Royal Artillery could now do with their guns. During trials with the Ehrhardt gun the Royal Artillery batteries found that they could easily maintain fire at twelve rounds a minute, as opposed to six with their previous guns. At extreme rapid fire for a short burst they were able to fire a staggering 28 rounds a minute.[14] It was from the trials with this gun that Brackenbury, in July 1901, drew up the conditions to be met for the new quick-firing gun for the Horse and Field artillery, which envisaged a gun firing an 18lb shell at up to 6,000 yards with a 16-degree elevation. Brackenbury listed in order of importance the features that were needed for the new gun with priority being given to shell power, ballistics

---

11  This company would later evolve into what is known today as the Rheimentall AG Group. For further details on the Ehrhardt Gun see Headlam, *The History of the Royal Artillery* Volume II, pp.113-119, Rogers, H.C.B., *Artillery through the Ages* (London: Seeley Service and Co Ltd, 1971) and 'Ordnance and ammunition from Germany', NA WO108/336. The latter is marked 'top secret' and perhaps illustrates the level of secrecy that was used. The document suggests that a merchant bank was used as an intermediary, possibly what is now known as the HSBC Group, although because it was regarded as top secret it is not clear.
12  *Elgin Commission Minutes of Evidence*, p.85.
13  Spiers, Edward, 'Rearming the Edwardian Artillery', *Journal of the Society of Army Historical Research* Volume 57 (1979), p.168.
14  Headlam, *The History of the Royal Artillery* Volume II (Woolwich: Royal Artillery Institution, 1937) p.160.

and rapidity of aimed firepower.[15] There were delays with the rearmament and the order was finally placed in December 1904 only after a sustained campaign in the press. Again this illustrates the effect the war had. It gave motivation to the process of rearmament that would have been lacking otherwise, but more than this it had led to a public and press outcry that it had not yet taken place only four years after the first quick-firing guns had been received.[16] Such a campaign on behalf of the Army would never have happened before the war. It showed not just what an impact the war had on the image and popularity of the Army, but also the increase in the importance of the Army that the war had shown was necessary. By urging this somewhat controversial and unconventional move Brackenbury had helped advance the British army materially and technologically, and the significance of this should not be lost.

---

15  Conditions to be fulfilled by a Quick-firing gun for Royal Horse and Field Artillery, 8th July 1901, British Library Add MSS 50325ff164. For further information on the process of rearmament of the artillery after the South African War see Chapter V of Headlam, *The History of the Royal Artillery* Volume II.
16  Headlam, *The History of the Royal Artillery* Volume II, pp.76-77. Parallels can be drawn with the famous 'we want eight and we won't wait' campaign that the press and public took on behalf of the Royal Navy (the eight being the number of new battleships desired), though it was never as vociferous. There exists a famous *Punch* cartoon concerning this from December 1904. *The Times* also featured an editorial article on this on 15th December 1904.

# Chapter 32

# The Conclusion of the South African War

The course and conduct of the war was such that demands were made on the military machine that had never been seriously considered prior to 1899. It is not the purpose of this study to look at why this was so, but to look at Brackenbury's role in how these demands were dealt with. It is sufficient to say that a machine largely set up to meet the peacetime demands would always struggle during wartime. The fact that the campaign saw nearly half a million men deployed meant that the conflict went in to territory for which all at the War Office were unprepared, given that the standard working field force had been envisaged at 40,000–50,000 men. This obviously created many supply problems and demands that were beyond the experience of the War Office.

### Small arms ammunition

A key area was that of ammunition. Mention has already been made of the incredulity with which the War Office replied to Sir George White's request for 4 million rounds in October 1899, yet orders far beyond this were later received. At its height some 3.7 million rounds a week were needed to maintain the army in South Africa. In such a situation reserves were quickly exhausted as the ordnance factories and the trade were struggling to meet the demands. In fact, it was only after the expansion of the new plant at the ordnance factories that the situation was brought under control. It was not simply a fault of the supply system. The trade quickly proved that they could not be relied upon, because commercial interests were quite understandably driving the large majority of them, and the ordnance factories could only produce 1.5 million rounds a week working flat out including weekends.

In such a situation the reserves were quickly used up, and Brackenbury took steps to try and cope with this. He stopped the shipping of ammunition to all other commands and raided the supplies of overseas garrisons. Gibraltar and Malta supplied about 8 million rounds between them. The situation deteriorated to the extent that the General Officer Commanding in Malta was ordered by Lord Lansdowne to disarm the garrison if necessary to provide ammunition for South Africa.[1] We clearly see a situation with possibly dire consequences. If all the ammunition supply was needed for what remained essentially a colonial campaign how could the army possibly cope with a much wider war that saw the army fighting on several continents? In such a situation not supplying other commands, or disarming garrisons, was not feasible. To an extent Brackenbury's response to problems of supply is aimed as much at a future conflict as the present one. In expanding and reequipping the ordnance factories he is trying to avoid a repeat. The problems in the First World War came when the 'game' had changed again and the British army was moving from hundreds of thousands of men to millions of men. By March 1900 the reserves held in Britain had run out and, according to Brackenbury, "there were just three boxes of ammunition in the entire country".[2] Fortunately that was as bad as it got. The new plant at Woolwich and the borrowing of ammunition from all over the Empire had given the trade time to catch up, a delay which was caused largely by their need to retool to produce the new pattern of ammunition. Saying that it was the excessive demand that was the biggest problem sums up the basic ammunition situation. The orders received were far beyond that which had been considered possible beforehand.

All this was not without consequences for the ordnance factories. The wear and tear caused by the increased production made Brackenbury's proposed replacement of plant not only desirable but also essential. By the end of 1899 things were at breaking point for both men and machines and had it not been for Brackenbury's persuasion of a reluctant Army Board to close the factories for five days over Christmas, there might have been a total collapse.[3] The work of the ordnance factories was excellent and they did all they could under the circumstances. The irony was that the trade was meant to cover up for the deficiencies in the ordnance factories, but it ended up the other way around. The factories were worked hard, and plant increased, because of the unreliability of large sectors of the trade. The change in control of the ordnance factories was vindicated by the South African War, where Brackenbury's overall control, and more to the point the *de facto* control of spending he was given, prevented the large scale collapse in supply which would inevitably have come if he had had to work through the procedures and rigours of the highly bureaucratic War Office purchasing system. In time of war the Financial

---

1  Lansdowne to G.O.C in Malta, 27th January 1900, NA WO108/66
2  Brackenbury to Balfour, 16th May 1901, Balfour papers, British Library, Add Mss 49683.
3  Page, Andrew, 'The Supply Services of the British Army in the South African War 1899-1902', p.196.

Secretary was an unnecessary intermediary who did nothing but delay purchase of equipment.

The system of reporting expenditure as soon as possible to the Army Board and then following it up with the necessary paperwork at a later stage that Brackenbury adopted, with the permission of the Secretary of State for War, was vital in maintaining the supply of the army in South Africa. It will be remembered that without this burden Brackenbury was only just able to keep the Army supplied; with the added bureaucracy, and more to the point the added time that this entailed, it is doubtful it could have been achieved. There was only one accounting system, with no provision being made for the rigours and immediate demands of war. In the early days of the war the department attempted to carry on with this system, and it has been suggested that this attempt may account for the number of nervous breakdowns that were suffered amongst the staff of the department.[4] Brackenbury also had to contend with the fact that no plans existed for the expansion of the factories in time of war because of the belief in the ability of the trade to produce anything at any notice. He soon found that this was not realistic and as a result the ordnance factories had to be expanded and foreign suppliers, of which his department had no prior knowledge or experience, had to be used.

## Artillery Ammunition

Artillery ammunition was also subject to unprecedented demands during the war. Before the war the total reserve of 15pdr shells in Natal was 5,000 but in the early engagements an estimated 1,000 shells were fired in a day. Brackenbury underestimated the weekly demand for shells and General Buller asked for almost double what Brackenbury had planned to send out.[5] Two things come out of this. First that Brackenbury, his department, and the War Office in general were into uncharted territory, and second that Brackenbury's experience as an artillery officer probably meant that he was better able to envisage such demands than a non-gunner. Very few, if any, artillery officers would have contemplated engagements where batteries were firing 1,000 shells a day, particularly in a 'colonial campaign'. Brackenbury did his best to keep the level of supply maintained. The demands were such that it was calculated that the reserve would be used up in two months. Brackenbury took shells from wherever he could find them. Batteries still in the British Isles had their stocks raided to the extent that in February 1900 the only field gun ammunition still in Britain were the remaining rounds in the limbers of the batteries.[6] Brackenbury

---

4   Page, 'The Supply Services of the British Army in the South African War 1899-1902', p.228.
5   *Elgin Commission Minutes of Evidence*, pp.73-74.
6   Page, 'The Supply Services of the British Army in the South African War 1899-1902', p.199.

deliberately sent out guns to South Africa that he knew could be supplied from Royal Navy stocks but he saw the danger of such a move. It was undoubtedly his evidence to the Mowatt Committee that led that body to conclude that:

> The time might come when the country would find itself simultaneously engaged in a great war by sea and by land, during which India and the Navy so far from being able to lend to the Army, might themselves have to make very heavy demands.[7]

Despite all the problems there is no account of the guns ever falling silent for want of ammunition.

**Henry Brackenbury. This photograph was taken after his promotion to General in 1902 and before retirement in 1904, and is quite possibly the last picture of him taken in military uniform. (Private collection)**

## Establishing Reserves

There were many problems in supplying the troops but despite this the quality of the equipment supplied was remarkably good. Andrew Page concluded that:

> The quality of the stores provided is difficult to assess. However apart from swords, lances and pistols, most items had more defenders than detractors.

---

7   Mowatt Committee, p.10.

It is easy and entertaining to amass a list of absurdities (helmets and saddles that disintegrated in the rain, caps so inadequate that dozens of troops could get sunstroke on Salisbury plain, rifles where the butt fell off if it got too hot, and so on) but to do so is misleading. Most stores, including most headgear, saddles and rifles, were perfectly serviceable. Occasions where there was a shortage of stores, or those provided were of poor quality, were publicised by those expecting, perhaps subconsciously hoping for, another example of administrative chaos like the Crimean War.[8]

In a memorandum of January 1904 Brackenbury, soon to leave the War Office, wrote that much of the reserve, for what in effect was the B.E.F., had been established.[9] He was 250 guns short of the required reserve but 78 were on order and another 100 had been budgeted for in the army estimates of 1904–05. He also reported that 233,000 rifles were missing from the reserve. This was accounted for by an unprecedented demand from India, due to the reorganisation that Lord Kitchener was undertaking and the fact that the department was still recovering from the war. Another reason for this was the decision to move over to the 'short' rifle with the introduction of the SMLE Mk I. Brackenbury, obviously remembering previous problems regarding the thoroughness of testing, not only issued 1,000 rifles to the Royal Navy, Royal Marines and British Army for trials but also despatched 100 to Somaliland. The latter would give the rifle a thorough trial in hot, dusty, and dry conditions.

The fact that the reserve had not been completed two years after the end of the South African War should not be regarded too harshly as such success as there was had been due only to Brackenbury persuading the cabinet to re-equip over three years as opposed to the usual ten. He could also point to the fact that the amount of small arms ammunition in reserve was over the authorised figure. He could be proud of the way things were going. Whilst dealing with demands of 'standard' equipment he was also finding demands for more unusual equipment. There exists an interesting letter between Henry Evelyn Wood, then commanding at Salisbury plain, and Brackenbury, which discussed the military use of bicycles.[10] The Boers had used them in the recent conflict, most notably a unit under the command of the controversial Danie Theron, but this was an area in which most armies were now experimenting. Brackenbury managed to obtain some 'experimental' models for Wood to work with. This was just one example of new equipment and material which the war had created an interest in.

---

8   Page, 'The Supply Services of the British Army in the South African War 1899-1902', p.250.
9   Report by Director General of Ordnance on the armaments and materials of war 1st January 1904. British Library, Add MSS 50325ff164-177b.
10  Evelyn Wood to Brackenbury, 3rd January 1902, private collection.

In February 1902 a new uniform was issued for the British Army and from now on the army would train in the uniform it would fight in. Whilst for the soldier this made sense it also made sense from a production point of view, and would reduce the problems of production for any future conflict. Uniformity was now the name of the game not simply in clothing but now artillery, rifles, ammunition and all manner of equipment was being designed so that there were fewer patterns to produce. In this sense the war allowed such things to be sorted out before the trials of the First World War and in this Brackenbury undoubtedly played a significant part.

## Brackenbury and Secretaries of State

Brackenbury was clearly helped in his task by his personal relationship with Lord Lansdowne, who allowed him a freedom that made his task easier. It was fortunate that Lansdowne was Secretary of State when the most serious demands were placed upon Brackenbury and the Ordnance Department. The relationship was not just one-way however, and Lansdowne regularly sought Brackenbury's opinion. When Lansdowne was called before the Royal Commission on the War in South Africa he had a conversation with Brackenbury about the evidence he would give, and it is clear from their correspondence that Brackenbury gave him assistance.[11] Obviously Brackenbury could provide Lansdowne with facts and figures to support his evidence, but there was clearly more to it than that. In a letter the following year Lansdowne throws more light on the matter.

> No one is more conscious than I am of the shortcomings of my administration at the War Office. How differently many things would be done, if one had to do them again! But the difficulties were very great, and no one understands them better than you do.[12]

This letter clearly illustrates a mutual respect and support existing between the two men. As Brackenbury was always apolitical, even refraining from voting whilst serving in the army, it is not a case of him trying to support a particular government or cause. It is more a case that he can understand the pressure and difficulties his friend is working under and wishes to support him.

Brackenbury also had a good personal relationship with Arnold-Forster who served as Secretary of State for War during Brackenbury's last year at the War Office. Arnold-Forster clearly admired and respected Brackenbury's ability, but again there was something of a personal relationship above that normally associated with work colleagues. Brackenbury was a weekend guest of the Arnold-Forsters

---

11  Lansdowne to Brackenbury, 9th November 1902, private collection.
12  Lansdowne to Brackenbury, 10th September 1903, private collection.

on several occasions, and somewhat unusually there exists a number of letters between Brackenbury and Mary Arnold-Forster, mostly of a personal and social nature. Indeed the same sort of relationship existed with the third Secretary of State during Brackenbury's time in office, William St John Brodrick. The relationships he enjoyed with these individuals made Brackenbury's job easier. Firstly it meant they trusted him, and all three allowed him remarkable freedom. A letter from Arnold-Forster in May 1904 illustrates this clearly. The letter discusses the new 18 pounder field gun. Brackenbury supports its introduction, whilst Arnold-Forster disagrees. However after a discussion between the two men Arnold-Forster agreed to accept Brackenbury's recommendation even though he still disagrees.[13] This might not sound like much but the willingness to trust a soldier against their better judgement is not one that any politician has ever taken lightly. That trust had been built up not only during his time as Director General of Ordnance but through a lifetime of service in the army. We clearly see a case that Brackenbury's reputation went before him in his relationships with the three Secretaries of State he served under.

---

13    Arnold-Forster to Brackenbury, 18th May 1904, private collection.

# Chapter 33

# Ill-Health and Retirement

The South African War took a considerable toll on the health of Sir Henry Brackenbury and it will be remembered that by the end of the war he was sixty-four. In a letter to Lady Wolseley in November 1903 he wrote "A few more weeks and active employment will be over for me, as for him [Lord Wolseley]. I shall have had forty-eight years of work, and shall not be altogether sorry for a rest".[1] He had good reason to look forward to a rest. His department had to deal with supplying an army ten times the size of that for which it had been set up. Page best sums up his achievements:

> ... He insisted on the change in control of the factories, did his best to ensure that contracts were adhered to, first recommended a general policy of buying abroad, expanded the Ordnance Factories as far as he was allowed and overrode the paralysing delays of War Office accounting. Neither he nor anyone could create in a moment productive capacity to meet any demand, and this was really what the pre-war system, with inadequate reserves required.[2]

There was no repeat of the collapse of supplies to South Africa as there had been in the Crimean War. In fact the main supply problems were in South Africa itself, especially after Lord Kitchener's attempt to centralise all transport had failed. It must be remembered that once items had reached South Africa Brackenbury's role was largely over. Brackenbury and his department, whilst trying to undertake a series of reforms and changes and cope with the series of committees that were set up, managed to keep up the supply and maintenance of the largest army that Britain had ever had up to that point. The final point cannot be stressed enough.

---

1   Brackenbury to Lady Wolseley, 16th November 1903, Wolseley papers, Central Library, Hove.
2   Page, Andrew, 'The Supply Services of the British Army in the South African War 1899-1902', p.212.

The scale and size of the South African War can easily get overlooked in the light of the two world wars of the twentieth century. Almost half a million men was far beyond anything that had been reasonably expected before the war. Whether this was short-sightedness on the part of the War Office and the state, or simply recognition of Britain's position as largely a maritime power, is difficult to say.

Brackenbury was fortunate to have some very able officers in his department including Colonel (later Lieutenant-General Sir) Robert A. Montgomery, his deputy for much of the period and the man who took temporary command in Brackenbury's absence. The Principal Ordnance Officer charged with inspection of material supplied was Colonel (later Major-General Sir) John Steevens, and Brackenbury obviously appreciated his abilities as he recommended him for promotion, which came in June 1902. Steevens wrote an admiring letter to Brackenbury in 1902, first thanking him for his promotion writing, "The prize is the more valuable to me, coming from that recommendation (from Brackenbury), and it is only one more, added to the many and great kindnesses which I have received at your hands". He went on to give an assessment of his time serving under Brackenbury.

> I have been fortunate in my travel of service, all my official life, but no period has brought me as much fortune as that which has fallen to my lot in having had the privilege of serving under, and in a small way being associated with, you, at a time when work was to be done.[3]

To an extent the relationship between Brackenbury and his staff was one of having jointly shared great trials and difficulties. However there is a little more than that, and it is clear that there was mutual respect and admiration. There was also a level of trust and Brackenbury had confidence enough in Steevens to allow him a fairly free hand in control of the Ordnance Office at Woolwich. Indeed before the Royal Commission and a court of inquiry Brackenbury publically praise the work of his staff, particularly Montgomery and Steevens.[4]

## OVERWORK AND ILL-HEALTH

The strain on Brackenbury and his department was enormous and on 15th December 1902 he offered his resignation on the grounds of ill-health saying, "I had become

---

3 Steevens to Brackenbury, 23rd June 1902, private collection.
4 Brackenbury gave evidence to a court of enquiry into the behaviour of Lt Col Hobbs and Colonel Clarke of the Ordnance Stores in South Africa. Brackenbury insisted that it be placed on record that both he and Col Steevens had no control over the 'accused' officers whatsoever. Brackenbury went on to defend Col Steevens from any blame and praised his behaviour and professionalism. He even stated that his confidence in him was so high that he had given him a fairly free hand in controlling his branch. NA WO32/7026.

sleepless and nervous, and was no longer fit to carry on responsible work".[5] He informed the Commander-in-Chief, now Lord Roberts, and the Secretary of State for War, Mr St John Brodrick, that he intended to resign from 1st January 1903. It is worth observing that by now the war was over, but the reforms continued.

> I have a great longing for rest, but on the other hand I have a strong desire myself to see through the work begun in 1899. By the end of March 1904, the modern armament of our fortresses should be complete, and we should have everything ready in the ordnance stores and clothing to equip an army of 135,000 men for service abroad, and maintain them in the field for 6 months. You will understand that I want to see this through, lest anything should slip before it is accomplished.[6]

Brackenbury was persuaded, largely by St John Brodrick, to stay on until the end of his five-year term in 1904. He agreed, but was ordered to go on leave until February in an attempt to recover.[7] It has been said of Brackenbury that, "His contribution to the successful prosecution of the war, and the placing of the army on a sounder footing after it, probably exceeded that of any other single individual", so one can understand why there was a reluctance to lose him altogether.[8] Brackenbury's reluctance to step down is also understandable after all the work he had put in. Cynically one could say he did not wish anyone else to take the credit for his work, but it is more accurate to say that after all the hard work he had put in he did not want anyone else to 'mess it up'.

The level of ill-health he was experiencing was such that those around him had begun to notice, and had been doing so for some time. Indeed when he had decided to offer his resignation in December 1902 he had already been suffering for some time. On 7th February 1900 Lansdowne had written to him saying:

> I was grieved, but not surprised, to hear that you have had to surrender to the doctors. I trust you will not try to resume your work too soon. You have done so splendidly for us, and for the sake of the office, if not for your own, you must husband your strength and not test your powers too soon.[9]

The date is important to note as the South African War, and therefore the demands upon Brackenbury and his department, was still escalating. Just before he offered his resignation he had confided in Lord Wolseley. In a letter that was otherwise sympathetic Wolseley remarked to Brackenbury "I warned you that you were

---

5  Brackenbury to Wolseley, 26th December 1902, Wolseley papers, Hove Central Library.
6  Brackenbury to Wolseley, 26th December 1902, Wolseley papers, Hove Central Library.
7  Part of this extended leave was spent in Nauheim and then Lucerne.
8  Page, 'The Supply Services of the British Army in the South African War 1899-1902', p.354.
9  Lansdowne to Brackenbury, 7th February 1900, private collection.

overstretching yourself by too hard a work". Although we do not know the exact extent of it he had been ill in 1901, but had recovered to a degree. In September 1901 Evelyn Wood wrote to Brackenbury "I am delighted to see your handwriting, and so firm and true, just as if you had not been ill, which I devoutly hope may prove to be but a temporary trouble, and that your health may soon be restored for the good of the country and this office, for which you have done so much".[10] Although we do not know the exact details it sounds like exhaustion and the severe strain that the demands of the war had placed on him personally both physically and mentally. It is important to recognise both forms of exhaustion and to acknowledge that physical exhaustion can be easier to recover from than mental exhaustion. This was harder for people to understand or appreciate. A soldier who is wounded in battle and needs time to recover is much easier to appreciate than a soldier in an office many thousands of miles from the front line who has worked himself to exhaustion so that the army in the field can be maintained in the best condition possible.

## Honours

Brackenbury was in effect left out of the honours that followed the war, although when he retired he was appointed a Privy Councillor. The reason for his omission is claimed to be because the King feared that awarding an honour to a Head of Department during the war would cheapen the honours system. Whatever view he held regarding this matter there is no doubt that His Majesty appreciated and understood the significance of the work that Brackenbury had done at the Ordnance Department. Rather than belittling the work of Brackenbury this should be seen as a matter of principle regarding the honour system. Sir Arthur Bigge, who served as Private Secretary to Queen Victoria, King George V and was close to King Edward VII, recorded His Majesty as saying that Brackenbury had "Pulled the army out of the hole in the South African War".[11] This is a simple, yet accurate, way of describing what Brackenbury had achieved, and illustrates that even the highest in the land were familiar with the extraordinary work that he had done.

The Secretary of State for War, by this time H.O. Arnold-Forster, felt Brackenbury deserved a more significant award for his service during the South African War, but as he wrote "I acquiesce (to the King) having no option". Arnold-Forster had written to the Prime Minister Balfour, who had succeeded Salisbury in 1902, about Brackenbury saying that:

---

10 Wolseley to Brackenbury, 1st November 1901, private collection and Wood to Brackenbury, 24th September 1901, private collection.
11 This conversation was reported to Henry Brackenbury via his nephew, Hereward Irenius Brackenbury, to Henry Brackenbury, 19th February 1907, private collection.

**Henry Brackenbury seen in his uniform and robes as member of the Privy Council. Circa 1904. (Private collection)**

> He has done the state splendid service. I should like him to receive a distinguished mark of favour. He has no children and in my opinion a peerage would be an appropriate and not excessive reward.[12]

Arnold-Forster was a great admirer of Brackenbury's skill and also wrote to Balfour that, "Brackenbury, to my great regret, is leaving us in a few weeks".[13] No doubt Brackenbury also regretted the fact that he was leaving just as secretaries of state were coming along with a mandate to carry out so many of the reforms that he had championed during his career. Only a matter of months after he left the army in 1904 the office of Commander-in-Chief was abolished and replaced by a Chief of Staff. Arnold-Forster wrote to Brackenbury on the occasion of his retirement:

> I am permitted to inform you that the King proposes to mark the conclusion of your great career by summoning you to the Privy Council. I am told that under the circumstances this honour is exceptional, to which I can only reply that the services have been exceptional.[14]

---
12  H.O. Arnold-Forster to Balfour, 13th January 1904, Balfour papers, British Library Add MSS 49722. He was not completely left out of the honours list. His K.C.B. was raised to a G.C.B.
13  H.O. Arnold-Forster to Balfour, 13th January 1904, Balfour papers, British Library Add MSS 49722.
14  H.O. Arnold-Forster to Brackenbury, 4th February 1904, Arnold-Forster papers, British Library Add MSS 50336.

## Assessment

It is easy to condemn the lack of foresight within the army but no one in the War Office had any experience of a conflict on such a scale. Even the Crimean War is not a fair comparison in size. The South African War was a 'wake up call' for the army and politicians alike. It made many realise the demands of modern warfare. Whilst there were still great failures of the military machine in the First World War, the army took the field in far better shape because of the South African experiences. In later years it was remarked that it was "a blessing in disguise" and even contemporaries appreciated the value of the South African War, with the great chronicler of Empire, Rudyard Kipling, writing a poem entitled 'The Lesson', which included the lines "Let us admit it fairly, as a business people should, We have had no end of a lesson: it will do us no end of good!".[15] It can be argued that the problems of the First World War largely came about after the conflict had changed in size again. Before South Africa, the Army had prepared for conflicts using tens of thousands of troops at most. South Africa brought about the realisation that it needed to be prepared for hundreds of thousands of troops at the very least. The supply problems of the First World War came when it had changed yet again to millions of troops.

The level to which Brackenbury's work was appreciated has now been lost, but in the years after the war it remained strong. Indeed when the tributes to him came in after his death in 1914 many of the newspapers were fulsome in their praise of his work as Director General of the Ordnance. Spenser Wilkinson, a renowned writer on military matters and the first Chichele Professor of Military History, wrote a glowing tribute in the *Morning Post*:

> So it came about that on him devolved the responsibility, at a time of unprecedented stress and emergency, of making good the alarming deficiencies in warlike stores of all kinds which became apparent as soon as the conflict with the Boers developed into a test of our preparation for war far severer than anybody had foreseen. He was now in his element. While many of his old campaigning associates and numberless officers far junior to him in rank were gaining distinction in the face of the enemy, the Director-General of Ordnance was labouring untiringly and with remarkable results to furnish them with the means of carrying on their operations, was overcoming difficulties of no common order arising out of previous years of improvident parsimony, and was effectually solving problems which might well have proved beyond the capacity of a less resolute man.[16]

---

15 Field Marshal Lord Carver, *The National Army Museum book of The Boer War* (London: Pan Books, 2000), p.259. 'The Lesson' by Rudyard Kipling, first published in *The Times*, 29th July 1901.
16 *The Morning Post*, 21st August 1914.

Wilkinson was a knowledgeable judge of such matters and his praise is not to be taken lightly. He makes an interesting point regarding 'old campaigning associates' and 'junior officers' and one does have to wonder whether there was a part of Brackenbury that wished he could have taken the field. This desire for active service in war is one which generations of civilians have struggled to understand. It is not to say that Brackenbury wanted war or gloried in it. He had seen enough of the, as he once put it, "seamy side of war" to have no illusions about it. Let us not forget that he had seen the horrors of the Franco-Prussian War at close hand and in particular the wounded in the hospitals. To put it simply it was his job and the profession to which he had devoted his life. It would have been the ultimate test of his skills, his training, and his experience. This was particularly so given that an important factor in the success of the war would be logistics, and how geographical and climatic difficulties were dealt with. Brackenbury may well have found himself equally 'in his element' in the field. Had he not been occupying such an important and prestigious office one wonders whether Lord Roberts might have sought his services when he was sent to take over operations in South Africa. We have already seen that even before they worked together so well in India, Roberts had been considering the possibility of employing Brackenbury as his Chief of Staff.

Whatever the likelihood of such events they ignore the fact that he was needed where he was, and had extremely important, if somewhat overlooked, work to do. Perhaps Lord Wolseley put it best in a letter to Brackenbury in July 1901 when he wrote:

> What Wonders you have effected since you came into office! When I think of the state we were in before your advent to your present position and compare it with what you tell me in your letters I scarcely know how much the country owes you.[17]

Brackenbury continued in office as Director General of Ordnance until January 1904. Despite all the stresses and strains he had reached the end of his five year tenure of office. It also marked the point at which he retired from the army. After forty-eight years in the army he retired in February 1904 aged sixty-six. Towards the end of his time at the War Office there was the suggestion that he should sit with Lord Esher and Admiral Sir John Fisher on the War Office Reconstitution Committee, more commonly referred to as the Esher Committee. According to General Sir Thomas Kelly-Kenny, at that time Adjutant-General, the Secretary of State for War St John Brodrick had recommended that this be "a council of three

---

17 Wolseley to Brackenbury, 6th July 1901, private collection. It is worth pointing out that by this time Wolseley had retired as Commander-in-Chief, in a somewhat acrimonious manner, and so was only aware of the goings on at the War Office through his communications with former colleagues such as Brackenbury.

you, Esher and Fisher".[18] One has to question whether his health could have stood the extra strain. Only a year after his retirement Brackenbury was too ill to accept Lord Roberts invitation to attend the Military Administration Committee. Had he spent the majority of 1904 sitting on the Esher Committee it could well have been the end of him.

## Retirement

It is perhaps unsurprising that after he retired his health began to pick up for a time. Although he had always been ambitious, and a devoted servant to the army and the state, he settled into retirement quite easily. He had now retired to Nice in the south of France with his second wife. If there was ever a part of him that regretted leaving the service he never made any mention of it. He had cause to be satisfied with his career when looking back on it. There must have been mixed emotions about the fact that the Army now had a Chief of Staff. On the one hand the position he had been campaigning for since 1867 was now established, but unfortunately he was not the first Chief of Staff, and it is logical to conclude that he regretted this. However, in the final years of his career it is clear that he was looking forward to retirement, not least of all because his health was failing him. After almost fifty years of hard work it was clear that he yearned for rest. There is also a degree to which he wanted to enjoy the happiness he had found with his new wife; a happiness he never enjoyed with his first. It also appears that he had no major financial problems, and could enjoy his retirement in comfort. Strange as it may sound part of his financial freedom came from the fact that he no longer had to 'keep up appearances' as an officer in the army. Although mainly residing in France he did return to Britain from time to time, retaining his flat in Queen Anne's Mansions. Indeed, his retirement was envied by some. Lord Lansdowne, in a letter written in December 1909, tells Brackenbury "How I envy you your escape from the atmosphere climatic and political which we are weathering". This has the feel of a letter between two old friends, discussing as it does politics, the forthcoming general election, and their health. There will always be a suggestion that many people appeared friendly with Brackenbury whilst he was in office and was 'useful' to them. Whilst this might be the case in some instances it is clearly not relevant to the relationship with Lord and Lady Lansdowne, which continued for the remainder of Henry's life with genuine affection.[19]

---

18   Kelly-Kenny to Brackenbury, 25th September 1903, private collection.
19   Lansdowne to Brackenbury, 6th December 1909, private collection. It is interesting to note that in this letter Lansdowne believes that in the January election that "they [Conservative and Unionists] will lose, but not be beaten to badly". As it was they gained 116 seats, mostly from the Liberals, and repaired much of the damage done in 1906 when they had lost 246 seats. The result in 1910 was a

Henry Brackenbury in retirement, circa 1909. This photograph was used for his book *Some Memories of My Spare Time*. (Private collection)

In retirement he started to write again, most notably *Some Memories of My Spare Time*. This was initially serialised in *Blackwood's Magazine* before been published as a book in 1909 by the same company. On 17th April 1914, with his health failing fast, Brackenbury recorded a final message to his friends:

> My dear friends, you have been very good to me and I cannot tell you how much your gifts of flowers have been loved by me. Edith will tell you personally what I have felt about each of you. God bless you all.

Three days later he died. *The Times* recorded that this was after a short illness, but the reality was that he had been ill for almost fourteen years, during which time his strength had come and gone at various intervals. In 1910 his nephew, Hereward Irenius Brackenbury, recorded that Henry was "often too unwell for visitors".[20] Yet he lived for another four years.

There followed a series of tributes in every leading newspaper and magazine. Many rushed to pay tribute to a man who had worked tirelessly behind the scenes. Mention has already been made of Spenser Wilkinson's tribute in *The Morning Post*. He also wrote to Lady Brackenbury:

> May I add the expression of my sympathy with you in your bereavement and the hope that you are maintained by the knowledge that your husband

---

hung parliament and a Liberal government supported in coalition by 82 Irish MPs.
20   His final words are found in the private collection written in what is presumably Edith Brackenbury's handwriting. Hereward Irenius Brackenbury to Lady Edith Brackenbury, 27th January 1910, private collection.

was the ablest soldier of his day and that his services to England though not much known by the public were fully appreciated by those who had the means of knowing.[21]

Many people wrote to Lady Brackenbury paying their respects and offering their condolences.[22] None would have been more welcome than that from His Majesty George V who sent a telegram which read "I am grieved to hear of the heavy sorrow which has befallen you, and, with the whole Army, regret the loss of so distinguished an officer as Sir Henry Brackenbury".[23] Lady Lytton, whom Brackenbury had known from his days in India, also wrote to Lady Brackenbury expressing their regret and simply adding "We mourn with you and England on a great loss".[24] *The Daily Telegraph* recorded on 21st April 1914 that, "With a sorrow which will be widely shared we have to announce the death of General Sir Henry Brackenbury". Further on in its tribute it made the observation that "The War Office still lacks a department of military history, though the section of the staff charged with the service of information has now days its proper status and value. In those matters the nation owes much to General Brackenbury". This obviously referred to his time as Head of the Intelligence Branch, and whilst quite true is perhaps an unusual way of putting it. Perhaps again it is Wilkinson in his article in *The Morning Post* who better explains the whole significance of Brackenbury's career and legacy.

> It is the senior officers of the army to-day who best know how great were Henry Brackenbury's services to the country and how great the talents which enabled him to perform them.

Although his funeral and burial were in Nice, France, a memorial service was held in St George's Church, Hanover Square, London on 24th April. This was largely so that his friends and former colleagues who could not get to France had the opportunity to pay their respects. Unfortunately even some of his closest friends were unable to attend what appeared a hurriedly arranged event. This was largely to accommodate the War Office whilst all its officers happened to be in London. As a result Lord Lansdowne was unable to attend. In a letter to Lady Brackenbury it is clear that he deeply regretted this. "In India and at the War Office I was closely connected with him, and my admiration for his ability and powers of work was unbounded. I found in him a loyal colleague and an invaluable adviser. What the War Office would have done without him during the dark days of the South African

---

21  Spenser Wilkinson to Lady Edith Brackenbury, private collection. This letter is undated but is clearly just after Henry's death so was likely written between late April and early May 1914.
22  Although Henry's first wife (Emilia or 'Milly') technically became Lady Brackenbury when he was first knighted, the term is often used merely for his second wife (Edith). Certainly this is the case within the documents of the Brackenbury family and was presumably done to make it easy to differentiate between the two.
23  George V to Lady Edith Brackenbury, 22nd April 1914, private collection.
24  Lady Edith Lytton to Lady Edith Brackenbury, 24th April 1914, private collection.

War I do not know".[25] The Hymns included *Now Labourer's task is o'er, Lead kindly light* and *The Lord is my Shepherd.* The service concluded with Chopin's funeral march.

In early May 1914 Major-General Sir Stanley von Donop, the Master-General of the Ordnance, wrote to Lady Brackenbury that "I have been requested by Lord Roberts to write and tell you that he proposes, subject to your approval, to convene a meeting for the purpose of forming a committee to raise a memorial to the late Sir Henry Brackenbury".[26] There is perhaps something of an irony in the fact that it is Roberts who proposes and undertakes this venture given the supposed rivalry between the Roberts and Wolseley 'rings'. It is another example of the respect that Roberts had for Brackenbury. The memorial fund with Lord Roberts as President and Lord Methuen as Chairman raised the sum of £507 3s 4d, almost £28,000 in modern money, for a permanent memorial. In June 1915 a plaque was placed on a pillar in St George's Garrison Church, Woolwich. Given his close association with Woolwich it was perhaps the most appropriate site. It simply read "Sacred to the memory of General the Right Hon. Sir Henry Brackenbury, G.C.B., K.C.S.I."[27]

---

25   Lord Lansdowne to Lady Edith Brackenbury, 26th April 1914, private collection.
26   Major-General Sir Stanley Von Donop to Lady Edith Brackenbury, 6th May 1914, private collection.
27   The exact status of this plaque is uncertain. The Royal Artillery Museum holds the records book for the Church and lists the unveiling of the plaque in 1915 and that it was added to by the family in 1933, although exactly what was added is not recorded, and no one in the Brackenbury family today is aware of what happened. During World War Two the Church was largely destroyed by bombing. Some of the plaques have been removed but it is unclear as to the status of Sir Henry Brackenbury's. After consultation with the authorities responsible I am still unable to identify the exact status of the memorial.

# Chapter 34

# Conclusion and Assessment

This book started with a quote from the 17th Earl of Derby and in conclusion we return to the same speech in the House of Lords in 1916 with a quotation that illustrates the intellectual and tactical astuteness of Henry Brackenbury alongside the quite visionary nature of the man.

> There had been a discussion—I do not know whether my noble friend remembers it—at the time when there was a reckless fit of economy after the Boer War, on the subject of the provision of sheds, I think at Aldershot, for dirigible balloons. I had taken the line of opposing them as being an unnecessary expense. Sir Henry Brackenbury came to my room and insisted. I have never forgotten the words he used. He said— "I wish you would help me to get this through. I shall not live to see it. You may. But I believe that England is more in danger from the air than she has ever been since the Spanish Armada." That seemed to me the most extraordinary foresight.[1]

The original conversation referred to in the speech was in 1903. The statement in the House of Lords was two years after Henry Brackenbury's death. Even then it could not have been known how prophetic his words would be as dirigible balloons gave way to aeroplanes as the means of aerial bombardment. Perhaps even Henry Brackenbury did not realise the full significance of what he said and just how far that threat from the air would go in the future, but it is clear than he had identified a future tactical threat and that even at the twilight of his career he still had a tactical vision ahead of his time. To the end of his career he remained a visionary.

---

[1] *Hansard*, House of Lords Debate 23rd May 1916, Volume 22 cc101-126.

## Conclusion and Assessment

In many ways this illustrates the ability he would have shown as a Chief of Staff. On a material level he could appreciate new technology and how it would alter the battlefield. One only needs to think of his introduction of a quick firing gun, the experimentation with bicycles, the use of traction engines to tow artillery, and it is clear what he could have achieve if he had been a Chief of Staff with even greater authority to shape the army. It is pure speculation, but one cannot help but wonder how different things would have been had the recommendations of the Hartington Commission been put in to practice and Brackenbury had been appointed Chief of Staff in the run up to the South African War.

It is difficult to assess the full impact of Henry Brackenbury's career and his legacy. He was clearly an extremely significant figure both in terms of his achievements but in wider terms of what he represented. He was one of the first of a new breed of officer: A staff officer in the best sense of the word. His skills of organisation, planning, and an ability to prepare was becoming more and more important in an era when tactical and technological changes had altered the nature of military planning and battlefield conduct. This was an era in which railways, the telegraph, the telephone, and even early motorised vehicles and aircraft were starting to alter the way battles were fought, to say nothing of the technological advances in weaponry such as machine guns, magazine rifles, breech-loading weapons, and so on. Indeed the army was slowly moving away from the era of Commander-in-Chief to Chief of Staff. In truth there was room for both. A Commander-in-Chief could in effect become the senior commander of the field army training it for war and ultimately leading it on campaign whereas a Chief of Staff would fight a war from the War Office, keep the commander in the field supplied and equipped, deal with the wider elements of strategy, plan future operations, and coordinate all departments of the army. For the latter role Brackenbury was ideally suited. His ability to organise was never better illustrated than during the South African War. It is testament to his skill and ability that he kept the army supplied and maintained despite all the problems and the fact that the conflict went far beyond anything ever previously planned for.

It would be wrong to dismiss completely Wolseley's suspicions over Brackenbury's championing of a Chief of Staff. Clearly he was ambitious, and he realised that in 1890 when the Hartington Commission proposed it, he was the logical choice. There was obviously personal ambition, and perhaps a degree of arrogance, but also a sense that this was where he could best serve the army and the state. However it would be wrong to ignore the fact that he had been recommending the creation of a Chief of Staff for many years. The first public record of this is in 1867 in his fifth article on Military Reform for *Fraser's Magazine* but one presumes that it was not a new idea to him even then. It must also be remembered that he probably envisaged a situation where in any future conflict he 'fought' from the War Office whilst a Wolseley-type figure led the army in the field. This would have been the best use of their skills. Whilst Brackenbury's writing and his lectures showed that he understood military tactics and how to control an army on the battlefield, there is a great distance between the theory and the practice. We will never know whether he could have put his knowledge into practice on the battlefield. Had the River Column been required to fight a battle after Brackenbury assumed command we might have a better idea, however the important role Brackenbury played in the tactical victory of Kirbekan should not be underestimated. What we do see clearly illustrated from his command of the river column is his ability to organise an army in the field. He led the column from a logistical and administrative point extremely well in very difficult circumstances.

William. C. Beaver makes an interesting remark in relation to this when stating that, "Brackenbury was acknowledged to be the brightest officer in the Army and Wolseley was very jealous of him, despite the fact that Brackenbury had been in his Ashanti ring".[2] There is perhaps something to the idea that Wolseley was jealous of Brackenbury, although it would be unwise to make too much of it. Perhaps in some ways it was a realisation that Brackenbury's style of professional officer, a staff officer and Chief of Staff, was the future. Since the reorganisation of the War Office during and after the Crimean War the 'senior' soldier in the army was becoming more and more of an administrator rather than a field commander. It might also be argued that Wolseley's admiration of Brackenbury's capacity for work, his sagacity and general ability, was in the form of envy if not quite jealously. In short Brackenbury could work and operate in a way that Wolseley could not.

As we have seen, Henry Brackenbury had a long and varied career. Although he would have liked to have reached the position of Chief of Staff, it can be said that in many ways he had reached the peak of his profession by the end of his career, and few would have predicted that someone whose main strength was administration would become a full General. He followed a common route into the army, being a younger son of a minor landowning and professional family with something of a military tradition. However the career that followed was far from conventional. His administrative, literary and active service achievements would have stood out individually. His education was a common enough path for a young officer, Tonbridge, Eton and then Woolwich. However, between Eton and Woolwich Brackenbury had an experience which undoubtedly affected his approach to his future career. The almost two years that Brackenbury spent in a notary's office in Quebec had a profound effect on him. That period immersed in a business, indeed professional, atmosphere gave him an experience that few of his contemporaries had. Most officers went straight from education to the army. Brackenbury had a wider experience. Not only had

---

2   Beaver, William C., 'The Intelligence Division Library 1854-1902', *Journal of Library History* 11/3 (July 1976).

he travelled to part of the empire, he had worked in a profession. He had knowledge of the wider world, and was not blinkered to simply the life of the 'gentry' or soldiering. Although his time there was relatively brief it obviously went a long way to explaining his professional approach to work, and study.

Given this early professional experience, which obviously held some interest for him, it could be considered somewhat surprising that he entered upon a career in the army. It was not the obvious port of call for a young man with a professional approach to work. It is likely that the reason for his decision was very much linked to his family history. As he wrote, in 1899, "In three generations sprang from my grandfather, who was himself a soldier, we have given twelve officers to the army including two generals".[3] This was an obvious family link. Both his father and uncle had been soldiers in the Peninsular War, and as his father died when Henry was only six years old, his military career was probably the part of his life he knew best. Indeed almost every reference that Henry makes to his father in his literary work is prefaced or followed by the observation that he was a Peninsular War veteran, a fact that clearly he took pride in. We must also remember that in the era Henry grew up the Napoleonic Wars would still have been very relevant and within living memory of many people. More than that, it was the largest conflict that Britain had ever been involved in up to that point. An attempt to emulate his father, and uncle, was perhaps part of his motivation for joining the army, as was the recent commissioning of his brother Charles into the Royal Artillery.

The other influence that Charles had upon him was his literary work. Whilst the other reasons for embarking on a literary career have already been examined, such as using his spare time constructively, and financial gain, the fact that he had seen his brother rise in importance due to his literary career, particularly as a war correspondent, was obviously appealing. It must have played a role in his desire to see the Franco-Prussian War at first hand. Initially he witnessed it as a 'tourist', then he wrote about it from London, including the 'Diary of the War', and finally he was right at the front working for the National Aid Society. There were obviously other motives behind his work, such as patriotism, the chance to enhance his administrative credentials and experience, but there was also a clear desire to help his own career advancement.

Henry Brackenbury was an ambitious and practical man. In his Sudan campaign journal Wolseley remarked of Brackenbury that, "... he is very able and will serve you with real interest and great ability as long as he thinks that doing so will be to his advantage. He has 'Greek' blood in him and consequently does not know what loyalty to any man – except to himself – can possibly mean or why it should be cultivated in man".[4] Whilst perhaps a little exaggerated, there is some truth in Wolseley's

3   Brackenbury, Henry, *A Letter about the Family of Brackenbury* (London: Blackwood's, 1899).
4   Wolseley's Sudan Campaign Journal 31st December 1884, National Archives, WO147/8.

comments. One sees in Brackenbury a man who was determined to rise as high as he could and to get there he would 'use' people to advance himself. Indeed, it was the only way he could get on. He had no power, wealth or influence of his own. Nor was he the sort of soldier, despite his talents in this direction, who could make himself a legend on the battlefield.

So yes, he did rise firstly on the coat tails of Wolseley, and then to an extent Roberts and Lord Lansdowne. However it would be wrong to believe that this was not a reciprocal arrangement. Wolseley did not employ Brackenbury simply out of the goodness of his heart, or because of philanthropic motivates to help a talented but unrecognised young officer. Wolseley 'used' Brackenbury for his talents as an administrator, as a man whose skill in this direction helped to enhance the Wolseley legend. To an extent the same could be said of Roberts, who also got an 'inside-man' in the British, as opposed to Indian based, army. Even Lansdowne, with whom there was no doubt a genuine friendship and warmth, used Brackenbury as a military expert and trouble-shooter. The pressure on and criticism of Lansdowne would have been far greater than it was if he had not had Brackenbury to shoulder so much of the burden during the South African War. Yet at the same time we see a suggestion of his selfish streak. When Lansdowne was being publically criticised for his conduct as Secretary of State, with the journalist W.T. Stead even going so far as to suggest he should be tried for treason, he wrote to Brackenbury that "I need not say how glad I should be if, some day or other, you should think it worthwhile to 'tell the truth'".[5] This is clearly a plea to a friend for help when read in the context of the fierce debate and criticism of Lansdowne that was going on at the time. With the letter being written in 1903 it is understandable that Brackenbury did not feel it proper to write in defence of Lord Lansdowne, as he was still a serving officer. Surely Lansdowne would have understood that, but he must have been disappointed that someone who had worked closely with him, was his friend, and knew just how difficult the situation was, never took up his pen to defend the actions of Lansdowne. Perhaps it was simply a continuance of Brackenbury's desire to keep clear of politics. However it fits in with Wolseley assessment of a man who would only do what was "... to his own advantage".

This brings us to the nature of Brackenbury's ambition. It is hard to see exactly what his ambition was. This is where the lack of private papers for the early period of his life is a problem, as we get no clear picture of whether he initially embarked upon his military career as a means to an end. In short did he intend to make his reputation in the army and then make his 'fortune' elsewhere? This was a common enough occurrence during this period. If that was the original plan it is interesting that he did not leave the army on the occasions that his career appeared to have

---

[5] Lord Lansdowne to Brackenbury, 10th September 1903, private collection.

stalled. If we therefore presume that he always intended to remain in the army and if, as he said, his "heart was in the army" then what was his ambition?[6] It is clear that from day one he is attempting to advance his career, something which will be better understood by the modern reader than his contemporaries. His desire, indeed desperation, to see active service should be seen in this light. It was in the field that reputations were made, and the system of promoting officers to high office as a reward for service in the field was to continue for many years. His own career would illustrate this as it was only after his success as a field commander in the Sudan that he was finally appointed to the War Office staff. His literary career was also an attempt to advance his career, and was another way he could get noticed.

Wolseley would later accuse Brackenbury of self-interest and a lack of loyalty and gratitude concerning his military career. There was undoubtedly truth behind this. Wolseley remained convinced that those who had been part of the 'ring' owed him an undying debt of gratitude. However all of them to a lesser or greater extent had made their own careers after his initial help. As has already been said, Wolseley had equal right to be grateful to those members of his ring who had helped to make his name by their support of his campaigns, and Brackenbury had played a key role in making sure that his campaigns had run smoothly and successfully. Brackenbury was never afraid to use whatever influence he could to help his career along. Active service and writing were all means to an end. Wolseley's comments always need to be taken with a pinch of salt, particularly during the Gordon Relief Expedition. At this time Wolseley was ill, initially with dysentery but one can also trace the beginning of his mental decline. He was also an increasingly worried man as the campaign appeared to unravelled and ultimately cost the life of one of only two men Wolseley ever referred to as his hero.[7] As was mentioned in the introduction, his criticism of all his staff is scathing but contradictory.

Brackenbury also made great use of his political connections. There were several occasions when he used such links to try and obtain future employment in the army. His three key administrative appointments were very much the result of political influence rather than military. His appointment at the Intelligence Branch owed a great deal to the intervention of W.H. Smith the newly appointed, but short-lived, Secretary of State for War. On returning from the Sudan he had found himself promoted to Major-General, but unemployed. Brackenbury had used his friendship with the future Lord Egerton, at that time Conservative M.P. for Mid-Cheshire, to canvas the support of W.H. Smith for employment at the War Office. Brackenbury recorded that W.H. Smith had said that he "had his eye on Brackenbury" and was keen to employ him at the War Office.[8] At the same time he was trying to use

---

6 Brackenbury to Wolseley, 4th February 1883, Wolseley Papers, Hove Central Library.
7 The other somewhat surprisingly was the Confederate General Robert E Lee.
8 Brackenbury to Wolseley, 13th August 1885, Wolseley Papers, Hove Central Library.

military contacts to find employment, but without success. Wolseley had tried to have him appointed Deputy Adjutant General and Lord Roberts had been keen to employ him in India. Neither had been successful. It was also political influence, at Brackenbury's prompting, that obtained his appointment as Military Member in India. He had become concerned that his recent activities, particularly on the Hartington Commission had alienated him from much of the army, particularly Wolseley and the Duke of Cambridge. Brackenbury believed, somewhat justifiably, that his career was over, and that he would simply be reduced to half-pay and not employed again. One can see through his correspondence with Stanhope that he was using all his political contacts to obtain future employment. Knowing that the appointment in India would soon be vacant he wrote to Lord Salisbury, W.H. Smith, Stanhope and Lord Knutsford, urging them all to support his case by writing to Lord Cross, Secretary of State for India.[9] It is perhaps a mark of his standing by this point that some of the most powerful men in the government were all prepared to write on his behalf, including the Prime Minister. This again leads weight to the argument that it was the politicians who truly appreciated his skills and achievements. Even his final appointment as Director General of Ordnance owed a great deal to political support. The relationship he had built up with Lord Lansdowne, when the latter was Viceroy of India, played a key part in the decision to appoint Brackenbury.

His use of such contacts and influence does suggest a somewhat 'pushy' individual. This was perhaps true, but it could be argued that he did not really have an alternative. He had no power, or influence of his own. He was not a Wolseley or Roberts with a great reputation gained on the battlefield, nor did he have the connections and background of either the Duke of Cambridge or the Duke of Connaught. He was in a difficult position. His real skill lay away from the battlefield. Even his active service career illustrates this. The key work he did was before the battle, it might even be argued before the campaign, in making sure that the preparation had been done and that the army took the field in the best condition. Even when he commanded the River Column in the Sudan it helped him that it was more a logistical battle than anything else. This was a vital part of a campaign, and indeed soldiering in general, but it was often ignored.

His ideal appointment would have been Chief of Staff. As head of a General Staff he could have planned for future operations, sorted out the administrative system of the army, improved the staff system and generally improved the efficiency of the army. When one sees the improvements in the Intelligence Branch, the Indian Army, and the Ordnance Department, he was able to achieve it can be considered a tragedy that he had not been appointed Chief of Staff in 1891, in line with the Hartington Commission's recommendation, and given the chance in the next eight

---

[9] Brackenbury to Stanhope, 3rd November 1890 and 6th November 1890, Stanhope Papers, Centre for Kentish Studies.

years before the South African War to have put right much of what was to cause the army and the nation such distress and loss of life in South Africa. To this end it is worth repeating the words of the Esher Committee of 1904 that:

> We unhesitatingly assert that if the recommendations of the majority of the Hartington Commission had not been ignored, the country would have been saved the loss of many thousands of lives, and of many millions of pounds, subsequently sacrificed in the South African War ... Upon many material points we have done no more than adopt and develop the principles laid down by the Hartington Commission, especially as regards the creation of the branch of a Chief of the General Staff.[10]

Brackenbury was an intellectually gifted officer. His administrative skills were just one part of this. His ability, and more importantly his willingness, to think and study his profession make him stand out in an era when this was not generally the case. The work of Brian Bond and Gwyn Harries Jenkins illustrate just how unusual this was and the work of Edward Spiers has illustrated that even the more gifted officers turned to the army as a last resort, having failed to enter the civil service, at home or in India, or university or even the legal profession.[11] However this was an era of change, albeit gradual. The rise of such organisations as the United Service Institute illustrated that there was a growth in study. Yet Brackenbury's hope that the officer would study his profession in the same way as someone did for the law or medicine was still someway off.

In Brackenbury it can be argued that we see something of a new style of officer. He was the first officer of truly intellectual leanings to reach high office. Whilst Wolseley recognised the importance of study, he was more inclined to have others do it for him, hence that men like Maurice and Brackenbury were sometimes referred to as 'the pen of Wolseley'. Certainly no one had ever achieved such high officer who had written so much concerning his profession. More than this Brackenbury's administrative abilities meant that he was able to put his ideas into practice when in positions of power. In this way his time at the Intelligence Branch is key. The emphasis was on, study, hard work and professionalism. By doing this he was able to produce an end product that, as we have seen, was on a par with that of their German counterpart, despite the latter's greater manpower and money. Key in this was his appointment of equally professional individuals. It is important to

---

10 *Report of the War Office Reconstitution Committee* [Esher Committee] Part I (London: H.M.S.O, 1904), p.161.
11 This is a continuing theme throughout Brian Bond's work but in particular in 'The Late Victorian Army', *History Today* 11:9 (Sept 1961). In Gwyn Harries-Jenkins' *The Army in Victorian Society* (Trowbridge: Kegan Paul Ltd, 1977), this is a constant theme, but in particular Chapter 5. Spiers, Edward, *The Late Victorian Army 1868-1903* (Manchester: Manchester University Press, 1992) chapter 4.

emphasise the role Brackenbury played in the early careers of many of the future leaders of the army. It was he who gave the likes of Robertson, Wilson, Gleichen, Wolfe Murray, Grierson and others their first chance to really prove themselves at the War Office. From reading their accounts of him you can see that they admired and looked up to him. In many ways he had developed his own 'ring', handpicking his own staff out of those best suited for the role.

The fact that Brackenbury, or a member of his family, failed to write an autobiography dealing with his military career mean that most of his own thoughts have been lost. It would have been intriguing to have read his account of the work he did at the Intelligence Branch, in India and as Director General of Ordnance. The fact that at some point in the future he did not perhaps contradicts the view that he was a self-publicist who sought to exaggerate his importance. The problem of this is that to a large extent we have to go on the accounts left by others. Had he himself left a record of the achievements of his career this could have been read, analysed and criticised by historians. Too often his point of view is lost and has been replaced in the historiography by another person's view about him. Despite the fact that his final appointment at the War Office meant that his career had reached par with Evelyn Wood or Redvers Buller, in that he was a member of the Army Council and holder of one of the top jobs at the War Office, his achievements have gone unrecorded. The factor of no children and that many of his papers have remained in a private collection probably explains a lot.

The reforms he had put in place in the Intelligence Branch and Ordnance Department paid dividends during the South African War. Indeed, the few areas of the army that came out of the war with any credit attached to them owed it largely to Brackenbury. The mobilisations scheme worked extremely well, and the ease and efficiency of it was a surprise to all. Whilst Ardagh deserved credit for the work he had done in fine-tuning the scheme, it was essentially Brackenbury's scheme that allowed the army to mobilise and deploy to South Africa with such relative ease and the same scheme, again with minor changes, that took the B.E.F. to France in 1914. It was his perseverance with the scheme, despite many problems, that had brought it to fruition. Although strongly criticised at the time the Royal Commissions into the war exonerated the Intelligence Branch. They found that the intelligence provided had been extremely accurate and that it was a failure higher up the chain of command that was to blame. The accuracy of their reports was a credit to the reforms and system of intelligence gathering that Brackenbury had introduced.

Even his work at the Ordnance Department was a successful part of the war. Given all the problems faced it is remarkable that the department, and the supply system in general, did not collapse under the strain of the conflict. That it worked as well as it did was down to the reforms that Brackenbury was able to introduce during the war itself. As Wolseley recorded:

> Had he never accomplished anything else for the State than the great service he rendered England throughout our recent and curiously prolonged war in South Africa, he might indeed be well satisfied with what he had done for his country. I do not know an officer who could have performed equally well the heavy and responsible duties which fell to his lot at the War Office during the last three years.[12]

In looking at the life and military career of Henry Brackenbury it is quite clear that here was a man of great intelligence, brilliant administrative skill and with an understanding of tactical, technical and scientific military matters that was beyond many of his contemporaries. Even within the group of bright young officers that formed the 'Wolseley ring' his ability stood out. His literary career was extraordinary, and the amount of material he produced was almost akin to that of a professional journalist. Indeed there were times when his writing seemed to take up more of his time than his military work. Yet his literary output should not be viewed as the product of a lifetime. Indeed his literary career only began in 1865 and by 1878 he was no longer writing regularly. After that year he only contributed occasional articles and books. The value of his literary career to both his financial security and career advancement cannot be ignored. As Brackenbury wrote "I attribute to a great extent whatever measure of success I had in my profession to it".[13] It was his literary work that led to his being asked to work for the National Aid Society, and this and his literary work brought him to the attention of Wolseley. As a consequence he enjoyed a considerable active service career that would have been the envy of many of his contemporaries. This in turn led to his opportunity to undertake key administrative positions in the War Office and India.

The career of Henry Brackenbury illustrates the period of change that the army was undertaking. Had he been in the army a generation before he would have found it almost impossible to reach the heights he did. Had he been born a generation later he would have played a key role in the development of the army up to World War One. A generation later and his abilities might have been more greatly appreciated. Men of a similar style, such as Wilson, Grierson, Gleichen, Callwell and Robertson are an example of this. It also seems highly likely that he would undoubtedly have been Chief of the General Staff. This was the ideal appointment for him. His championing of the creation of such a position was obviously, and naturally, partly motivated by a desire to fill such a post. However to say this was the sole reason for his campaigning

---

12  Wolseley, Field Marshal Viscount, *The Story of a Soldier's Life* Volume 2 (London: Constable & Co, 1903), p.281.
13  Brackenbury, Henry, *Some Memories of My Spare Time*, p.354.

would be to do him an injustice and would also ignored the fact that it was in the best interest of the army to have one. Britain was the last major power to create a General Staff, even though the need had been visible for some time. It took the South African War to finally prove the necessity of such a body. It was indeed ironic that the office of Commander-in-Chief was abolished and a Chief of Staff created in its place only a matter of months after Brackenbury retired from the army.

The day after his death *The Times* recorded that:

> By the death of General Right Hon. Sir Henry Brackenbury, P.C., G.C.B., K.C.B., K.C.S.I., formerly Director-General of Ordnance and Colonel Commandant of the Regiment of Royal Artillery, which occurred in Nice yesterday, the Army loses the services of one of the most able of its officers of senior rank.[14]

Indeed it was right that he should be called one of the ablest officers of senior rank, and it illustrated now far he had come. The Intelligence Branch had taken his profile to another level. His time in India was such a success that his name was being mentioned, although not by him, as a possible Commander-in-Chief in India. He had received high praise for his role in the South African War. Much of what he had campaigned for in military reform had been vindicated by the South African War. There was now a mandate to carry out such reform.

His achievements were recognised at the time, but years of neglect by historians mean that his role has largely been forgotten. Indeed he had been relegated to just one of the 'Wolseley ring'. This biography has illustrated that he was far more than that and should be recognised as such. His importance to the army and the state was above his connection with Wolseley. Brackenbury was a man who became important in his own right, and had a career that deserves to stand out on its own merit. Had he become Chief of Staff it is certain that he would be extremely well known to historians. He might even have been an English von Moltke or von Schlieffen. However we shall never know. His administrative skills would have been put to great use had he been Chief of Staff in the years leading up to the South African War and World War One.

More than anything else Brackenbury's career illustrated that it was possible for a man of high intellect, learning and limited financial means to achieve high office in the late Victorian British army. To say he was a trailblazer is perhaps a slight exaggeration but the vital role in encouraging young officers of a similar leaning, and proving that they could reach the heights of the army should not be underestimated. Many of those young officers who served under him praised his example. It is disappointing that neither Ardagh or Grierson wrote autobiographies as the two

---

14   *The Times*, 21st April 1914.

men were closer to Brackenbury, in professional terms at least, than any other, and could in a way be called his protégés.

On mere length of service alone, some forty-eight years, Henry Brackenbury's career is worthy of note and despite the many problems with undertaking such a study, it is still slightly surprising that no work about his military career and life has, until now, been written. This is especially so when one considers the many, and varied, areas in which he served and the significant events for both the army and the state in which he was closely involved. That Brackenbury achieved such a career, given his modest private means and the fact that he supplemented his pay through considerable literary work, again makes his life all the more interesting and significant. This, added to his ability to write, and to write well, his zeal for his work, both literary and military and the careful study of his profession make it no surprise that he was in many ways 'The Thinking Man's Soldier'.

# Appendix I

### Timeline of the Career of General Sir Henry Brackenbury

| | |
|---|---|
| 1837 | Born on 1st September at Bolingbroke Hall, Lincolnshire. Fourth son of William and Maria Brackenbury. |
| 1838 | Family move to Usselby Hall, Lincolnshire. |
| 1842 | Henry's father is left paralysed by a stroke. |
| 1843 | Family move to Ahascreagh, Ireland. |
| 1844 | William Brackenbury dies. |
| 1846–49 | Henry attends Tonbridge School. |
| 1850–52 | Attends Eton. |
| 1852–54 | Training in legal profession under Her Majesty's Notary in Quebec, Mr Archibald Campbell. |
| 1853 | Commission as Ensign in the Seventh battalion of the Quebec Militia. |
| 1854 | Sits exam for Royal Military Academy, Woolwich. Passed with fifth highest score. Joins as gentleman cadet and is appointed senior under officer. |
| 1856 | Commission Lieutenant in the Royal Artillery. Appointed to garrison artillery, Plymouth. |
| 1857 | Sails for India in August as part of force to suppress the Mutiny. |
| 1858 | Sees first action at Battle of Banda. Invalided home later that year. |
| 1860 | Appointed Adjutant of Royal Artillery in the western district. |
| 1861 | Married Emila Morley (died 1905). |
| 1862 | Appointed Lieutenant of Company of gentleman cadets at Royal Military Academy Woolwich. |
| 1864 | Appointed Assistant Instructor in Artillery at Royal Military Academy, Woolwich. |
| 1866 | Promoted to Captain in August. |
| 1868 | Appointed Professor of Military History at Royal Military Academy, Woolwich. |
| 1869 | Promoted to Major in April. |

# Appendix I

| | |
|---|---|
| 1870–71 | Service for the National Aid Society during Franco-Prussian War. Awarded Iron Cross and Legion of Honour. |
| 1873–74 | Served in Ashanti Campaign as Military Secretary to Wolseley. |
| 1874 | Garrison Artillery at Sheerness. |
| 1875 | Went to Natal serving as Military Secretary to Wolseley as Governor and High Commissioner. |
| 1875 | Returns to England Promoted to brevet Lieutenant Colonel and placed in command of depot at Woolwich. |
| 1877 | Given command of garrison battery at Dover. |
| 1878 | In May 1878 moved with his battery to Newhaven. |
| 1878 | In July goes to Cyprus with Wolseley. Brackenbury appointed Assistant Adjutant and Quartermaster of force. In August appointed Chief Commandant of Police and inspector of Prisons. |
| 1879 | Appointed Military Secretary to Wolseley as the latter travels to take command in Zulu War. In September as Chief of Staff plans campaign against Chief Sekukuni. Made a Brevet Colonel. |
| 1880 | Appointed Private Secretary to Viceroy of India, Lord Lytton. Continued in this appointment until August of that year. |
| 1881 | Appointed Military Attaché in Paris. |
| 1882 | Arrives in Ireland to take over command of Police, with exact title still unknown. Later given position of Assistant Under Secretary for Police and Crime. Position ends badly and is placed on half-pay, and returned to regiment with rank of Major. |
| 1883 | Appointed to command of garrison artillery in Gibraltar. Promoted Lieutenant-Colonel, and brevet Colonel. |
| 1884–85 | Serves in Gordon Relief Expedition, eventually commanding the River Column. Acting Brigadier-General. |
| 1885 | Returns from Sudan and promoted to Major General. |
| 1886–91 | Director of Military Intelligence at the War Office. Promote Lieutenant General in April 1888. |
| 1891–96 | Military Member of the Council of the Viceroy of India. Knighted on leaving office in 1896 (Knight Commander Order of the Star of India). |
| 1896–99 | President of the Ordnance Board. |
| 1899–1904 | Director General of the Ordnance. Temporary General, confirmed in that rank in 1902. |
| 1904 | Retires from the army and is made a Privy Councillor. |
| 1905 | Marriage to Edith Desanges and moves to Nice, France. |
| 1914 | Dies in Nice, France. |

# Appendix II

### List of books and articles by Sir Henry Brackenbury

Any such list can never be complete. Largely this is due to the fact that many of the articles he wrote were anonymous due to their controversial nature and his position as an officer of the Crown. It is only where Brackenbury or someone else has claimed credit for him that they can be recorded. Hence some of these articles do not appear on lists such as the Wellesley Index[1] or P.C.I. Full Text, but are claimed by Brackenbury in *Some Memories of My Spare Time* or are confirmed by the private letters of Blackwood's. It is unknown how much he contributed to *The Times of Natal*. Brackenbury, Colley and Butler took it in turn to write the leading article for the paper. No record exists of which were contributed by him. Of his lectures at Woolwich, a few survive in the private collection of the Brackenbury family.

### Books[2]

*Les Maréchaux de France, Étude de leur Conduite de la Guerre en 1870* (Paris: Lachaud Place du Theatre, Francais, 1871).[3]

*The Ashanti War: A Narrative prepared from the Official Documents* (London: Blackwood's, 1874, 2 volumes).

*The River Column: A Narrative of the Advance of the River Column of The Nile*

---

1  Houghton, Walter E. *The Wellesley Index to Victorian Periodicals 1824-1900* (London: Routledge & Kegan Paul, 1972).

2  Some would regard 'The Tactics of the Three Arms' as a book, as Mitchells of London first published it as a pamphlet in 1873. It was originally a lecture to the Royal United Service Institute, and subsequently published in their Journal. If one is to count this as a book it would be necessary to count 'A Letter from Salamanca' in the same vein, as this was published in the same format by Blackwood's at a later date. It has been decided here to count neither as a book and include them as journal articles for the sake of clarity and simplicity.

3  This is the book that Brackenbury had suppressed before publication for fear that it might prejudice the trial of Marshal Bazaine. Only six copies survived, one with the Emperor Napoleon III, one with Marshal Canrobert, one with Sir Lintorn Simmons, one with the Staff College Library and one to the French Journal *République Francaise*. The final copy remains in the Brackenbury family to this day.

# Appendix II

*Expeditionary Force* (London: Blackwood's, 1885).
*Some Memories of My Spare Time* (London: William Blackwood & Sons, 1909).

## Journal Articles and Published Lectures

'Ancient Cannon in Europe' Part I 1865.
'Ancient Cannon in Europe' Part II 1866.[4]
'Operations against Charleston', *Fraser's Magazine* Volume 74 (July 1866).
'Military Reform' Parts I to V *Fraser's Magazine* Volumes 74–76 (December 1866 to August 1867).
'Warfare in the Middle Ages', *The Gentleman's Magazine*, December 1866.
'The Military Armaments of the Five Great Powers', *Saint Paul's: A Monthly Magazine*, Volume I (November 1867).
'Our Army as it is, and as it should be', *Saint Paul's: A Monthly Magazine*, Volume I (February 1868).
'Parliament and Army Reform', *Saint Paul's: A Monthly Magazine*, Volume II (July 1868).
'Army Reform', *The Athenaeum* (August 1868).[5]
'Army Reform', *The Athenaeum* (February 1869).
'The Influence of Modern Improvements Upon Strategy', *Saint Paul's: A Monthly Magazine*, Volume III (March 1869).
'Military Education', *St Paul's; A Monthly Magazine* (February 1870).[6]
'The Last Campaign of Hanover', *Journal of the Royal United Services Institution* (1870).
'The Tactics of the Three Arms as modified to meet the requirements of the Present Day', *Journal of the Royal United Services Institution* (1873).
'Fanti and Ashanti: Three papers read on board the S.S Ambriz on the voyage to the Gold Coast', (London: Blackwood & Sons, (1873).
'Philanthropy in War', *Blackwood's Magazine* Volume 119 (February 1877).
'Crete', *Blackwood's Magazine* Volume 121 (April 1877).
'The South African Question', *Blackwood's Magazine* Volume 124 (July 1878).
'The Troubles of a Scots Traveller', *Blackwood's Magazine* Volume 124 (October 1878).

---

4   It has already been mentioned that this was meant to be a series of three articles, but his archival research was lost in a fire, and he had neither the time nor inclination to start again. The original handwritten copies of the first two articles survive in the archives of the Royal Artillery Museum at Woolwich.
5   The two articles on Army Reform, whilst linked, are not entitled part I & II, so they have been listed individually.
6   In *Some Memories of My Spare Time* Brackenbury claims to have written this article anonymously.

'Shadwell's Life of Lord Clyde', *Blackwood's Magazine* Volume 129 (April 1881).
'Midsummer in the Soudan', *Fortnightly Review* Volume 44 (August 1885).
'Life Insurance for Officers of the Army', *United Service Journal* (October 1891).
'Stonewall Jackson', *Blackwood's Magazine* Volume 164 (December 1898).
'A Letter about the Family of Brackenbury to William Blackwood Esq.', *Blackwood's Magazine* (2nd January 1899).
'A Letter from Salamanca' *Blackwood's Magazine* Volume 165 (March 1899).
'Sir George Pomeroy-Colley: Some Personal Recollections', *Blackwood's Magazine*, (March 1899).
'The Transvaal Twenty Years Ago', *Blackwood's Magazine* Volume 166 (November 1899).
'Lord Wantage, V.C, K.C.B', *Blackwood's Magazine* Volume 183 (February 1908).
'The Ashanti Campaign', *Blackwood's Magazine* Volume 185 (March 1909).
'Lord Lytton's Indian Administration', *Blackwood's Magazine* Volume 166 (December 1899).
'Military Attaché in Paris', *Blackwood's Magazine* Volume 185 (April 1909).
'Prince Napoleon', *Blackwood's Magazine* Volume 185 (April 1909).
'Sir John Ardagh', *Blackwood's Magazine* Volume 185 (May 1909).
'James Douglas, M.D. Surgeon Venturer', *Blackwood's Magazine* Volume 191 (January 1912).
'Sir Frederick Richards and Sir Garnet Wolseley', *The National Review*, (September 1913).

## Newspaper Articles

Brackenbury wrote far more for the daily press than is known. Much was either deliberately anonymous or credit was not given.
Leading article on corporal punishment in the army, *The Standard* 18th March 1867. A second article on the same subject was published in *The Standard's* sister paper *The Morning Herald* on 30th March 1867.
'Help for the Sick and Wounded', *The Standard* (January 1868). Two articles.
'A Tour in the Cockpit of Europe', *The Standard* (14th September 1868).
'The Kermesse in Belgium', *The Standard* (23rd September 1868).[7]
'The Armies of France, Prussia and Spain', *The Standard* (12th July 1870).
'French and Prussian Tactics', *The Standard* (14th July 1870).
'Diary of the War', *The Standard* (6th August 1870). This continued every day until 1st September 1870, when he left to start his work for the National Aid Society.

---

7   The articles in question were written during one of his vacation tours of the Continent's battlefields which he undertook whilst Professor of Military History at Woolwich. He undertook a similar tour in 1869, but no record of the articles he wrote exists.

'The Paris Commune', *The Times* (17th April 1871).
'Russia at Constantinople', *The Daily Telegraph* (18th November 1876).
'Diplomatic Parallels', *The Daily Telegraph* (20th November 1876).
'England's Greatest Danger in the East' *The Daily Telegraph*. Two articles on 18th and 20th February 1877.[8]*
'Five French Plays and a Moral', *The World* 14th March 1877.
'England's Threatened Interests', *The Daily Telegraph* April 1877.*
'Why do we hesitate?' *The Daily Telegraph* April 1877.*
'The Russian Advance Through Roumania', *The Daily Telegraph* April 1877.*
'The Passage of the Danube', *The Daily Telegraph* May 1877.*
'The Lines of Gallipoli', *The Daily Telegraph* June 1877.*

## Miscellaneous

*Brande's Dictionary of Literature, Science, and Art* (London: Messrs Longmans, Green & Co, 1866). Brackenbury contributed the military articles for this edition.

Smith, Major-General Michael W., *Drill and Manoeuvres of Cavalry combined with Horse Artillery* (London: Longman's, 1865). At the request of Mr Longman Brackenbury edited the book.

---

[8] The articles were written under the signature of 'Anglophile'. Any articles marked * were written under that pseudonym. Their nature was highly politicised. Reading between the lines it can be suggested that they might have been written with the collusion of Lord Hartington. See Brackenbury, Henry, *Some Memories of My Spare Time* (London: William Blackwood and Sons, 1909), pp.247-248.

# Bibliography[1]

## Archives

Brackenbury Family Archive
    Private manuscript collection of unsorted papers held by Mr Mark Brackenbury.

British Library
    Arnold-Forster Papers Add MSS 50300, Add MSS 50336
    Balfour Papers Add MSS 49683, Add MSS 49722
    Campbell-Bannerman Papers Add MSS 41233, Add MSS 41238
    Chief of Staff's Journal of the military operations in the Transvaal, 1879. By Lt Colonel H. Brackenbury (London, 1880).
    T.H.S. Escott Papers Add MSS 58775
    Gladstone Papers Add MSS 44308
    E.T.H Hutton Papers Add MSS 50078
    Report by Director General of Ordnance on Armaments and material of War Add MSS 50325
    Report of the Inter-Departmental Committee on Reserves of guns, stores for the Army (Mowatt Committee) 1900 Add MSS 50306
    Spencer Papers Add MSS 77088

British Library, Asia, Pacific and Africa Collection
    Brackenbury Official Papers, MSS Eur.D.735.

Centre for Kentish Studies, Maidstone
    Stanhope Papers

Devon Records Office, Exeter
    Buller Papers

Hove Central Library
    Wolseley Papers

---

[1] Except for his books, the works of Sir Henry Brackenbury have not been recorded in this bibliography. For a list of his publications see Appendix II.

Military Intelligence Museum, Chicksands
    Intelligence Archives

National Archives, Kew
    HO73/35/3 Minutes of Evidence of Hartington Commission
    HO73/36/4 Report of the Hartington Commission
    PRO30/40/2 Ardagh Papers
    WO32/6136 Lord Wolseley's Sudan Campaign Dispatches
    WO32/6349 Memorandum by Brackenbury & Newmarch
    WO32/6352 Brackenbury correspondence with Buller
    WO32/7026 Committee of Enquiry
    WO32/7860 Reports of Director General of Ordnance
    WO33/46 Intelligence and Mobilisation Reports
    WO33/50 Brackenbury to British Ambassador in Berlin
    WO106/16 Chapman Papers
    WO106/6157 Secret Military Despatch No 180
    WO108/66 Secretary of State for War Papers
    WO108/79 Proceedings of the Army Board
    WO108/336 Ordnance and Ammunition from Germany
    WO147/3 & WO147/4 Wolseley Ashanti Campaign Journal
    WO147/5 Wolseley Journal whilst in Natal
    WO147/6 Wolseley Cyprus Journal
    WO147/7 Wolseley Zulu War Journal
    WO147/8 Wolseley Sudan Campaign Journal

National Army Museum, Chelsea
    Roberts Papers R11/42

National Library of Scotland
    Blackwood Papers

Royal Artillery Museum Woolwich
    Brackenbury Letter Books

## British Public Documents

Reports from the Select Committee on Army and Navy Estimates; together with the proceedings of the committee, and minutes of evidence. (1887)

Report of the Royal Commission appointed to inquire into the system under which patterns of warlike stores are adopted and the stores obtained and passed for Her Majesty's service (Stephen Commission) (Cd.5062, 1887)

Minutes of evidence taken before the Royal Commission appointed to inquire into the system under which patterns of warlike stores are adopted and the stores obtained and passed for Her Majesty's service (Stephen Commission) (Cd.5062–1, 1887)

Report of the Committee appointed to inquire into the organisation and administration of the Manufacturing Departments of the Army; with minutes of evidence, appendix and index (Morley Committee) (Cd.5116, 1887)

Report of the Royal Commission appointed to inquire into the civil establishments of the different offices of state at home and abroad, with minutes of evidence, appendix (Ridley Commission) (Cd. 5226, 1887)

Memorandum of the Secretary of State relating to the Army Estimates 1887–88 (Cd. 4985, 1887)

Final report from the Select Committee on Army Estimates; with the proceedings of the committee, 17th July 1888.

Royal Commission appointed to enquire into the civil and professional administration of the naval and military departments and the relation of those departments to each other and to the treasury (Hartington Commission) (Cd. 5979, 1890)

Memorandum showing the duties of the principal officers and departments of the War Office and details of office procedure, under the Order in Council dated 21st November 1895 (Cd. 7987, 1896)

Memorandum showing the duties of the principal officers and departments of the War Office and details of office procedure, under the Order in Council dated 7th March 1899 (Cd. 9230, 1899).

Report of the Committee appointed to enquire into War Office organisation (Clinton Dawkins Committee) (Cd. 580–1, 1901)

Report of His Majesty's Commissioners appointed to inquire into the military preparations and other matters connected with the war in South Africa (Elgin Commission) (Cd. 1789, 1903)

Minutes of evidence taken before the Royal Commission on the war in South Africa (Elgin Commission) Part I (Cd. 1790, 1903) Part II (Cd. 1791, 1903)

Report of the War Office Reconstitution Committee (Esher Committee) Part I (Cd. 1932, 1904) Part II (Cd. 1968, 1904) Part III (Cd. 2002, 1904)

Appendices to the minutes of evidence taken before the Royal Commission on the war in South Africa (Cd. 1792, 1904)

## Newspapers and Periodicals

*The Academy*
*The Athenaeum*
*Blackwood's Magazine*
*The Daily Telegraph*
*Fortnightly Review*
*Fraser's Magazine*
*The Illustrated London News*
*Review of Reviews*
*Saint Paul's: A Monthly Magazine*
*The Standard*
*The Times*
*The United Service Journal*


## Edited Diaries

Arthur, Sir George, *The letters of Lord and Lady Wolseley 1870–1911* (London: William Heinemann, 1923).

Brett, M.V., (ed) *Journals and Letters of Reginald Viscount Esher* (London: Ivor Nicolson, 1934–35, 4 volumes).

Cavendish, Anne (ed), *Cyprus 1878: The Journal of Sir Garnet Wolseley* (Nicosia: Cultural Centre of the Cyprus, 1991).

Laband, John, *Lord Chelmsford's Zululand Campaign 1878–1879* (Stroud: Alan Sutton Press, 1994).

Preston, Anthony, (ed) *The South African Journal of Sir Garnet Wolseley* (Cape Town: A.A. Balkema, 1971).

Roberts, Bryan (ed), *Roberts in India: The Military Papers of Field-Marshal Lord Roberts 1876–1893* (Stroud: Alan Sutton, 1993).


## Contemporary Books, Autobiographies and Journal Articles

Adye, Sir John, *Recollections of a Military life* (London: Smith, Elder & Co, 1895).
— *Soldiers and others I have known* (London: H. Jenkins, 1919).
Amery, Leo. S., *The Times History of the War in South Africa* (London: Sampson Low, 1900–09, 7 volumes).
Arnold-Forster, H.O., *The Army in 1906: A policy and a vindication* (London: Duttton, 1906).
— *The War Office, the Army and the Empire* (London: Cassell & Co Ltd, 1900).

Arnold-Forster, Mary, *The Rt Hon Hugh Oakley Arnold-Forster: A Memoir* (London: Edward Arnold, 1910).
Aston, Major-General Sir George, *His Royal Highness the Duke of Connaught and Strathearn: A life and intimate study* (London: Harrap & Co Ltd, 1929).
— *Secret Service* (London: Faber & Faber, 1909).
Baden-Powell, Lieutenant-General Sir Robert, *My Adventures as a Spy* (London: C.A. Pearson, 1915).
Balck, Major, *The lessons of the Boer War and the Battle-working of the three arms* (Translated from original German and published in the *Journal of the Royal United Services Institution* 48 Part 2 July/Dec 1904).
Barrow, General Sir George, *The Fire of Life* (London: Hutchinson & Co, 1941).
Battersby, H.F. Prevost, *In the Web of War* (London: Methuen & Co, 1900).
Beresford, Lord Charles, *The Memoirs of Lord Charles Beresford* (London: 1914, 2 volumes).
Bethell, Colonel H.A., *Modern Guns and Gunnery: A Practical manual for the officers of the Horse, Field and mountain Artillery* (Woolwich: Royal Artillery, 1910).
Brackenbury, Henry, *Ashanti War* (Edinburgh: Blackwood's, 1874, 2 volumes).
— *Some Memories of My Spare Time* (London: William Blackwood & Sons, 1909).
— *The Last Campaign of Hanover* (London: W. Mitchell & Co, 1870).
— *The River Column* (London: Blackwood's, 1885).
—*The Tactics of the three arms as modified to meet the requirements of the present day* (London: Mitchell, 1873).
Butler, Lewis, *Sir Redvers Buller* (London: Smith, Elder & Co, 1909).
Cairnes, William Elliot, *An Absent Minded War: Being Some Reflections on our Reverses and the Causes which Led to Them* (London: J. Milne, 1900).
Callwell, Charles E., *Small Wars: Their Principles and Practice* (London: H.M.S.O, 1896).
— *Stray Recollections* (London: Edward Arnold & Co, 1923, 2 volumes).
— *Field Marshal Sir Henry Wilson* (London: Cassell, 1927, 2 volumes).
Childers, Lieutenant-Colonel Spencer, *The life and correspondence of the Rt Hon. C.E. Childers 1827–1896* (London: John Murray, 1901, 2 volumes).
Conan-Doyle, Arthur, *The Great Boer War* (London: Smith, Elder & Co, 1900).
Director General of Ordnance (General Sir Henry Brackenbury), *Notes of Artillery Material and Experiments* (London: Ordnance Department, 1903).
Dilke, Sir Charles & Spenser Wilkinson H., *Imperial Defence* (London: Constable, 1892).
Dilke, Sir Charles, *Army Reform* (London: Service & Paton, 1898).
Durand, Sir Mortimer *The Life of Field Marshal Sir George White V.C.* (London: William Blackwood, 1915).

Escott, T.H.S., 'Henry Brackenbury and his school' *Contemporary Review* 105 (January/June 1914).
— 'Lord Wolseley and "Those about Him", chapter in *Personal Forces of the Period* (London: Hurst and Blackett, 1898).
Fleetwood-Wilson, Guy, *Letters to Somebody* (London: Cassell & Co, 1922).
Furley, John, *Struggles and Experiences of a Neutral Volunteer* (London: Chapman, 1872, 2 volumes)
— *In Peace and War: Autobiographical sketches* (London: Smith, Elder & Co, 1909).
Gleichen, Lord, *A Guardsman's Memories* (London: Blackwood's, 1921).
— *With the Camel Corps up the Nile* (London: Chapman & Hall, 1888).
Grierson, Lieutenant-Colonel James Moncrieff, *Scarlet into Khaki* (London: Sampson, Low, 1899).
Gudgin, Peter, *Military Intelligence: A History* (Stroud: Sutton Publishing Ltd, 1999).
Haldane, Richard Burdon, *An Autobiography* (London: Hodder & Stoughton, 1929).
Hamilton, Captain Ian S.M., *Listening for the Drums* (London: Faber & Faber, 1944).
— *The fighting of the future* (London: Kegan Paul, 1885).
Hamley, General E.B., *Operations of War* (London: Blackwood's, 1872).
Hicks Beach, Lady Victoria, *The Life of Sir Michael Hicks Beach, Earl of Aldwyn* (London: Macmillan & Co, 1932, 2 volumes).
Knollys, H., 'Awake! Lord Hartington!' *Colburn's United Service Magazine* (July/December 1884).
Lowe, Charles, *Our Greatest Living Soldiers* (London: Chatto & Windus, 1900).
Malmesbury, Susan Countess of, *The Life of Major-General Sir John Ardagh* (London: John Murray, 1909).
Maurice, Major-General Sir Frederick and Grant, M.H., *History of the War in South Africa* (London: Hurst and Blackett Ltd, 1906–10, 4 volumes).
May, Lieutenant-Colonel E.S., *A Retrospect on the South African War* (London: Sampson Low, Marston & Co, 1901).
Menpes, Mortimer, *War Impressions* (London: Adam & Charles Black, 1903).
Owen, Lieutenant-Colonel C.H., 'Modern Artillery as Exhibited at Paris in 1867 *Journal of the Royal United Services Institution* 12 (1869).
— *Principles and Practice of Modern Artillery* (London: John Murray, 1871).
—'The Employment of Artillery in South Africa', *United Service Magazine* (April/September 1900).
Pollock, Major A.W.A., *With Seven Generals in the Boer War* (London: Skeffington & Sons, 1909).
Repington, Lieutenant-Colonel Charles à Court, *Vestigia* (London: Constable and Co Ltd, 1919).

Roberts, Field Marshal Lord, *Forty-one years in India: From Subaltern to Commander-in-Chief* (London: Macmillan, 1902, 2 volumes).
Robertson, Field-Marshal Sir W., *From Private to Field-Marshal* (London: Constable and Co Ltd, 1921).
Smith-Dorrien, General Sir Horace, *Memories of Forty-Eight Years Service* (London: John Murray, 1925).
St John Brodrick, Earl of Middleton, William, *Records and Reactions, 1856–1939* (London: John Murray, 1939).
Stead, W.T., *How Britain goes to War* (London: Review of Reviews, 1903).
— *The War in South Africa: Methods of Barbarism* (London: 1901).
— 'What is the Truth about the Navy?' *Pall Mall Gazette* (15th September 1884).
Waters, Colonel W.H.H., *Private and Personal* (London: John Murray, 1928).
— *Secret and Confidential* (London: John Murray, 1926).
Waters, Col H.H. & Du Cane, Colonel Herbert (transl.), *The War in South Africa: Prepared in the Historical Section of the Great General Staff, Berlin* (London: John Murray, 1906, 2 volumes).
Wilson, H. W *With the Flag to Pretoria* (London: Harmsworth Brothers Ltd, 1900, 4 volumes).
— *After Pretoria: The Guerrilla Campaign* (London: Amalgamated Press, 1902, 2 volumes).
Wilkinson, Spenser, *Lessons of the War* (London: Constable & Co, 1900).
— *The Brain of an Army: A popular Account of the German General Staff* (London: Constable & Co, 1890).
— *The Brain of the Navy* (London: Constable & Co, 1895).
Wolseley, Field Marshal Viscount, *The Story of a Soldier's Life* (London: Constable & Co, 1903).
Wood, Field Marshal Sir Henry Evelyn *Midshipman to Field Marshal* (London: Methuen Press, 1906, 2 volumes).

## Later published sources – Books

Arthur, Sir G., *Life of Lord Kitchener* (London: Macmillan & Co, 1920).
Andrew, C.M., *Secret Service: The Making of the British Intelligence Community* (London: Heinemann, 1985).
Ascoli, David, *A Companion to the British Army 1660–1983* (London: Harrap Ltd, 1983).
Asher, Michael, *Khartoum: The Ultimate Imperial Adventure* (London: Viking Books, 2005).

# Bibliography

Altholz, J.L., *Victorian England 1873–1901* (Cambridge: Cambridge University Press, 2002).

Badsey, Stephen, *The Franco-Prussian War 1870–1871* (Oxford: Osprey Publishing, 2003).

Baker, A., *The Battles and Battlefields of the Anglo-Boer War 1899–1902* (Milton Keynes: Military Press, 1999).

Barnett, Correlli, *Britain and Her Army 1509–1970* (London: Cassell & Co, 1970).

Barthorp, Michael, *Queen Victoria's Commanders* (Oxford: Osprey Publishing, 2000).

Bastable, Marshal J., *Arms and the State: Sir William Armstrong and the remaking of British Naval Power 1854–1914* (London: Ashgate, 2004).

Beaver, William, *Under Every Leaf: How Britain played the Greater game from Afghanistan to Africa* (London: Biteback Publishing, 2012).

Beckett, Ian and Gooch, John (eds), *Politics and Defence studies in the formation of British Defence policy 1845–1970* (Manchester: Manchester University Press, 1981).

Beckett, Ian, *The Victorians at War* (London: Hambeldon Press, 2003).

— *Victoria's Wars* (Princes Risborough: Shire Publications, 1998)

Belfield, Eversley, *The Boer War* (London: Leo Cooper, 1975).

Best, Geoffrey, *Humanity in Warfare: The Modern History of the International Law of Armed Conflicts* (London: Weidenfeld and Nicolson, 1980).

Best, G. & Wheatcroft, A. (eds), *War Economy and the Military Mind* (London: Croom Helm, 1976).

Bidwell, Shelford, *The Royal Horse Artillery* (London: Leo Cooper, 1973).

Biddulph, Sir Robert, *Lord Cardwell at the War Office* (London: John Murray, 1904).

Blake, R., *The Conservative Party from Peel to Churchill* (London: Eyre & Spottiswoode, 1970).

Bond, Brian, *The Victorian Army and the Staff College 1854–1914* (London: Eyre Methuen, 1972).

—*Victorian Military Campaigns* (London: Hutchinson, 1967).

—*War and Society in Europe, 1870–1970* (London: Fontana Press, 1984).

Bonham-Carter, Victor, *Soldier True: The Life and Times of Field-Marshal Sir William Robertson, 1860–1933* (London: Muller, 1963).

Brackenbury, Charles E., *The Brackenburys of Lincolnshire* (London: The Society for Lincolnshire History and Archaeology, 1983).

Brereton, J.M., *The British Soldier: A Social History from 1661 to the present day* (London: The Bodley Head, 1983).

Brigland, Tony, *Field Gun Jack Versus the Boers: The Royal Navy in South Africa 1899–1900* (London: Leo Cooper, 1998).

Brown, L., *Victorian News and Newspapers* (London: Clarendon Press, 1985).

Brookes, Kenneth, Battle Thunder: The Story of Britain's Artillery (Reading: Osprey, 1973).
Bywater, Hector & Ferraby, H.C., Strange Intelligence: Memoir of Naval Secret Service (London: Constable & Co, 1931).
Carver, Field Marshal Lord, The Seven Ages of the British Army (London: Weidenfeld and Nicolson, 1984).
— Britain's Army in the 20th Century (London: Pan Books, 1999).
— The National Army Museum Book of The Boer War (London: Pan Books, 2000).
Chandler, David (ed), The Oxford Illustrated History of the British Army (Oxford: Oxford University Press, 1994).
Charteris, Brigadier-General John, Field Marshal Earl Haig (London: Cassell & Co Ltd, 1929).
Clayton, Anthony, Forearmed: A History of the Intelligence Corps (London: Bassey's, 1993).
Coetzer, Owen, The Anglo-Boer War: The Road to Infamy 1899–1900 (London: Arms and Armour Press, 1996).
Cooter, Roger, Harrison, Mark & Sturdy, Steve, War, Medicine and Modernity (Stroud: Sutton Publishing, 1998).
Corfe, T.H., The Phoenix Park Murders: Conflict, Compromise and Tragedy in Ireland 1879–1882 (London: Hodder & Stoughton, 1968).
Corvi, Stephen J. & Beckett, Ian F.W. (eds), Victoria's Generals (Barnsley: Pen & Sword, 2009).
Davey, A., The British Pro-Boers (Cape Town: Tafelberg, 1978).
Deacon, Richard, A History of the British Secret Service (London: Frederick Muller, 1969).
Denis, Peter & Grey, Jeffrey (eds), The Boer War: Army, Nation and Empire (Canberra: Army Historical Unit, 2000).
Duckers, Peter, The British-Indian Army 1860–1914 (Princes Risborough: Shire Publications Ltd, 2003).
Dunlop, Colonel John K., The Development of the British Army 1899–1914 (London: Methuen Press, 1938).
Ehrman, John, Cabinet Government and War 1890–1940 (Cambridge: Cambridge University Press, 1958).
Eldridge, C.C., Disraeli and the rise of a new Imperialism (Cardiff: University of Wales Press, 1996).
Elletson, D.H., The Chamberlains (London: John Murray, 1966).
Emery, Frank, The Red Soldier: Letters from the Zulu War, 1879 (London: Hodder and Stoughton, 1977).
Ensor, Sir Robert, England 1870–1914 (Oxford: Clarendon Press, 1968).

Farwell, Byron, *Armies of the Raj: From the Great Indian Mutiny to Independence, 1858–1947* (London: W.W Norton & Co, 1989).
— *Eminent Victorian Soldiers* (London: W.W Norton, 1985).
— *For Queen and Country* (London: Allen Lane, 1981).
— *Queen Victoria's Little Wars* (London: Allen Lane, 1973).
— *The Great Boer War* (Ware: Allen Lane, Wordsworth Editions, 1999).
Featherstone, Donald, *Weapons and Equipment of the Victorian Soldier* (Poole: Blandford Press, 1978).
Fergusson, Thomas G., *British Military Intelligence, 1870–1914: The Development of a Modern Intelligence Organisation* (Frederick, Maryland: University Publications of America, Inc, 1984).
Fisher, John, *Gentleman Spies: Intelligence agents in the British Empire and beyond* (Stroud: Sutton Publishing, 2002).
Forbes, General Archibald, *A History of the Army Ordnance Service* (London: The Medici Society Ltd, 1929, 3 volumes).
Foreman-Peck, James (ed), *New Perspectives on the Late Victorian Economy* (Cambridge: Cambridge University Press, 2003).
Forester, C.S., *The General* (Harmondsworth: Penguin Books, 1975).
Fortescue, Sir John, *A History of the British Army* (London: Macmillan Press, 1902 to 1930, 13 volumes).
—*Military History* (Cambridge: Cambridge University Press, 1923).
— *The Empire and the Army* (London: Cassell, 1928).
—*The Royal Army Service Corps: A history of transport and supply in the British Army* (Cambridge: Cambridge University Press, 1930).
Frankland, Noble, *Witnesss of a Century: The Life and Times of Prince Arthur Duke of Connaught 1850–1942* (London: Shepherd-Walwyn, 1993).
Fraser, Peter, *Lord Esher: A Political Biography* (London: Hart-Davis, 1973).
French, David & Holden Reid, Brian, *British General Staff: Reform and Innovation 1890–1939* (London: Frank Cass, 2002).
French, David, *Military Identities: The Regimental System, the British Army, and the British People c1870–2000* (London: Oxford University Press, 2005).
French, Hon Gerald, *Lord Chelmsford and the Zulu War* (London: Unwin Brothers Ltd, 1939).
Gibbs, Norman H., *The Origins of Imperial Defence* (Oxford: Oxford University Press, 1955).
Gilmour, David, *The Long Recessional: The Imperial Life of Rudyard Kipling* (London: John Murray, 2002).
Glover, Michael, *Rorke's Drift* (Ware: Wordsworth Editions, 1997).
Godwin-Austin, Major A.R., The Staff and the Staff College (London: Constable and Company, 1927).

Gooch, John (ed), *The Boer War: Direction, Experience and Image* (London: Frank Cass, 2000).

— *The Plans of War: The General Staff and British Military Strategy* (London: Routledge & Kegan Paul, 1974).

— *The Prospect of War: Studies in British Defence Policy 1847–1942* (London: Frank Cass, 1981).

Goodwin, John E., *Fortification of the South Coast: The Pevensey, Eastbourne and Newhaven Defence 1750–1945* (Worthing: JJ Publications, 1994).

Gordon, Hampden, *The War Office: Past and Present* (London: Methuen, 1914).

Graves, Charles, *Mr Punch's History of Modern England 1841–1914* (London: Cassell & Co, 1921).

Grigg, John, *The young Lloyd George* (London: Methuen Press, 1973).

Gourvish, T.R., 'The Rise of the Professions' in Gourish, T.R & O'Day, A (eds) *Later Victorian Britain 1867–1900* (Basingstoke: 1988).

Guy, Alan & Harding, Marion (eds), *Ashes and Blood: The British Army in South Africa 1795–1914* (London: National Army Museum, 1999).

Hamer, W.S., *The British Army: Civil-Military Relations 1885–1905* (Oxford: Clarendon Press, 1970).

Hannah, W.H., *Bobs, Kipling's General: The life of Field-Marshal Earl Roberts of Kandahar* (London: Leo Cooper, 1972).

Harries-Jenkins, Gwyn, *The Army in Victorian Society* (Trowbridge: Routledge & Kegan Paul Ltd, 1977).

Hastings, Max, *The Oxford Book of Military Anecdotes* (Oxford: Oxford University Press, 1985).

Haswell, Jock, *British Military Intelligence* (London: Weidenfeld & Nicolson, 1973).

Haythornthwaite, Philip J., *The Colonial Wars Source Book* (London: Caxton Publishing Group, 2000).

Headlam, Major-General Sir John, *The History of the Royal Artillery* Volume II (Woolwich: Royal Artillery Institution, 1937).

— *Six Centuries of Royal Artillery History* (Woolwich: Royal Artillery Institution, 1944).

Heathcote, T.A., *The Indian Army: The Garrison of British Imperial India 1822–1922* (David & Charles: Newton Abbot, 1974).

— *The Military in British India: The Development of British land forces in South Asia 1600–1947* (Manchester: Manchester University Press, 1995).

Howard, Michael, *The Franco-Prussian War: The German Invasion of France 1870–1871* (London: Methuen Press, 1981).

Holmes, Richard, *Sahib: The British Soldier in India* (London: Harper Collins, 2005).

Hopkirk, Peter, *The Great Game: On Secret Service in High Asia* (Oxford: Oxford University Press, 1990).

Hutchinson, John, *Champions of charity: War and the rise of the Red Cross* (Colorado: Westview Press, 1996).
Jackson, Patrick, *The Last of the Whigs: A Political Biography of Lord Hartington* (Cranbury, New Jersey: Associated University Presses, 1994).
Jackson, Tabitha, *The Boer War* (Basingstoke: Macmillan Press, 2001).
James, D., *The Life of Lord Roberts* (London: Hollis & Carter, 1954).
James, Lawrence, *Raj: The making and unmaking of British India* (London: Abacus Books, 1997).
— *The Rise and Fall of the British Empire* (London: Abacus Books, 1995).
Jeal, Tim, *Baden-Powell* (London: Pimlico Press, 1995).
Jerrold, Walter, *Earl Kitchener of Khartoum: The Story of his Life* (London: W.A Hammond, 1915).
Johnson, F.A., *Defence by Committee* (London: Oxford University Press, 1960).
Judd, Denis & Surridge, Keith, *The Boer War* (London: John Murray, 2002).
Judd, Denis, *Empire: The British Experience from 1765 to the present* (London: Harper Collins, 1996).
— *Radical Joe: A life of Joseph Chamberlain* (Cardiff: University of Wales Press, 1993).
— *Someone has Blundered: Calamities of the British Army in the Victorian Age* (London: Arthur Baker Ltd, 1973).
Kennedy, Paul M., *The War Plans of the Great Powers 1880-1914* (Winchester, Massachusetts: Allen & Unwin Inc, 1985).
Kennedy, P.M., *The Rise and Fall of British Naval Mastery* (London: Macmillan, 1983).
— *The Rise of Anglo-German Antagonism 1860-1914* (London: Allen & Unwin, 1980).
Keown-Boyd, Henry, *A Good Dusting: The Sudan Campaigns 1883-1899* (London: Guild Publishing, 1986).
Kochanski, Halik, *Sir Garnet Wolseley: Victorian Hero* (London: Hambledon Press, 1999).
Knight, Ian, *Brave Men's Blood* (London: Greenhill, 1990).
— *Colenso 1899: The Boer War in Natal* (London: Osprey, 1995).
— *Go to your God like a soldier* (London: Greenhill, 1996).
— *Great Zulu Battles 1838-1906* (London: Cassell & Co, 1998).
— *The National Army Museum Book of the Zulu War* (London: Pan Books, 2004).
Kruger, Rayne, *Goodbye Dolly Gray: A History of the Boer War* (London: Pan Books, 1974).
Laband, John & Thompson, Paul, *The Illustrated Guide to the Anglo-Zulu War* (Pietermaritzburg: University of Natal Press, 2000).
Laband, John, *The Anglo-Zulu War: The War Correspondents* (Stroud: Alan Sutton, 1996).
— *Lord Chelmsford's Zululand Campaign 1878-1879* (Stroud: Alan Sutton for Army Records Society, 1994).
Laffin, John, *Tommy Atkins: The Story of the English Soldier* (London: Cassell, 1966).
Lee, John, *A Soldier's Life: General Sir Ian Hamilton 1853-1947* (Basingstoke: Macmillan Press, 2000).

Le May, G.H., *British Supremacy in South Africa 1899–1907* (Oxford: Clarendon Press, 1965).
Lehmann, Joseph H., *All Sir Garnet: A Life of Field-Marshal Lord Wolseley* (London Jonathan Lane, 1964).
— *The First Boer War* (London: Buchan and Enright, 1972)
Lloyd, A., *The Drums of Kumasi: The Story of the Ashanti Wars* (London: Longmans, 1964).
Loades, Judith (ed), *The Life and Times of David Lloyd George* (Bangor: Headstart History, 1991).
Longford, Elizabeth, *Jameson's Raid: The Prelude to the Boer War* (London: Weidenfeld & Nicolson, 1982).
Lowry, Donal (ed), *The South African War Reappraised* (Manchester: Manchester University Press, 2000).
Luvaas, Jay, *The Education of an Army: British Military Thought 1815–1940* (London: Cassell, 1964).
MacDiarmid, D.S., *The Life of Lieutenant General Sir James Moncrieff Grierson* (London: Constable & Company Ltd, 1923).
MacKenzie, J.M. (ed), *Imperialism and Popular Culture* (Manchester: Manchester University Press, 1986).
— *Propaganda and Empire: The manipulation of British public opinion 1880–1960* (Manchester: Manchester University Press, 1984).
Magnus, Phillip, *Kitchener: Portrait of an Imperialist* (London: Butler & Tanner, 1958).
Makepeace-Warne, Anthony, *Brassey's Companion to the British Army* (London: Brassey's, 1998).
Marsh, P.T., *Joseph Chamberlain: Entrepreneur in Politics* (New Haven: Yale University Press, 1994).
Mason, P.A., *Matter of Honour: An Account of the Indian Army, its officers and men* (London: Jonathan Cape, 1974).
Maurice, Major-General Sir Frederick, *The Life of General Lord Rawlinson of Trent* (London: Cassell & Co Ltd, 1928).
Maurice, Sir Frederick & Arthur, Sir George, *The Life of Lord Wolseley* (London: William Heinemann, 1924).
Maxwell, Leigh, *The Ashanti Ring: Sir Garnet Wolseley's Campaigns 1870–1882* (London: Leo Cooper, 1985).
Melville, Charles Henderson, *Life of General the Right Hon. Sir Redvers Buller* (London: Edward Arnold & Co, 1923, 2 volumes).
Messenger, Charles, *History of the British Army* (London: Bison Books Ltd, 1986).
Miller, Stephen M., *Lord Methuen and the British Army* (London: Frank Cass, 1999).
Millman, R., *Britain and the Eastern Question 1875–1878* (Oxford: Clarendon Press, 1979).
Molony, Senan, *The Phoenix Park Murders* (Cork: Mercier Press, 2006).
Montgomery, Field-Marshal Viscount, *A Concise History of Warfare* (London: William Collins, 1968).

Morris, Donald R., *The Washing of the Spears* (London: Sphere Books, 1976).

Murray, Williamson (ed), *The Making of Strategy: Rulers, States and War* (Cambridge: Cambridge University Press, 1994).

Nasson, William R., *The South African War, 1899–1902* (London: Hodder & Arnold, 1999).

Newton, Lord, *Lord Lansdowne: A Biography* (London: Macmillan Press, 1929).

Newton, Scott & Porter, Dilwyn, *Joseph Chamberlain 1836–1914: A Bibliography* (London: Greenwood Press, 1994).

Nicoll, Fergus, *The Mahdi of Sudan and the death of General Gordon* (Stroud: Sutton Press, 2005).

Nutting, A., *Gordon: Martyr and Misfit* (London: Constable, 1966).

Omissi, D. & Thompson, A.S. (eds), *The Impact of the South African War* (Basingstoke: Palgrave Macmillan, 2002).

Owen, Frank, *Tempestuous Journey: Lloyd-George his life and times* (London: Hutchinson & Co, 1954).

Pakenham, Thomas, The Boer War (London: Abacus Books, 1992).

— *The Scramble for Africa 1876–1912* (London: Abacus Books, 1992).

Parritt, Lieutenant-Colonel B.A.H., *The Intelligencers: 'The Story of British Military Intelligence up to 1914* (Ashford: The Intelligence Corps: 1971).

Pearce, Malcolm & Stewart, Geoffrey, *British Political History 1867–1990: Democracy and Decline* (London: Routledge, 1992).

Peck, John, *War, the Army and Victorian Literature* (Basingstoke: Palgrave Macmillan, 1998).

Perkin, Harold James, *The Rise of Professional Society: England since 1880* (London: Routledge, 1989).

Perrett, Bryan, *Last Stand: Famous Battles against the odds* (London: Cassell Military Paperbacks, 1991).

Porter, A.N., *The Origins of the South African War: Joseph Chamberlain and the Diplomacy of Imperialism* (Manchester: Manchester University Press, 1980).

Porch, Douglas, *Wars of Empire* (London: Cassell & Co, 2000).

Powell, Geoffrey, *Buller: A Scapegoat?* (London: Leo Cooper, 1994).

Preston, Adrian, *In Relief of Gordon* (London: Hutchinson & Co, 1967).

Pretorius, F., *The Anglo-Boer War 1899–1902* (Cape Town: D. Nelson, 1985).

Price, Richard, An Imperial War and the British Working Class (London: Routledge & Kegan Paul, 1972).

Regan, Geoffrey, *Military Blunders* (London: Carlton Publishing Group, 2001).

Richards, D.S., *The Savage Frontier: A History of the Anglo-Afghan Wars* (London: Pan Books, 2003).

Roberts, Andrew, *Lord Salisbury: Victorian Titan* (London: Phoenix, 1999).

Rogers, Colonel H.C.B., *Artillery through the Ages* (London: Seeley Service & Co, 1971).

— *The Mounted Troops of the British Army 1066–1945* (London: Seeley Service & Co, 1959).

— Weapons of the British Soldier (London: Seeley Service and Co, 1960).
Rose, Kenneth, *Superior Person: A Portrait of Curzon and his circle in Late Victorian England* (London: Weidenfeld & Nicolson, 1969).
Rowland, Peter, *David Lloyd George: A Biography* (London: Barrie & Jenkins, 1975).
Samuels, Martin, *Command or Control: Command, Training and Tactics in the British and German Armies 1888–1918* (London: Frank Cass, 1995).
Selby, John, *The Boer War* (London: Arthur Baker Ltd, 1969).
Searle, G.R., *A New England? Peace and war 1886–1918* (Oxford: Oxford University Press, 2004).
— *Entrepreneurial Politics in Mid-Victorian Britain* (Oxford: Oxford University Press, 1993).
— *The Quest for National Efficiency: A Study in Politics and Political Thought, 1899–1914* (London: Ashfield Press, 1990).
Shannon, Richard, *The Age of Salisbury, 1881–1902: Unionism and Empire* (Harlow: Longman Press, 1996).
Sheffield, Gary (ed), *Leadership and Command: The Anglo-American Military Experience since 1861* (London: Brassey's, 1997).
Sheppard, Captain Eric William, *A Short History of the British Army to 1914* (London: Constable & Co Ltd, 1934).
Short, Kenneth R.M., *The Dynamite War: Irish-American Bombers in Victorian Britain* (Dublin: Gill and Macmillan, 1979).
Skelley, A.R., *The Victorian Army at Home* (London: Croom Helm, 1977).
Skentelbery, Norman, *Arrows to Atom Bombs* (London: Ordnance Board, 1975).
Smith, Iain R., The Origins of the South African War 1899–1902(Harlow: Longman, 1996).
Smith, Paul, *Government and the Armed Forces in Britain 1856–1990* (London: Hambeldon Press, 1996).
Smyth, Brigadier The Rt. Hon Sir J., *Sandhurst: The History of the Royal Military Academy Woolwich, The Royal Military College, Sandhurst and the Royal Military Academy Sandhurst 1741–1961* (London: Weidenfeld & Nicolson, 1961).
Snook, Mike, *Into the Jaws of Death: Epic fights of the Victorian Army* (US Naval Institute, 2007).
Sommer, Dudley, *Haldane of Cloan: His life and time* (London: Allen & Unwin, 1960).
Spiers, Edward M., *The Army and Society 1815–1914* (London: Longman, 1980).
— *The Late Victorian Army 1868–1902* (Manchester: Manchester University Press, 1992).
— *The Victorian Soldier in Africa* (Manchester: Manchester University Press, 2004).
Stafford, David, Churchill & Secret Service (London: John Murray, 1997).
Strachan, Hew, The Politics of the British Army (Oxford: Oxford University Press, 1997).
Streets, Heather, *Martial Races: The Military, Race and Masculinity in British Imperial Culture 1857–1914* (Manchester: Manchester University Press, 2004).
Stone, Jay & Schmidl, Erwin A., The Boer War and Military Reform (London: University Press of America, 1988).

Strong, Maj-General Sir Kenneth, Men of Intelligence (London: Cassell, 1960).
Surridge, Keith, British Civil Military Relations and the South African War 1899 1902 (London: University of London, 1994).
— Managing the South African War 1899–1902: Politicians Vs Generals (Woodbridge: Royal Historical Society Publications, 1998).
Symons, Julian, *Buller's Campaign* (London: Cresst Press, 1963).
— *England's Pride: The Story of the Gordon Relief Expedition* (London: Hamish Hamilton Ltd, 1965).
Taithe, Bertrand, *Citizenship and War: France in Turmoil 1870–1871* (London: Routledge, 2001).
— *Defeated Flesh: Welfare, Warfare and the making of Modern France* (Manchester: Manchester University Press, 2000).
Terraine, John, *Douglas Haig: The Educated Soldier* (London: Hutchinson & Co, 1963).
Thompson, George C., *Public Opinion and Lord Beaconsfield 1875–80* Volume II (London; Macmillan & Co, 1886).
Thompson, Brian, *Imperial Vanities: The Adventures of the Baker brothers and Gordon of Khartoum* (London: Harper Collins, 2002).
Trebilcock, C., 'War and the Failure of Industrial Mobilisation, 1899–1914' in Winter, Jay M (ed), *War and Economic Development* (Cambrdige: Cambridge University Press, 1975).
Trawin, Len, *Early British quick-firing artillery: Field and Horse* (London: Nexus, 1997).
Trew, Peter, *The Boer War Generals* (Stroud: Sutton Publishing, 1999).
Turner, E.S., *Gallant Gentlemen: a portrait of the British Officer 1600–1956* (London: Michael Joseph Ltd, 1956).
Urban, Mark, *Generals: Ten British Commanders who shaped the world* (London: Faber & Faber, 2005).
Van Hartesveldt, Fred, The Boer War (Stroud: Sutton Publishing, 2000).
Van Thal, Herbert (ed), The Prime Ministers Volume III (London: George Allen & Unwin Ltd, 1975).
Verner, Willoughby, The Military Life of H.R.H. George, Duke of Cambridge (London: John Murray, 1905, 2 volumes).
Walker, A. (ed), The Cambridge History of the British Empire: Volume VIII South Africa (Cambridge: Cambridge University Press, 1963).
Wantage, Baroness, *Lord Wantage, V.C, K.C.B: A Memoir* (London: Smith, Elder & Co, 1907).
Warner, Phillip, *Dervish: The Rise and Fall of an African Empire* (London: Purnell Books, 1973).
Warwick, Peter (ed), *The South African War: The Anglo-Boer War 1899–1902* (London: Longmans, 1980).

Wawro, Geoffrey, *The Franco-Prussian War: The German Conquest of France 1870–1871* (Cambridge: Cambridge University Press, 2003).
Wessels, Andre, *Lord Roberts and the War in South Africa 1899–1902* (Stroud: Sutton Publishing, 2000).
Wheeler, Captain Owen, *The War Office Past and Present* (London: Methuen and C Ltd, 1914).
White, Arnold, *Efficiency and Empire* (London: Harvester Press, 1973).
Wilson, K. (ed), *The International Impact of the Boer War* (Chesham: Acumen, 2001).
Williams, R., *Defending the Empire: The Conservative Party and British Defence Policy 1899–1915* (New Haven: Yale University Press, 1991).
Woodward, David, *Armies of the World* (London: Sidgwick and Jackson Ltd 1978).

## Later published sources – Articles

Allen, Dan, 'Boer War Field Orders', *The Journal of the Victorian Military Society, Soldiers of the Queen*, Issue 115 (December 2003).
Bailes, Howard, 'Patterns of thought in the Late Victorian Army', *Journal of Strategic Studies*, Volume 4 Part 1 (March 1981).
— 'Technology and Imperialism: a case study of the Victorian Army in Africa', *Victorian Studies Journal*, No 24 (1980).
Barthorp, Michael, 'Guardsman and Intelligencer: Lord Edward Gleichen', *The Journal of the Victorian Military Society, Soldiers of the Queen*, Issue 97 (June 1999).
Beaver, William C., 'The Intelligence Division Library 1854–1902', *Journal of Library History* 11/3 (July 1976).
Beckett, Ian, 'Edward Stanhope at the War Office 1887–1892', *Journal of Strategic Studies* 5 (1982).
— 'Personality and the Victorian Army; Some Reflections', *The Journal of the Victorian Military Society, Soldiers of the Queen*, Issue 100 (March 2000).
— 'The Indian Expeditionary Force on Malta and Cyprus 1878', *The Journal of the Victorian Military Society, Soldiers of the Queen*, Issue 76 (March 1994).
— 'The Pen and Sword: Reflections on Military Thought in the British Army 1854–1914', *The Journal of the Victorian Military Society, Soldiers of the Queen*, Issue 68 (March, 1992).
— 'The Stanhope Memorandum of 1888: A Reinterpretation', *Bulletin of the Institute of Historical Research*, 57 (1984).
— 'Wolseley and the Ring', *The Journal of the Victorian Military Society, Soldiers of the Queen*, Issue 69, (June 1992).
Bond, Brian, 'The Late Victorian Army', *History Today* (September 1961).
— 'Judgment in Military History', *Journal of the Royal United Services Institution* (Spring 1989).

— 'Prelude to the Cardwell Reforms, 1856–68', *Journal of the Royal United Services Institution, Journal* 106 (1961).
— 'Recruiting the Victorian Army 1870–1892', *Journal of Victorian Studies* No 5 1961).
— 'The Effect of the Cardwell Reforms in Army Organisation 1874–1904', *Journal of the Royal United Services Institution* 105 (1960).
— 'The Retirement of the Duke of Cambridge', *Journal of the Royal United Services Institution* 106 (1961).
Cooke, A.B. & Vincent, J.R., 'Lord Spencer and the Phoenix Park Murders', *Journal of Irish Historical Studies*, 18 (72) (1973).
Corfe, T.H., 'The Phoenix Park Murders', *History Today*, 11:12 (December 1961).
Darwin, J., 'Imperialism and the Victorians: The Dynamics of Territorial Expansion', *English Historical Review*, 122, (1997).
Dawson R.N., Lieutenant A.T., 'Modern Artillery', *Journal of the Royal United Services Institution*, No 45 (1901).
Elliot, W.J., 'The Military Intelligence Departments of England and Germany in Contrast', *Colburn's United Service Magazine*, (June 1885).
Ellison, Lt-General Sir Gerald, 'Lord Roberts and the General Staff', *The Nineteenth Century and After* 112 (December 1932).
Escott, T.H.S., 'Henry Brackenbury and his School', *Contemporary Review*, 105 (Jan/Jun 1914).
Griffiths, Major Arthur, 'The War Office: Past, Present, and to Come', *Fortnightly Review* (April 1903).
Hall, Darrell, 'Artillery in the Zulu War –1879', *South African Military History Society Journal* Vol 4 No 4 (December 1978).
— 'Artillery of the First Anglo-Boer War 1880–1881', *South African Military History Society Journal* Vol 5 No 2 (December 1980).
— 'Field Artillery of the British Army' Part III, *South African Military History Society Journal*, Volume 2 No 6 (December 1973).
— 'Guns in South Africa' Parts III & VI, *South African Military History Society Journal*, Vol 2 No 2 (December 1971).
— 'Guns in South Africa' Part I & II, *South African Military History Society Journal*, Vol 2 No1 (June 1971).
— 'The Naval Guns in Natal 1899–1902', *South African Military History Society, Journal* Vol 4 No 3 (June 1978).
Harvie, Ian, 'A Very Dangerous Man: A Profile of Henry Brackenbury' *The Victorian Military Society Journal, Soldiers of the Queen*, Issue 96 (March 1999).
— 'The Raid on Essaman, 14th October 1873', *Journal of the Society for Army Historical Research*, 77, (1999).

Hughes, Major A.T., 'Field Artillery fire and Okehampton experiences' *Journal of the Royal United Services Institution*, No 39 (1895).

May, Major E.S., 'The Actions of Cavalry and Horse Artillery Illustrated by Modern Battles', *Journal of the Royal United Services Institution*, No 38 (1894).

— 'The Analogy between the tactics of Field Artillery and those of the other arms', *Journal of the Royal United Services Institution*, No 40 (1896).

McEldowney, John, 'Miscarriages of Justice? The Phoenix Park Murders 1882', *Journal of Criminal Justice History*, 14 (1993).

O'Brien, Jim, 'The Anglo-Boer war: Soap and Tinned Meat', *The Journal of the Victorian Military Society, Soldiers of the Queen*, Issue No 125 (June 2006).

— 'The Second Anglo-Boer War: Getting there', *The Journal of the Victorian Military Society, Soldiers of the Queen*, No 112 (March 2003).

— 'Victoria's Army: A brief overview of army organisation', *The Journal of the Victorian Military Society, Soldiers of the Queen*, Issues 119 & 120 (December 2004 & March 2005).

Owen, Major-General Charles H., 'The Value of Artillery in the Field', *Journal of the Royal United Services Institution* No 33 (1888).

Preston, Adrian, 'British Military Thought 1856–1890', *Army Quarterly*, No 89 (October 1964).

— 'Frustrated Great Gamesmanship: Sir Garnet Wolseley's Plan for War against Russia, 1873–1880', *International History Review*, No 2 (1980).

— 'Sir Garnet Wolseley and the Cyprus Expedition 1874', *The Journal of the Society for Army Historical Research*, Volume XLV (1967).

— 'Wolseley, the Khartoum Relief Expedition and the Defence of India 1885–1900', *Journal of Imperial and Commonwealth History*, Volume 6 (May 1978).

Robson, Brian, 'The Banda and Kirwi Prize Money', *The Journal of the Victorian Military Society, Soldiers of the Queen*, Issue 97 (June 1999).

Spiers, Edward M, 'Rearming the Edwardian Artillery', *Journal of the Society for Army Historical Research*, Volume 57 (1979).

Walford, Lt-Colonel N.L., 'The Development of Field Artillery Material', *Royal United Service Institution Journal*, No 35 (1891).

— 'The Drill Regulations of the German Field Artillery', *Journal of the Royal United Services Institution*, No 33 (1888).

Webb, J.V., 'The Trouble in the 2nd Grenadier Guards in 1890', *The Journal of the Victorian Military Society, Soldiers of the Queen*, Issue 95 (December 1998).

## Unpublished Dissertations

Bailes, Howard, 'The Influence of Continental examples and Colonial Warfare upon the reforms of the Late Victorian Army', PhD, University of London, 1980.

Kochanski, Halik, 'Sir Garnet Wolseley and the reform of the British Army 1870–99', PhD Thesis, University of London, 1996.

Mahaffey, Corrine L., 'Professionalisation in the British Army 1870–1914', PhD Thesis, Glasgow University, 2004.

Meriweather, Jeffrey L., 'Procrastination or Pragmatism? British defence policy, War Office administration and the South African War 1898–1903', Mphil Thesis, University of Exeter, 2001.

Moon, H.R., 'The Invasion of the United Kingdom: Public Controversy and Official Planning 1888–1918', PhD Thesis, University of London, 1968.

Page, Andrew, 'The Supply Services of the British Army in the South Africa War 1899–1902', PhD Thesis, University of Oxford, 1976.

Scales Jnr, Robert H., 'Artillery in Small Wars: The evolution of British Artillery Doctrine 1860–1914', PhD Thesis, Duke University, 1976.

Spiers, Edward M., 'The Reform of the Front-line Forces of the Regular Army in the United Kingdom 1895–1914', PhD Thesis, University of Edinburgh, 1974.

# Index

Note – military ranks have been omitted from the index.

Abyssinian Expedition 1868, 28, 83
Adye, Sir John, 149, 186
Afghanistan, 127, 166, 178, 181-182, 200-202, 216-217, 219, 224
Allison, Sir Archibald, 161, 164
Ardagh, Sir John, 14, 172-173, 177, 184, 196-197, 226, 300, 302
Army Reform, xvii, xix, 21-27, 41, 45, 47, 53-67
Arnold-Forster, Hugh, xviii, xxii, 279-280, 284-285
Artillery, 25, 36-37, 40-41, 46-49, 59, 78, 100-102, 119, 127, 147, 169-170, 210, 232, 257, 267-271, 276, 279, 293
   Coastal artillery, 232-233, 248
Ashanti War 1874, 28, 44, 50, 107, 116-117
Austro Prussian War 1866 (Seven Weeks War), 50, 54, 80, 82, 102, 269

Baden-Powell, Robert, 179-180
Baker, Valentine, 68, 101-102, 148-149
Balfour, Arthur (later 1st Earl Balfour), 239, 256, 284-285
Bazaine, Marshal François, 77, 93, 103-104
Bigge, Sir Arthur, 284
*Blackwood's Magazine*, 51, 289
Boers, 27-28, 117, 127-128, 196, 235-236, 250, 265, 267-268, 270-271, 278, 286,
   1881 War with, 27, 128, 236
Brackenbury, Charles (brother), 6-10, 14, 42, 68, 71, 106, 295
Brackenbury, Edith (second wife), 73-74, 289-291
Brackenbury, Sir Edward (uncle), 4, 34
Brackenbury, Emilia (first wife), 69-74
Brackenbury, Hereward (nephew), 289
Brackenbury, Hilda (sister-in-law), 71
Brackenbury, Maria (mother), 68, 76
Brackenbury, Richard (grandfather), 3-5
Brackenbury, William (father), 4, 6, 11, 13-14, 68, 295
British Expeditionary Force (B.E.F), 17, 27, 31, 175, 278, 300

Buller, Sir Redvers, 150, 207-208, 300

Callwell, Charles, 30, 174-177, 189, 301
Canada, 13, 107, 110, 152, 164
Cambridge, H.R.H. Duke of, xvi, xx, 7-9, 20, 60, 63, 67, 110, 125, 140, 150, 159, 162, 186-190, 225, 298
Campbell, Archibald, 13
Campbell-Bannerman, Sir Henry, xviii, 132, 162, 184, 186-189
Canrobert, Marshal François, 72-73, 77, 93, 99-100, 103-104, 121, 132
Canrobert, Leila Flora, 72-73, 94, 98, 131
Cardwell, Edward, 20-24, 28, 31, 54, 56-57, 59, 64, 66, 86, 107, 109, 164
    Cardwell Reforms, xviii, 22, 28, 54, 59, 66
Cavendish, Lord Frederick, 133-134
Chamberlain, Arthur, 256-257, 262
Chamberlain, Joseph, 236, 239, 256, 259
Chapman, Edward, 195-196, 209
Chelmsford, Lord, 24, 28, 125-126, 139
Chesney, Charles, 86, 209
Chief of Staff, xii, xvi, xix, 8, 20, 63-67, 126, 148, 150, 167, 185-192, 204, 233, 285, 288, 293-294, 298, 302
Childers, Hugh, 135, 143, 186, 188
Churchill, Lord Randolph, xxiii, 24, 184-187, 189-190, 251
Churchill, Winston, xi, 12
Colley, George, 28, 52, 106, 117, 125-126, 129, 154, 236
Connaught, Prince Arthur Duke of, 105, 188, 298
Conservative Party, xii, 147, 185, 239
Cowans, John, 68, 197
Cricket, 12, 15, 34, 38-39, 62, 117, 147
Crimean War 1854-56, xxiv, 14-15, 17, 19-20, 22, 25, 27, 34, 52, 54, 84, 164, 278, 281, 286, 294
Crown Prince of Prussia (later Kaiser Frederick III), 91, 104
Cyprus, 115, 117, 119, 121-123, 125, 136, 141, 206

Danish-Prussian War 1864, 46, 48
Derby, Edward Stanley 17th Earl of, xv, 292
Director General of Ordnance, 9, 63, 222, 230, 232, 235, 237-238, 240-241, 257, 280, 286-287, 298, 300, 302
Disraeli, Benjamin, 1st Earl of Beaconsfield, 23, 125
Dover, 105, 121

Earle, William, 152-157, 159
Edward VII, King, 284
Egypt, 23, 27, 30, 118, 132, 135, 140, 142, 147, 149, 151, 153, 161, 166, 172, 208
Egyptian War 1882, 29, 142-143
Ehrhardt Gun, 267, 271-272
Elgin Commission, 234, 250, 258, 264, 267-268
Elgin, Victor Bruce 9th Earl of, 234
Elles, Sir Edmond, 205, 222
Elphinstone, Sir Howard Craufurd, 105
Escott, T.H.S., xi, xii, xviii, 120, 147, 162
Esher, Reginald Brett 2nd Viscount, 148, 187, 234, 287, 288
Esher Committee, 192, 287-288, 299
Eugénie, Empress, 98

First World War, xix, 17, 21, 23, 27, 176, 210, 268, 272, 275, 279, 286
*Fraser's Magazine*, 41, 51, 53, 56, 293
Franco-Prussian War 1870-71, xi, xvii, 28-29, 50, 68, 73, 75, 79, 82, 85, 87, 97-99, 101-103, 105, 111, 119, 122, 131, 163-164, 170-171, 269, 287, 295
French Army, 18, 47, 65, 77, 80, 95, 99-100, 103-104, 121, 131, 178
Furley, Sir John, 83-84, 88

George V, King, 74, 284, 290
General Staff, xviii, xix, 8, 49, 77, 141, 168, 170, 176, 178-179, 183, 185, 188-190, 193, 195, 204, 298-299, 301-302
Gibraltar, 147, 149, 275
Gladstone, William Ewart, 23, 97, 133, 135-136, 138-140, 142, 145, 186, 201, 236, 239
Gleichen, Lord Edward, xvi, xix, 164-165, 175-176, 180, 300-301
Gordon, Charles, 139
Gordon Relief Expedition 1884-85, xi-xvii, xxi, 44, 130, 149, 162, 217, 233, 244, 297
Grierson, Sir James, x, 175, 178-179, 189, 195-196, 209, 219, 227, 300, 301-302
Grove, Sir Coleridge, 183

Hague Convention, 265
Hale, Lonsdale, 29, 46
Hamber, Thomas, 77
Hamilton, Sir Ian, xx-xxi, 60
Hamley, Sir Edward, 52, 106
Harcourt, William, 140, 143, 145
Hartington Commission, 168, 184-185, 187-188, 190-193, 231, 240, 293, 298-299

# INDEX

333

Hartington, Marquis of (later 8th Duke of Devonshire), 133, 135-136, 184, 186, 190, 240 I

Hicks Beach, Sir Michael, 240, 249, 251-252

Home, Robert, 113

Imperial Defence, xxiii, 8, 18, 25-27, 58, 66, 168, 186

India, x-xi, xiv, xvii-xxiv, xxvii, 6, 10, 18, 26, 29, 32-38, 53, 58-59, 69, 118, 120, 125-126, 129-131, 144, 148, 161, 166-167, 178, 180, 182, 196, 198-232, 235, 238, 248, 254, 264, 277-278, 287, 290, 298-302

    Army, 122, 150, 166-167, 175, 199, 204-208, 210, 213-215, 219, 221, 226-228, 298.

    Governance, 26, 198-9, 203-207, 215, 219, 224

Indian Mutiny 1857-59, xvii, 6-7, 16, 32-33, 43, 111, 144, 199, 203, 219

Intelligence Branch, xii, xvii, xix, xxiv, 7-8, 58, 106, 118-119, 138, 161-164, 167-168, 172-177, 179-184, 189, 191, 194-198, 208-212, 216, 218, 222, 224, 228, 232, 290, 297-300, 302

Invasion scares, 18-19, 25, 58-59, 166-170, 183-184

Ireland, xvii, xviv, 5, 11, 14, 133-147, 164, 195, 206, 227, 233, 239, 246

Iron Cross, 97-98

Kabul, 200-201, 213, 215, 217

Kandahar, 201, 215, 217

Kelly-Kenny, Sir Thomas, 287

Khartoum, 150-152, 154, 158, 201

Kipling, Rudyard, 200, 286

Kirbekan, battle of 1885, 157-159, 294

Kitchener, Lord, xx, xxv, 87, 90, 204-205, 222, 278

Krupp Guns, 127, 271

Kynoch & Co., 254-257, 259-262

Lansdowne, Lord, x, xviii, xxiii, 70, 182, 210, 212, 214, 225-226, 228-233, 239-241, 245-246, 250, 252, 255-256, 261, 275, 279, 283, 288, 290, 296, 298

Lefroy, Sir John, 39, 41

Legion of Honour, 97-98

Liberal Imperialists/Unionists, 135, 239

Liberal Party, 64, 66, 135, 139, 142, 147, 239

Lloyd-George, David (later 1st Earl Lloyd George), 259

Longman, William, 41, 51

Lyons, Lord, 78-79, 100, 104

Lytton, Lord, 70, 129-131, 203

MacDougall, Sir Patrick, 106, 118-119, 164
MacMahon, Marshal Patrice de, 106, 118-119, 164
Mahdi, Mohamed Ahmed the, 150-151
Major, Alfred, 254, 263
Markham, Sir Edwin, 226, 232, 235
Maurice, Sir (John) Frederick, 24, 52, 114, 125, 162, 299
Methuen, Lord, 291
Military Member of the Council, x, 22, 195, 198-199, 203-211, 221-222, 228, 231, 235.
Mobilisation plans
    British Army, 27, 166, 168-173, 177, 184-187, 197, 210, 218, 243-244, 247, 250, 300
    Indian Army, 213, 215, 225-228
Montgomery, Sir Robert, 282
Mowatt, Sir Francis, 248
    Mowatt Committee, 248-252, 256, 259-260, 263, 277

Napier of Magdala, Lord, 123
Napoleon III, Emperor, 98-99, 104
Natal, 72, 115, 117-119, 121, 123, 129, 276
National Aid Society, xvii, 43, 82-86, 88, 90, 94, 97-98, 102, 111, 119, 295, 301
Newspapers
- *The Daily News*, 77, 143
- *The Daily Telegraph*, 44, 51, 120-121, 290
- *The Illustrated London News*, 50, 121
- *The Morning Herald*, 43
- *The Standard*, xvii, 23, 43, 76-77, 79-80, 82-83, 85-86
- *The Times*, 7, 61, 76, 84-85, 102, 145, 289, 302
- *The World*, 44, 120-121
Noble, Sir Andrew, 240, 257
Nolan, John Phillip, 77-79

Ordnance Factories, *see* Woolwich, Ordnance Factories

Paris Commune 1871, 99-102
Parnell, Charles Stewart, 134
Phoenix Park Murders, 139
Pless, Prince, 90, 94
Plymouth, 15-16
Powell-Williams, Joseph, 238-240, 256, 262
Prussia, 22, 29, 48-49, 54, 76, 89, 91, 104
    Imitation of, 8, 18, 29, 48-50, 54, 57-59, 63, 269

Military reform, 18, 21-23, 54, 57, 66, 105
Military success of, 46, 48-50, 54, 63, 64, 80, 102, 164, 269

Quebec, 13-15, 38, 123, 294
    Militia, 13-15

Railways, 48, 145, 154, 224, 243, 293
Recruitment, xxi, 8, 19, 22-24, 46-47, 58, 60, 63, 66
Red River Expedition 1870, 28, 107, 110, 152
Repington, Charles à Court, 68, 178
Richardson, Sir W.D., 258
River Column (Gordon Relief Expedition of 1884-85), 44, 150, 152-153, 160, 162, 294, 298
Roberts, Lord, x, xviii, 47, 127, 161, 167, 180, 196, 200, 205, 207, 210-211, 214, 223, 225-226, 229, 233, 246, 263, 272, 283, 287-288, 291, 298
Robertson, Sir William, 176, 300-301
Royal Artillery, xx, 6, 9, 14-16, 34-36, 39-40, 53, 82, 86, 117, 122, 127, 143, 165, 272
Royal Navy, 3, 13, 18, 27-29, 58, 166-167, 171, 217-218, 231, 240, 245, 277-278
Russell, Sir Baker Creed, x, 125-127
Russia, 18, 48, 120, 148, 170, 178, 269
    Alliance with France, 166-167, 216-218
    Invasion of India, 166-167, 181-182, 196, 200-202, 204, 209, 212-220, 222, 224, 228
    Threat of War with, 120, 122-123, 161, 196, 209, 212

*Saint Paul's Monthly Magazine*, 46, 48
Salisbury, Robert Gascoyne-Cecil 3rd Marquess of, 183, 186, 240, 284, 298
Sekhukhune Expedition 1879, 44, 125-126
Sheerness, 117-118, 121
Shepstone, Helen, 72, 74
Shepstone, Theophilus, 117
Shepstone, Theophilus Jr, 72, 118
Simmons, Sir Lintorn, 86, 104-105, 186
Smith, W.H, 162, 184, 186, 297-298
South African War 1899-1902, xi, xviii, xxii, 27, 31, 47-48, 163, 172, 192-193, 196-197, 204, 211, 217, 222, 229, 233, 235-236, 238, 241-242, 244, 246-247, 253, 258, 267-268, 271, 274-275, 278, 281-284, 286, 293, 296, 299-300, 302
Spencer, John 5th Earl, xii, 135-142
Staff College, xix, 21, 30, 45, 86, 104, 106, 176
Stanhope, Edward, xii, xviii, xx, xxiii-xxiv, 21, 24-25, 27, 56-57, 59, 147, 149, 183, 186, 188, 191-192, 215, 226, 239, 298

Stanhope Memorandum, 25, 30, 169, 197, 243
Stead, W.T, 296
Steevens, Sir John, 262, 282
Stewart, Sir Donald, 212
Stewart, J.D.H., 158
St John Brodrick, William (later 1st Earl of Middleton), 239, 280, 283, 287
Sudan, xi, xix, 24, 27, 139, 147, 149-151, 154, 158-160, 162, 164, 172, 201, 207, 228, 244, 295, 297-298

Thackeray, William Makepeace, 16
Thompson, Sir Ralph [sometimes spelt Thomson], 9, 165, 172, 186, 206
Transvaal, 117, 127-128, 236
Trollope, Anthony, 130
Tulloch, Alexander, 118-119

Ulundi, Battle of 1879, 126

Victoria, Queen, 15, 20, 97, 105, 148, 284

Waddington Family, 132
Wantage, Lord (Robert Loyd-Lindsay), xxiv, 84, 256
War Office, xx, 21-25, 53-57, 63-66, 110, 126-127, 135, 143, 147-150, 163-165, 169, 172, 183-197, 235, 238-239, 245-258, 261-264, 272-279, 286-287, 290, 293-297, 300-301
Wellington, Duke of, 20
White, Sir George, xxiii, 197, 205, 209-210, 225-226, 228, 263
Wilkinson, Spenser, 8, 286-287, 290
Wilson, Sir Henry Hughes, 24, 176, 300-301
Wolfe-Murray, Sir James, 176, 217, 300
Wolseley, Viscount, vii-viii, x-xii, xvi-xv, 7, 21, 30, 52, 54, 60, 66, 68-69, 72-73, 106-119, 122-129, 132, 135-136, 139-143, 145, 148-162, 167-169, 172, 176, 183, 186, 188-191, 194, 207-208, 211, 214, 231-233, 250, 259, 283, 287, 293-299, 301-302
    Lady Wolseley, xi, 68-69, 72-73, 281
Wood, Sir Henry Evelyn, x, 68, 125-126, 149, 153, 155, 159, 250, 268, 178, 284, 300
Woolwich, vii, x, xiv, xxii, 6-7, 9, 12, 14-15, 38-39, 40, 53, 71, 75-76, 79, 86-87, 95, 98, 102-107, 111, 118, 132, 136, 148, 163, 179, 222, 241, 275, 282, 291, 294
    Ordnance factories, 237-240, 242, 244-251, 261, 264, 266, 274-276, 281
    Royal Military Academy, vii, xxii, 6-7, 12, 14-15, 39, 75-76, 163, 222

Zulu War 1879, xvii, 72, 112, 125, 127-128

# Helion Studies in Military History

No 1     *Learning from Foreign Wars. Russian Military Thinking 1859–73*
        Gudrun Persson (ISBN 978-1-906033-61-3)

No 2     *A Military Government in Exile. The Polish Government-in-Exile 1939–45, a Study of Discontent*
        Evan McGilvray (ISBN 978-1-906033-58-3)

No 3     *From Landrecies to Cambrai. Case Studies of German Offensive and Defensive Operations on the Western Front 1914–17*
        Capt G.C. Wynne (ISBN 978-1-906033-76-7)

No 4     *Playing the Game. The British Junior Infantry Officer on the Western Front 1914–18*
        Christopher Moore-Bick (ISBN 978-1-906033-84-2)

No 5     *The History of the British Army Film & Photographic Unit in the Second World War*
        Dr Fred McGlade (ISBN 978-1-906033-94-1)

No 6     *Making Waves. Admiral Mountbatten's Radio SEAC 1945–49*
        Eric Hitchcock (ISBN 978-1-906033-95-8)

No 7     *Abolishing the Taboo. Dwight D. Eisenhower and American Nuclear Doctrine 1945–1961*
        Brian Madison Jones (ISBN 978-1-907677-31-1)

No 8     *The Turkish Brigade in the Korean War Volume 1. Kunu-Ri Heroes (November-December 1950)*
        Dr Ali Denizli (ISBN 978-1-907677-32-8)

No 9     *The Diaries of Ronnie Tritton, War Office Publicity Officer 1940–45*
        Edited by Dr Fred McGlade (ISBN 978-1-907677-44-1)

No 10    *The Thinking Man's Soldier. The Life and Career of General Sir Henry Brackenbury 1837–1914*
        Dr Christopher Brice (ISBN 978-1-907677-69-4)

No 11    *War Surgery 1914–18*
        Edited by Thomas Scotland and Steven Heys (ISBN 978-1-907677-70-0)

No 12    *Counterinsurgency in Africa. The Portugese Way of War 1961–74*
        John P. Cann (ISBN 978-1-907677-73-1)

No 13    *The Armed Forces of Poland in the West 1939–46*
        Michael Alfred Peszke (ISBN 978-1-908916-54-9)

No 14    *The Role of the Soviet Union in the Second World War*
        Boris Sokolov (ISBN 978-1-908916-55-6)

No 15    *Generals of the Danish Army in the First and Second Schleswig-Holstein Wars, 1848–50 and 1864*
        Nick B. Svendsen (ISBN 978-1-908916-46-4)

No 16    *A Considerable Achievement. The Tactical Development of the 56th (London) Division on the Western Front, 1916–1918*
        Matt Brosnan (ISBN 978-1-908916-47-1)

No 17    *Brown Waters of Africa. Portugese Riverine Warfare 1961–1974*
        John P. Cann (ISBN 978-1-908916-56-3)